The Grand Dukes

*Sons and Grandsons of Russia's Tsars
Since the Reign of Paul I*

Volume I

By

*Janet Ashton
Arturo E. Beéche
Zoia Belyakova
Lisa Davidson
Coryne Hall
Ilana Miller
Greg King
William Lee
John van der Kiste*

Introduction by Charles Stewart

EUROHISTORY.COM

ISBN 978-0-9771961-8-0
Copyright © 2010 Arturo E. Beéche
First Hardback Edition March 2013

Published by:

Eurohistory.com

6300 Kensington Avenue
East Richmond Heights, CA 94805 USA
Telephone: (510) 236-1730
Fax: (510) 778-8465
Email: books@eurohistory.com
URL: http://www.eurohistory.com

Cover design by David W. Higdon and Henry Wong
Editing by Arturo E. Beéche, Katrina Warne & David W. Higdon
Layout & Design by Arturo E. Beéche & David W. Higdon
Printed and bound in Berkeley, CA

To the Imperial Family...

Source of such great passion!

The Romanov Dynasty

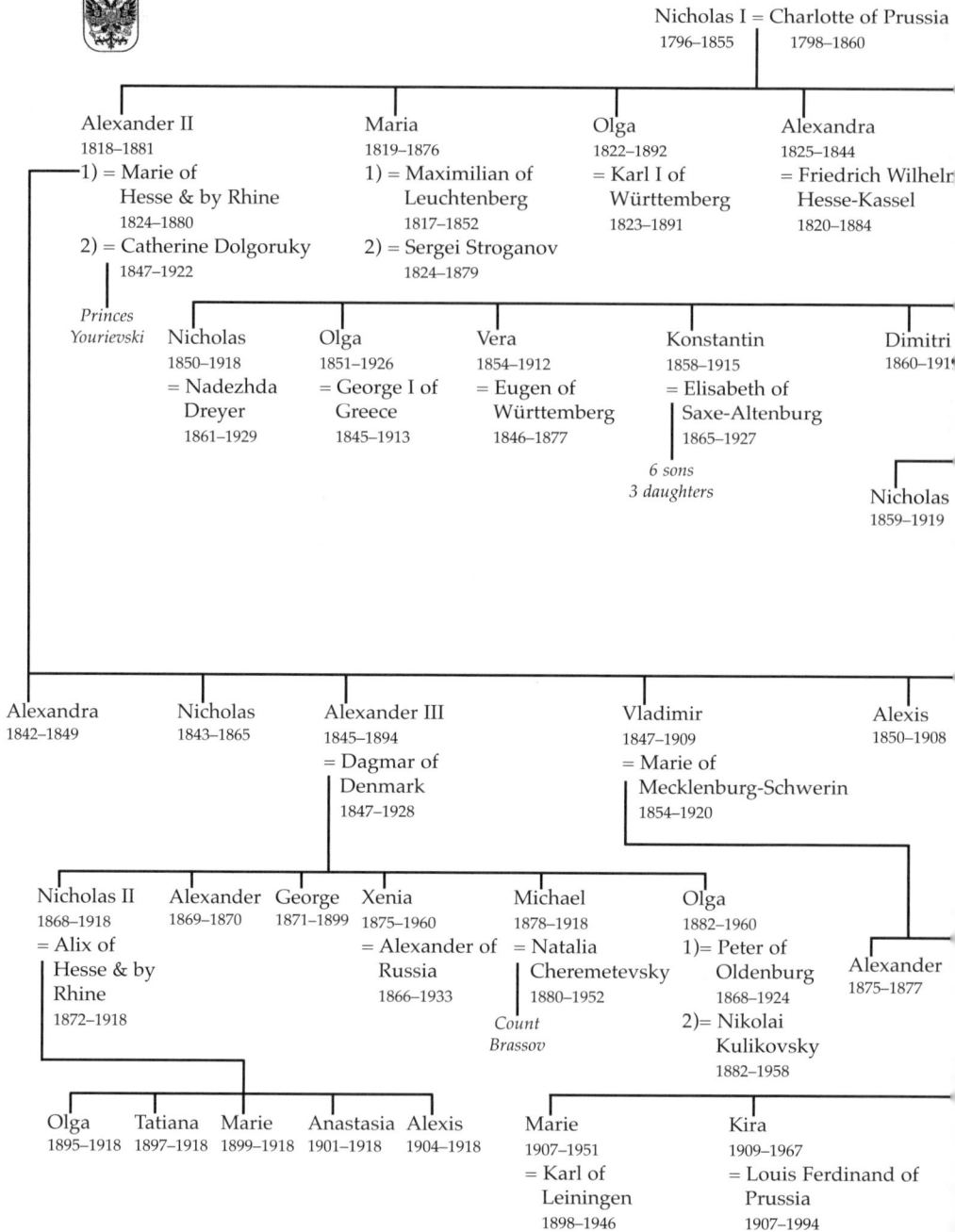

Nicholas I = Charlotte of Prussia
1796–1855   1798–1860

Alexander II	Maria	Olga	Alexandra
1818–1881	1819–1876	1822–1892	1825–1844
1) = Marie of	1) = Maximilian of	= Karl I of	= Friedrich Wilhelm
Hesse & by Rhine	Leuchtenberg	Württemberg	Hesse-Kassel
1824–1880	1817–1852	1823–1891	1820–1884
2) = Catherine Dolgoruky	2) = Sergei Stroganov		
1847–1922	1824–1879		

Princes Yourievski

Nicholas	Olga	Vera	Konstantin	Dimitri
1850–1918	1851–1926	1854–1912	1858–1915	1860–191?
= Nadezhda	= George I of	= Eugen of	= Elisabeth of	
Dreyer	Greece	Württemberg	Saxe-Altenburg	
1861–1929	1845–1913	1846–1877	1865–1927	

6 sons
3 daughters

Nicholas
1859–1919

Alexandra	Nicholas	Alexander III	Vladimir	Alexis
1842–1849	1843–1865	1845–1894	1847–1909	1850–1908
		= Dagmar of	= Marie of	
		Denmark	Mecklenburg-Schwerin	
		1847–1928	1854–1920	

Nicholas II	Alexander	George	Xenia	Michael	Olga	Alexander
1868–1918	1869–1870	1871–1899	1875–1960	1878–1918	1882–1960	1875–1877
= Alix of			= Alexander of	= Natalia	1)= Peter of	
Hesse & by			Russia	Cheremetevsky	Oldenburg	
Rhine			1866–1933	1880–1952	1868–1924	
1872–1918					2)= Nikolai	
			Count Brassov		Kulikovsky	
					1882–1958	

Olga	Tatiana	Marie	Anastasia	Alexis	Marie	Kira
1895–1918	1897–1918	1899–1918	1901–1918	1904–1918	1907–1951	1909–1967
					= Karl of	= Louis Ferdinand of
					Leiningen	Prussia
					1898–1946	1907–1994

The Romanov Dynasty

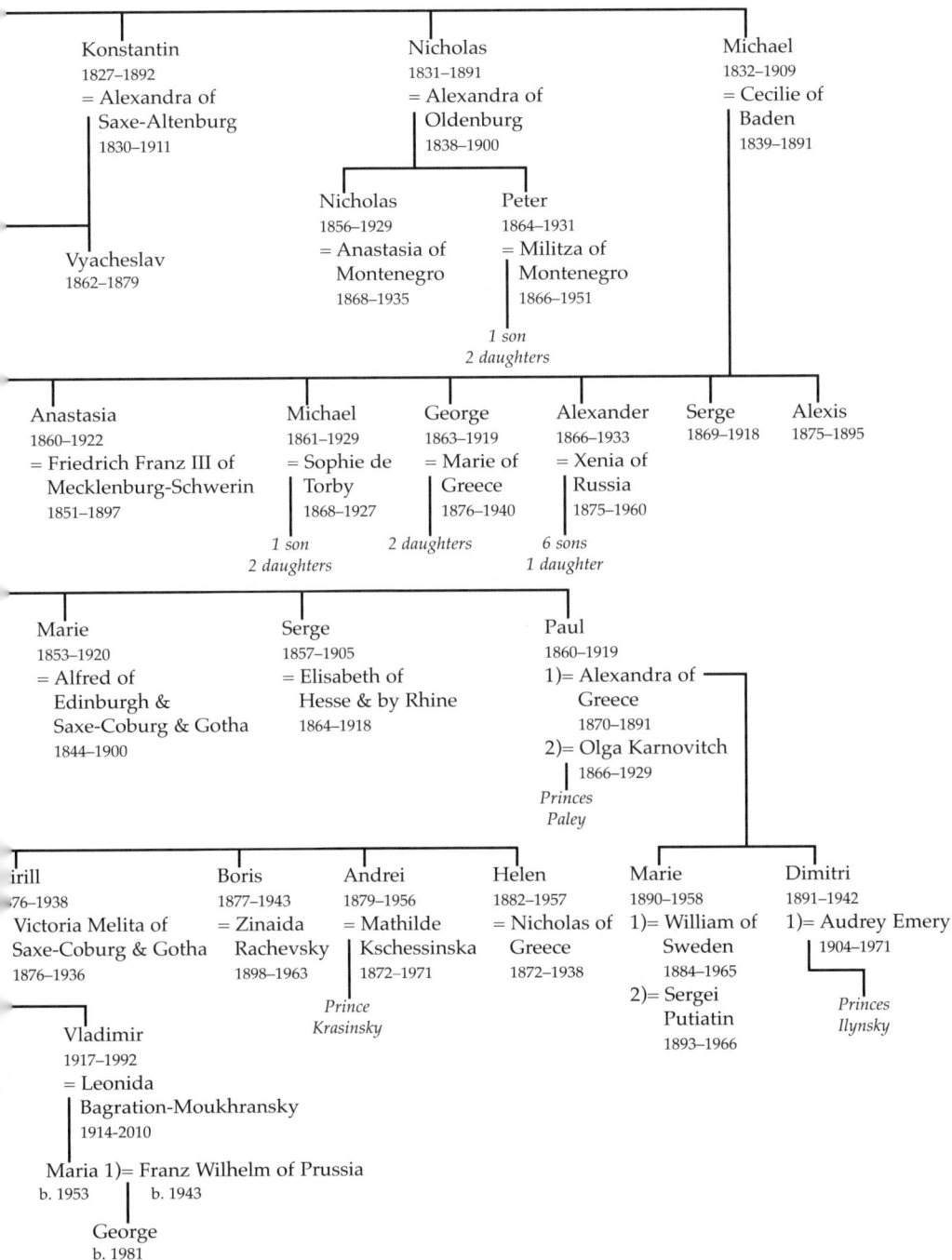

Konstantin
1827–1892
= Alexandra of
  Saxe-Altenburg
  1830–1911

Vyacheslav
1862–1879

Nicholas
1831–1891
= Alexandra of
  Oldenburg
  1838–1900

Nicholas
1856–1929
= Anastasia of
  Montenegro
  1868–1935

Peter
1864–1931
= Militza of
  Montenegro
  1866–1951

1 son
2 daughters

Michael
1832–1909
= Cecilie of
  Baden
  1839–1891

Anastasia
1860–1922
= Friedrich Franz III of
  Mecklenburg-Schwerin
  1851–1897

Michael
1861–1929
= Sophie de
  Torby
  1868–1927

1 son
2 daughters

George
1863–1919
= Marie of
  Greece
  1876–1940

2 daughters

Alexander
1866–1933
= Xenia of
  Russia
  1875–1960

6 sons
1 daughter

Serge
1869–1918

Alexis
1875–1895

Marie
1853–1920
= Alfred of
  Edinburgh &
  Saxe-Coburg & Gotha
  1844–1900

Serge
1857–1905
= Elisabeth of
  Hesse & by Rhine
  1864–1918

Paul
1860–1919
1)= Alexandra of
    Greece
    1870–1891
2)= Olga Karnovitch
    1866–1929

Princes
Paley

irill
876–1938
Victoria Melita of
Saxe-Coburg & Gotha
1876–1936

Boris
1877–1943
= Zinaida
  Rachevsky
  1898–1963

Andrei
1879–1956
= Mathilde
  Kschessinska
  1872–1971

Prince
Krasinsky

Helen
1882–1957
= Nicholas of
  Greece
  1872–1938

Marie
1890–1958
1)= William of
    Sweden
    1884–1965
2)= Sergei
    Putiatin
    1893–1966

Dimitri
1891–1942
1)= Audrey Emery
    1904–1971

Princes
Ilynsky

Vladimir
1917–1992
= Leonida
  Bagration-Moukhransky
  1914-2010

Maria 1)= Franz Wilhelm of Prussia
b. 1953   b. 1943

George
b. 1981

TABLE OF CONTENTS

PHOTO SECTION

I *INTRODUCTION*

*T*here may never have been a time when "Grand duchy" didn't conjure a castle in Fairyland, nor when "Grand Duke" did not evoke a silver-haired aristocrat sporting a monocle whose chest was festooned with too many sashes and medals, and whose life was adorned with too many comforts and sycophants. Unlike kings, who come in a variety of images, ranging from paternally wise to battle horse-mounted to gold-greedy, grand dukes are quaint stereotypes, at best vague, at worst absurd. Even when the last living member of this species, the ruler of Luxembourg, is remembered, no substantially different figure comes to mind. Rather the reverse.

But once upon a time there were grand dukes of a different sort. Medieval grand dukes, bearded and wrapped in fur-lined capes wielded sword and icon against pagans on the steppes. Soldier grand dukes swarmed on the capital between wars filling theatre balconies with applause or waiting impatiently in closed carriages for a prima ballerina to make her last curtsey on stage. And émigré grand dukes sipping someone else's champagne in the lounge of a 20th century Parisian hotel they could no longer afford. Russia's dukes, throughout their history, were like Russia's literature; sweeping, mysterious, and tragic. In short, grand. These men grew Russia, and spent it, and their like is no more to be seen.

Grand Duke is the traditional English rendering of the Latin *magnus dux* and *magnus princips*. After the fall of the Byzantine Empire in 485 C.E., Europe's marauding tribes spread out and began to settle down and establish boundaries which they could defend against rivals. Skilled warriors made themselves chieftains and, if they could aggrandize the tribe's territory and pass leadership down among kinsmen, they emerged from the Dark Ages as dukes and princes, adopting those titles from the commanders of the old Roman Empire.

Among these, Gonçalo Mendes (fl. 950–997) in northwestern Iberia may have been the first to take a higher title, *magnus dux portucalensium* ("great duke of the Portuguese") in rebellion against his liege lords, the kings of León around 980 C.E. In 1435 Duke Philip *the Good* of Burgundy (1396–1467) declared himself "Grand Duke of the West," but neither he nor his son Charles the Bold (1433–77) achieved broad recognition of the title or succeeded in expanding their Flemish base into a revived kingdom of Arles. In 1569 the Medici family rendered permanent their domination of Florence when Pope Pius V conferred upon them the rule of the new Grand Duchy. In 1576 the Holy Roman Emperor dropped his protest against this elevation and confirmed the Grand Dukes of Tuscany as vassals within the Empire. Tuscany passed, upon extinction of the Medici, to the Habsburgs and remained Europe's best known independent grand duchy until absorbed into the kingdom of Italy in 1859.

In Eastern Europe, duchies and principalities evolved differently than in the West and South. Unlike "grand dukes" whose territories were of insufficient size and clout to obtain international recognition as kings, the typical grand prince in Eastern Europe was more likely to lead a loose confederation of tribes in war or migration. The princes over whom he exercised jurisdiction were likely to be kinsmen or allies, authority over sub-tribal groups being retained by each group's own leaders. The Grand Prince (Nagyfejedelem) of the Magyars emerges in the 9th century with a following of seven tribes. They merged with three Khabar tribes of Turkish origin by 881, spreading out over the Carpathian mountains. The grand princedom thrives until 1000 C.E., when St Stephen converts this Magyar/Turk amalgamation into the Christian kingdom of Hungary.

The "grand dukedoms" of Transylvania and Finland were largely titular, as no independent prince ever held them. The titles simply identified these territories as subject provinces of foreign monarchs. In 1765 Empress Maria Theresia upgraded her province, the Principality of Transylvania, into a grand princedom (Großfürstentum), but it continued to be administered by a Hungarian governor in her name. Pursuant to the Austro-Hungarian Compromise of 1867, Transylvania ceased to be administered separately within the Austro-Hungarian Empire, and was fully integrated as an additional province into the kingdom of Hungary, although the Habsburgs continued to include "Grand Prince of Transylvania" among their hereditary titles.

Under Sweden, Finland was also a sovereign grand princedom in name only from 1581 to 1809, sending representatives to Stockholm's Parliament and having no independent government. Following the defeat of Sweden in the Finnish War in 1809, the country switched allegiance from the King of Sweden to the Emperor of Russia who became the new grand duke. Although Russia remained an autocracy, during the war resistance to its conquest was sought by promising the Finns internal autonomy. Thus, Finland was governed separately, according to the laws and administrative system closer to that developed under its old suzerain, Sweden. Russia's tsar contented himself with appointment of a Finnish governor-general resident in Helsinki. However, from 1899 until the Russian Revolution, Finland's independence and progressive legislation was thwarted as the tsar's regime imposed "russification" in an effort to consolidate Russian rule and to thwart nationalist tendencies. With the abolition of the Russian monarchy in 1917, the Finnish grand princedom ceased to exist. The Finnish Diet looked briefly to the Duke of Urach (a morganaut of the German royal House of Württemberg, like the Duke of Teck) and a Prince of Hesse to establish an independent monarchy – this time as a kingdom. But revolutionary fervor for a republic prevailed and the Hessian's invitation to a royal coronation in Helsinki was rescinded on 14 December 1918.

Another medieval dynastic model of grand ducal status is illustrated by the Gedyminids in Lithuania. Grand Duke Mindaugas (c.1200-1263) arose in 1220 to form a Baltic state in Lithuania, becoming a Christian and allying with the Order of Livonian Knights. Although in the last decade of his reign he was crowned king, he is the first known Grand Duke of Lithuania, having been recognized in youth as inheriting senior rank among Lithuania's 16 native Balt princes and dukes. Considered a nation-builder despite constant struggles with Tatars and rebellious relatives who finally assassinated him, he remains a heroic grand ducal figure.

Gediminas (c.1275-1341) was a successor, though not a descendant, of Mindaugas. He rejected Lithuania's Chrisian royal crown in favor of grand ducal status in 1316 and spent his reign fending off Christian encroachment in defense of the predominant pagan population. His numerous sons and daughters firmly entrenched his dynasty in Lithuania as the House of Jagiellon, where they reigned as grand dukes while ruling Poland as kings until 1572. Subsequent rulers of Poland retained rule of the grand duchy of Lithuania but it became one of many subordinate lands and titles held by these Polish kings. However, several prominent families of the nobility in Russia and Poland legitimately descend from Gediminas.

Contrary to popular opinion, at no time was there a "Grand duchy of Warsaw." Napoleon would reduce Poland to a mere duchy. Then after 1807 Poland was divided as the spoils of war, the emperors of Russia ruling as kings of "Congress Poland" and the kings of Prussia as "Grand Dukes of Posen."

Grand duchies came late to Germany arriving, in fact, only after the abolition of the Holy Roman Empire in 1804 and Napoleon's elevation of his brother-in-law Joachim Murat as Grand Duke of Berg. In the vacuum left by the Habsburgs, the landgraviate of Hesse-Darmstadt declared itself henceforth to be the Grand Duchy of Hesse and by Rhine and the margrave of Baden took the title of Grand Duke. They were soon followed by the now independent dukes of Saxe-Weimar, Mecklenburg-Schwerin, Mecklenburg-Strelitz and Oldenburg. Even the Congress of Vienna engaged in title inflation, carving out the grand duchy of Luxembourg for the Princes of Orange as newly-minted kings of the Netherlands in 1830.

Unlike some of the earlier, titular grand princedoms, these small 19th century realms were real and the internal authority of their grand dukes was undiminished, theoretically, by any overlord. But they were dwarfed by the imperial powers aggrandizing around them, forged by 19th century nationalism. The German grandduchies were obliged in 1815 to join the German Confederation and, in 1871 the German Empire established under Prussia's Hohenzollerns. Luxembourg joined too, despite its allegiance to the Dutch king and Tuscany's Habsburg grand duke was replaced by a 95% vote of his subjects to transfer their allegiance to the Savoyard king of Italy.

There remained one more grandduchy from the medieval era on the outskirts of Europe which, unlike those which became secondary statelets, evolved into the main realm of its dynasty and ultimately, into a European super-power. During the course of that evolution, the title of grand duke changed in usage and meaning in Russia, but survived there for as long as monarchy did.

Slavic lore once maintained (and now resists) the notion that Rurik (c.830–c.879) was a Viking prince who led a migration of Scandinavians (the Varangians) to Russia. He established his rule as a prince ("knyaz"), in Novgorod among a host of warring Slavic and Baltic petty rulers around 860 CE. His numerous descendants successfully expanded their authority in all directions over generations to follow. Primogeniture was unknown among them, so at every generation each Rurikid prince received a fraction of the patrimonial territory, liegemen and his kin's support to establish or conquer his own principality. Thus Kiev was taken by Rurikid Varangians in 882 and the grandduchy of Kieven Rus' was born, the political and cultural womb of modern Russia, the Ukraine and Belarus. Ruled by Rurik's descendants, Kiev became the first Russian grandduchy in 1015, until fratricidal conflict and invasion by the Mongols in 1237 brought about its collapse.

Scattered and reduced, Rurik's descendants nonetheless survived. A few climbed back up to grand ducal status, now under the dominion of the Golden Horde. It was at this point that a distinction arises among the Rurikids between those who held only princely rank and their theoretical suzerains, the grand dukes of Vladimir-Suzdal, Muscovy and Galicia–Volhynia. Previously, the distinction between the 'velikiy knyazi' (grand princes) and the 'udyelniye knyazi' (local princes) was largely a matter of prestige. The Mongols made it a matter of authority. In 1252 Sartak Khan made Prince Alexander Nevsky of Novgorod the new Grand Duke of Vladimir-Suzdal, then foremost of the Rurikid principalities. Muscovy transformed from principality to grand duchy in 1283. With the approval of the Mongol overlords, the grand dukes exercised authority over the other Rurikid princes, their policies reflecting awareness of the fact that rival Rurikids were eager to supplant them.

Once Peter, Metropolitan of All Rus, moved his seat from Vladimir to Moscow in 1325 it was clear that Muscovy had become the premier Rurikid power in the Rus. In 1328 Ivan I Kalita ("the Moneybag"), Prince of Moscow, obtained appointment from the Great Khan of the Golden Horde as Grand Duke of Vladimir, thereby becoming suzerain over the other Rurikid princes, in particular Ivan's rivals, the princes of Tver and Nizhny Novgorod. His descendant Ivan III the Great repelled the Golden Horde's exactions and tripled Muscovy's area in what is known as "the gathering of the Russian lands."

Ivan IV the Terrible took the decisive step, having become Grand Duke of Muscovy in 1533 (occasionally styling himself tsar as had some of his ancestors, notably Ivan III) of officially crowning himself Tsar and Autocrat of All Russia in 1547. Henceforth the sons and daughters of Russia's rulers added to their grand ducal title that of 'tsarevich' or 'tsarevna'.

'Tsar' was the Russian term for the ancient rulers of Byzantium and other monarchs of imperial stature, and the word is related to the Latin 'Caesar'. Nonetheless by the time of Peter the Great, the word was no longer synonymous with 'emperor'. The only European monarch of imperial rank was the Holy Roman Emperor, who had long been referred to in Russia as "kesar" rather than as tsar. However, the tsar was also Autocrat ("Samoder-ec"), a title which unequivocally implied the monarch's absolute authority over the Russian land and people.

Ivan the Terrible gave meaning to tsarist autocracy by introducing the Oprichnina ("separation") to Russia. A time of terror for prince and peasant alike, during this period of focus on the rights and lands of the Tsar, now become absolute, those of the nobility were deprecated. Ivan pursued a policy of isolating himself from and degrading the nobility, including his own kin who until recently had reigned over principalities inherited, like Ivan's tsardom, from their common ancestor Rurik the Varangian. Officially, all subjects of the realm were declared to be serfs of the Autocrat and, while retaining their personal estates, the rights of the many Rurikid families over their properties and peasants were curtailed, their princely privileges revoked and effaced. Princes and boyars, including those like the Gedyminians who descended from foreign sovereigns, while not stripped of their nobility relative to the rest of society, were declared to share neither status nor prerogatives with the Tsar. Thanks to Ivan's own familial brutality his line soon came to an end, and with him the rule of the Rurikids in Russia.

The first Romanov to become Tsar in Russia did so through an obscure connection in the female line to the last tsars of the House of Rurik. After an interregnum (the so-called "Time of Troubles") during which the country was occupied by Polish-Lithuanians, Russia's Zemsky Sobor (assembly of the land) bypassed the numerous squabbling Rurikid princely branches who had, anyway, lost any claim to dynastic status during the Oprichnina, to award the vacant throne to Michael Romanov in 1613. Descended from Muscovite boyars, his paternal grandfather's sister, Anastasia Romanova, had become the first consort of Ivan the Terrible in 1547. Officially, Michael was not elected tsar from among the Russian people at large, but was 'called' to the throne as one of the nearest collaterals of Tsar Theodore I. Every sector of Russian society was called upon to prevent recurrence of the Time of Troubles by publicly and unreservedly swearing allegiance to Michael and the heirs of his body as their new dynasty of sovereigns.

In 1721 Peter assumed a different title, one unknown in Russia save to those fluent in Latin: Imperator. The consort of the imperator was declared to be the 'Imperatritsa'. The titles for imperial children of 'tsarevich' and 'tsarevna' were abandoned in favor of similar but newly-coined terms; 'Caesarevich' ('Tsesarevich' in Russian) and 'Caesarevna' ('Tsesarevna') essentially blended together the Slavic and the Latin, East and West — just the image Peter intended to evoke. Grand Duke and Grand Duchess fell into desuetude, although they remained titles belonging to the older generation of Romanovs, Peter's siblings and nieces.

When the childless Caesarevna Elisabeth Petrovna Romanova became empress, she summoned from Germany her late sister Anna Petrovna's son, Duke Karl Peter of Holstein-Gottorp, to take up his place in Russia as her heir. After converting to Orthodoxy, he was proclaimed successor to the throne, granted the title of grand duke and the style of Imperial Highness. Use of the old titles for this new heir was apparently intended to re-assure Russians that a new, foreign dynast could be inserted into the line of succession to Russia's throne without alarm. After all, Karl Peter was a grandson of the revered Peter the Great, whose name he adopted. When the young Peter's own son Paul Petrovich (by Princess Catherine of Anhalt-Zerbst) was born he, too, was proclaimed a grand duke – although designation as the official heir to the throne was omitted. When Peter's wife seized the throne from him, beginning her reign as Catherine the Great, Paul Petrovich was, again, promptly recognized as 'Grand Duke', but not as heir, in keeping with the Emperor Peter's law which allowed the Autocrat to name his or her successor. For the next 40 years, Russia's heir presumptive was known to the public simply as the Grand Duke Paul Petrovich.

Traditionally the title velikiy knyaz had no specific rules of descent: it belonged to all dynasts, and additionally, dynasts were created by the act of granting the title to some other heirs. Until the 19th century, the Russian Imperial House was usually in a precarious situation, often having no more than a couple of living male dynasts, if even that many. Empress Elisabeth, after all male-line descent had been exhausted, made her sister's son, the future Peter III of Russia a dynast and a Grand Duke.

In 1797, Peter III and Catherine II's disaffected son, Emperor Paul, having languished during his mother's reign under fear of being disinherited by imperial fiat, decreed the Fundamental Laws of the Russian Empire, which fixed the rules of succession for the duration of the monarchy. It is widely believed that Catherine's mistreatment of Paul left him in such a state of misogynistic paranoia that as soon as he became tsar he banned women from the throne forever. The opposite is true: Not only did he affirm that Romanov descendants in female line could inherit the throne, but Paul stipulated that any female dynast was to reign in her own right if the succession fell to her, and could not be bypassed in favor of her male issue. He also stipulated in law that every male Romanov upon attaining adulthood, and each new monarch during coronation, had to swear to uphold the succession laws unaltered.

However, no woman could succeed to the throne of Russia so long as there remained any males in the dynasty. Despite the execution of several males of the Imperial family besides her father and brother, there were still many Romanov grand dukes and princes who escaped from the Russian Revolution, the last of whom died in exile only in 1992.

Russian monarchical law stated that once the last Romanov male died (who would also have been emperor/tsar, at least in theory), that male's nearest female relative, or her descendant, automatically inherited the throne. This is known in Europe as 'semi-Salic' succession because, unlike the Salic law of history, it did not ban female succession altogether. But it meant that instead of an emperor's daughter or sister succeeding to the crown, a distant male relative, perhaps of a junior branch of the family, might inherit. Moreover, if he died without male issue his own daughters and sisters would have a prior claim to the crown than those of the previous emperor.

Semi-Salic law only distinguishes between females based on nearness of kinship to the last emperor, not dynasty. Thus it gave no preference to Romanovs per se, and none to Russians over foreigners, or to the Orthodox over the non-Orthodox.

Another complexity is the application of requirements for 'equal' marriage to Russia's dynasts. In 1820, the Fundamental Laws were modified to require that spouses of Romanovs had to be born of a "royal or sovereign family" if the issue were to have rights of succession to the Russian throne. Although Alexander III tightened this law in 1886 by altogether forbidding unequal marriages, in 1911 Nicholas II eased the restriction by ukase, allowing princes and princess of the Blood Imperial – but not grand dukes or grand duchesses – to marry unequally under three conditions: 1. the marriage had to obtain the emperor de jure's prior consent; 2. the issue would have no succession rights or membership in the imperial house; and, 3. Imperial consent would only be granted if the prince or princess first renounced his/her own personal right of succession as well.

Although three Romanovs complied with this law when they married (Princess Tatiana Konstantinovna in 1911, Princess Irina Alexandrovna in 1914, and Princess Catherine Ioanovna in 1937), three Romanovs violated it: Grand Duke Michael Aleksandrovich in October 1912, Grand Duchess Olga Alexandrovna in November 1916, and Grand Duchess Maria Pavlovna Jr. in September 1917 (in post-revolution Russia). Under monarchical law, these last three weddings were void, since a 1797 Fundamental Law declared that marriages of members of the imperial dynasty were only legal if contracted with the emperor's prior approval, and such approval could not legally be granted to dynasts of grand ducal rank.

Because the Fundamental Laws only applied to sons and daughters of the imperial dynasty in the male line, the marriages of female Romanovs (whether grand duchess or princess) were fully subject to restriction, while those of their offspring – even though possessing Russian succession rights if descended from an approved marriage – were not (the sole exception were the children of Nicholas II's sister, Xenia, who had married a Romanov cousin).

The emperor was traditional and legal head of the Orthodox Church in Russia and his consort was expected to be Orthodox as well. Included in Russia's Fundamental Laws were Articles 184 and 185. The two laws regulated, but distinguished between, the marriages of male dynasts who were distant enough in the line of succession that their wives were unlikely to become empress, and those who, by contrast, could be expected at the time of marriage to be called to wear Russia's crown.

Article 184 applied to the former group, allowing them to marry non-Orthodox princesses dynastically. Article 185 was unspecific, affording the sovereign discretion, but in practice it was applied to the emperor's heir-apparent or heir-presumptive and their near heirs, to require them to marry Orthodox brides. Who decided which dynasts could only marry within the church? The Emperor. Of course it was always possible that a distant cousin would unexpectedly succeed to the crown. But in that case his or her consort could, under law, convert.

This religious compromise reflected the fact that when the Fundamental Laws were adopted, Russia was the only Orthodox dynasty reigning in Europe. It would have limited the bridal selection pool too much if the Romanovs had been rigid about Orthodoxy. Contrary to a popular misconception, it made no legal difference in the Romanov dynasty whether the child of an equal and approved marriage was born to an Orthodox mother so long as the child adhered to Orthodoxy in the event of inheritance of the throne.

Strictly speaking, all of Peter III's male-line descendants and their wives were also "Duke/Duchess of Holstein-Gottorp, Count/Countess of Oldenburg." In practice, these titles were only added to the Emperor's long string of secondary titles. Russia exchanged its claim to Gottorp for Oldenburg in 1777, and then donated the latter to a German branch of Holstein cousins. But the ducal and county titles continued to descend according to the rules of the Holy Roman Empire and, later, those of the German Empire within which the territories lay.

In 1762 Catherine II's son Grand Duke Paul Petrovich was accorded the title 'Tsesarevich' as heir apparent (or more commonly spelled *Tsarevich*). Until then, there had been no special title for the emperor's or tsar's eldest son. Paul's eldest son, Alexander, was likewise tsesarevich from 1797, after Paul was crowned Emperor. Paul's children, mostly born while he was heir apparent, were grand dukes and grand duchesses, which became the customary style for the emperor's children and other male-line descendants.

When Catherine the Great introduced French as the court language at St Petersburg, 'grande duchesse' was already the customary translation in that language, as was 'grand duchess' in English. Some linguists and historians consider this usage a modern mistranslation. But Catherine, being fluent in German, Russian and French, was better situated than anyone to assess the relevant nuances and alternatives. Thus, whatever its provenance, 'grand duchess' reflects sovereign choice rather than ignorant error.

In 1886, Alexander III restricted the title of grand duke to children and male-line grandchildren of an emperor, along with the attribute of Imperial Highness. Great-grandchildren were princes of the Blood Imperial with the style of Highness. Each of these great-grandsons' heirs-male in perpetuity (and their consorts) was also entitled to be addressed as Highness, while the remainder of male-line descendants were princes and Serene Highnesses. This latter style being fairly common among Russia's many non-royal princely families, in 1911 a group of grand dukes petitioned the emperor to extend the grand ducal title to additional generations of Romanovs, and to allow princes to marry unequally while retaining their dynastic rights. Nicholas II formally rejected these requests as is documented in the Frederiks Memorandum.

What, then, of the claim to be a 'grand duke' made by Vladimir Kirillovich (1917-1992)? And of his even more ambitious claim to be the de jure Emperor, entitled to exercise the Imperial prerogative even in the long years of Romanov exile following the Russian Revolution? And finally, what of the claim that his daughter, Maria Vladimirovna (b.1953) inherited headship of the Imperial dynasty upon her father's death despite the fact that there are a dozen or more males alive who descend in the legitimate male line from one or another of Russia's emperors?

These questions are closely bound together and usually accompanied by many more questions and doubts as to the rightful claimant to the defunct throne of the Romanovs. But upon examination, they appear answerable by reference to a few facts, seldom acknowledged in this context.

The rules governing succession and titles are legally non-existent and unenforceable since the overthrow of Russia's monarchy in 1917. Most Romanov descendants have lived outside Russia for generations now and use either no title at all or one conveniently made up and recognized by others as a courtesy. On the other hand, any discussion of Romanov claims and titles, whether historical, genealogical, political or purely hypothetical is meaningless unless the rules that were in force when the monarchy existed structure the conversation. Yet the challenges to the dynastic claims of Kirill Vladimirovich, Vladimir Kirillovich, Maria

Vladimirovna and/or George Mikhailovich invariably ignore – and demand that others ignore – the steps taken by them to comply with Russia's Fundamental Laws governing the succession at enormous personal sacrifice, while ignoring the contradictions or inadequacies of the objections raised to their claims. Sometimes it seems as if only the Vladimirovichi are held to a standard of legality or tradition in order to qualify as claimants to headship of the Romanov dynasty. Others who assert such leadership or repudiate claims, too often do so without addressing questions about their own standing, according to law or tradition, as Romanov dynasts, or about the reasoning they apply in determining the validity of others' claims to dynastic status: a chorus of "never mind!" is too often submitted as the only reply to any questioning of alternative rationales or assertions.

Never mind, for instance, that other dynasties have lost thrones, wealth, citizenship, and lives (Spain, Bulgaria) during revolution, but equal status (so-called "*ebenbürtig*") marriage remained the norm in their dynasties (even during exile) until the heads of their dynasties changed the norms – and not before.

Never mind that post-Revolution the Vladimirovichi branch of the Romanovs managed to contract four marriages between 1925 and 1976 into families previously recognized as ebenbürtig, apparently not finding it impossible to comply with Russia's dynastic (Pauline) law on marriages in exile.

Never mind that twenty years after the 1917 revolution, three of the four surviving grand dukes and two adult Romanov princes not only recognized Vladimir as the rightful head of the dynasty according to Pauline law, but signed an affidavit affirming "*that the rights of each one of the Members of the Imperial House of Russia are precisely defined by the Fundamental State Laws of the Russian Empire and the Statute on the Imperial Family, and are well known to all of us and we have all committed ourselves by a special oath to observe them.*"

Never mind that as soon after the revolution as 1924, Grand Duke Alexander Mikhailovich provided his signature and those of four of his adult sons on a similar pledge of allegiance to Grand Duke Kirill Vladimirovich, which stated, "*We submit ourselves to you and are ready to serve our beloved country as our fathers served it, and according to their principles.*" Excluding the two of Alexander's sons who never signed (Dimitri and Vassily, both of whom pre-deceased Vladimir Kirillovich, leaving no sons), there were only two adult male Romanovs living who, by 1938, had not agreed in writing to continue to be bound by the Pauline succession laws: Prince George Konstantinovich, who died unmarried the next year, and Prince Roman Petrovich.

Never mind that Roman Petrovich's son, Nicholas Romanovich, as President of the Romanoff Family Association, stated in an official declaration published in *Point de Vue* on 12 May 1992, that "*Kirill's rights were incontestable,*" yet Kirill, as acknowledged head of the dynasty, never recognized the 1921 marriage of Roman's parents as dynastically valid. Never mind that of the four members of the Romanoff Family Association (alleged to be dynasts) who have rejected the dynasticity of Vladimir Kirillovich and/or his daughter Maria Vladimirovna, two are themselves children of marriages deemed morganatic by the man they or their fathers accepted in exile as rightful head of the Romanov dynasty. The other two are Dimitri Romanovich (b. 1926) and the late Princess Vera Konstantinovna (1906-2001), neither of whom produced dynastic offspring eligible to claim legal heirship to Nicholas II, Peter the Great or Michael Romanov.

For émigrés, monarchists, sticklers and dreamers, article 53 of the Fundamental Laws remained crucial long after the Romanovs were executed or exiled: *"On the demise of the Emperor, his heir accedes to the Throne by virtue of the law of succession itself, which confers this right upon him. The accession of an Emperor to the throne is counted from the day of the demise of his predecessor."*

Properly, this means that for those who reject the legality (if not the reality) of the Russian Revolution, there has been no interregnum since 1917. The laws that governed Romanov succession and titles under the monarchy are considered still valid, regardless of de facto obstacles to their enforcement. Therefore, if one applies the formula of the Fundamental Laws to the House of Romanov to determine who would today be Russia's monarch, that person's right to use of the titles and prerogatives of the Russian Emperor follows automatically, regardless of what discretion is deemed politic to employ in the real world.

There are, in other words, living grand dukes in today's world. We have but to acknowledge the tradition they incarnate to know them.

Charles B. Stewart
Los Angeles, CA
June 2012

P   PUBLISHER'S NOTES

During the Summer of 2004 I was busily preparing for two events: the publication of *The Grand Duchesses – Daughters and Granddaughters of Russia's Tsars*, and our wedding. Both took place the same week. It was a stressful time, as the reader can imagine.

However, both events have brought me, as a publisher and a husband, endless joy. Soon after *The Grand Duchesses* began selling, I realized that we had to produce a companion book, which logically would be titled "*The Grand Dukes – Sons and Grandsons of Russia's Tsars.*" Two years later I had finished choosing the authors, every single one of them an expert in their field, and work began in earnest. The end result amunted to nearly six hundred pages, which just before going to print forced us to make the decision to print the book in two-volumes. This allowed for an easier book to handle, as well as giving us the chance for more pictures to be used than if we had retained the original idea of having the book as a stand-alone volume.

It was not the easiest enterprise. The contributors came from the USA, the United Kingdom, Canada and Russia. We had to have guidelines, spelling consistency, cohesiveness, agreeing on editing, formatting and content. Getting a dozen people to accept every decision proved a challenge, and the source of countless delays, and yet we remain close friends. We did it!

What the reader now holds is the product of an amazingly talented group of today's leading royal biographers. Among us we have written more than 50 books, something to be extremely proud of.

The Grand Dukes came to life after a challenging Summer 2010 during which I battled a life-threatening illness and faced countless radiotherapy sessions. Thinking about completing the book provided me with ample sources of inspiration and the will to overcome the challenges I faced. Once the medical team seeing me through this illness allowed my return to the office at Eurohistory.com, I jumped in the fray and three weeks later the book went to print.

I am inspired by the end result. *The Grand Dukes* is sure to become one of those "must-have" titles in our European royal history book collection. Hopefully, the reader will agree with our own perception of the book we have written.

Before letting the reader continue, one word of caution. Imperial Russia followed the Julian calendar, "a reform of the Roman calendar, was introduced by Julius Caesar in 46 BC, and came into force in 45 B. It was chosen after consultation with the astronomer Sosigenes of Alexandria and was probably designed to approximate the tropical year, known at least since Hipparchus. It has a regular year of 365 days divided into 12 months, and a leap day is added to February every four years. Hence the Julian year is on average 365.25 days long."

The rest of the Western world followed the Gregorian calendar. "The Gregorian calendar, also known as the Western calendar or the Christian calendar, is the internationally accepted civil calendar. It was introduced by Pope Gregory XIII, after whom the calendar was named, by a decree signed on 24 February 1582." Furthermore, The motivation for the Gregorian reform was that the Julian calendar assumes that the time between vernal equinoxes is 365.25 days, when in fact it is about 11 minutes less. The accumulated error between these values was about 10 days when the reform was made, resulting in the equinox occurring on March 11 and moving steadily earlier in the calendar. Since the equinox was tied to the celebration of Easter, the Roman Catholic Church considered that this steady movement was undesirable.

Consequently, countries following the Julian calendar were behind a few days. Russia was one of them. In the XVIII century Russia was eleven days behind the Western world. In the XIX century the difference was 12 days, while in the XX century that number rose by one to 13. Hence, when appropriate, authors have used Western dates, and if Julian calendar dates were used, we have added the "O.S." after the used date. O.S. stands for Old Style, meaning the Julian calendar.

One last word. Of late some authors have taken to addressing members of the Imperial Family by the title of "Grand Prince" or "Grand Princess." Although this is a translation perhaps closer to the original Russian title, we feel it erroneous. The Imperial Court was quite clear about this. The manual published by it and handed to Western diplomats serving in Russia established that the title of members of the Imperial Family was "Grand Duke" and "Grand Duchess." For some modern authors to contradict the Imperial Court itself, I personally find erroneous, historically inaccurate and jarring.

Also, and for obvious reasons, we have not included in this volume those Russian Grand Dukes who died in infancy.

With that said, enjoy *The Grand Dukes* – we hope it brings alive a world long gone, a world devoured by the passions of men and their inability to appreciate history.

Arturo Beéche, October 10, 2010.

A | **ACKNOWLEDGMENTS**

*T**he authors would like to extend their appreciation to everyone involved in the publication of this extensive two-volume book, a truly unique work of royal biography in itself, and one that we expect will become one of the books of choice when readers wish to learn about the Romanov dynasty and Imperial Russia.*

Furthermore, Grant Hayter-Menzies would like to express his appreciation to for their assistance and encouragement to the following: Arturo Beéche, Xenia von Besack, Carl Reeves Close, Peter Kurth, Marion Mienert, Stephen O'Donnell, and Odette Terrel des Chenes.

Janet Ashton would like to thank Katrina Warne, William Lee, and, as always, Greg King.

Lisa Davidson would like to thank "Jeff for being my dearest love and constant support; thank you Erika and Alexis for constantly reminding me what it's all about; thank you Jean and Jim for loving me always; ditto to Hoyt and Barbara and also for a loving home; thank you Charlotte, Carolynn and Lynn and the Bottom Line folks for keeping me on the right track, and to David L. for the precious gift of self reliance.

John van der Kiste would like to "thank my wife Kim Van der Kiste who read through the drafts for me as ever."

William Lee is deeply thankful to Prince David Chavchavadze and to Janet Ashton.

Last, but by no means least, Arturo Beéche would like to thank, "my husband David W. Higdon for his unquestioned support of every single project I have designed at Eurohistory.com – as well, I must thank our son Zac Higdon Beéche for allowing his stay-at-home dad the time and space to complete this book. I would also like to thank several of our collaborators and supporters, in particular: Charles Stewart, Katrina Warne, Mary Houck, Geoff Teeter, Mark Andersen, Larry Russell, Katie Tice, Leslie Sieren, and Phil Perry. I would also like to express my deepest appreciation to all the contributors for their diligence, enthusiasm and patience. Henry Wong has been instrumental in the design of the book cover and for his tireless work I am deeply thankful. Lastly, as Founder of Eurohistory.com, I must thank the readership of our magazine and books for their incredible support.

The printing staff at Thomson-Shore and their expertise are a great addition to our myriad projects amf we look at many more yeras of collaboration with them!

1

THE SONS OF TSAR PAUL I

TSAR ALEXANDER I
(1777-1825)

By Janet Ashton

*I*n 1834, in the Square before the Winter Palace in St Petersburg, a Victory Column was erected. A single red granite monolith topped by an angel holding a cross, it survived the Soviet years unscathed, a symbol of Russian resistance to foreign invasion, raised to celebrate the defeat of Napoleon in 1812. Though its base is decorated with military images, the angel atop it, his face modeled on that of the victorious Tsar Alexander, lends a pacific and transcendent edge. The monument embodies the profound duality of the Emperor whose face it bears: Alexander the Blessed, all things to all men; the autocrat and spirit of Enlightenment; the mystic and giver of temporal laws; the European and victor over the revolutionary European invader. Alexander, "our Angel," presiding serenely over the Tsarist capital, over Soviet Leningrad, and over capitalist Petersburg again; the aloof, apolitical figure, held in place like the column by nothing more or less than the force of his own weight.

He was born, appropriately enough to his messianic image, just before Christmas 1777, on 12 December (O.S.), at the Winter Palace in St Petersburg. Though he was the firstborn child of the future Tsar Paul and of the Grand Duchess Maria Feodorovna, this fact mattered to few at court. To all intents and purposes, Alexander Pavlovich was the property of his grandmother the Empress, Catherine the Great, who took him when he was a few days old and gave his parents a patch of land to build a palace in return. Perhaps unexpectedly, it was his parents who were responsible for choosing his portentous name: its classical grandeur actually annoyed Catherine at first, but she soon reconciled herself, and when Alexander's eldest sibling was born, she selected a Greek name for him too: Konstantin. She took Konstantin away from his parents as well, so Alexander would at least be raised with a companion his own age.

Catherine superintended every detail of the little boys' upbringing, right down to designing a one-piece romper suit for them. Their parents were not to be trusted with anything: her own relationship with Paul had been damaged by his being taken away from her as a baby, in exactly the manner she had now done with his sons, and personality clashes added to the difficulties as he grew. Their mother Maria, who herself was to mature into a formidable grande dame in time, was for now an inexperienced young girl, no match for the Empress. *"Monsieur Alexandre,"* Catherine wrote archly when her grandson was still a toddler, *"is ahead of his age in everything: strength, intelligence, good temper, knowledge; he'll grow into an excellent person, as long as his parents' tricks don't get in my way."*[1]

The Empress, of course, was doing more than simply over-indulging the maternal instinct that had been frustrated when her own son was a baby: she was raising a future Emperor. She was fond of Alexander's and Konstantin's younger sisters, but being unlikely to succeed to the throne they failed to excite the same interest from her as the boys did, and she left them to be raised by their parents at Pavlovsk, the palace Paul and Maria built on the land she had swapped them for Alexander.

His education and Konstantin's was to be organized along modern lines, according the philosophy of Jean-Jacques Rousseau: the interests a child revealed in play would become an intrinsic part of his training. This meant that the boys were observed even in their leisure hours, of course. The ultimate aim was to produce "Enlightened Despots" in the eighteenth-century mode: to become what Catherine herself had first striven to be as a monarch: just, thoughtful, and honest rulers, legislators rather than conquerors, to whom the dictates of Reason and their consciences were incomparably superior to the opinion of those around them. Inevitably, the reality of their educations fell somewhat short of the aspiration.

They started their education with Sophie Benckendorf as Governess, assisted by nursemaids called Mrs Nichols and Miss Gessler. The Empress looked after their well being in every possible way: vaccination against smallpox being the latest medical wonder, she had a doctor brought in from England where the vaccine had been developed to inoculate them. The technique at that time was to inject a child with smallpox pus, giving him a mild dose of the disease, but Alexander became sicker than expected and the household was on tenterhooks, despite the doctor's assurance that he was in no real danger. Any trivial thing the young grand duke asked or desired sent his household into a rush to procure it for him, and he rewarded those he liked by giving them coins from a little purse he owned and had near him at all times. Both his doctor and his grandmother were favoured recipients while he was sick.[2] His and Konstantin's nursery was full of expensive toys, including silver clockwork barges which when wound up would move through real water with toy men rowing them. Each had their own suite of rooms with footmen and guards at the door.[3]

After the elderly governess's death, a tough military governor, Nicholas Saltykov, was appointed, along with other tutors including a secularized beardless priest who taught agriculture and the radical Swiss pedagogue Fredric-Cesar La Harpe. The tutors divided into factions, with "westernizers" – including the Orthodox priest Samborskii – uniting against the autocratic thinking of the Russian tutors, who complained that Alexander's education was too European, too republican. But all left their mark on his political thinking to different degrees, achieving a better synthesis than might be expected. Alexander was to be viewed throughout his life and by many historians as a political chameleon, changing his colours according to the company or the times, but from several principles he did not deviate: all reform came from him, the Tsar; and the rule of law was paramount. Thus he was able to be true simultaneously to both his liberal and his conservative heritage in the confusing times surrounding him. Even La Harpe, ostensibly the most liberal of his tutors, emphazised continually that Alexander alone would be the font and initiator of reform in Russia, and counselled him accordingly throughout his life: *"In the name of your people, preserve as inviolable the authority bestowed upon you which you want to use for the supreme good."*[4]

Now he had left the nursery, Alexander lived in the Winter Palace, sleeping on a leather mattress stuffed with hay, his rooms notoriously close to the sound of the gun salute from the Admiralty, which was intended to harden him to battle, but instead damaged his hearing. Despite his fairly Spartan rooms and close supervision, all of the tutors worried that Catherine's court would spoil him: he was a tall blond boy, reasonably handsome, a good dancer and mimic: as he reached his teens the Empress liked to show him off and buy him all the clothes he wanted. Even in his parents' homes, where he was expected to wear uniform and rise at 4a.m., he was treated with the exaggerated deference due his rank: possibly even more so than in the Empress's circles. Somewhat to people's surprise, he enjoyed himself very much in his father's homes, marching on the parade ground Paul worshipped and taking part in gun practice. To counter all the flattery, La Harpe had a policy of forcing both boys to engage in constant strict self-criticism. This had the result of damaging their confidence considerably. *"Instead of redoubling my efforts to profit from the years of study that remain to me,"* Alexander wrote aged fourteen, *"I grow every day more careless, inattentive and incapable. What shall I become? Nothing, according to all appearances."*[5]

His education was about to be disrupted permanently by his grandmother's marital plans for him. In 1792 she had the fourteen-year-old Princess Louise of Baden brought to St Petersburg, and watched hopefully for signs of developing romance between the young girl and fifteen-year-old Alexander. *"It's a devilish trick I am playing on him,"* she wrote rather salaciously to her habitual confidant Melchior Grimm. *"For I am leading him into temptation."*[6] – The Princess entered the Orthodox Church with the name Elisabeth Alexeievna and she and Alexander were married on September 28 (O.S.), 1793, but their union failed to blossom into the grand passion Catherine hoped. Some court observers thought Elisabeth intellectually more mature than her groom, for all his tutors' efforts. The somewhat reserved young bride certainly found Alexander inattentive, occasionally sarcastic in the face of her attempts to be romantic, and she soon developed instead an inappropriately intense relationship with a lady-in-waiting. Alexander found distraction elsewhere, chiefly but far from exclusively with Princess Maria Narishkina, who bore him several children while married to another man. The situation was notorious in society: long after Alexander's own death, the great poet Pushkin was provoked to his fatal duel by a satirical letter which announced his election to The Serene Order of Cuckold Husbands, presided over by Prince Dimitri Lvovich Narishkin, Maria's spouse.

Members of Alexander and Elisabeth's household, under the spell of Alexander's charm, were not slow to lay the blame for the failure of the marriage entirely at his wife's feet. *"An ardent and passionate imagination came, in her case,*

3

alongside a heart incapable of true affection," wrote a lady-in-waiting. *"These few words explain her story. Her noble sentiments; her high ideals; her virtuous ways, made her the idol of the masses but never attracted her husband."*[7] Even her sympathizers admitted that poor Elisabeth's shyness made her seem cold.

Sowing his wild oats and enjoying himself while he could, Alexander contemplated his eventual heritage with misgivings. *"There is incredible confusion in our affairs,"* he observed of Russia's political system. *"In such circumstances is it possible for one man to rule the state, still less correct abuses within it?"*[8] He was aware that his grandmother, to whom belonged the legal right to name her successor, was considering settling the throne directly on him rather than upon his father, and he was in two minds about this possibility. Catherine's death following a stroke in her bathroom in November 1796 put an end to the discussion: Paul mounted the throne and at once began a series of reforms that created both personal and political conflict for him.

Tsar Paul, who traditionally has had a bad press from historians and in popular conception, was a man of strict moral standards whose reforming zeal stemmed from his disgust at what he saw as the degeneracy of the ruling class around his mother. He was certainly not the mad man of legend, but some of his overly melodramatic actions on ascending the throne frightened his subjects and annoyed his family. Exhuming the body for familial displays of sorrow, Paul insisted for instance on declaring mourning for his long-dead father Peter III in conjunction with that for Catherine, and he turned the Tauride Palace – the home of his mother's most enduring lover Grigory Potemkin – into a barracks. Yet he did not avenge himself directly upon Catherine's friends and admirers: he took out his wrath in symbolic rather than personal ways. At the funeral, Catherine's coffin was bare, while that of the husband her favourites had murdered bore the imperial crown she had taken after his death. Paul, whose own paternity had never been clear to anyone, wished the world to see that his throne came to him through heredity, as the son of Peter and scion of the Romanovs, rather than the heir of the usurping German princess who had almost disowned him in turn.

Alexander and his wife, meanwhile, were piqued by his parents' petty attention to such matters as what they wore out in public: both Elisabeth and Konstantin's new bride Anna complained that the Empress Maria treated them like ladies-in-waiting who must perpetually be ready for her call. The imperial family was now expected to spend the majority of its time together in a public show of devotion and unity, with morning given over to military exercises for the men, while evenings were passed in audiences and assemblies or at the theatre. Court balls ceased to be the fun they had been in Catherine's day; instead, they were simple exercises in obedience to etiquette, and transgressions could result in actual punishment. United in adversity, Alexander and Elisabeth grew closer than they had been previously, and in 1799 their first child, the Grand Duchess Maria Alexandrovna ("Mauschen"), was at last born. Rumours at court attributed her paternity not to Alexander but to his great friend Adam Czartoryski: but if this was true, Alexander himself showed no bitterness to either his wife or his friend. In truth, he actively encouraged their relationship while enjoying in turn a flirtation with his sister-in-law Anna, herself Elisabeth's inseparable friend. When Anna went home to Coburg, ostensibly for her health, shortly before Elisabeth's confinement, the Grand Duchess was inconsolable.

Luckily, her little Maria thrived at first. She cut her teeth, a stage of life considered dangerous in the early nineteenth century, with minimal problems, to the pride of her mother. But when she was one year old she was taken to live in the gloomy Marble Palace, described by one tourist as *"the most repulsive building in all St Petersburg…One who, expecting an orangery, falls into an ice cellar, cannot experience a more bitter deception, or a severer chill."*[9] Coincidentally or not, the baby developed several weeks of fever and diarrhoea, dying of convulsions in July 1800. Elisabeth was devastated, her anguished letters to her mother showing a quite different side of the personality her staff found so cool and distant. *"Oh Mama – how dreadful an irreparable loss is! You can understand the emptiness, the utter death, that has come over my existence! You lost a child, but you had others; I have none!"*[10] Two months later, envisaging little chance of another baby to console her, she was still struggling to live normally. *"There's not an hour in the day that I don't think of her, and certainly not a day when I don't weep bitter tears for her."*[11] It was indeed to be six years before she had another child, the Grand Duchess Elisabeth, "Lisinka", who in turn succumbed to convulsions at two years old.

In time, the personal annoyances of living in his father's court were joined for Alexander by misgivings about the speed and purpose of changes his father wrought. *"Everything has been turned upside down at once…The military take up almost all of his time, and that in parades. For the rest, he has no plan to follow; he orders today what a month later he countermands,"* the Heir to the throne wrote, perhaps not quite fairly. And then he added, portentously. *"When my time comes it will be necessary to work little by little to create a free constitution."*[12] He was still far from confident in his own ability to run the state unaided, and in any case he was increasingly surrounded by friends and advisers for whom constitutional government was highly desirable: they included his own close friend Adam Czartoryski, a Polish aristocrat raised in that country's republican tradition, and some of his grand-mother's former intimates. A constitution for Alexander's circle meant the system-atic rule of the law: he was certainly not envisaging a fully representative system in the sense understood today. But his friends and fellow travelers used his belief in this system to help him overcome his misgivings about ascending the throne at all.

Ironically, many of Paul's reforms tended to the same end of strict and systematic legality. He began by regularising the succession, abolishing the Petrine system that allowed a monarch to select a successor at will, and insti-tuting a semi-Salic system of primogeniture that gave Alexander the inalienable right to expect the throne on his father's death. He also laid out quite clearly the rights and responsibilities of the imperial family and the aristocracy, and institut-ed certain laws designed to improve the lot of Russia's serfs. It was these measures as much as his rather erratic foreign policy – driven by a loathing of revolutionary France – and his much-ridiculed obsession with uniform and military display that turned parts of the aristocracy against this new Emperor whose obvious aim was to turn them into blindly loyal servants of his paternal-istic state.

For a time, the Tsar showed a clear preference among his sons for Konstantin, naming him "Tsarevich" in recognition of military success, though this title belonged in theory and law to the heir alone. Alexander began to fear that in spite of the Pauline Law he himself was about to be replaced by his brother as Catherine had contemplated replacing his father with him. But before long, Paul grew suspicious of both his adult sons. Educated by his mother, they evoked her despised world for him, and both were known to criticise him publicly. He talked of his intention to adopt a German nephew as heir, and withdrew – dragging his reluctant family with him - into his vastly fortified new home, the Mikhailovsky Castle, in St Petersburg. Here he would be safe from the conspiracies that he suspected – and certainly not without reason – were being hatched against him.

Alexander was aware of these plots, and affected to believe the protestations that all they sought to achieve was his father's abdication. On March 11, 1801 (O.S.), a group of conspirators that included his friend Peter Alexeievich von Pahlen, the Governor of the city, and Nicholas Zubov, brother of Catherine's one-time lover, got into the Castle with the assistance of Paul's own guard. Entering his bedchamber, they found the terrified Tsar crouching behind a screen, his bare feet giving him away, and they demanded his abdication. A struggle ensued, lights went out, and within a short space of time Paul was dead.

For the rest of his life, the dreadful event and his own complicity in it preyed on Alexander's mind. He was inclined to view the deaths in childhood of both his daughters by Elisabeth and four of his likely six children by Maria Narishkina as Divine retribution for this most Biblical of crimes, a parricide. There were further children attributed to Alexander, and most survived, but these were born of brief transient relationships with maids-of-honour and other men's wives, and raised or adopted by other people. Even the paternity of his sister-in-law Anna's secret son, born some years after her separation from Konstantin, is laid by some sources at Alexander's door, though there are other candidates too. Alexander was irresistible to women: contemporary memoirs leave no doubt as to the mystique wrought by elevated rank combined with gentle charm and reasonably good looks.

Notwithstanding the regularity and delicacy of his features," wrote one Polish countess who came to know him well, *"the brightness and freshness of his complexion, his beauty was less striking, at first sight, than that air of benevolence and kindness which captivated all hearts and instantly inspired confidence. His tall, noble and majestic form, which often stooped a little with grace, like the post of an ancient statue, already threatened to become stout, but he was perfectly formed. His eyes were blue, bright and expressive; he was a little short-sighted. His nose was straight and well-shaped, his mouth small and agreeable. The rounded contour of his face, as well as his profile, resembled that of his august mother. His forehead was somewhat bald, but this gave to his whole countenance an open and serene expression, and his hair of a golden blond, carefully arranged as in the heads on the antique cameos or medallions, seemed made to receive the triple crown of olive, myrtle and laurel. He had an infinity of shades of tone and manner. When he addressed men of distinguished rank, it was dignity and affability at the same time; to persons of his retinue, with an air of kindness almost familiar; to women of a certain age, with deference; and to young people, with an infinite grace, a refined and attractive manner, and a counte-*

nance full of expression.

> *This prince in his early youth had had his hearing seriously impaired by the discharge of artillery, in consequence of which his left ear was somewhat deaf, and he usually turned the right toward the speaker to hear better. No painter, with out exception, has ever been able to catch the likeness of his features, especially the expression and refinement of his countenance....More fortunate than his brother artists, [François] Gerard obtained several sittings with the Emperor Alexander. In his portrait of the prince, as in all his chefs d'oeuvre, he has shown a great talent and a beautiful touch, but still it is not Alexander."* [13]

Alexander actually spent the early part of his reign in a condition of intermittent depression, struggling to re-establish a state of equilibrium in foreign affairs while acting the part of the "hesitant reformer" at home, bound by his desire to *"govern the people entrusted to us by God according to the Laws and the heart of Our late August Grandmother,"* the Enlightened Despot, Catherine the Great.[14] In the light of subsequent events, many concluded that Alexander's reforming bent in the early part of his reign was mainly due to his desire to keep the conspirators who had killed his father on his side. But all the while he was corresponding enthusiastically with Thomas Jefferson on matters constitutional, and he declared of serfdom that, *"Nothing could be more degrading or humiliating than the sale of people. To the shame of Russia slavery still exists."*[15]

It was during this period that the Tsar engaged Michael Speranskii to draw up a potential constitution for Russia, which envisaged a series of elected bodies or Dumas with a State Council to mediate between them and the autocrat. *"The existence of a Russian constitution,"* Speranskii wrote, *'should be owing not to the inflammation of passions and the extremity of circumstances, but to the beneficent inspiration of the supreme power."*[16] The system eventually approved was much-modified from the original proposals, but revolutionary enough in itself, being based on the ministerial system of Napoleonic France: this was the basis for government in the last century of Romanov rule. The guiding principal was that sovereign will rather than factional interests would lie behind the imposition of laws designed to achieve the happiness of Russia and her people. Alexander and Speranskii also took steps to raise the educational level of the bureaucracy, instituting examinations to ensure that unqualified aristocrats could no longer jump straight in to the upper echelons.

Around the centre of St Petersburg, Alexander commissioned ministerial buildings whose vast, neo-classical symmetry consciously echoed the rationalism of his new government. Alongside them were barracks and parade grounds, for the symbolic display of a well-ordered society. Alexander was as fanatical about uniforms and parades as his father had been, but when he took to the battlefield himself at Austerlitz against France – the first Emperor since Peter the Great to lead his troops into battle - the results were less stunning. He treated his ministers as fellow-officers, comrades-in-arms, even when dismissing them, and kept his distance from everyone else: as his father had done before him, he used military rank to create a gap between himself and the nation he ruled, never so visible as when he faced the massed troops on parade. History records love affairs exclusively with women, but there was also something undeniably homoerotic about the imagery of Alexander's regime: from the muscled atlantii on public buildings, to the tearful displays of deep personal friendship with his ministers, he evoked the preoccupations of the classical world quite successfully.

Despite his cool distance from his people, Alexander was always at pains to present himself as a gentle Tsar: he did not use the military to intimidate or coerce as his father had done. Within the family he played the same role: his mother and his younger siblings called him *"Our Angel"* and looked up to him as to a demi-god, the source of all reason and sense, whose judgment was never questioned. Apart from Konstantin, he had had little to do with them all as a child. His other brothers Nicholas and Michael were so much younger that he treated them more as sons, planning their education and marriages. The Lycée or grammar school at Tsarskoe Selo, designed to put Speranskii's educational principles into practice among the sons of the nobility, was originally conceived as a college for the young Grand Dukes.

Unfamiliarity with his five surviving sisters, four of them relatively close in age to him, led when Alexander came to know them as adults to some rather odd relationships, much as in the case of his younger contemporary Lord Byron in a similar situation. The arrogant and blunt-spoken Grand Duchess Catherine, his fourth sister, was probably the only sibling besides Konstantin who dared question him, and Alexander appreciated her in particular, writing letters to her in which he extolled her nose, *"which I love to flatten and kiss,"*[17] so managing to make his wife jealous.

Catherine's ready ire was particularly aroused by the 1807 Treaty of Tilsit, in which Alexander and Napoleon formed a rapprochement designed to divide Europe between them, with Russia gaining her long-term prize, Constantinople, in exchange for abandoning her absolutist intention, initiated by Paul, to rid Europe of the revolutionary French. Alexander and Konstantin were basically admirers of the Napoleonic system of government; Napoleon in turn liked the Tsar, and declared arrogantly that if Alexander had been a woman he would have made him his mistress. The two were united in their dislike and mistrust of the British, Alexander's former allies, who he felt had let him down. But to Russian conservatives including the Dowager Empress and Catherine Pavlovna the Treaty was no more than a panic response to Russia's recent defeats. Misgivings about it all seemed confirmed when Napoleon failed to honour his promise to withdraw from Poland, or indeed from Prussia, whose King and Queen had been subject to loud public vows of friendship by Alexander not long before. Napoleon, who had consoled himself for his inability to take Alexander to his bed by opening negotiations for the hand of the Tsar's very youthful sister Anna, was discouraged by Russian reluctance to let her go, and suddenly announced that he was to marry the Austrian Archduchess Marie Louise instead. It was clear that he had been wooing both simultaneously. Russia also began to suffer from the lack of imports of British grain, embargoed by the alliance, and thus in 1810 Alexander broke the conditions of the Treaty by allowing British ships back in. His ally Napoleon began to prepare an invasion.

On June 12, 1812, the Emperor of the French crossed the River Nieman into Russian Poland with a Grande Armée of 450,000 men. *"The peace we shall con-*

clude will carry with it its own guarantee," he declared ominously. *"It will terminate the fatal influence which Russia has for fifty years exercised in Europe. I have come to finish for once and for all with the colossus of the barbarian north."*[18] Alexander was equally resolute. *"Once the war has begun, one of us, either Napoleon or I, Alexander, must lose his crown."*[19] A colourful mixture of Frenchmen, Italians, Portuguese, Germans, Danes and Poles, the invading troops were surprised to meet with little resistance. Alexander's army, which was about one third the size of the invader's, retreated before them, burning crops and slaughtering animals as it went so as to leave the Grande Armée nothing to eat, avoiding direct confrontation but drawing Napoleon's followers deep into the heart of Russia as autumn approached. Hungry troops and horses began to die in the vast empty landscape.

Although it was deliberate policy, the retreat did nothing to endear Alexander to his already cynical aristocracy. Catherine wrote to tell him this in no uncertain terms: *"Dissatisfaction has reached its highest point, and your person is far from being spared."*[20] Konstantin urged him to sue for peace with their former idol. But the Tsar, thinking it wise for once to take some notice of public opinion, allowed his forces to engage in the one major battle of the conflict, the slaughter that was Borodino, from which neither side emerged as victor. Napoleon pressed on to Moscow, expecting to meet surrender, and overjoyed at last to be seeing civilization. *"The sun was reflected,"* wrote one of his followers, *"on all the domes, spires and gilded palaces...the effect was to me – in fact to everyone – magical. At that sight, troubles, dangers, fatigues, privations, were all forgotten, and the pleasure of entering Moscow absorbed all our minds."*[21] To their surprise, they found another empty city. Puzzled, Napoleon set up home in the Kremlin, and that very same night his troops were disturbed by the unmistakable smell of burning from the wooden buildings all around. The Russians, in retreat, had apparently torched their own ancient capital.

For the Tsar, the moment was an epiphany. It came home to him how bitterly the invader was hated; how Russia conceived opposition to Napoleon as something close to a religious crusade against the anti-Christ – and the church, from Metropolitans to village priests, were encouraging them in this.

"The burning of Moscow at last illumed my spirit and the judgment of God filled me with a warmth of faith I had never felt before," he wrote his friend Friedrich Wilhelm of Prussia. *"From that moment I learned to know God....to the deliverance of Europe from ruin do I owe my own safety and deliverance."*[22]

He made his famous pledge to the nation.

> *"I will not make peace until I have driven the enemy back across our frontiers....As long as I am defending Russian territory I will only ask for munitions and arms from England. When, with the aid of Providence, I have repulsed the enemy beyond our frontiers, I will not stop there, and it is only then that I will reach agreement with England on the most effective assistance that I can ask for to succeed in liberating Europe from the French yoke."*[23]

Napoleon waited a few more weeks in vain for Alexander to offer peace talks, and then he left, besieged now by the advancing winter. Cold and hungry, his army was subjected to guerrilla attacks by gangs of Cossacks as they marched, and peasants who first offered hospitality had a tendency to cut throats while the Grande Armée slept. In desperation, the troops took to sleeping inside the warm bodies of their dead horses, drinking the animals' blood as Ghenghis Khan had done a millennium before. A mere fraction of the 450,000 made it back to France with their lives.

Within a year, Napoleon had been driven from Spain by the British and was at war with his own father-in-law in Austria. Neither the King of Prussia nor Alexander wasted the opportunity to settle scores and honour pledges: it was Russian troops who took the keys to Paris while the Emperor of the French was engaged in battle nearby, and Alexander who led the Allies on their triumphant march into the city. But he wanted no one to think that he came to destroy them.

> *I esteem France and the French, and I hope they will give me the opportunity to do good for them...I am not entering their walls as an enemy, and it is for them to accept me as a friend...I have but one enemy in France and with him I am irreconcilable.*[24]

Returning from Paris in 1814, Alexander left behind one immediate legacy and carried away another. His troops, beating on the doors of the bars and cafés in their anxiety for a drink, urged the owners to open *"Quickly!" "Bistro!"* and thus a new word entered the French language. Meanwhile, Alexander himself took away a baby, Maria Alexandrovna Parizhskaia, whose mother was an actress at the Theatre Français, and whose parentage was officially ascribed to Russian nobles killed in the conflict. She was to be raised at court as Elisabeth's beloved adopted child, and tutored by the same governess Alexander's sisters had had.

After Paris, with Napoleon banished to exile in Elba, the Tsar was at the height of his confidence and popular acclaim, traveling about Europe and England hailed as the magnanimous saviour of civilization. He attended the Congress of Vienna to work out the terms of peace with a vast entourage that included the ubiquitous Grand Duchess Catherine, even appearing in drag on one occasion, dressed in her clothes.[25] All of his youthful gaiety and spirit seemed to have returned – by contrast with Elisabeth, who attended the Congress but avoided everyone save her own sister. But both Napoleon and Alexander carefully attributed the French disasters in Russia, which were the beginning of the end for Napoleon, to supernatural rather than human agency. Napoleon declared that had it not been for the Russian winter he would have won that war; Alexander in turn gave all credit to God, with Moscow as a martyred bit player but the peasants and Cossacks, the men who had rallied at his own call to defend their nation, distinctly downplayed. Perhaps this was a deliberate political gesture as much as a religious one: Alexander was all too aware of how bitterly he had been criticized for his failure to make a stand, and he perhaps feared that by emphasizing the role of the ordinary people he might weaken himself further among his own people. But others in Russia took note of what had happened, and in the years after 1812 he had to contend with a new, nationalistic and popular spirit that exalted the ordinary people of Russia and sought their active involvement in government lest the government fail them again. The later years of

Alexander's reign were ones of pride in the Russian language and a flowering of vernacular poetry: no one wanted to emulate France any more.

Alexander was quietly in awe of France too, and of the revolutionary spirit she epitomized. At the Congress of Vienna, settling the war, he played the role of constitutional legislator handing down rational government, but when unrest failed to abate in Europe generally, he grew less enthusiastic in his plans for reform of his own government lest he unleash something bigger. He never forgot his father's fate at the hands of a group of enraged subjects, and like many reformers before and since he was irritated by the insatiability of the demands: the more he gave, the more they wanted. The great triumphal event of his career as Tsar was the military pageant at Vertus after the Congress of Vienna, in which he used troop display to advertise the civilized harmony of the Russian state to all Europe. To him, the army remained the supreme exemplar of well-organized society, and one of the most infamous acts of his later reign was the development of camps and villages in which his soldiers' families were to live. For Alexander, these were a means to provide homes and good food to his loyal troops, but punishment for infractions was so severe that the camps became notorious to history as a sign of his retreat into the brutal conservatism of his father's regime. In truth, he showed no active support for or opposition to reform; he was aware of societies that talked of popular government, but he did nothing about them in either direction. As in the days before his father's murder, he simply let things happen while preserving his angelic aloofness, increasingly wrapped up in religion. He made many journeys around Russia – avoiding government, his critics said. Pushkin immortalized him in verse at this stage of his reign as the Tsar of the disastrous 1824 flood: the man who could not tame God's elements and hold back the torrent engulfing St Petersburg, while the bronze horseman, Peter the Great, stood firm.

Court life revolved not so much around Alexander and Elisabeth as around his mother, the Dowager Empress Maria Feodorovna, who took precedence over the reigning Empress and retained her vast establishments at Gatchina and Pavlovsk. She was frequently visited by her daughters and grandchildren from abroad, and the younger Grand Dukes, Nicholas and Michael, with their wives, were also expected to be there in attendance when possible, whatever their own inclinations. Elisabeth and her mother-in-law had a poor relationship: the quiet, well-educated empress avoided the rigid etiquette and juvenile games of Maria's homes, preferring to shut herself away on Elagin Island in the north of St Petersburg, where she had her summer palace, designed by Rossi in Palladian style. Alexander favoured the Stone Island palace, a small, neoclassical building built for his father as Tsarevich. Containing less than fifty rooms behind a yellow, colonnaded façade, the two-storey palace was simply furnished and surrounded by a huge park for privacy.

South of the capital, they gravitated not to Gatchina or Pavlosk but to Tsarskoe Selo, taking up residence in the enormous Catherine Palace, while Grand Duke Nicholas lived in the nearby Alexander Palace, which Catherine the Great had built for Alexander himself as a youth. Tsarskoe Selo was renowned for its immaculate appearance. *"The whole garden is kept with extraordinary care,"* wrote one visitor. *"The lawns are splendid and the paths so well looked after that you hardly pass before a little workman appears to clear your traces. The Emperor likes to be able to walk in his park as if he were in his salon, without a speck of dust on his shoes. Eight hundred to a thousand men are constantly kept busy keeping up this ravishing retreat, with instructions to stay out of sight of walkers whenever possible, so that the whole place seems like fairyland.*"[26] On one of the lakes a small ship cruised perpetually in memory of Alexander's beloved sister Catherine, who had used it during her last visit. The controversial Catherine Pavlovna died suddenly aged just thirty in 1819. Elsewhere was a farm, with an infamously spotless cow house, where the imperial family played at farming in the daintiest manner imaginable, feeding the international selection of cattle with black bread from plates that a servant first handed them. Even the milk pails were covered in little tents to prevent contamination by the smallest speck of dust.[27]

Alexander refused to have a formal court at Tsarskoe Selo with him, and he did the household accounts himself, rising at five to start work and give audiences. His diet was strict for the sake of his health, and after dining alone he went to bed early, serenaded by a band of guards beneath his window. Elisabeth lived in a suite of apartments connected to his by a long gallery with a view of the park. She received no one, and struck those who did see her as being *"a creature not made for this world"* with languid manners and a sad smile. She loved to talk mainly of literature and history, and struck people as being afraid of Alexander. In particular, it was noted that she did not go out into the park until evening, for fear of encountering him and annoying him. *"They seemed to have been made for each other; the same goodness, the same gentleness and intellectual power. Yet there seemed to have been one point on which their hearts could not meet."*[28]

Konstantin Pavlovich, at variance with his brother's policy in many regards, remained as Viceroy of Poland, living quietly with his new, morganatic wife, a situation that suited everyone. According to their father's law, he should have been heir to the throne: it was clear that Alexander and Elisabeth would have no more children. But Konstantin felt unequal to the task of being Tsar, and later, on his second marriage, he quietly renounced his claim, passing it on to the strong-minded third brother, Nicholas, who was happily married within the terms of Paul's laws, and already had a son of his own. The country at large remained unaware of the situation, but Nicholas knew about it, contrary to some of the tales that were to circulate at the time of his succession. *"We felt struck as if by a bolt of lightning,"* wrote Nicholas's future Empress Alexandra Feodorovna of the day that Alexander informed them of their destiny. *"The future seemed sombre and without happiness."*[29] A manifesto appointing Nicholas as heir, along with letters from Konstantin announcing his intention to renounce the throne, were placed with the State Council, the Synod, the Senate, and in the Cathedral of the Assumption in Moscow, where the next Tsar would be crowned. Yet somehow Alexander failed to actually promulgate this manifesto, and Nicholas and Alexandra apparently retained some hope that Konstantin would change his mind. This hope was to have dire consequences.

Alexander's new, Christian spirit eventually led to a certain improvement in his relationship with Elisabeth, and possibly even guilt on his part at the numerous infidelities of his earlier days. *'she has an agreeable voice but has let her figure go and her whole appearance is marked by the sorrows she has had to endure,"* wrote one lady who came to their court late in his reign, on meeting the Empress. *"Though nowadays the Emperor tries to make up for the wrongs he has done her and is very much attached to her, it is hard to heal the wounds she has received."*[30] Elisabeth's beauty had vanished and her health was very poor: a bout of an illness that was probably rheumatic fever damaged her heart irreparably, and in 1825 she was advised to go south for the winter. She went to the Naval base Taganrog on the Sea of Azov, where Alexander joined her after a tour of various sites in the near-by Crimea. He had a slight fever too, for which he took only purgatives, and kept on working. Within a few days, he was no longer able to leave his room, but according to the accounts of his suite he still refused medicines. By the time they were given him it was too late. *'stop tormenting me!"* he pleaded again and again as his medical staff applied leeches and other drastic measures; he asked the Empress for only lemon ice cream.[31]

On November 19 (O.S.) he died, apparently of typhus, aged only forty-eight. Elisabeth survived him by just three months. *"Don't abandon me now, I'm all alone in this world of sorrows,"* she wrote pathetically to her unloving mother-in-law. *"His smile proved to me that he is happy and that he sees things more beautiful than here on earth. My only consolation is that I will not survive him long."*[32]

The suddenness of the Emperor's death, far from his capital, combined with the otherworldly image he cultivated, led to legends that he had not died but had faked his own demise in order to live quietly as a hermit. Feodor Kuzmich, a Siberian Holy Man who died as late as 1864, was believed by many to be the man Alexander became. To this day the historiography of this case flourishes, buoyed by the fact that on the several occasions it has been opened, the Tsar's grave in the Peter-Paul Fortress has been found to be empty. Some think that Alexander's body was moved at the behest of his nephew Alexander II to the graveyard of the Nevsky Monastery near his two infant daughters. But legend is often more appealing than the prosaic truth – and one of the most intriguing and entertaining variations on the legend of Kuzmich states that in old age he fathered a child who went on to become a starets in turn. The name of that child was Grigorii Rasputin.[33]

GRAND DUKE KONSTANTIN PAVLOVICH
(1779-1831)

By Janet Ashton & William Lee

Konstantin Pavlovich should according to the Pauline Law have succeeded Alexander I as Tsar. The second son of Tsar Paul, he was a curious and contradictory personality who most resembled his father physically, being shorter than his brothers, with Paul's characteristic pug nose. Heir to the throne for the majority of Alexander's reign, by his own decision he never became Tsar, and instead occupied a pretender's role in the history of the Russian monarchy: the might-have-been Emperor, the bright white hope – whose glorious popular image among the Russian working class was decidedly at variance with the grim impression history has of him. Konstantin had his admirers, though: family and friends saw a side of him in private which neither wishfully-thinking subjects nor irritated courtiers were privy to. He is interesting on two levels: both for what he really was and for what he represented historiographically to the Romanov dynasty and the Russian monarchy. Konstantin Pavlovich is the only non-reigning member of his family to have had a whole book devoted to his cult.[1]

He was born on April 27, 1779 (O.S.), at Tsarskoe Selo, and the event was occasion for considerable rejoicing. It was the first time in several generations that the dynasty had consisted of so many eligible males. His father Paul, the Heir to the throne, was an only son, born after many barren years in his own parents' marriage. Paul's legal father, Peter III, had been another solitary heir, a German prince – Romanov through his mother only– grafted onto Russia because there was no other available boy. But now Paul himself was founding a dynasty. Konstantin's grandmother, Catherine the Great, overjoyed at the arrival of a second boy to secure the succession, appropriated him at birth as she had done his brother. *'so here's Konstantin, as fat as a fist; and here am I, with Alexander on my right and Konstantin on my left,"* she gloated to her confidant. *"I love musical names, and since the Greek Church only bestows one, there are plenty left for the dozen to come!"*[2]

She was to be disappointed on two counts. To begin with, the expected dozen more boys failed to arrive; instead, six sisters gradually filled the nursery at Pavlovsk. Then, Konstantin himself was to prove less than an ideal child, prone to short-lived enthusiasms, rebellious behaviour and outbursts of temper – and his snub nose and small stature that reminded her unpleasantly of his father. Konstantin's position as junior Grand Duke was extremely difficult. His ugliness was a burden, but had he been more attractive than Alexander, this itself might have been resented. In the event, Konstantin's buffoonery gained him a certain popularity among *"unrefined"* people,[3] and it is hardly difficult to see why he might embrace such behaviour. When they were still babies, Catherine bluntly compared Alexander to an angel and Konstantin to the devil, and thus the die was cast; but she had plans for him and he was to have an intellectually rigorous upbringing in spite of his own inclinations.

Young Konstantin's name was a deliberate choice: Catherine, at war with the Ottoman Empire from which she soon wrested the Crimea, dreamed of restoring Christian rule to Turkey and its dependencies. Thus her grandson, named for the last Byzantine Emperor, was to be sovereign of a revitalised eastern Roman Empire, and to this end he was even given a Greek nurse where Alexander's was English, and taught to speak in Greek from infancy. As a toddler, he was painted holding the Christian cross aloft in his hands, while Alexander, alongside, brandished a sword with which to cut the Gordian Knot and thus, like his ancient namesake, acquire the right to rule all of Asia. Konstantin was even exposed to Greek political affairs, receiving the knife that had used to assassinate a prominent Turkish figure, and being hailed by Greek visitors to Russia.[4] But he seemed perversely bent on frustrating every plan Catherine made for him. In 1786, when he was seven, she intended taking both boys to the Crimea with her, to view the conquered territory and place Konstantin within spitting distance of his future dominions for the first time. At the last minute, to the relief of the boys' parents and the annoyance of the Empress, Konstantin – of course it had to be Konstantin rather than the paragon Alexander – developed German measles, so neither could go.

Around the same time, Konstantin received another tentative offer of a throne – one which his grandmother refused to accept, but which was to prove far more prescient than her own plans for him. The King of Poland, Stanislaw August Poniatowski, her one-time lover, pledged Catherine that if she support his new constitution and give him help in his own war against Turkey, he would ensure the election of Konstantin as his successor. Catherine turned this down on the grounds that her own plans for her grandson were paramount. In any case, she had no desire to see him become a Catholic or a constitutional monarch on a throne that she had done her fair share to destabilise.

Of course, the Greek project was far from stable. By the time he was eleven years old, events in Europe had inclined his grandmother to adopt a "rather more modest" ideal. In 1794, with war looming between Turkey and Austria, the Greek project was briefly revived, and although she finally recognised the impossibility of realising her original vision for her grandson, Catherine seemingly never relinquished the idea altogether. She never designated any other role for him.

Konstantin shared Alexander's tutors, from the Swiss philosopher LaHarpe to the military governor Saltykov, and as in Alexander's case was schooled in harsh self-criticism by the former. Aged twelve, he wrote, "*I know nothing, not even to read. To be rude, coarse, impertinent, that is to what I aspire. My knowledge and ambition are worthy of any army drummer. In a word, I will never amount to anything.*"[5] Alexander as we know wrote similarly shame-faced letters, and both boys clearly learned passive-aggressive behavioural patterns, but Alexander was compliant by nature, at least as a child, whereas Konstantin was defiant. This quality is perceivable even in his most self-abasing statements, with words which seem meant to say, if you insist on telling me I'm worthless, then I'll be worthless, and we shall see if it pleases you. On one occasion, when admonished to follow the example of his elder brother, he replied: "*He is the future Tsar and I am a soldier;*

who am I to imitate him?"[6] Disappointing as he apparently was to his liberal, western tutor, Konstantin fared no better with the Russian absolutists in his schoolroom, who complained of his insubordinate temper. At any moment, given the opportunity, Konstantin would run away and jump from a window to freedom. LaHarpe responded by shaming the boy, with Alexander paraded before him as a model of perfection. Consequently the boy, who was pandered to by lackeys and weak-willed tutors on the one hand, and made to feel his inadequacies and relative unimportance on the other, developed a glaringly apparent inferiority complex along with a an equally heated, albeit contradictory, resentment of all those who failed to recognise his imperial dignity, and a determination to assert it. He was, in short, a rebellious and angry youth, who acted out his frustrations but nonetheless craved approval.

As for the relationship between the brothers, one might guess, given the constant reminders of Alexander's superiority, that Konstantin would nurture a resentment toward him. In fact, he seemingly accepted Alexander's perfection, adored him, and sought, albeit with little success, to imitate him. No such close relationship would ever have emerged without Alexander's enthusiastic participation. By and large, he appears to have been the soul of patience with the younger boy. In the classroom, he guided Konstantin through his lessons, and on the social front he interceded with the members of his own 'set" to ensure that his brother was treated amicably.[7]

In 1795, each boy was named honorary colonel of a line regiment, and Konstantin was permitted to make an inspection tour of fortresses in Finland. The brothers were drawn to their father's military activities. Paul, unlike Catherine, trusted them with what they perceived as real commands. Moreover, their participation won them their father's approval. Catherine had usurped his role in their lives, but the result of this was that all their adolescent rebellion was directed against her instead. Their masculine self-identity demanded an identity rooted in service, not grandeur. Czartoryski, Alexander's friend, remembered:

> *Alexander and Konstantin gave themselves up to their duties with the zeal of young men who are for the first time given something to do, and the Court and the public compared them to children playing at soldiers...all they thought of was to obey the wishes and even the eccentricities of their father...the regulated uniformity of their Grandmother's court...was often inexpressibly tedious to them*[8]

The same year, when the Grand Duke was sixteen, his grandmother decided that the time had come for him to marry: his brother had been married at the same age. As in Alexander's case, three German princesses were brought to Russia, with the intention that both Konstantin and the Empress would decide which one they liked most. The three girls presented him were all daughters of the Duke of Saxe-Coburg-Saalfeld. The bourgeois manners of their mother created a poor impression: Catherine's court complained that the Duchess Auguste shoved her children forward as if the girls were *"goods for sale;"* but the youngest, fourteen-year-old Julie, caught everyone's fancy at once. Alexander's lonely wife Elisabeth was delighted by the prospect of having a girl close in age at court; she sighed in rapture at Julie's fair complexion and auburn hair. Unlike Elisabeth, the Coburg princess was not shy in the least; she flirted with Konstantin and he in turn was witty and cheerful with her. In due course, he did what was expected of him and, *"trembling,"* asked her mother for her hand in marriage.

The Duchess of Saxe-Coburg's estimation of Konstantin at this stage in his life was thoroughly favourable and thoroughly at variance with some of the pictures of him that were emerging already. *"Not in all the world,"* she declared, *"is there a more spiritual and moral young man!"*[9] In this rather unusual opinion she did not waver, even later in the light of events. At the same time, one of Catherine's courtiers contrasted his *"lively and penetrating"* intelligence very favourably with that of Alexander, who seemed mainly interested in superficialities. The Duchess was happy to leave her daughter with him, and the two were wed on February 15, 1796 (O.S.) , once Julie had converted to the Orthodox religion and taken the name Anna Feodorovna.

Konstantin and Anna received the vast, cold Marble Palace in St Petersburg, built for one of the Empress's lovers, as a wedding present, and it was here that they spent a wedding night attended by rumour. According to the gossip of the day, Konstantin spent the night railing against some guards who had committed a minor infraction, and failed to perform his marital duties. This set the tone for the relationship: Anna flirted openly with the Grand Duke's brother while Konstantin, emotionally immature and intoxicated by the freedom his new adult status afforded, endlessly drilled soldiers on parade grounds. Some tales held that he went to bed in his boots. Ironically, Alexander, who now at eighteen played the devoted swain to Anna, had been as immature at the time of his own marriage as Konstantin was, and had messed up his own relationship with Elisabeth just as obviously.

Contemporary scribes observed the difficulties of husband and wife and drew their own conclusions about the Grand Duke's character. *"Grimace serves him for wit,"* wrote one acerbically,

> *and buffoonery procures him popularity....He possessed the germs of a sound heart and understanding, which his first masters neglected to culti-vate....It will be happy for Constantine when he arrives at an age of more dis cretion, should he revive and cultivate them himself. In other respects, he is a son worthy of his father: the same eccentricities, the same passions, the same severi-ty and the same turbulence distinguish him; but he will never possess the same information which his father has acquired, nor his capacity, though he promises in time to equal or even surpass him in the art of manoeuvring a dozen automata.*[10]

In due course, the Empress moved Anna and Konstantin back into the Winter Palace so she could keep an eye on them and guide them. Here, Konstantin found other avenues for offending and demonstrating his contempt for the court. One of his public displays of bad behaviour occurred when Gustavus Adolphus of Sweden came to Russia, the intended bridegroom of Konstantin's sister Alexandra Pavlovna. The young prince was conspicuously more genteel than either

Alexander or Konstantin, but the latter in particular made a public display of himself with *"rough tricks and coarse horse play,"* prompting Catherine into placing him under arrest.[11] Not long afterward, she herself was dead.

Whatever they may have expected, the two young Grand Ducal couples found their freedom curtailed by the petty regulations and enforced familial closeness of the new court. *"Anne was my only consolation and I hers,"* Elisabeth wrote sadly about these times, *"Our husbands were practically never at home."*[12] Paul not only agreed with Catherine that members of the dynasty could not have personal lives, but he took a particularly rigid stance in relation to his elder children. The brothers were kept very close to their father and held in a *"state of dependence."* Konstantin was watched by an adjutant called Safonov, instructed by Paul to act as a "nanny" to the young man, and report on *"all his highness's actions."* Nor was Konstantin left in any doubt as to the man's role.[13]

Konstantin's military career occupied his full attention in the early days of his father's rule. He is said to have carried out Paul's order that Catherine's last favourite Platon Zubov, a man of immense power in the preceding reign, should be turned out of his chancery. The role he played vis a vis Zubov was a prototype for a future Grand ducal function, to wit, handling sensitive matters at risk of reputation or image. In this instance, the symbolic importance of direct Romanov involvement in Zubov's fall from power was achieved without exposing the sovereign or the heir to political taint.

Russia was also at this point at war in Italy with revolutionary France, and Paul sent Konstantin to serve under the great general Suvorov, recently brought out of retirement to rout Napoleon. Proving his courage appears to have been a high priority for the Grand Duke, and one which he equated with the establishment of his status as a "real" officer. When danger threatened during an early skirmish, Suvorov recalled Konstantin, who then made use of his royal privilege to defy this command, dispatching the adjutant Komarovsky to give Suvorov the news. Rather than precipitate a showdown, Suvorov railed at the adjutant, informing him that his irresponsible behaviour would be reported to Paul. For the moment, Suvorov contented himself with strengthening the Grand Duke's bodyguard, and it looked as though Konstantin would retain the advantage, until his first effort at military leadership ended in catastrophe. He goaded a general into confronting the enemy against Suvorov's orders, and nearly 1,300 Russian troops were lost! Konstantin was ushered into Suvorov's room in privacy, remained there for a long time, and emerged with a distressed mien. The power dynamic had shifted in Suvorov's favour.

Despite these initial set-backs, the young Grand Duke eventually proved to be rather a good military strategist, and he was both generous to and usually popular with the troops. For his victory and bravery at the battle of Novi Paul bestowed on him the title "Tsarevich," limited in theory to the heir to the throne. This prompted speculation that the Emperor intended disinheriting Alexander, and no doubt Paul was motivated at least partially by the intention to keep his heir on his toes. It might also have been simply a spontaneous expression of the Tsar's pleasure at Konstantin's realization of the cherished military ideal.

That same year, Anna left Russia for a time, ostensibly for the sake of her health. The home she had first shared with Konstantin, the Marble Palace, became for a short while the refuge of Stanislaw August Poniatowski, last King of Poland, deposed in 1796 by Catherine's troops as practically her final act as Empress. Paul half believed himself to be Stanislaw's son, and the former King came to Russia at his invitation, spending some weeks amassing the art works he so loved before dying there in the Marble Palace with Alexander and Konstantin both in attendance. Having the King there in his own home was a second, curious hint that Konstantin's fate was linked in some way to Poland.

The Marble Palace, a neoclassical edifice designed by Antonio Rinaldi and located on the Neva Quay to the east of the Winter Palace, was conveniently near the new parade ground called the Champ de Mars, allowing Konstantin to indulge his passion for military display. At the same time, however, he also became owner of a summer estate on the Baltic, where he was to reveal a more thoughtful side of his character. Strelna, lying on the Peterhof highway some way west of St Petersburg, was conceived by the Peter the Great as a palace to rival Versailles. He lived there, as was his wont, in a small wooden building, while commissioning from Niccolo Michetti a huge stone palace with a vast triple archway opening onto the clear blue water of the Gulf of Finland. Like many of these northern palaces, Strelna was rendered in pale yellow to draw light from the all-pervasive sky. Beneath the terrace was a grotto, the first step toward realising what Peter hoped would be a park full of fountains and cascades. But the marshy terrain proved unequal to supporting such a garden, and the Tsar transferred his attention to Peterhof, further west, instead, leaving Strelna incomplete. Some changes were made in the century that followed, mainly by Bartolomeo Rastrelli, the favoured architect of Peter's daughter Elisabeth and the man responsible for both the Winter Palace and the Catherine Palace at Tsarskoe Selo. But Konstantin was the first Romanov to actually live at Strelna. Under his auspices, new gardens were laid out and Andrei Voronikhin was commissioned to make improvements to the palace itself, while remaining true to the early eighteenth century feel. Here at Strelna Konstantin began an art collection, with pictures by such fashionable portraitists as George Dawe, as well as older works from Poussin, Cuyp and Rubens. He also built up a vast aviary of rare birds in the grounds.

Konstantin found distraction in taking care of Strelna from the increasingly strained situation at home with his parents. Paul now made scenes over the pettiest infractions of court or family politeness, and then sulked immoderately until his adult sons delivered the expected apologies.

> *I want to protest before God, dear father,* wrote Konstantin after some breach of etiquette related to dinner, "*...that the reproach you gave me and my brother made both of us very unhappy. We didn't deserve it, and we will try to prove to you that the whole of our upbringing has been based on our sacred duty to you.*"

This apparently went some way to placating the Tsar. "*Dear children,*" wrote their mother to both Konstantin and Alexander, "*Papa spent the whole after-dinner period with me and he seemed a little calmer....I advise you both to go and see him and tell him with your own mouths what you want to say. It's better that you're turned away twenty times than have to reproach yourselves that you didn't do everything you could.*"

"My father has declared war on common sense and he's vowed never to make peace," complained Konstantin.[14]

Such elaborate and even pathetic displays of offence may be common in lesser families with moody parents who fear that their children do not love them; but rarely are the stakes so high. In lesser families such confrontations do not lead to regicide.

Paul in his latter days suspected Konstantin's loyalty as well as Alexander's, but the Grand Duke had no involvement in the plans for his father's murder. *"I knew nothing and I was sleeping, as youngsters of twenty [he was actually twenty-four] can sleep,"* he remembered later, thinking back to the night of the murder, *"when Platon Zubov [his grandmother's former lover, presumably back to have his revenge on Konstantin in return], drunk, burst noisily into my room. He roughly wrenched my covers aside and said rudely, 'Get up and go to the Emperor Alexander; he's waiting for you.' You can imagine my shock and terror. I looked at Zubov still half asleep and thought I was dreaming. Zubov wrenched me up by force. I put on my trousers, my shirt, my shoes, and followed him mechanically. Cautiously, I took my Polish sword...I went into my brother's room, where I found a noisy, excited, crowd of officers...As for my brother, I found him stretched out on a sofa weeping. The Empress Elisabeth was there too. Then I understood that my father had been murdered."*[15] The bitterness and self-doubt, already native to his character, were aggravated by this shock, and the scar left by the affair appears to have borne a negative impact both upon his dynastic identity and his relationship toward the state.

Differences in policy quickly emerged between him and Alexander, since Konstantin's instinct was conservative and he feared the consequences of the reforms his brother started making. Moreover, the second son who enjoyed his brother's trust and regard inevitably became an object of resentment to jealous courtiers, and these were often successful in pushing him away, even when they could not alienate his brother's affections. Having experienced life in his older brother's shadow, and now finding himself driven back by courtiers, it was rare man who would not begin to resent the established order, and to look elsewhere for a place to establish his own identity. Any such assertion of independence violated the principle of self-abnegation, however, and could be interpreted as a sign of illegitimate ambition. It thus offered ammunition for sowing discord between the heir and his eldest brother.

Only months elapsed before Konstantin's loyalty was questioned. In a June 1801 letter to Alexander, S. R. Vorontsov expressed a fear that the grand duke might provide a power base for a new coup d'etat, writing:

> *The Emperor should look to his family, because, if Konstantin doesn't follow his brother's example and distance himself from those scoundrels who surround him, then there will be two parties: one composed of good people, and the other of immoral people, and because the latter, as is usually the case, will be the more active, it will overthrow both the sovereign and the state.*[16]

Clearly the threat of which Vorontsov spoke was never realised, and Konstantin never expressed a desire to supplant his elder brother. He continued to demonstrate his sense of alienation from, and even hostility toward the court.

He stayed away from politics and devoted himself to his military career and to Strelna, where, in 1803, there was a tragic fire that obliged him to re-do many of his previous improvements. Anna Pavlovna took advantage of the relaxation of sexual rules under the new Tsar and left Russia altogether to take up residence in Switzerland. Two years later, Konstantin, in love with another woman, finally begged his mother for permission to seek a divorce. This could not be attributed solely to dislike of his wife. Dynastic duty did not, after all, demand that he lived with the Grand Duchess, or refrain from taking mistresses.

Maria Feodorovna was furious: it was bad enough to her that both he and Alexander rather publicly flouted their marriage vows, but to seek a dissolution was totally beyond the pale. She accused him of ruining the nation's morals and even the future of the monarchy:

> *The peasant will presume that Faith is less sacred for the imperial family than for him and such an opinion is enough to tear hearts and minds away from the Tsar and the entire imperial house...Morals, already corrupted and spoiled, will decline into still greater depravity through the ruinous example on the steps of the throne...Believe me, only unwavering virtue will enable us to instil in the people confidence in our superiority, which together with the feeling of reverent respect, secures the tranquillity of the empire.*[17]

So for the time being Konstantin remained trapped in a still-born marriage that helped damage his image and standing with his royal contemporaries. He briefly attempted a reconciliation, visiting her in 1814 with her brother, the future King Leopold of the Belgians, in attendance. Her response was not positive, and humiliated him considerably. *"He felt her hesitation showed revulsion for him,"* wrote Leopold. *"And he was totally mortified. For my own part, I didn't think her reasons were very good...youth can excuse much. She'd have to shut her eyes to certain things, and he'd do the same."*[18] "Certain things" included illegitimate children. At Strelna in 1808 Konstantin's mistress, a French actress named Josephine Friedrichs, bore him a child, Paul, who was acknowledged by the Grand Duke and raised in his homes. Josephine also lived with Konstantin for a number of years. Anna, meanwhile, had two illegitimate children of her own, the paternity of the first, who received the name and style of Eduard, Count von Löwenfels, sometimes attributed to Alexander.

Empress Maria, though, was totally wrong about Konstantin's behaviour damaging the imperial house in the country at large. His affairs, his displays of short temper, his apparent recalcitrance in the face of expected standards and behaviour, all contributed to an extraordinary popularity among ordinary Russians, particularly those who hoped for some genuine relaxation in autocratic government. Konstantin came to be perceived as a rebel, their own representative at court, and the hope for the future.

His conduct during the wars with France led Konstantin's detractors to claim that he was pacifistic when faced by battle but brutal if provoked. In this latter characteristic he was actually no more than typical of the soldier princes of his generation. Many people speculated that his main interest in the army was as a showpiece: like his father and brother he was hyper-pedantic about the details of uniforms. Malicious gossip held it that he was opposed to war chiefly because it would mess the clothes up.[19] One rather thinks however, that it might have had something to do with his first hand experience of the unpleasantness of war. At any rate, when called upon to do his part, he performed commendably, and outshone Alexander, whose attempt to prove himself as a commander ended with routing of his troops at Austerlitz in 1805. Konstantin, in his capacity as Chairman of the War Commission, had advocated non-intervention. In 1807, he again took an anti-war stance, and not without reason. Of Alexander's generals, only one favoured action, and even he was concerned that Russia lacked sufficient troop strength to defeat Napoleon. Konstantin was strongly in favour of the Treaty of Tilsit and – having met Napoleon when Alexander did at the time of that treaty, on a barge in the middle of the River Nieman – he became an admirer of the French Emperor's.

In 1812 after the fall of Moscow, Konstantin's was one of the loudest voices urging his brother to sue for peace. None of this appears to have weakened Alexander's esteem for his brother, however. Now recognised as an experienced general and war hero, Konstantin continued to rise in the service. In 1812 he was made a corps commander, and given a place among the country's top military strategists, sitting on the Smolensk War Council. After Napoleon's retreat, he led the allied reserves in the first army, performing with such distinction *"that his command of his troops and brilliantly planned attacks were praised as being among the most outstanding of the entire Napoleonic Wars."*[20]

The most interesting aspect of Konstantin's service, however, was not his battlefield performance, but his relationship with his superiors. In peacetime, his position of corps commander would have been an independent post, but in wartime it subjected him to the authority of General Barclay de Tolly, the commander of the Army in the west, and Konstantin clashed with the general almost immediately. When the war council supported his call for an offensive, Barclay de Tolly ignored its decision. Of course, as the Tsar's chosen military leader, he represented Alexander's own authority, but Konstantin, overcome with passion, apparently failed to consider this when he sought to involve the people of Smolensk in his dispute with the general, proclaiming loudly, *"Russian blood does not flow in him who commands!"* The general responded by sending the Grand Duke to Moscow with a message for the Tsar, thus gingerly but effectively removing the *"dissident voice"* from Smolensk. Nor did Alexander force a reconciliation, despite the fact that Konstantin insisted upon returning. Rather, he was assigned the task of raising a new cavalry company, a considerable demotion from the position of corps commander!

The next assignment offered was even more far-flung and demeaning. Alexander suggested that Konstantin should form a provincial militia. Faced with his brother's resistance, the Tsar relented, but when Konstantin began to speak out against Barclay de Tolly again, he was dismissed on the general's own authority. Alexander approved, and Konstantin's participation in the campaign came to a halt. He went to live with his sister Catherine Pavlovna in Tver, remaining there until after the French retreat. Once the Russian army had adopted an offensive position, Konstantin's conflict with Barclay de Tolly disappeared, and Alexander was able to reintroduce him. It was then that he took command of the allied reserves and proved once again that he was capable of serving with merit so long as his heart was in his task.

The Tsar was clearly canny enough to realize that he could not disregard either public opinion, or the desires of his commanders, merely to gratify Konstantin. But there is no evidence that he looked upon his brother as threat to himself or wished Konstantin's foes to be able to sneer at him. He seized upon the opportunities that presented themselves to publicly demonstrate his favour toward the Grand Duke. His recall saw his inclusion in the Emperor's suite for his journey to Warsaw. Then, in June, Alexander sent him to Russia to proclaim the end of the war, news which aroused such joy that the messenger was treated as a hero. Thereafter, he was allowed to accompany his brother to the Congress of Vienna. His inability to adapt himself to situations contrary to his own convictions would remain a constant feature of his character, however, and one which never ceased to bedevil his sovereigns.

At the Congress of Vienna, much of what had been the Napoleonic Duchy of Warsaw was awarded to Alexander, King rather than conqueror, and it became Poland again, albeit a much smaller Poland than it had been before its partition by the great powers. Alexander promised, much as Napoleon had before him, that he would reinstate the pre-partition boundaries of the country, re-uniting the Duchy with its eastern provinces, long since part of Russia. Inevitably, he did not do this. He further committed in the rump state he acquired to rule according to the Polish constitution and to respect Polish laws and customs. Konstantin Pavlovich was sent there to work on merging its Army with that of Russia – largely it appears by matching their uniforms as closely as possible. All the negative characteristics associated with him followed him to his new post. He insisted upon relentless drill and seemed to be preparing his troops for a pageant rather than a war. It was not his military role which distinguished Konstantin's sojourn in Poland, however, but his evolution into the virtual ruler of the Kingdom. In time he was accorded vice regal powers – though without the title of Viceroy – and after 1815 he lived there more or less permanently, which suited everyone. Undoubtedly it was his alienation from events – and his brother's court – in Russia that made him prefer to be in Warsaw. Equally, the Grand Duke's presence was a potent symbol to Russians, who could look upon him as a symbol of Russian dominance in Poland. More important, however, than his role as representative of crown and country was his ability to free Alexander from the political taint of Poland. As unofficial ruler, he could act toward the realization of Russian ambitions in the region, while allowing the Emperor to adopt a disingenuous tone toward western European leaders who complained of the sabotaging of their own interests, thus preserving his reputation as an enlightened sovereign. Konstantin had already rendered similar aid, albeit on a much smaller scale, to his father.

Konstantin at first regarded the Polish parliament as a joke, and he played fast and loose with political appointments. But the country's resulting gradual slide toward revolution was only one significant development in the kingdom at that time. Konstantin's personal evolution into a supporter of Polish constitutionalism and reunification was another more surprising event.

The factors which brought about this transformation had little to do with Poland itself. There was, to begin with, the fragility of Konstantin's identity – his inability ever to forgive the Russian court and state for the grief they had caused him, and his burning desire to find his own place in the world. On the other side of the equation, Alexander was confronted by the difficulty posed by Konstantin's place in the succession hierarchy. His marital problems, his insistence that he would never accept the crown, and his tendency to play the maverick all made the Tsarevich a danger to dynastic cohesion. The appointment to Warsaw signalled both brothers' recognition of Konstantin's real position. His status as a working grand duke, residing outside Russia and involved in sensitive activity, was not compatible with his official designation as heir. Alexander's willingness to grant him extraordinary power in 1819 was a compensatory prelude to the dynastic disenfranchisement that would follow.

The matrimonial issue was the centre-point to the whole affair. In 1820, Alexander finally granted his brother the right to seek a divorce from Anna. The rest of his siblings responded gallantly and with pleasure to a sudden announcement of his intention to marry a Polish woman, Joanna Grudzinska, one of three daughters of a palace commandant known as "The three Graces" in Warsaw society.[21]

"It was with the greatest excitement, my friend and very dear sister, that I have just received your kind and charming letter dated April 27," wrote the Grand Duke to Anna Pavlovna, his youngest sister, when she congratulated him. *"I just admit to you in all happiness that I wept like child while reading it."* And then he explained his thinking about the whole situation.

> *I felt I should do it to bring about a permanent solution. It becomes painful to remain separated from my wife and involved in an illegal union as I grow older; a youthful folly may be excused, but at the age of refection it is no longer good. Nor do I feel called to become a monk...Were I to remarry with a princess of my rank, able to have children, I would be putting them all directly in front of my brother Nicholas. This is repugnant to my conscience and my scruples, especially for him who is married to a princess of Prussia* [i.e. they wouldn't want to see a lesser German princess come ahead of Nicholas's wife]. *To resolve everything and to give me some peace in a home, I felt it would be best to seek the hand of a private person. For all this I had the Emperor's authorisation....she is well-bred in all ways...I am happy, content, and I have my home established the way I wish it, with a wife who is not, thank God, a Grand Duchess and does not wish to be one.*[22]

Anna Pavlovna knew nothing of her brother's intention at this same point to renounce the Russian throne, though one can read it between the lines of his concern not to upstage Nicholas or have a wife of equal rank. She and her husband sent a lace shawl as a gift to Princess Lowicz, the title Alexander conferred upon Joanna, and even the dowager Empress was gracious.

In 1822, Konstantin made his renunciation of the throne official by signing a secret declaration in which he confessed that he had neither the "gifts" nor the 'strengths" nor the 'spirit" to rule Russia. He thus dared to ask the sovereign to pass his birthright to Nicholas *"and by doing so to secure forever the immovable position of OUR state."*[23]

Whatever the boorishness of his private behaviour in early youth,

Konstantin had grown into a calm and affectionate man where his family were concerned, full of humour and sensitivity in counselling his son, Paul Alexandrov, and his younger siblings. He took much pleasure, as he had done in Russia, in redesigning and decorating his various homes. In Warsaw there was Warsaw Castle, the official seat of government, where he had an apartment; but more significantly there was also the Lazienki estate to the south of the city centre, which had been the private paradise of Stanislaw II. In 1817, Alexander bought the exquisite little Lazienki Palace as a residence for himself when he visited Warsaw.[24] He transformed the riverside reaches of the palace grounds into a botanical garden, but the main work was on the Belweder, a former porcelain factory in the grounds of the palace, which became an elegant residence for Konstantin. On the Grand Duke's behalf, Jakub Kubicki transformed the Belweder into a simple Neo-classical palace. Inside, he introduced some radical features: for example, the reception rooms were on the ground floor instead of the first, an unusual feature at the time.[25] Konstantin's favourite was the so-called Blue Room, after the colour of its upholstery, where he spent his evenings. The garden, newly created, was laid out in the Romantic style, with bushes, trees and winding lanes. There was also a pond with an island and bridge, and temples to various Greek, Roman and Egyptian deities.

The new princess's health was poor; she had migraines and fevers and rheumatism, so the couple led a quiet life. Konstantin going to Warsaw on business in the morning before spending the afternoon asleep. After dinner, the household might go to the theatre before retiring early. Otherwise, the Grand Duke spent the evening in front of his fire, contentedly smoking cigars and contemplating his home and garden.[26] Joanna filled the rooms with a clutter of souvenirs, mostly chosen for sentimental associations rather than artistic merit.[27]

They also owned the former hunting estate of the Archbishop of Gniezno at Skierniewice south-west of Warsaw, in the region from which Joanna's family came. Remodeled for Konstantin by Petersburg architect Carlo Rossi, the palace at Skierniewice consisted of two principal storeys on a raised basement, stuccoed and washed with the bright lemon-yellow of St. Petersburg's official structures. The interior was strictly classical, with Corinthian pilasters and allegorical paintings. This palace was to serve as the official residence of later generations of Romanov Tsars in Poland.

From time to time, the couple went to Germany so Joanna could take the cure. *"I am so bored I could swallow my tongue!"* Konstantin joked affectionately after one such sojourn among the sick.[28] He worried about the obviously less stable marriage of his brother Michael and Michael's new wife, and although – or perhaps because - in many ways the situation paralleled his own with Anna, he blamed his boorish brother entirely for their difficulties. *"I found her very likeable in every way and especially in private,"* he wrote to his sister Anna.

> *In public she has a very noble bearing and expresses herself wonderfully well; it is to the point and [touching], added to which is a charm which suits her. In spite of this, she is less capable of discretion than Nicholas's wife. As far as I was able to judge, she is very witty and feels things keenly and intensely, with a great deal of sensitivity…As for Michael, he is incomprehensible to*

me…he maintains a unique coldness and unawareness toward her. Whether it is the newness of the situation, shyness or another reason, I was not able to make it out…the two things he cares about are giving service and sleeping. The rest hardly concerns him.[29]

Michael was in Warsaw with Konstantin when Alexander suddenly died in Taganrog on November 19, 1825 (O.S.). Nicholas remained in St Petersburg. News of the tragedy reached the Polish capital two days before it arrived at the Winter Palace. That interval allowed Konstantin to compose a letter to Nicholas, acknowledging him as Emperor. On November 27, without knowledge of Konstantin's reaction, Nicholas did his duty in accordance with the 1797 statute and swore allegiance to the new "Emperor." The subsequent revelation of the abdication documents failed to effect an immediate change. Nicholas declared that he had no right to recognise acts which had never been publicized. He did not seek to oppose Konstantin's will, still less Alexander's, but to uphold the law, and *"protect our beloved Fatherland from even the smallest momentary confusion as to the identity of its lawful sovereign."*[30] When the contents of the abdication documents were revealed to the State Council, including the letter in which Konstantin described himself as incapable of ruling, this breach of family secrecy was viewed by him as an act of gross disrespect on the part of his brother. So great was his rage that he threatened to mobilise the Polish and Lithuanian troops *"in defence of his rights against Nicholas."*[31]

Nicholas's response to Konstantin's anger was so obsequious that it suggested a wariness bordering on fear. But the deference proved a wise strategy insofar as it mollified Konstantin.

Unfortunately for Russia, while Konstantin and Nicholas sized each other up, rebellion was afoot. The Decembrist conspirators were drawn principally from the nobility, but their patriotic idealism was, in most cases, sincere. The crown had ceased to provide progressive leadership and they had reached the conclusion that *"they themselves would have to take up the course of realising the western political ideal in Russia"*[32] Events reached a head on December 14 when Nicholas issued a manifesto confirming the succession, and instructing that the oath be taken to him and his heir, identified as Grand Duke Alexander Nikolaevich, without the title Tsarevich. In response, the rebel members of the Northern Society of Decembrists filled Senate Square yelling "Konstantin and constitution!" Their use of his name was disingenuous, since they had no reason to believe he supported their cause, but they believed rightly that the soldiers would rally to him. Nicholas in response used the vulnerable figure of the seven-year-old Alexander Nikolaevich to rally the troops to the cause of the crown.

Their sister provided a lightly ironic note which serves as a post-script to the whole terrible affair: *"It will perhaps be a unique example to see two brothers fighting over who will not have the crown!"* wrote Anna Pavlovna.[33]

There was a strong Polish element involved in the Decembrist rebellion, and Nicholas's repercussions against them were harsh in spite in some instances of his brother's protests. One of Konstantin's personal friends got twenty years in Siberia, despite the viceroy's protestations that he had not been in touch with the conspirators in some while.[34] Nicholas also attempted to interfere with the judicial independence of the Polish police and merge them with Russia's, and he strongly opposed his brother's plans – which were originally Alexander's – to reunite the Congress Kingdom with the one-time eastern provinces of Poland. Yet to keep the peace at home and in the family he never recalled him from Warsaw. Meanwhile, a line seems to have been drawn between the familial and official realms, within warmth and affection manifested within the former, and mild disapprobation in the latter. Nicholas made his nephew, Paul Alexandrov, a fligel-adjutant, and in September 1827 named his new-born son Konstantin after his brother.

In November 1830 an insurrection against Russian rule finally began, led by young officers from the Cadets School in the Lazienki Park. Their plan was first to march on the Belweder and murder Konstantin, who remained extremely unpopular as symbol of Russian rule, despite his latter-day conversion to Poland's cause. 1830 was a year of European revolutions. In July, as Konstantin noted, *"Paris had a horrible revolution,"* and one in Belgium followed. These were followed with delight in Warsaw, where some wit wrote a sign outside the Belweder, *"From the beginning of the New Year – for rent."*[35] The November Insurrection was very much a product of the Romantic Era: in addition to cadets, the rebellion was led by writers and dreamers infused with national spirit. Luckily for the viceroy, this meant that the young conspirators bungled his attempted assassination. Several hours after retiring to bed his household was woken by a crowd making its way down the road from town to the Belvedere. On the horizon was the unmistakeable sign of a fire.[36] The conspirators from the Cadet School planned to burn down a brewery as signal to their allies, but the fire was put out before most of them saw it. Just fourteen people turned up at the Belweder and Konstantin escaped quite easily, although they got as far as the antechamber next to his bedroom and killed a member of his household who they apparently took for him. They then hurried back to the barracks to report to their fellow conspirators.[37] The crowd of insurrectionists outside the Belweder moved onto the working class areas of the city to find more supporters and thus succeeded in storming the Arsenal, from which they stole weapons and so took Warsaw.

Konstantin retreated over the Russian border with his Russian troops: not through cowardice, but because he could not bring himself to crush the revolution.

"Fundamentally," he told the Polish parliament, *"I am a better Pole than all of you. I have spoken your language for so long that it is difficult for me to speak Russian. I have proved my sympathy with you by forbidding the imperial troops to fire on you."*[38]

Nicholas had no such scruples. Nor did he hesitate the close down parliament, ban the official use of the Polish language, and subject the nation to twenty-five years of military rule under General Paskevich.

Konstantin Pavlovich died of typhoid in Vitebsk in 1831, still pleading for mercy for Poland and mourning that his career had ended *"in such a deplorable way."* Not long afterward, his wife Joanna followed him to the grave.

TSAR NICHOLAS I
(1796-1855)

By Janet Ashton

Nicholas Pavlovich, the man on whose head the unwanted crown had eventually come to settle, was a different character again from his two elder brothers, and he had a very different training. Born on June 25, 1796 (O.S.), he was almost twenty years younger than they were, and he came after a succession of six sisters. *"Mama has been delivered of an enormous boy,"* wrote Catherine his grandmother, with pleasure. *"He has a bass voice which cries in a most astonishing way. His hands are almost as big as mine."*[1] Her own death shortly afterward deprived her of the chance to take him away from his parents, and thus he was the first son raised according to Paul's and Maria's precepts.

Unlike his elder brothers, Nicholas saw only the benevolent side of Paul. He and his sister Anna, one year older, and brother Michael born two years after him, formed a discreet unit in the family, since seven years divided Anna from their next sister, Catherine; the child between them, Olga, having died as a toddler. It is very well known that they formed a little club, calling themselves "The Triopathy," and wearing a ring to denote membership. They remembered Paul as an affectionate figure who had them in his room when his hair was done in the morning, and called them *"my little sheep."* They were far too young for their loyalty to be questioned by him, but certainly old enough to idolise the memory of this kind man who vanished from their lives so suddenly and in such horrible circumstances. Nicholas was the son whose career was most unambiguously faithful to his father's memory in all regards.

He had a Scottish nanny, two governesses from the Baltic States, and a military governor, Count Lamsdorf, appointed when Nicholas was four. At an age when most boys were still in dresses, he was put into uniform, and by the time of his father's death he wore regimental tunics more frequently than ordinary clothes. Lamsdorf employed harsh military discipline: he hit the boys with rifle ramrods, and even threw them against walls when they failed to obey. Their mother was aware of this and raised no protest, though in general she was wary of a totally military training and attempted to introduce more humanistic elements to their education. *"We had six other tutors who bore the title Gentleman of the Court,"* Nicholas remembered later, *"and each took us in turn for twenty-four hours. We liked some and detested others. But none gained our confidence. The constant changing of people around us instilled, right from childhood, the habit of discovering their weakness so as to profit by it when we wished."*[2] They did not trust their mother, largely because she permitted their abuse by the military governor, and this in turn must have increased their tendency to idolise their dead father and all he represented – forgetting of course that he had been he man who appointed Lamsdorf to begin with. In any case, their mother was rarely present: according to the court calendar for 1798, Nicholas saw her for just six or seven hours a month.

Classical languages, cosmology, pianoforte – all abstract topics introduced at Maria's behest were lost on Nicholas. *"I saw only coercion and I had no pleasure in learning,"* he said, baldly. And yet he loved the very subjects Lamsdorf originally represented: military science and engineering. He had a good memory and did well at these topics. He came to know a lot about architecture, too, perhaps for its mathematical aspects and link with fortification.

As young children, Nicholas and Michael were educated with friends, but when the elder was thirteen his mother took these away, believing outsiders to be corrupting influences on princes. The lycée at Tsarskoe Selo was built with their secondary education in mind, but ultimately they were not permitted to attend. They remained imprisoned within the walls of Gatchina, the severe and gloomy palace their father had adored, where an atmosphere of rigid virtue and duty prevailed, along with the shouts of the guardsmen who drilled endlessly outside. Bored silly, the two longed to go to war against Napoleon, but in the event they were permitted only to visit Paris after it fell, and take part in the parades and victory celebrations at Vertus. *"I hope military service will not make you adopt a brutal, harsh and imperious manner,"* wrote Maria to her son. *"It is most unpleasant in anyone, but unbearable in people of your birth."*[3]

Nicholas's education culminated in tours of Europe and Russia, during which he made a mixed impression. His mother conceived it all as a mind-broadening experience, and wanted him to be popular with his future subjects. But Nicholas, who had grown up as puritanical, aloof and suspicious as the education she had imposed would appear to intend, seemed to feel that he was being sent as an inspector of the empire, and he uttered many criticisms of all he saw, and was criticized in turn as cold and unbending. Of all the nations he saw abroad, he found Prussia, the infamous "army with a state" most to his taste – as his father had done before him.

His chosen bride – chosen by Alexander, but Nicholas happily acquiesced – was a Prussian princess, Charlotte, the eldest daughter of Friedrich Wilhelm III and Queen Louise, whose stubborn stand against Napoleon had won them a Europe-wide cult of their own, as well as Alexander's friendship. As one contemporary observer put it, Russia had never before *"carried her matrimonial pretensions so high"* as to woo a daughter of Prussia.[4] Previous empresses had been drawn from small German states whose rulers were so dazzled by the Romanovs that they acquiesced easily to the demand that their daughter relinquish her own faith for Orthodoxy. To require the same of a princess of powerful Prussia was more audacious, but no demand was too great to be refused the Blessed Alexander's brother. Charlotte had been brought up in a family at once territorially insecure due to the wars but emotionally close to one another. Queen Louise died when her daughter was still a child, leaving all the children bereft and worshipping her memory. The self-sure Nicholas, brother of the saviour of Europe and extremely handsome to boot, offered a future that seemed to answer Charlotte's every need for both personal and dynastic security. She in turn was the object of his most gentle and chivalrous behaviour: he cocooned and overwhelmed her, in truth.

Charlotte became the Orthodox Grand Duchess Alexandra Feodorovna and married her prince on July 13, 1817, after an engagement period of two years.

Maria Feodorovna, learning from the lesson of her elder sons, was not anxious to push Nicholas into marriage before he was ready, and she was thinking of the bride too: her own two first daughters had died in childbirth after teenage marriages, so when it came to the younger ones she had deliberately left them unwed until fully mature. Thus Charlotte of Prussia also was not to marry Nicholas until she was nineteen years old and he almost twenty-one. In the meantime, the groom took occasional lectures on law and politics, and continued with his reviews.

The wedding was a grand affair in the Winter Palace, after which the couple proceeded along the Nevsky Prospect to the Anichkov Palace, their future home, where Alexander and Empress Elisabeth awaited with bread and salt. The fireworks and illuminations continued for three days: this sort of celebration, with the imperial family's private events treated as occasions for the entire nation, had been another Pauline innovation, and one which Nicholas was to continue with enthusiasm.

His life and Alexandra's was something close to a fantasy one for the first years of their marriage. They made changes to their home at the Anichkov, removing some of the colder classical features inside and installing fountains, plants and cages full of birds, to the Grand Duchess's taste. Nicholas occupied himself with the army in the fairytale sense of participating in periodic grand parades, while Alexandra gave birth to first a son, Alexander, and then a daughter, Maria. Nicholas thus became the first of his brothers to bear a legitimate son, and in fact the first to bear a surviving legitimate child of either gender. He was disgruntled at first not to have had two sons, and with extraordinary insensitivity he let his wife know it, but Maria rapidly became his favourite. *"My children are really delightful,"* he wrote when they were toddlers. *"The little boy is definitely a soldier; the little girl is becoming a delicious little creature; she has the neck and shoulders worthy of a fifteen-year-old! She turns my head. My boy shoots with a big army-issue rifle and rides horseback with me."*[5] Considering the heirless state of his brothers, the thought that he and certainly his son would eventually sit on the throne can have been no stranger to him, for all the shock that he and Alexandra evinced when the possibility was mentioned. *"Both of us,"* Alexandra recalled, *"had a horror of everything that was the court."*[6] *"He and I were only really happy and pleased when we were alone in our rooms, with me sitting on his knees while he was being loving and tender."*[7] But she had won her mother-in-law's rare approval, and they were expected to spend much time with the Dowager Empress at Gatchina, or in particular at Pavlovsk, congregating for family visits and afternoon drives in the summer. Sometimes they resorted to dissimulation. In 1825, when Alexandra was expecting their fourth child (the third, Olga, was born in 1822) a visitor to the Dowager Empress's court noted,

> *A letter arrived for the Empress from the Grand Duchess Alexandrine. They had long been arguing where she was to lie in. The Grand Duke wanted to remain in St Petersburg, but the Anichkov Palace is not habitable during the great summer heat. The Grand Duchess did not want to come to Pavlovsk, where the Empress wanted her, preferring to stay at Tsarskoe Selo. As the doctors had been told to say the palace at Pavlovsk was too damp, the letter which had just*

arrived could announce her wish to come to Pavlovsk. The Empress at once with drew to answer it – and refuse in view of the opinion of the doctors. Thus it was settled that the Grand Duchess Alexandrine would occupy the Alexander Palace at Tsarskoe Selo.[8]

The baby, Alexandra Nikolaevna, was born three weeks later at the Alexander Palace. Her name, hardly unique in the imperial family, was eventually abbreviated to "Adini," which sounds like a child's own formation from Alexandrine, the para-French form that was favoured by the family in place of the Russian Alexandra. Her mother, known as Alexandrine or Aline to the Dowager Empress, was "Charlotta" to others and "Mouffy" to Nicholas. Alexander, Nicholas and Alexandra's son, went by the traditional Russian diminutive 'sasha," and thus avoided confusion with anyone.

Within a few months of his youngest daughter's birth, Nicholas faced the horrible inter-regnum of December 1825, when he and Konstantin *"threw the crown back and forth to one another as if it were an india rubber ball,"*[9] and the Decembrist conspirators took advantage of the disarray to attempt a revolution. Having finally accepted his legal right and obligation to take the throne, Nicholas showed considerable personal courage, firstly appearing before the palace with the heir, Alexander, whom he symbolically placed in the arms of the chevaliers of the Order of St George of Sapper Grenadiers, commending him and by extension the dynasty to the protection of the regiment. Then he rode out into Senate Square to meet the rebels and attempt to persuade them to surrender. The Governor-General of St Petersburg had already been killed, and one of those present attempted to shoot Grand Duke Michael. At the same time, workmen on the roof of the new St Isaac's Cathedral began to throw logs down onto the imperial troops. Only at this point did Nicholas order that they open fire, that they *'spill the blood of my subjects on the first day of my reign,"* as he wrote sorrowfully later.[10] He was always careful to present this act as one of sacrifice on his own part, abandoning his earnest desire for popularity and peace for the sake of the preservation of his family and state. The Decembrist revolt was to act as a symbolic justification for the whole system of government that he instigated. Nicholas was as devoted to the principle of law as Alexander was – both selected *"Law, the arc of all safety for each,"* as a personal motto[11] – but unlike his brother he had no intention of presenting himself as the font of reform, using law primarily in the service of transformation. As Richard Wortman has written, Nicholas saw the Decembrist Revolt as a reason to pose as the lonely and heroic defender of autocracy against its assailants, and more importantly still as the *"champion of good and morality, embodied in the imperial family, over the subversive forces of evil."*[12]

At his coronation, which took place in Moscow on August 22, 1826, he took care to emphasise the centrality, submissiveness and almost otherworldly nobility of his family. Eight-year-old Alexander, born in the Kremlin, took part in the ceremony and was greeted ecstatically by the crowds. But the defining moment was the swearing of allegiance by the Grand Duke Konstantin. *"no one among the numerous spectators beheld that affecting scene unmoved,"* wrote a historian. *"Constantine was crowning the glorious act of abnegation...he was humbling himself in the presence of all before a throne which might have ascended, and did so with fervour and enthusiasm, in a way that removed ever doubt as to his candid and free determination. This was the most string scene of all in that imposing drama; compared with it, all the rest was formal and languid."*[13]

Nicholas struck people who met him with his extraordinary good looks: his height, and his perfect classical profile ensured that he would eventually be remembered as the most handsome of all Tsars. Nevertheless, as heir he had been neither particularly popular nor particularly well known in the country at large. Like all of his brothers, he was pedantic about military detail and often harsh with his soldiers, and his demeanour in all situations was coolly correct and formal.

> *The Grand Duke has received from nature one of the finest gifts that could be granted to an individual in his high rank, that of the most noble figure I ever saw,"* wrote a contemporary. *"The general expression of his countenance has in it something of something of severity and misanthropy which does not set one quite at ease. His smile is one of courtesy, not the expression of gaiety or enjoyment; the constant suppressing of which has become so habitual to him that there is no apparent effort or constraint, and every word or gesture is perfect harmony with this expression. He speaks with animation and simplicity his conversation is always easy and appropriate and whatever he says is intellectual and in good taste. There is nothing in the tone of his voice or the character of his discourse which indicates pride or dissimulation, and yet you feel that his heart is closed, that the barrier is insurmountable....he has even to a certain degree communicated the same characteristic to his wife, who often displays and expression of suspicion and scrutiny which ill accords with the pleasing regularity of her naturally sweet and gentle countenance.*[14]

If Alexandra was suspicious, she probably had reason to be: as a naïve girl from the relatively unsophisticated Prussian court, she found it bewilderingly easy to give offence in Russia by simply saying the wrong thing. Peoples' willingness to see insults everywhere rather shocked her when she was a Grand Duchess.

But as Tsar and Empress, Nicholas and Alexandra were able to remodel the court they claimed to hate, forming it rather in their own image with an emphasis on family life and constant dances and balls that allowed the Empress to relax and grow popular. *"When animated, the unpleasing expression of her piercing glance disappears,"* wrote the same observer. *"The princess becomes lost in the more pleasing form of woman."*[15] Nicholas remained necessarily majestic in formal situations, *"towering over everyone in the room,"* the all-seeing eye who *"directed everything, even to the smallest minutiae"*[16] but warmer to those who saw him in private with his young children. Family life became the supreme exemplar of national values: love for and duty to his imperial family equaled patriotism and duty to nation, and if he adhered to a high moral standard at home so too was he entitled to demand similar standards and sacrifices and devotion from his subjects. His pretty children, an invaluable asset to him, played a crucial role in promoting this image, receiving their fair share of public caresses from both parents, and often playing in semi-public palace gardens beneath the admiring gazes of both Russians and foreigners. In addition to the four they had at the time of his succession, there were three more born "in the purple" to a reigning Tsar: the Grand

Dukes Konstantin, Nicholas and Michael Nikolaevich, dutifully named in order after the previous generation of Romanov men. *"In those days,"* wrote one resident of Tsarskoe Selo, where Nicholas favoured the small Alexander Palace,

> *Our favourite occupation was to watch how the children played on the lawn in front of the Alexander Palace. I also remember that every evening this lawn was surrounded by the residents of Tsarskoe Selo who would not miss an opportunity to admire those lively family scenes of imperial life. We were among those people and with avid eyes followed each move of Tsar Nicholas Pavlovich, his Empress Alexandra Feodorovna, and their beautiful children.*[17]

The family spent the festive season and winter in St Petersburg at the Winter Palace, beginning with a party for the Emperor's nameday on December 6 and undergoing the usual round of social obligations and balls, all presented to the world as pageants organized for the entertainment of the Empress, around whom both family and court revolved. There were Christmas trees in the German style and presents for the children and all their friends. In the first years of the reign, New Year's Eve was a holiday for the whole town, the Winter Palace being literally open to everybody. More than 30,000 people would be admitted that evening, and many would return home with their clothes torn to pieces by the crowd.[18] Lent followed, and the family moved to the quieter and most beloved Anichkov Palace on the Nevsky, which had been their home before Nicholas became Tsar. Next came Easter, the most elaborate celebration of the Orthodox year, and then a few weeks south of the city at Tsarskoe Selo. The Alexander Palace was redecorated several times according to their tastes, with an enormous slide being added to one hall so that the children could amuse themselves when it rained.[19] The sons lived in the left wing, near the road, while Nicholas, Alexandra and their daughters inhabited the right side, overlooking the grounds. On an island at the centre of the lake visible from their windows, there was a play-house for sunny days. Here few affairs of state intruded on their lives. The Empress, whose health was never very good and whose physical delicacy became part of her mystique, relaxed and saved her strength while her husband consciously found time to romp with his children in the evenings.

In summer, the family moved usually to Peterhof, where they had a house on the shores of the Baltic. Completed in 1829 the Gothic "Cottage Palace" was regarded by the imperial family – and particularly by the Empress - as their true home. It was designed by the Scottish architect Adam Menelaws, and is full of rich colour, with parquet and friezes throughout, lace and velvet curtains, thick carpeting and elegant wooden furniture decorated with the rose and sword motif that the Empress adopted as her own. As in the family rooms at the Alexander Palace, the impression created is of both luxury and simplicity, with plenty of light and none of the stifling clutter that characterised houses built or decorated later in the century for their descendants. The Cottage stands at the top of a meadow looking down toward the Gulf of Finland, and was of such modest size that before long they had outgrown it. In 1841, the Russian architect Andrei Stakenschneider was commissioned to add extra rooms to the house and at the same time convert some of the outbuildings for the use of the young Grand

Dukes. Thus the former Guardhouse – another Gothic structure – became the Konstantin or Admiral's house, while the old kitchen buildings and stables were adapted into a school for the two youngest brothers. There was also a schoolroom on the first floor of the Cottage itself, and a covered balcony where the children learned to fence and played when young if it was raining outside[20] The Cottage stands in the Alexandria Park, named of course for the Empress, which adjoins the main Peterhof estate and under the auspices of Nicholas was developed from imperial hunting grounds into a romantic idyll of woods, ruins, rivers and bridges. There was even a private church, the distinctly un-Orthodox looking Gothic Chapel, dedicated nevertheless to St Alexander Nevsky and filled with icons and Russian art.

The main ceremony of summer was the Empress's birthday party, at which hordes of Russians and foreigners arrived by boat from the capital to enjoy fireworks and dancing around the grounds of the Grand Palace. *"To this ball everyone, without exception, is welcome,"* marveled a German visitor.

> *The country people, in their, ordinary garb, mingle with the wearers of elegant dresses and brilliant uniforms...Suddenly the musicians strike up; through the folding doors, thrown wide open, two chamberlains enter, and with the utmost courtesy entreat the assemblage to make room for their Majesties, who are near at hand. Everyone draws back....and the Polonaise is danced, with the Emperor at its head, through all the extensive suite of apartments...At a signal from the Empress all of the vast garden is now suddenly illuminated. This takes place as by enchantment. With lightening speed the countless flames ascend from the lowest branches to the very top sprigs of the trees. In less than quarter of an hour, park and garden appear in a blaze. The waters of the fountain splash and ripple over steps which seem to burn. Lamps, ingeniously sheltered from extinction, gleam through the falling waters whose every drop glistens, diamond-like, through all the tints of the prism. Eye cannot behold a more striking and beautiful scene. The finest sight of all is the Golden Staircase next to the Hercules fountains with which even the Grands Eaux at Versailles cannot be compared. And now imagine effect of the monster illuminations, reflected on all sides in the colossal cascades and waterworks, and in the adjacent arm of the sea; imagine the melodious murder of music, issuing from the palace, and mingled with the whizzing of rockets, and with the booming of cannon from the vessels at Kronstadt, and with the joyous songs of countless groups, who, having selected spots for their bivouac, lie around the fires in various and picturesque attire...*[21]

The following day, the crowds were entitled to approach the Cottage, the only day of the year on which they might do so. Beneath the eyes of spectators, the imperial family had tea like animals in a zoo, this curious ceremony recalling similar events in eighteenth-century England, when subjects were entitled to watch the royal family at certain dinners.

For all his fondness, Nicholas was an exacting father. All four of his sons were given military commissions in their cradles and were put into uniform at an early age. *"I wish to make a man of my son before I make an Emperor of him,"* he once said sternly, discussing his educational plans for his heir.[22] *"He has an angelic but very absent minded character so one must combine kindness with firmness in order to be useful to him."*[23] When the boys overstepped the mark or – worse – showed signs of weakness, they were soundly beaten, often by their father himself. Even Alexander's tutor, the romantic poet Vassily Zhukovsky, selected as tutor mainly for his fundamental belief in humane autocracy, worried that the Tsar's harshness would rob the children of the ability to do right of their own volition. *"Discipline is the complete antithesis of lawfulness,"* he wrote. *"It is a priceless pearl of military service; without it there cannot be an army. But God protect the state from legality based upon that model...then it is goodbye to justice and truth"*[24] Nicholas rather broke Alexander's spirit, and in his character, easily knocked back or depressed, the future Tsar grew up to resemble his namesake far more than his father. Konstantin the second son, a clever child who *"had an answer for everything"* and was destined for the Navy, was assigned at five years old to the twenty-four hour care of peremptory and blunt Feodor Petrovich Litke, an explorer and Naval geographer who was deeply ambivalent about being required to give up his career to teach a little boy. He seems to have wreaked some of his own frustrations on that boy. For a time as a young adolescent, the apparently resilient Konstantin behaved in a troubled manner: he had an imaginary friend as a much younger child would, talking to this friend, receiving replies, and showing little interest in his real life.[25] Some historians have seen Konstantin Nikolaevich's eventual career as a reformer as a rebellious Oedipal reaction against his strict father's system.[26]

Nicholas's relationship with his daughters was easier, since their education fell chiefly under their mother's gentler jurisdiction: Olga was to remember her childhood as a halcyon, "golden time." But from them too he expected *"the most strict obedience"* in all things.[27] Into all of the children he instilled a worshipful adoration of their mother, and strict reverence for the person of the Emperor and for the dynasty: only the lively and energetic Maria, who was his favourite, proved cheerfully recalcitrant in his own lifetime. Her first marriage was to Maximilian Beauharnais, Duke of Leuchtenberg, a scion of the Bavarian royal house but also son of Napoleon's step-son Eugène. The elder Beauharnais, most significantly, had been in the Grande Armée that marched on Moscow, and thus the marriage was not popular with Russians, though Nicholas approved it, happy that Maximilian could live in Russia and Maria would not be leaving her parents. Maria further transgressed by marrying morganatically after the death of this first husband, and some believe that the youngest child born during her first marriage was actually the offspring of her eventual second husband. The Tsarevich Alexander had his share of flings as a young man, which caused his mother great disquiet, but settled dutifully into marriage, and the scandal that eventually engulfed him came long after his parents' death.

Nicholas's own marital fidelity is also moot: gossip attributed strings of illegitimate children to him despite his public and private stance as the most devoted of husbands, and maintained that he used the maids of honour like a harem. His biographers have generally been wary of accepting this. He certainly had at least one significant mistress in his fifties when Alexandra's health failed and he himself began to grow stout and fear impotence, but any earlier dalliances may have been no more than temporary physical relief when his wife was under medical orders to avoid pregnancy. This sort of double standard would not have been seen in his day as inconsistent with romantic love for the pure angel of the hearth who was his wife, and Nicholas's clear discomfort when forced to abstain from sex was noted by even his mother.

Out in public among his people, Nicholas also consciously projected the image of a courageous, strict and loving father. He liked to drive around without guards, stopping at intervals to kindly but firmly lecture malefactors on poor behaviour, or to give assistance to the deserving. His reign saw the publication of tales about beggar children who – ignorant of his identity – asked for a ride in his sleigh and were taken home to see the Winter Palace. He was also reputed to have led the mourners in the funeral of a poor bureaucrat whose coffin he saw pass without family or friends. When the Tsar took his place behind it, hundreds instantly followed him in paying their respects.

The story of the poor bureaucrat, the loyal servant honoured by his Emperor, had particular resonance because the bureaucracy itself was central to Nicholas's rule as Tsar. Under his auspices, the Imperial Chancellery founded by Paul developed into an enormous trans-Russian administrative body, responsible for everything from Decrees and Orders to the charities run by the Dowager Empress. It was in Nicholas's reign, acting through the Second Section, that Michael Speranskii resumed the reforms he had commenced in Alexander's with the foundation of the State Council and the creation of the ministries. He now worked on the systematic codification of the imperial laws, providing Russia with sixty-five volumes of law each around 800 pages long by 1830. But the most notorious institution of the Chancellery and reign was to be the Third Section, which Nicholas originally intended to help enforce justice and moral purity in the nation: he wanted people to trust the gendarmes, whom he charged to lead the righteous along the correct path, reward the just, and investigate corruption wherever that existed. There was censorship of books and journals, which again had a positive, paternalistic intent: he wanted to encourage the best of Russian art while removing what he saw as corrupt elements. This censorship certainly did not impede the flowering of the real golden age of Russian literature, even if some of the ideas that that age engendered flourished precisely because of the always somewhat oppressive atmosphere of Nikolaievan Russia. Inevitably though the Section soon became unwieldy, and its power over every aspect of life engendered further corruption in itself. For much of the reign, it effectively ran a vast network of spies, observing even the activities of the imperial family. It was easier to imprison than properly to investigate. The Marquess of Custine, the famed travel writer who enshrined the image of Nicholas's police state in western literature and minds, commented that if a man wanted to keep a secret in Russia, the only person he might tell it to was the Tsar.[28]

The Third Section also became notorious for the particular scrutiny of foreign nationals, since they were now considered to be the source of the ideas that led to revolt. Nicholas went some considerable way to harnessing the spirit of nationalism that awoke in Russia after 1812. This was more than a cynical move to gain some popularity: it reflected his own belief that the European, enlightenment ideas imported by his grandmother and brother had done little more than engender the Decembrists revolt and, a little later, the Polish rebellion of 1830, which ended Nicholas's own solitary experiment in constitutional monarchy. The favoured historian of his regime was Nikolai Karamzin, author of the vast *"History of the Russian state"* which had greatly impressed Alexander I in the latter more conservative part of his reign. Karamzin had been around the court freely criticizing government policy since Nicholas was a boy. He extolled autocracy and worked Russian folk traditions into his history of the nation in a manner that a modern historian would find uncritical or sentimental, but which won high favor in the Romantic era of the early nineteenth century, searching for a truly national spirit. Inspired by Karamzin and others, Nicholas's reign saw the creation of the official doctrine of Autocracy, Orthodoxy and National Character, entwining the three inextricably and using them as a counter to the French revolutionary slogan of Liberty- Equality and Fraternity. It was the first broad-based ideological justification anyone had attempted for autocratic government. *"The Russian, devoted to his Fatherland, will as little agree to the loss of a single dogma of our Orthodoxy as to the theft of a single pearl from the Tsar's crown,"* wrote S.S. Uvarov, the Minister of Public Instruction credited with developing the doctrine of Official Nationality in the 1830s. *"Autocracy constitutes the main condition of the political existence of Russia. The Russian giant stands on it as the cornerstone of his greatness....Together with these two national principles there is a third, no less powerful: Nationality"*[29] In this as in all things, Nicholas's government started with actions intended as positive and paternalistic but progressed rapidly to oppression: it scrutinized and held down minority religions, particularly the Jews, and began to view Russia's own religion and government as the moral saviour of the corrupted western world. *"In the Christian world autocracy is the highest level of power,"* added Zhukovsky, the Tsarevich's poet-tutor. *"It is the last link between the power of man and the power of God."*[30]

Nicholas's nationalism was aesthetic as well as political. He favoured the gothic style for his own little Cottage and chapel at Peterhof because it had developed as a "national" style – albeit not Russia's – and in the public buildings he commissioned he moved away from the formal neoclassicism of his brother's reign toward something that sought to express a specific national idiom for Russia. He was a ferociously prolific builder: in Moscow he commissioned Konstantin Thon to refurbish the Great Palace of the Kremlin, destroyed by the fire of 1812, and build in celebration of the Russian victory the Cathedral of Christ the Saviour, which adopted the cupolas of Muscovite tradition but was vastly larger than any ancient Russian church: it was supposed to represent the universality of the Russian idea and religion, heir of Byzantium and the Roman Empire.[31]

In his capital, Nicholas was responsible for the first public art museum in Russia, the New Hermitage, which opened in 1852 and displayed the imperial collections to the world. He also perforce presided over the restoration of his own official home adjoining it, the Winter Palace. One evening in December 1837, he and the Empress were enjoying an evening's entertainment at the theatre when they began to receive reports of a fire in the Palace, where the children were asleep. The Empress, treated as ever as one too frail to withstand life, was dispatched straight back to the Anichkov Palace, but her husband participated in the evacuation and fire-fighting as crowds began to throng the streets. The children were hurried to safety quite easily, the tiny Grand Duke Michael asleep and wrapped in blankets throughout the operation, but before the flames were extinguished the Neva wing of the palace was horribly damaged, and the family's private apartments also took fire. It was thirty hours before the flames were all extinguished. Enormous importance was attached to a restoration project due to the Palace's status as the physical embodiment of the greatness of the Russian monarchy: it could not be allowed to stand empty and burned out. Thus, through Herculean effort by architects, designers and workmen, it was all refurbished and restored within two years. Vassily Stasov looked after the state rooms, sticking to the original Baroque in places but introducing changes in others. Alexander Briulov, who also worked on the Marble Palace, took charge of the private apartments, introducing the famous Malachite Room that divides the state rooms from the private ones. Apartments were also prepared for the Tsarevich Alexander Nikolaevich, shortly to marry and set up his own home there.

Nicholas commissioned or refurbished a palace for each one of his children who were to live in Russia as adults, allocating the imposing Marble Palace, empty since the departure of Konstantin Pavlovich for Poland, to his brother's godchild and namesake Konstantin Nikolaevich, and having Andrei Stakenschneider design a palace apiece for Maria Nikolaevna and for the third imperial son Nicholas in the area of the city around Senate Square. Both these palaces were in the eclectic style with Russian nationalist elements as well as more obviously neo-classical forms, and they completely dominate their surroundings. Michael his youngest son was to live on Palace Embankment in a house that stood out less from those adjoining it, but was equally vast and grand on the inside.

Nicholas's view of himself as the defender of all that was right and just in the world had as much of an impact on his foreign policy as it did on his domestic government and the way he chose to design his homes. He began his reign with a war to assist Greece in liberating itself from the Ottoman Empire. Alexander's failure to support the Greeks in this had been one of the factors that disillusioned liberals about him; but Nicholas's reasoning was not liberal: he supported less the principle of Greek self-determination than the principle that Christian, Orthodox citizens should not be subject to the Turks. If there was any doubt in western Europe after this as to where Nicholas stood, his actions in crushing the 1830 Polish rebellion and subjecting the country to military rule under General Paskevich left no doubt. Henceforth he was the "crowned policeman" and for better or worse a bulwark against revolution. In 1848, another year of revolution in which the French government was overthrown, the King of Bavaria forced to abdicate and the heir to the Prussian throne driven abroad, Nicholas actively supported the Austrian monarchy against Hungarian rebels demanding their own parliament. His main concern was to stop all this spreading to Poland, but after the successes of 1848 his nation and system of government looked invincible to the world.

At home, he was less sure of himself. Despite his own espousal of Russian nationalism, a number of arrests were made in Slavophile circles, largely because the Slavophile advocacy of Russia as protector to all Slavic peoples – including the turbulent Bohemians in the Austrian Empire – tended to undermine the legitimate authority of other Emperors. These arrests went almost to the very heart of the court: Ivan Aksakov the young Slavophile thinker went to prison for a short while: he was a habitué of the artistic salons held by Nicholas's sister-in-law Elena Pavlovna, and knew Konstantin Nikolaevich from them too. The novelist Dostoevsky was sent to jail as well, and after that to Siberia via a death sentence commuted last minute in the most sadistic manner. *"We were taken to Semenovskii Square,"* he remembered later. *"Here the sentence of death was read to us, we were all made to kiss the cross, a sword was broken over our heads, and we were told to don our white execution shirts. Then three of us were tied to the stakes in order to be shot. For me, only one moment of life remained…then the drums sounded retreat and an order from His Imperial Majesty was read which granted us our lives."*[32] Dostoevsky was a member of the highly revolutionary Petrashevtsy discussion circle, but in later years as a reformed character enamoured of religion and Russia he came tutor several of Nicholas's grandsons. Thus the awkward dichotomy of Nicholas's own Slavic nationalism.

The Tsar went far further than the persecution of a few writers considered to be encouraging revolution. Nicholas now banned all discussion of reform; police surveillance increased, and censorship became still greater. In the country at large, the Tsar's latest actions caused great consternation, including in some surprising places. *"We were frightened by the revolution,"* one deeply conservative statesman commented with acid and vehemence, *"and thus we began to stop our education, to avoid thought, to persecute intellect, to humiliate the spirit, to kill the word, to destroy publicity, to put out enlightenment, to spread the theme of patronizing ignorance."*[33] In more radical quarters, Nicholas was actively detested by now. The man who had started with active and positive intentions had turned his own government into an instrument of petrification, stifling all development.

"You will not mislead Holy Russia
With your faithless soul.

No, you will not hold back
Russia's universal destiny,"

wrote the Slavophile poet Feodor Tiutchev of Nicholas's rigid foreign and domestic policy.[34] It was not too long before the limitations of that policy became utterly apparent.

On October 4, 1853, the Ottoman Empire declared war on Russia. This was the culmination ostensibly of a quarrel over the Orthodox Church's right to control the holy Christian sites within the Empire's borders, which the Empire had previously respected but was increasingly inclined to cede to the Catholics instead. In reality, the war was tied up with the situation in Europe too, because the Catholic Church's rights were aggressively promoted by France, reasserting its status as a Great Power after years of post-Napoleonic suppression by the rest of the continent. France was backed in turn by parts of the British cabinet, concerned lest Russia use the opportunity finally to dismember the Ottoman Empire and seize control of shipping routes to India. Nicholas had recently invaded the unsettled Danubian provinces of the Ottoman Empire, and this he came not to help the Sultan – a fellow absolute monarch – against recalcitrant subjects, but to protect recalcitrant Orthodox subjects against their Islamic overlord. Technically, he had the right as protector to do so, but it was at this point that the sultan declared war.

All attempts by Austria and others to mediate fell apart, and by spring 1854, Russia was at war not only with the Ottoman Empire, but with France and Britain as well, fighting invasion of the Crimean peninsula annexed from the Ottoman sultan by Catherine seventy years before.

The Crimean War was a disaster for all who participated. The western Allies, although victorious, sustained huge losses. Britain's military operations in particular became a by-word for aristocratic incompetence and arrogance at the expense of the ordinary soldier. Like Napoleon I (whose nephew and namesake was after all the current French Emperor), these allies came up against the force of the Russian winter, which even in the Crimea can be extreme. Russia in turn was bedevilled by poor internal communications which hampered military strategy, and – in a war which was after all being fought over shipping routes to the east – by a grossly inadequate Navy and by harbours into which her ships were blockaded by superior French and British forces.

Threatened defeat in the Crimea underscored the inadequacy of Russia's current economic, political and social structure, and in reformist circles there was a certain sense of anguished relief, even, at this strong possibility of being defeated. *"Now we shall wakeup. It's too bad about Sevastopol. It's too bad about the spilled blood. But it's all for the best, because now our eyes will open up,"* wrote one desperate historian.[35]

In February 1855, worn out with the struggle, the Tsar fell sick with influenza. *"I recall the memory of the night of the death,"* wrote a lady-in-waiting.

> *"It was two or three o'clock in the morning, but nobody slept. They had just called for the Court Chaplain. In the corridors, on the stairs every- where, I met (coming down from my rooms and shaking with apprehension) frightened, anxious faces. This silent anxiety in the semi-darkness of the Palace, feebly lit by a few wall-lamps, deepened the impression of that terrible moment. The dying Emperor was lying in his small study on the lower storey. The great domed vestibule was filled with silent courtiers. In this agonizing silence one heard only the howling of the wind in the enormous square courtyard."*[36]

He died in the early morning of March 2, urging his son *"Hold – hold all!"* with a sweep of a hand that indicated Russia.

The death of the Iron Tsar was greeted with a sense of relief in many circles both at home and abroad. Revolutionary Alexander Herzen was wildly effusive from exile, rejoicing *"at the fact that the hated tyrant in jackboots is finally returned to the elements."*[37] Others less radical still felt that it had *'somehow become easier to breathe."* The Empress, at his funeral, though, struck the world *"as if she was dying of sorrow."* For better or for worse, everyone knew that a change would come now.

GRAND DUKE MICHAEL PAVLOVICH

(1798-1849)

By Arturo E. Beéche

The benjamin of the family, Grand Duke Michael Pavlovich happened to be the object of much affection from his adoring parents and siblings. Tsar Paul felt a definite weakness for his three youngest children, doting on them constantly. Anna Pavlovna recalled how much her father Tsar Paul enjoyed the company of his younger children.

> My father," recalled the future Queen of the Netherlands, "*loved to have us about him and, particularly in his last years, used to send for Nicholas, Michael and me to play in his room while his hair was being dressed – the only leisure time he had. He was so kind and gentle to us that we used to love to go. He said that he had been estranged from his elder children, who had been taken from him as soon as they were born, so he wished to have the younger ones about him so that he could get to know them.*[1]

Paul's wife, Empress Maria Feodorovna, who was nearing the age of forty by the time she gave birth to their youngest child, felt no differently toward Michael. Doted on by all around him, Michael had a happy childhood, only marred by the untimely death of his father. However, the adulation that the youngster received was not only excessive, but it was to mold his future character. Michael, as nice as he could be, was also extremely selfish and self-centered. These character traits would make for an unhappy life in later years. Michael's brother, Alexander I, once tried to raise awareness in Michael, in an effort to show him how the common soldier functioned, by having his youngest brother, and Nicholas Pavlovich perform "*manual exercises on deck...before the crew of a ship which was being inspected in the harbour of Cronstadt.*"[2]

Michael Pavlovich was born at St Petersburg on January 28, 1798 (O.S.).[3] As was the case with all Russian grand dukes, Michael entered the imperial army at an early age. At the time of the Napoleonic invasion of Russia the youngster itched to be involved in the campaign to defend his motherland. His being just a teenager prevented Michael from much involvement. Yet, the military exploits of his older siblings, as well as Russia's role in expelling and eventually defeating Napoleon and his allies, made an indelible mark in Michael Pavlovich's mind. The army was to become a world in which he relished functioning. Michael's difficult personality was well-known within the armed forces, "*to ordinary men in the ranks he was a harsh disciplinarian, even brutal, but people who really knew him valued his cheerfulness and his generosity and his family adored him.*"[4]

By the time Michael entered his twenties, the need for him to seek a wife became a matter of imperial importance. Both Tsar Alexander I and Grand Duke Konstantin Pavlovich remained childless, at least legitimately. Grand Duke Nicholas finally became the father of a boy in 1818, the future Alexander II. A dearth of baby boys in the imperial nurseries made Michael's matrimonial prospects an issue of national importance. Unfortunately, at the time there was a shortage of marriageable princesses, a fact that even Michael's mother complained about.[5]

The search for Michael's bride finally settled on a close relation, Princess Charlotte of Württemberg. Born Princess Friederike *Charlotte* Marie of Württemberg, eldest daughter of Prince Paul of Württemberg and Princess Charlotte of Saxe-Hildburghausen. Her birth took place at Stuttgart on January 9, 1807.[6] However, her parents separated and Paul shocked everyone by moving to Paris with two of his children in tow, Charlotte being one of them. Paul, who was both artistic and non-conformist, found living in Paris far more exciting, than the staid surroundings he grew up in at Stuttgart. No amount of demands from his Württemberg relations made Paul change his mind to return home, or allow his daughters to do so. While residing in Paris, Charlotte, and her sister Pauline, lived in strained circumstances since their father did not possess much of a fortune. Yet, all seems to point that the girls retained fond memories of their Parisian interlude, even though their home was quite modest compared to royal standards. It was while in Paris that Charlotte first came under the tutelage of several intellectuals, a part of her life that would blossom in later years.

Michael Pavlovich and Charlotte met in 1822. The groom-to-be was twenty-four, his unsuspecting bride had just celebrated her fifteenth birthday. A noted author, Charlotte Zeepvat, pointed to the fact that by the time the couple finally met, their fate was sealed, she *"first met her husband in the summer of 1822, but the engagement was settled months before the meeting."*[7]

Charlotte was described as *"exceptional,"* if not *"exactly pretty."*[8] What was known about her was both her intellectual prowess, as well as how natural her personality seemed to be. Grand Duke Konstantin Pavlovich described Elena (the name Charlotte would adopt upon converting to Orthodoxy) as,

> *very likeable in every way and especially in private. In public she has a very noble bearing and expresses herself wonderfully well; is to the point...added to which is a charm that suits her. She is very witty and feels things very keenly and intensely, with a great deal of sensitivity. In short, she pleases me greatly in ever respect.*[9]

And yet, these two souls were destined never to find a common ground on which they could function as a couple. Elena found Michael's penchant for military life distasteful and hated having to experience barrack life. Contrastingly, Michael found Elena's intellect too much to handle, as well as her pursuit of intellectual matters tedious and boring. Grand Duke Konstantin Pavlovich tried his best to identify the source behind the couple's inability to coalesce.

> *As for Michael, he is incomprehensible to me. In spite of the fact that he could love his wife, he maintains a unique coldness and unawareness toward*

her. Whether it is the newness of the situation, shyness or another reason, I was not able to make it out, and to every question which I asked him about it he always answered me in such a way as to make me think that he was pleased. Thus, I took my leave of them, carrying away the conviction that the married state is an accessory which he might have been able to do without.[10]

Furthermore, Grand Duke Konstantin, to whom Michael felt closest among his brothers, also hoped that time would provide his brother with the necessary space to be a better husband. Konstantin was well aware that for Michael military service and sleeping were favored endeavors, while the young grand duke was most unconcerned with other aspects of his life. Konstantin, who never ceased expressing how much he cared for his brother, also hoped that in time both Michael and Elena would find the happiness that every married couple deserved. Sadly, and in spite of offspring, happiness was never to be an ingredient found in the marriage of Michael Pavlovich and Elena Pavlovna.

Elena first arrived in Russia in 1823. She immediately began the long process of becoming a future member of the imperial family. She learned Russian and became quite knowledgeable about her adopted country's history and politics. By 1824 she was ready to not only enter into a marriage she had had no say in, but also adopt a faith for which she held no particular passion. On August 2, 1824[11] (O.S.), Elena Pavlovna married Michael Pavlovich in St Petersburg.

Michael and Elena's first child, Maria Mikhailovna, was born in September 1825. The following year a sister, Elisabeth, joined her in the nursery. Catherine Mikhailovna was born in 1827. By then the marriage was on the rocks. Elena suffered greatly after every birthing and it took her considerable effort to recover from post-natal trauma. Added to this was the fact that Michael paid her less interest as weeks turned into months. Elena felt the loss of Alexander I and his wife deeply, as both had always been very kind, and understanding, toward her. Thus, after the birth of Catherine, Elena was ready to give up on her husband. To get the point across, she left Russia. The emperor would not allow Elena a long sojourn abroad, but she convinced Nicholas that spending time in a spa would be greatly beneficial to her shattered health. On her way to Germany, Elena visited her brother-in-law Konstantin, who lived in Warsaw. He shared his impressions, and attested to her predicament and pain when sharing his thoughts with Anna Pavlovna.

> *Her health is in a very wretched condition, but I hope she is not alto gether lost; however. It is very close to that. In her, everything has been affected, both physical and moral qualities…One must agree that this young and charming woman was very gratuitously and very uselessly sacrificed. Her position is frightful…and what is worse, no one wants to put themselves in her place to understand it…I hope that time will make both her and Michael see what there is to be done in order to come to an understanding.*[12]

Konstantin remained convinced that it his initial hesitation about the future of Michael and Elena had been listened to, much pain would have been avoided. Unfortunately, his concerns were never paid much attention to. Most members of the Imperial Family chose to ignore Konstantin's initial hesitations about Michael's inability to make his marriage work. In a letter to his sister Anna Pavlovna, Grand Duke Nicholas Pavlovich said,

> *he is working hard now to get children for them, but it appears that this is still unsuccessful. They do seem to be in perfect agreement, which makes us all very happy…You know how things were…so you can imagine how this change makes us feel. God grant that it may continue to last; progeny, especially would do them a lot of good.*[13]

Sadly, it did not.

While Michael's marriage crumbled, the young grand duke was otherwise engaged. The distraction was brought about by the start of the Russo-Turkish War, which exploded in 1828. The Greek uprising ignited the conflict and that subjugated people's desire to achieve independence from Ottoman oppression. To express his opposition to Russian involvement in Balkan affairs, the Sultan closed the Dardanelles for Russian ships and revoked previous international agreements.

Tsar Nicholas I, accompanied by Grand Duke Michael, led the main Russian forces. The Danube was crossed and Russian troops entered the Dobruja, a region shared by Romania and Bulgaria. The Russians took Bucharest and Grand Duke Michael's troops besieged Brailov. Nicholas I wrote Anna Pavlovna a letter in which he expressed his confidence in Michael's military abilities, *"Michael is in charge of the siege of Brailov and I hope will reduce them shortly to surrender and will take it by storm."*[14] Michael distinguished himself during the conflict and his imperial brother was very proud of the fact that Brailov was eventually taken, even though it cost the Russians greatly. Anna Pavlovna hoped that the trying experiences Michael lived through would *"please Heaven that the anxieties and dangers of the Turkish war may make Michael value his home-life; he is a dear but unique combination whom one must love with all one's heart because no one is better than he for spiritual qualities."*[15]

Upon returning from the Balkan front, Michael tried reconciliation with Elena. By then, she had returned to Russia after spending nearly a year abroad. In the meantime the Dowager Empress Marie Feodorovna had died, leaving Michael a considerable share of her private fortune, as well as countless estates. Elena inherited the administration of two charitable institutions, in an effort to give her something to invest her maple energy in.

At their home, the imposing Mikhail Palace, a détente was established. While Elena continued her interest in intellectual matters, as well as artistic endeavors, Michael did what was expected, no more further pregnancies arrived. In 1830 Elena had a miscarriage. One year later she gave birth to a fourth daughter, Alexandra. Unfortunately, the child died a year later. One last baby joined the nursery at the Mikhail Palace in 1834, Anna Mikhailovna. She was born in Moscow, but was to die in St Petersburg two years later.[16]

In late 1830 Michael's military knowledge was required once again. In Poland, where Konstantin Pavlovich served as Governor-General, an uprising began on November 29. Known as the Cadet Revolution, Polish conspirators stormed the palace where Konstantin lived. He managed to escape, but the uprising exploded across the country. Konstantin believed that the uprising had to be dealt with by Polish authorities and to assure that would be the case, he retreated into Russia. As the situation worsened, Nicholas I sent troops to Poland, Michael Pavlovich being one of the generals he relied on.

Upon returning from the Polish conflict, Michael settled to the life of a grand duke. He continued involvement with his military obligations, while trying to stay away from his wife's intellectual endeavors as much as possible. At the Mikhail palace, and the couple's other residences, Elena gathered a salon visited by the country's intellectual elite. They resembled those she had witnessed while living in Paris and turned Elena into a magnet for Russia's *"most creative and interesting people."*[17] As one of Russia's leading ladies, Elena carried much weight. Her salon not only raised her public image, but it also earned her derision from the most conservative sections of Petersburg society. Entry was provided by intellect, not by social position and wealth. In 1830s Russia that was an unthinkable act. Yet, Elena was not deterred and she continued her salon with unwavering dedication to learning, enlightenment and political discussion.

> *She invited the clever, the artistic and the musical, and the rigid censorship imposed by her brother-in-law seemed to stop at her door. Gogol, Pushkin and Turgenev all enjoyed [her] patronage, knowing that they could express any ideas in her house in safety and be sure of an audience.*[18]

Years later, and while a widow, Elena even welcomed her nephews, leading among them the future Tsar Alexander II, into her salon. It was to be one of the first gatherings within Russia where abolition of serfdom was openly discussed and supported. After Michael's death she had asked Nicholas I's permission to free the serfs in the Poltava estate, which she inherited from Michael. Fearful of what repercussions there would be, Nicholas refused her request.

Meanwhile, Michael kept away from Elena's intellectual pursuits by meandering around Russia and abroad. He visited Germany with frequency and in 1836 he also paid Anna Pavlovna a visit in The Netherlands. Michael was also very attracted by England and visited London several times. In 1846 he and his daughter Maria were visiting Vienna and while there the young Maria died unexpectedly. None of his daughters had enjoyed good health and in fact Elisabeth had predeceased Maria by almost two years. Elisabeth had married Duke Adolph of Nassau, a stepson of Elena's sister Pauline, in 1844. A year later she died in childbirth at Wiesbaden, her husband's capital. After Maria's death Michael and Elena were left with one living child, Catherine, who in 1851 married Duke George of Mecklenburg-Strelitz, who settled in Russia and served in the imperial army. Catherine and George were the parents of four children who were to be Michael and Elena's only grandchildren.

In 1849 Grand Duke Michael Pavlovich attended military maneuvers in Warsaw. He had never enjoyed a robust constitution and had frequently traveled to various spas around Europe in search of relief. The strains caused by the death of his daughters Maria and Elisabeth only complicated his already compromised health. Michael suffered a stroke while in Warsaw. He never recovered. Death came to him a few months later. No one better expressed the sense of loss felt by the imperial family than Anna Pavlovna, by then Dowager Queen of The Netherlands, *"Another cruel loss this year…it is too dreadful. Since I heard of his illness I have been in mortal terror…one cannot always resign oneself…His ring is on my finger and will never leave it again."*[19]

Widowhood seemed to bring Elena impetus to relish in her role as the leader of Russian's most progressive salon. Her vast wealth, which she inherited from Grand Duke Michael, the husband responsible for given her such distress while alive, made Elena's life amazingly comfortable. Her daughter's marriage in 1851 also brought into Elena's home a young man whose company she very much enjoyed, particularly as he made Catherine Mikhailovna very happy, while providing Elena with the grandchildren she had always longed for.

Elena also became a matchmaker of sorts. In 1848 she played a role in furthering the marriage of her nephew Grand Duke Konstantin Nikolaevich to the former Princess Alexandra of Saxe-Altenburg, whose mother was a Württemberg. She also played a role in furthering the marriage of Nicholas Nikolaevich to an Oldenburg, step-granddaughter of Pauline of Württtemberg. More importantly, Elena brought out of obscurity another young princess who was to emulate her benefactor's intellectual pursuits. Her name was Elisabeth of Wied. Born in 1843 she was the daughter of Hermann, 4th Fürst of Wied, and of his wife Princess Marie of Nassau, a stepdaughter of Elena's sister Pauline.[20] In fact, Marie of Nassau was a sister of Elena's former son-in-law, Duke Adolph, widower of Grand Duchess Elisabeth Mikhailovna. In Elisabeth of Wied Elena found a kindred spirit, someone with whom she could easily relate and discuss myriad intellectual issues that occupied her mind. Elisabeth visited Russia and was a guest of Elena's. She also accompanied her aunt on many travels around the continent. In 1869 Elisabeth married future King Carol I of Romania.

In 1873 Elena visited Stuttgart, her ancestral home. It was while there that she died on February 2.[21] Her death was deeply felt in Russia, where her role in support of liberal groups was much admired. Not only were Russian intellectuals much in debt to her, but she was also a patron to many artists, including noted musician Anton Rubinstein, who had taught Elisabeth of Wied. Several years before her death, Elena founded a nursing school, The Institute of Grand Duchess Elena Pavlovna, which would be responsible for training some of the empire's most notable doctors, while becoming the precursor of the Russian Red Cross.

By the time death brought an early end to a fulfilled life, Russia remembered Elena Pavlovna, while many had forgotten her unhappy husband Michael Pavlovich. Perhaps in the end, the success of this ill-starred alliance must center on the fact that Michael's marriage to Elena brought into Russia a woman who would play an important role in bringing much reform to a country in dire need of modernization.

Elizabeth Narishkin-Kurakin, a memoirist of imperial times, paid tribute to Elena. She remember the Grand Duchess's salon *"was the center of intellectual life. It was an era rich in eminent men, all the outstanding minds found in the Grand Duchess an encouraging and stimulating patroness…she received all the shining lights. Even the Emperor* [Alexander II] *liked to be present."*[22] Thus, one can argue that Elena Pavlovna was Michael Pavlovich's most lasting and important legacy to Russia.

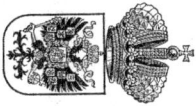

TABLE #1: THE CHILDREN OF TSAR PAUL I

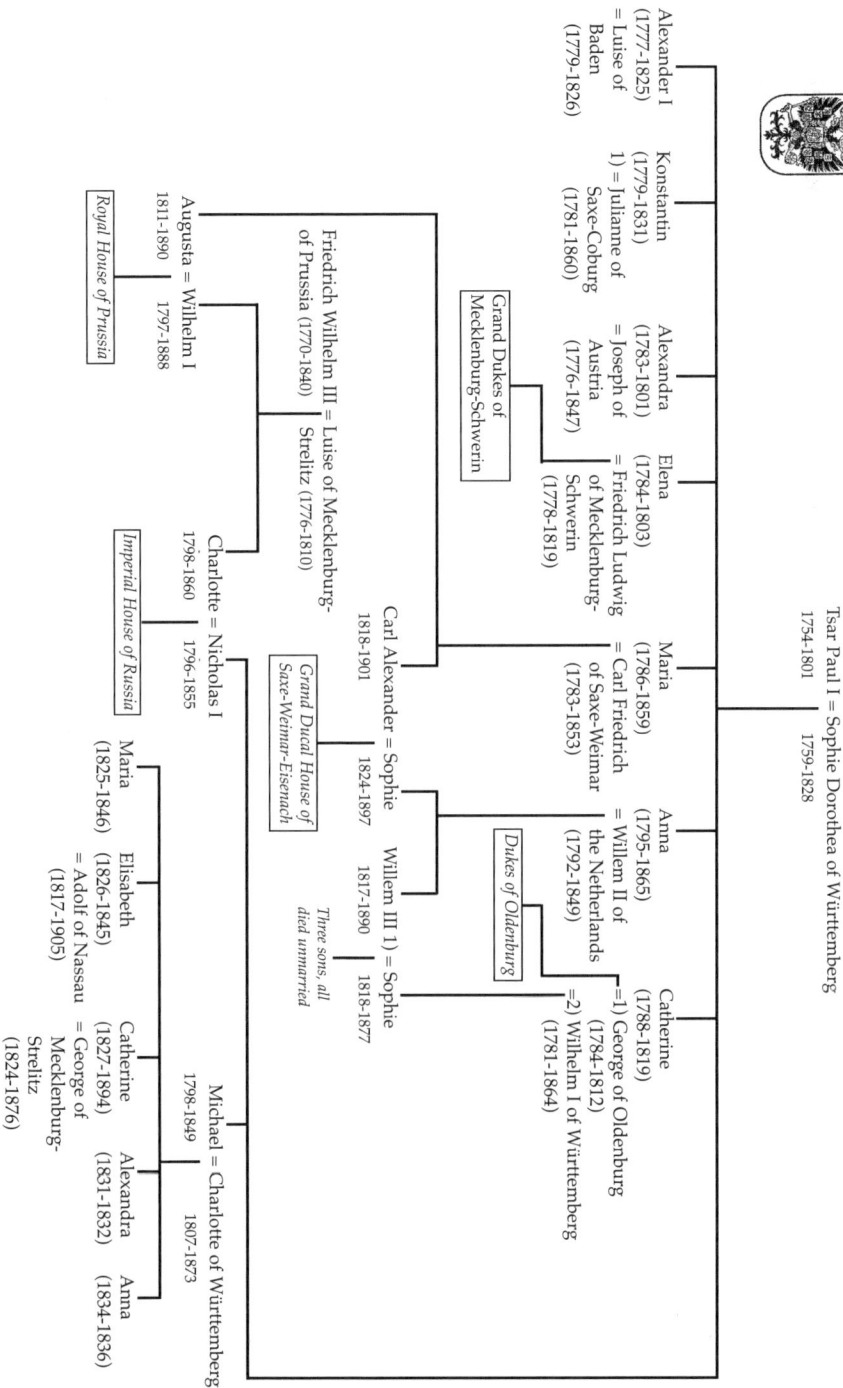

Tsar Paul I = Sophie Dorothea of Württemberg
1754-1801   1759-1828

Alexander I
(1777-1825)
= Luise of
Baden
(1779-1826)

Konstantin
(1779-1831)
1) = Julianne of
Saxe-Coburg
(1781-1860)

Augusta = Wilhelm I
1811-1890   1797-1888

Royal House of Prussia

Friedrich Wilhelm III = Luise of Mecklenburg-
of Prussia (1770-1840)   Strelitz (1776-1810)

Alexandra
(1783-1801)
= Joseph of
Austria
(1776-1847)

Grand Dukes of
Mecklenburg-Schwerin

Elena
(1784-1803)
= Friedrich Ludwig
of Mecklenburg-
Schwerin
(1778-1819)

Charlotte = Nicholas I
1798-1860   1796-1855

Imperial House of Russia

Carl Alexander = Sophie
1818-1901   1824-1897

Grand Ducal House of
Saxe-Weimar-Eisenach

Maria
(1786-1859)
= Carl Friedrich
of Saxe-Weimar
(1783-1853)

Anna
(1795-1865)
= Willem II of
the Netherlands
(1792-1849)

Dukes of Oldenburg

Willem III 1) = Sophie
1817-1890   1818-1877

Three sons, all
died unmarried

Catherine
(1788-1819)
=1) George of Oldenburg
(1784-1812)
=2) Wilhelm I of Württemberg
(1781-1864)

Michael = Charlotte of Württemberg
1798-1849   1807-1873

Maria
(1825-1846)

Elisabeth
(1826-1845)
= Adolf of Nassau
(1817-1905)

Catherine
(1827-1894)
= George of
Mecklenburg-
Strelitz
(1824-1876)

Alexandra
(1831-1832)

Anna
(1834-1836)

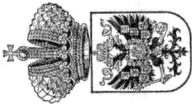

TABLE #3: GRANDCHILDREN OF TSAR NICHOLAS I

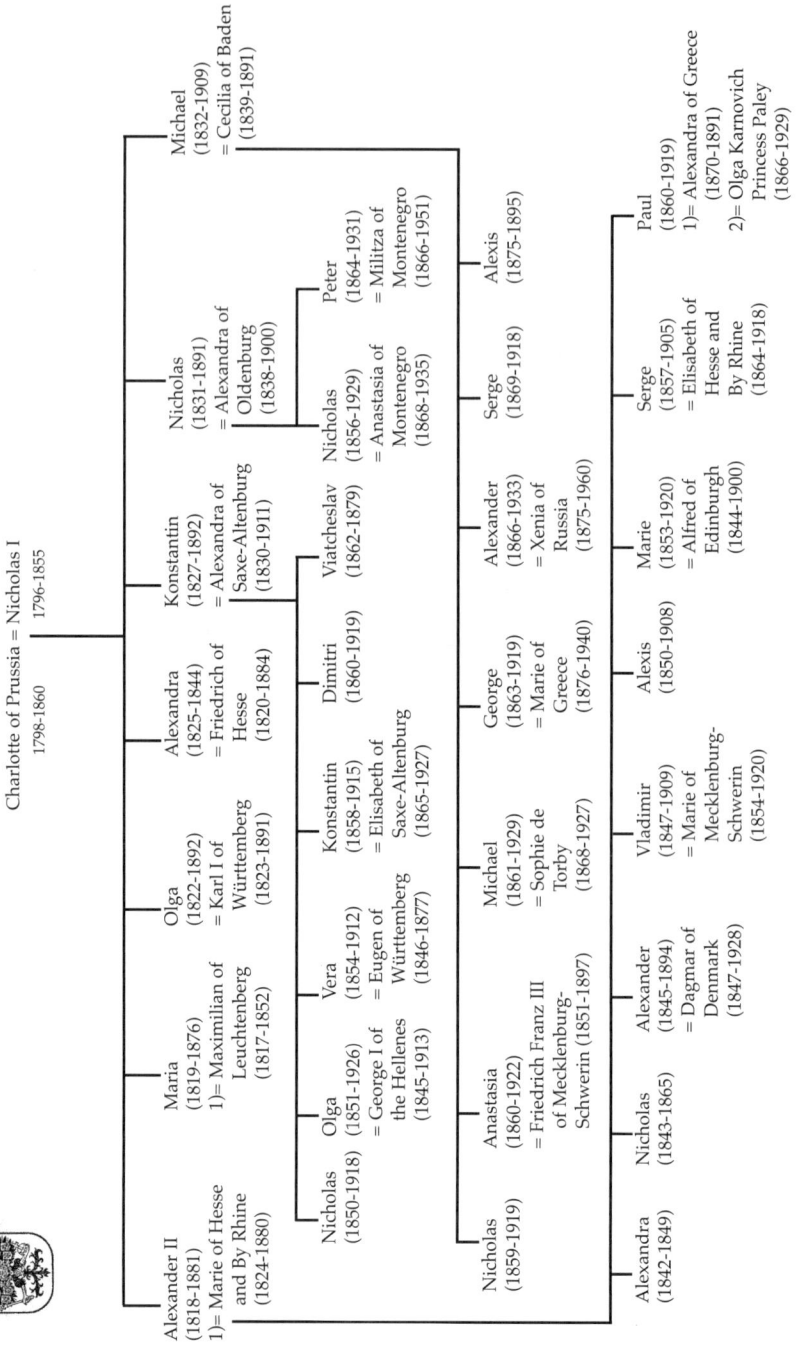

Charlotte of Prussia = Nicholas I
1798-1860   1796-1855

Alexander II
(1818-1881)
1= Marie of Hesse
and By Rhine
(1824-1880)

Maria
(1819-1876)
1)= Maximilian of
Leuchtenberg
(1817-1852)

Olga
(1822-1892)
= Karl I of
Württemberg
(1823-1891)

Alexandra
(1825-1844)
= Friedrich of
Hesse
(1820-1884)

Konstantin
(1827-1892)
= Alexandra of
Saxe-Altenburg
(1830-1911)

Nicholas
(1831-1891)
= Alexandra of
Oldenburg
(1838-1900)

Michael
(1832-1909)
= Cecilia of Baden
(1839-1891)

Nicholas
(1850-1918)

Olga
(1851-1926)
= George I of
the Hellenes
(1845-1913)

Vera
(1854-1912)
= Eugen of
Württemberg
(1846-1877)

Konstantin
(1858-1915)
= Elisabeth of
Saxe-Altenburg
(1865-1927)

Dimitri
(1860-1919)

Viatcheslav
(1862-1879)

Nicholas
(1856-1929)
= Anastasia of
Montenegro
(1868-1935)

Peter
(1864-1931)
= Militza of
Montenegro
(1866-1951)

Nicholas
(1859-1919)

Anastasia
(1860-1922)
= Friedrich Franz III
of Mecklenburg-
Schwerin (1851-1897)

Michael
(1861-1929)
= Sophie de
Torby
(1868-1927)

George
(1863-1919)
= Marie of
Greece
(1876-1940)

Alexander
(1866-1933)
= Xenia of
Russia
(1875-1960)

Serge
(1869-1918)

Alexis
(1875-1895)

Alexandra
(1842-1849)

Nicholas
(1843-1865)

Alexander
(1845-1894)
= Dagmar of
Denmark
(1847-1928)

Vladimir
(1847-1909)
= Marie of
Mecklenburg-
Schwerin
(1854-1920)

Alexis
(1850-1908)

Marie
(1853-1920)
= Alfred of
Edinburgh
(1844-1900)

Serge
(1857-1905)
= Elisabeth of
Hesse and
By Rhine
(1864-1918)

Paul
(1860-1919)
1)= Alexandra of Greece
(1870-1891)
2)= Olga Karnovich
Princess Paley
(1866-1929)

2

THE SONS OF
TSAR NICHOLAS I

TSAR ALEXANDER II
(1818-1881)

By John van der Kiste

G rand Duke Alexander Nikolaevich, the son of Grand Duke Nicholas Pavlovich and Grand Duchess Alexandra Feodorovna, was born on April 17, 1818 (O.S.), in the Kremlin during Holy Week. The Grand Duchess, daughter of King Friedrich Wilhelm III of Prussia, noted in her journal on the arrival of her firstborn that she could not but feel *'slightly melancholy at the thought that the tiny helpless thing would one day have to ascend the throne.'*[1]

Known by the family as 'le petit Sacha' during his childhood, the boy spent his summers at Pavlovsk, west of St Petersburg, and winters at the Anichkov Palace. His parents were affectionate but strict, bringing him up in relatively spartan surroundings and rooms which were quite austerely furnished. His tutor Colonel Karl Merder, appointed in 1824, reported that His Imperial Highness was 'extremely well-mannered, thoughtful about the comfort of others,' and though attentive and quick-witted at his lessons, was *"rather prone to tears and reluctant to struggle with the least difficulty."*[2]

At the age of seven his father ascended the throne as Tsar Nicholas I, and he became Tsarevich. A second tutor, the poet Vasili Zhukovsky, was chosen to assist with his education. His enlightened outlook was largely responsible for the future Tsar's open-minded way of thinking. In personality the boy was always polite, honest, willing to learn though only of average ability, sensitive and inclined to be dreamy. The tutors often found him mischievous and emotional by turns, erratic and sometimes hesitant when faced with problems. He showed no great enthusiasm for eventually becoming Tsar, and when his brother Constantine was born in 1827, he remarked that it was a relief, as *"Papa will be able to choose him as the Heir."*[3]

From his mother he inherited and always retained a strong affection for Prussian ways. At the age of eleven he paid his first visit to Berlin, and King Friedrich Wilhelm III appointed him Colonel-in-Chief of the 3rd Prussian Uhlan

Regiment. After returning to St Petersburg, every year he would attend the annual cadet camps organized under his father's personal supervision. Nevertheless he showed little enthusiasm for military affairs, much to the disappointment of his father, who wanted the boy to grow up every the perfect soldier and autocrat.

In 1834 he celebrated his sixteenth birthday, and the coming of age ceremonies in the Winter Palace included taking an oath of allegiance and solemn obedience to the Tsar and to the laws of the empire. He was granted a special inheritance, and asked for gifts to be made to his mother, sisters, tutors and school companions, and to the governors-general of St Petersburg and Moscow for the benefit of the poor and sick of both cities. The coming of age festivities ended with a ball at the Palace.

In the spring of 1837 his formal schooling was considered to be at an end, and he undertook a seven-month tour of Russia. Travels around Europe followed, and on a visit to Darmstadt he met Marie, daughter of the Grand Duke of Hesse and By Rhine. According to gossip the fourteen-year-old princess was said to be the child of the Grand Duke's master of the horse, but he had acknowledged her as his daughter in order to avoid scandal. Such rumours made no difference to the smitten Tsarevich, who may have thought that it was a ploy designed to try and put him off her. Before long he was passionately in love with her, and in April 1840 their betrothal was officially announced. She was received into the Orthodox Church in December and given the names Maria (Marie) Alexandrovna, and on the eve of the groom's twenty-third birthday in April 1841, they were married in the Chapel of the Winter Palace.

Between 1842 and 1860 Marie gave birth to six sons and two daughters. Much to the parents' grief their firstborn, Alexandra, died at the age of six, but the rest – Grand Dukes Nicholas, Alexander, Vladimir, Alexis, Serge and Paul, and Grand Duchess Marie – all attained their maturity. He was a devoted father, and his desk and the walls of his study were covered with miniatures and portraits of his wife and children.

In March 1854 Britain and France jointly declared war on Russia. The empire's defeats in one battle after another were a bitter blow to the already ailing Tsar Nicholas, and he died on February 18, 1855 (O.S.). Father and son had argued bitterly over the conduct of the war, and it was believed by some that the Tsarevich's appointment of the able Gorchakov as commander-in-chief to replace the inept Prince Menshikov was the final blow to the Tsar, who had not consented to the appointment and was enraged at being opposed by the son and heir who had taken an oath of loyalty to him.

Unlike his father Tsar Alexander II was not a natural leader of men. Inclined to be diffident, he was regarded by some as lacking in some of the more forceful qualities necessary for the head of the mighty Russian empire. Others were more hopeful, convinced that his accession would mean the dawning of a new era led by an enlightened, well-meaning man who genuinely believed in personal freedom but had inherited an empire in a sorry state, ill-equipped to meet the demands and challenges of the modern world. He also differed from his father in holding strong feelings, unusual for a ruler of the age, about the horror and futility of war.

His two main objectives were firstly to bring peace to the Russian empire, and after that to alleviate the general well-being of his people. Before his death Tsar Nicholas had consented to a conference in neutral Vienna to discuss peace terms. The peace congress met at Paris in February 1856. Although Tsar Alexander II found some of the initial proposals humiliating, such as the cession of territory to other nations, he was persuaded that he had no alternative but to submit, and a settlement was agreed in the following month.

This shock to Russia's system spurred him and his more forward-looking ministers into a new start for Russia. Among the first major pieces of legislation put into effect by the Tsar and his ministers were plans for new railways in the empire, and liberalisation on the freedom of the press. At the time of his coronation in August 1856 a manifesto granted amnesties to a large number of convicted conspirators and exiled revolutionaries.

The greatest achievement of his reign, and that for which he was destined to be associated with for all posterity, was the emancipation of the serfs. With this measure enacted in March 1861, around twenty million peasants were freed from the necessity of performing duties for their masters, became free citizens and were given land from their landlords. The statute was important in that it helped ameliorate the economy by increasing the mobility of labour, but it created unforeseen problems in that the peasants found themselves burdened with "redemption debts" which they could not pay at times of bad harvests. Moreover there was little consistency in the distribution of land, so that in the more fertile areas the peasants received less than his fair share, and felt badly done by.

There was widespread disappointment that emancipation did not herald a new golden age in Russia. Not only were some of the peasants dissatisfied with their lot, but landowners were aggrieved at having been "robbed" of much of their land; and university students, emboldened by relaxations in state censorship, demanded further reforms. It was almost as if a measure intended to benefit everybody perversely ended up by pleasing none. The Tsar was genuinely grieved that his efforts should have been misinterpreted and resulted in further unrest.

In 1864 his eldest son, the cultured but rather delicate Tsarevich Nicholas, was betrothed to Princess Dagmar of Denmark. Joy at the good news turned to grave anxiety when he fell ill shortly afterward, and to grief when he died on April 12, 1865 (O.S.). His bride-to-be dutifully transferred her affections to the new Tsarevich, Alexander, and they married on October 28, 1866 (O.S.), in the Winter Palace.

By the time the wedding took place, two further shadows had fallen across the life of the Tsar. The Tsarina had never been very healthy; her constitution had been taxed by a combination of several successive pregnancies and the severe Russian winters, and she and her husband gradually drifted apart. He began an extra-marital affair with Catherine Dolgorouky, a union which would bring him four further children (of which one died in infancy) but also estrange him from most of his family. In April 1866, he was returning to his carriage after a walk in the grounds of the Winter Palace when a self-proclaimed revolutionary fired on him. The Tsar was unhurt, but it was only the first of what would be several attempts on his life. To celebrate his narrow escape from death, several churches and chapels were built in cities throughout the empire.

Although a lover of peace, it was his misfortune to be drawn into war later in his reign. Unrest in the Balkans resulted in Russia's declaration of war on Turkey in April 1877. The Tsar joined three of his sons, Alexander, Vladimir and Serge at the front, though he was not permitted to join the army and fight himself, partly for reasons of security and partly because of ill-health. Now almost sixty years of age, he was a martyr to insomnia and asthma, and suffered from rheumatism so badly that he had a hot brick placed in his bed on cold nights. He wrote regularly to Catherine, assuring her that she would *"understand better than anyone else what I feel at the beginning of a war I so much wanted and hoped to avoid."*[4] Prince Cherkassky visited him in the summer, and had nothing but admiration for him.

> *When you see him, tired and unwell as he is, visiting hospitals, entering into the men's interests and needs, bearing himself with a sovereign's dignity and a friend's compassion, you cannot but love him as a man.*[5]

Fortunately the conflict lasted less than a year; Turkish resistance soon collapsed and a treaty, signed at San Stefano in March 1878, was ratified at the congress of Berlin three months later.

The passing years had done nothing to stem the tide of revolution, fomented by secret societies who were determined to kill the Tsar. In April 1879 he was again shot at while returning to the Winter Palace on his return from a walk, but the would-be killer fired four shots and missed him. Later that year a small fanatical organisation calling itself "The Will of the People" formally condemned "Alexander Romanov", whom they stigmatised as the embodiment of reaction and repression, to death for failing to summon a constituent assembly in Russia. Their first attempt on his life came in November, when he was returning to the capital from the Crimea by train. The imperial carriage was unharmed, but another train was mined and wrecked in the subsequent explosion.

Another, more serious, attempt was made in February 1880. A member of the revolutionary group managed to find employment with a group of builders undertaking repairs in the Winter Palace. Every day he carried a few dynamite charges into the palace with him, and before long he had enough explosives in the basement to precipitate what could so easily have resulted in a spectacular mass assassination. The Tsar, Tsarevich and Tsarevna and the Tsar's daughter Marie, who had married Queen Victoria's son Alfred, Duke of Edinburgh in 1874, were to attend a dinner party with their guest of honour Alexander, Sovereign Prince of Bulgaria. Mercifully for all of them, Prince Alexander's train was late and dinner had to be delayed by half an hour. When the company were assembled and the Tsar was about to lead them to the dining room, an explosion shook the palace, and the room was completely demolished. Eight men were killed and over forty seriously injured.

Outwardly the Tsar was calm, but inwardly he was shattered. His brother Grand Duke Konstantin compared their situation to that of those who had lived through the terror of revolutionary Paris, but with the difference that at least the Parisians had seen their enemy face to face; *"We neither see them not do we know them."*[6] After the Tsar attended the mass funeral of the victims, he remarked sadly that they "did break the Turk" during the recent war, and *"we must break this enemy also."*[7]

On the morning of May22/June 3, the Tsarina died. Her husband was too honest to make any public displays of grief, and a month later he told his chamberlain that he intended to marry Catherine Dolgorouky. The ceremony took place in secrecy in an apartment of the palace at Tsarskoe-Selo on July 6/18. Afterward he conferred on her the style and title of Most Serene Highness Princess Yourievsky, and the children were legitimized.

This move did nothing to redeem the Tsar or his young wife in the eyes of his children. The Tsarevich and Tsarevna were incensed, calling Princess Yourievsky 'the outsider', and the Tsarevich talked of moving with his wife and children to Denmark, though as he could succeed to the throne at any moment, this was no more than an idle threat. On the whole the younger Grand Dukes were reasonably tolerant if not forgiving of the affair, and if they disapproved, kept their thoughts to themselves, but the Grand Duchesses felt that the late Tsarina had been treated shamefully by her unfaithful husband, and remained implacably opposed to the presence of their sovereign's morganatic wife. Grand Duchess Michael, the Tsar's sister-in-law, declared that she would never recognize 'that scheming adventuress' who had broken up the family and was plotting to ruin the empire.[8] A more understanding view of the position of the whole family came from the German Crown Princess Friedrich Wilhelm, who considered that it was impossible not to feel bitterly the want of respect to the late Empress's memory, *"much as the children feel their father's marrying again, yet it must be preferable for them to feeling ashamed of the life he was leading."*[9]

Though the Tsar was saddened and frustrated at seeing that his reforms had had the unhappy effect of unleashing revolutionary discontent among those who wanted more than he was prepared to give, he did not shrink from continuing to take further steps to improve the lot of his people. A few days after the attempt on his life in the Winter Palace, he announced that he was considering granting a constitution, and to demonstrate his good intentions he ordered the release of a number of political prisoners from prison. Count Michael Loris-Melikov, his minister of the interior, was given the task of devising a constitution that would go some way toward satisfying the reformers while retaining the sovereign's autocratic powers. The Tsarevich was sceptical about the benefits of any such reforms. His advisers had convinced him that Russia needed a strong autocratic sovereign, and anything resembling a constitution was anathema. Such differences of opinion led to difficulties between father and son.

Nevertheless in January 1881 the minister presented his plans to the Tsar, comprising an expansion of the powers of the Zemstvo. Under his plan, each regional body would also have the power to send delegates to a national assembly that would have the power to initiate legislation. Concerned that this would grant too much power to the national assembly, Alexander appointed a committee to look at the scheme in more detail. This pace was too slow for the revolutionaries, increasingly angry at the government's failure to announce details of the new constitution, and determined to continue with their aim of assassination.

On the morning of February 28/March 12, the manifesto was handed to the Tsar. He read through it and promised he would sign it the following day, when it would be published in the press. At the same time Loris-Melikov warned him in the presence of the Tsarevich not to attend the parade ground the following day as some of the terrorists were still at large. The Tsar answered that he had only accepted a bodyguard with great reluctance, and if he was not safe when surrounded by his own loyal Cossacks he might as well abdicate. It was thought by some that the sovereign had been rejuvenated and was feeling more at ease with the world than he had for some time; that he intended to have Princess Catherine crowned as his Empress; and that when his political reforms had been achieved, perhaps no more than a year hence, he would abdicate and retire with his wife and their young children to France. This may have been merely hearsay, but several people who saw him at around this time thought he suddenly looked many years younger.

On the next day was the Tsar returning in a closed carriage to the Winter Palace. A bomb was thrown at his carriage but missed and instead landed among the Cossacks who were guiding him. He got out to check on the condition of those who were injured. Another bomb was thrown and this time reached its target. Hideously mutilated yet still semi-conscious, he was placed on a stretcher and carried back to the palace. Both legs were shattered below the knee, his face was horribly disfigured and streaming with blood, and it was probably only the intense cold which prevented him from bleeding to death on the spot. The explosion was so severe that Ignatius Grinevitsky, who had thrown the bomb, also died of his injuries. Two hours later, a bulletin was issued saying that there could be no hope for His Majesty's life. Holy Communion was administered, and a few minutes later his sufferings were over.

According to the Tsar's nephew, Grand Duke Alexander, "idyllic Russia" ceased to exist that day. *"Never again would a Russian Tsar be able to think of his subjects in terms of boundless confidence."*[10] It was ironic that the man whom posterity has judged as the most intelligent and humane of the Tsars was assassinated to be replaced by a reactionary son and heir who shared nothing of his father's vision.

GRAND DUKE KONSTANTIN NIKOLAEVICH
(1827-1892)

By Zoia Belyakova

His Imperial Highness Grand Duke Konstantin Nikolaevich is one of the most remarkable, complex and controversial characters among all grand dukes. A few wrote about him that *"with his death the House of Romanov lost its most educated, independent and advanced representative, an enlightened government official and a progressive reformer of his era."*[1] However, the majority considered him a stubborn, sharp and sinister man, a real "red" and a nihilist.

Konstantin was the second long-awaited son in the family of Nicholas I and Empress Alexandra Feodorovna. He was born in St Petersburg on September 27, 1827, and joined his siblings: the Tsarevich Alexander (Sasha, 1818-81) and three sisters born in a row: Maria (Mary, 1819-76), Olga (Olli, 1822-92) and Alexandra (Adini, 1825-44). The Tsar rejoiced. He was the third son of Emperor Paul I and only by accident became emperor.[2] He was now feeling more relaxed in the male succession to the throne. Konstantin (Kosti) was the first "born in the Purple", his four elder siblings were born as children of their not yet crowned father. Kosti was much proud of the fact, and in later years caused occasional problems and complications to Sasha, the heir to the throne.

From early childhood, Kosti was destined for a career in the navy, quite a rare Romanov profession. Therefore, when the boy became five years old, the traditional English nanny was replaced by a new tutor, the young naval officer, geographer and Arctic explorer Feodor Litke (later Count and President of the Academy of Science), who had twice circumnavigated the globe. At seven, Kosti was assigned A.Grimm as his second governor. A few funny episodes of his childhood circulated in the family. Once the little boy heard a story of an unlucky merchant who went bankrupt and had to sell off his last treasure – his dog. *"But why,"* little Kosti exclaimed, *"couldn't his valets and other servants collect some money for his sake?"* His parents and tutors decided to emphasize a practical side in the boy's upbringing, to raise him first as a human character and thereafter to fashion him as a grand duke or Grand Admiral of the Navy. He learnt carpeting, turning and other practical things in shipbuilding.

The little fellow showed eager interest in history and geography,

> *was able to translate a German rendition of the Odyssey...he lived and breathed the Homeric age, and sought out in the Hermitage all the pictures that represented Homeric or other mythical objects, repeating with the greatest animation what he had learned to his playmates on Sundays, and urging them to perform scenes from the Trojan War.*

His sister Olga remembered that Kosti acted as a wonderful cicerone conducting the sightseers during their visit of the Kremlin with its churches, played pranks, tried the boots of Peter the Great, sat in the throne chair, and nearly put on the hat of Monomakh, but the vigilant Litke stopped him.[3]

Nicholas I, regretting the gaps in his own education, did his best to ensure that his son received an all-round education whilst still in childhood. His intention was supported by Konstantin's demonstration from an early age of extraordinary talents, an inquisitive mind, tenacity and a strong will. His lessons in calligraphy, painting and music were later complemented with lessons in dance twice a week, as well as gymnastics, fencing, military drilling and armaments. To the two languages of his childhood (the four elder siblings spoke English among themselves, the "little treasures" Nizi and Misha spoke Russian) added a fluency in French and German. His natural gift for music developed to perfection: Konstantin Nikolaevich knew music, loved it and played cello excellently.

Zhukovsky, the tutor of Tsarevich Alexander, taught Konstantin to think logically, and kept up a correspondence with him that lasted to the end of the poet's life. Professor Shulgin taught Russian history in informal conversations. History in its wider scope was taught by Grimm in German. Mathematics and physics were the responsibility of the academician Lentz. Colonels and generals taught military sciences. Exams happened every three years, at the ages of eleven, fourteen and seventeen. The Emperor assigned a fortnight hearing for the exams, with two days devoted to each subject. To examine one's progress, Kosti (and other sons) had to withstand a crossfire questioning in the presence of the Tsar's family and the most select Court members. Konstantin acquitted himself with flying colors.

Nevertheless, he was not an ideal child. He exhibited an uncontrollable temper, behaved like a stubborn bully, unrestrained and uncouth. Count Sollogub recalled how in the drawing room, during a game of cards, the boy pulled a chair away that the minister Count I.M.Tolstoi was about to sit in, causing him to fall heavily to the floor. The Grand Duke ran out of the room laughing. Nicholas I put down his cards, and in French said to the Empress, who was sitting not far from him: *"Madam, arise."* The Empress stood up. *"We shall apologize to Ivan Matveyevich for having brought up our son so badly."*[4]

In 1837 Kosti was only ten years old.

> *He looked small, a little stooped and short-sighted, therefore Uncle Michael called him Aesop. When in good spirit and excited, he alone made more noise than the whole group of children. Very clever and developed for his age, he immediately caught the line of a conversation and never felt bored of the adults' talks. However, left to himself alone, he became intolerable. He was always ready to answer back, and his funny grimacing often put an end to Mama's patience.*[5]

By instinct Kosti seemed to feel that he was not the best favored child. He remained rather lonely as a teenager, quite aloof of the elder children, lacking the tenderness of the Empress who was such a kind and patient angel, however, often annoyed with Kosti's fiery temper and naughtiness. Olga recollected that both

Mama and Litke punished little Kosti. He lacked companionship, undergoing naval training. By age eight, he owned a small yacht on which he ate, slept and took classes. It anchored in the Neva, next to the Winter Palace, and in summers in Peterhof, where Kosti trained as a naval cadet sailing back and forth between Peterhof and Kronstadt in the Gulf and further to Finland's shores. It was both a rigid and rigorous upbringing to make a successful naval career.

The strict discipline enforced by Litke was an attempt to smooth over the fervid temper and the uncontrollable energy of his pupil. Olga blamed this attitude,

> *He often remained silent for days long, feeling so much insulted and angry about such a manner of his upbringing, and, at 20 years old, he decided to marry to get rid of the education burdens. Thus, straight from a nursery he found himself a husband, lacking any experience, without a chance to immerse in pleasures of youth or to enjoy companionship.*[6]

Litke succeeded in instilling in him endurance and cold-blooded grit in moments of danger. In the summer of 1854, a boat of American construction sank, which Konstantin and his adjutants were sailing to Kronstadt for testing, and he was the one of the crew to swim to the rescue craft without assistance, whilst some of the crew drowned.[7] Later Litke managed to involve Konstantin into the work of the recently formed Geographical Society, which was attended by leading economists, explorers and philosophers.

Konstantin completed his first sea voyage abroad before reaching the age of nineteen, journeying to Constantinople and then on to France, Spain and England. The Grand Duke's visit to the Turkish Sultan was sketched by the artist Ivan Aivazovsky. By using his diary with astute observations, Konstantin published his essays with detailed descriptions of the lands and countries that he had seen, displaying his power of imagination, intelligence and considerable writing skills.

In 1847, Konstantin gave his ceremonial oath of allegiance to the Throne and the Homeland, which Emperor Nicholas I had introduced for his sons as a crucial component in their education and upbringing.

In 1846, Grand Duke Konstantin saw for the first time his future wife, Alexandra Frederica of Saxe-Altenburg, the younger daughter of Duke Joseph of Saxe-Altenburg. The powerful effect of their first meeting was unforgettable. *"I don't know what has happened to me,"* eighteen-year-old Konstantin wrote, *"I am a completely different person. Only one thought moves me, I have only one picture before my eyes: always and only she, my angel, my star…I'm up to my ears in love."* Kosti astonished his parents when they received a letter from Europe explaining his intention to marry. *'she, or no one,"* wrote their son. Having considered the matter, Nicholas I said to the Empress, *"When I met you, I decided the same thing, you, and no other, and I was only eighteen. Write him our blessing."*[8] The permission was given on the condition that the marriage would only be possible in two years' time, as the bridegroom was nineteen and the bride sixteen at the time of their engagement.

For a year before the marriage ceremony, the princess lived as a bride-guest of the Empress in Tsarskoe Selo, learning Russian and getting prepared for conversion to Orthodoxy. Her good looks, natural manner and joyful mood delighted everyone. Their wedding on August 30/September 11, 1848, was celebrated with great pomp. On the day of the ceremony, Konstantin was promoted to the rank of Rear-Admiral, and was appointed Head of the Naval Cadets' Corps and commander of the Life-Guards Finnish Regiment. At only twenty-four years of age he already headed the Marine Department (dubbed "ministry of progress") in the rank of Rear-Admiral, was a member of the State Council, President of the Russian Geographical Society, and was known as a liberal and an enlightened patron of art and literature.

Following the death of Grand Duke Konstantin Pavlovich the magnificent Marble Palace on the Neva Embankment remained empty. In March 1832, the palace was granted to Grand Duke Konstantin Nikolaevich, and was put under the management of the Department for Crown lands. The famous architect Alexander Bruillov was commissioned to reconstruct and entirely renovate the interiors of the palace (1846-1851). On December 10, 1849, an order was issued by Nicholas I presenting the palace to His Imperial Highness Grand Duke Konstantin Nikolaevich, to be held for life and to be passed on to his heirs. The order also renamed the building the Konstantinovski Palace.

The Marble Palace received a new hostess, Grand Duchess Alexandra Iosifovna (1830-1911). Having grown up at a small modest German court, "Sanny", as her relatives called her, quickly mastered the tone and style of the Winter Palace, and loved the Russian extravagance and magnificence, which was entirely in keeping with her extraordinary beauty, her marvelous wealth of hair in particular. A few considered that she resembled Mary Stuart, Queen of Scots, whose style to dress Sanny copied. All of Europe spoke of her astonishing jewels, of her pearl necklace, in which each pearl was the size of a nut. She never suffered any homesickness. The lady-in-waiting Anna F. Tiutcheva believed that Sanny was neither clever, nor well educated. *'she takes the place of a spoilt child in the family and they treat her frequent tactlessness and lapses in behavior as jolly pranks."*[9] However, others believed that the Grand Duchess Konstantin enjoyed a lively mind and wits, a few called her silly, her only distraction being a strange, hoarse and high-pitched voice. Sanny always took a passionate interest in anything, which related to the beauty of other women. With typical feminine jealousy she would ask: *"Who is the more beautiful, the Empress of Austria or I?"* The Empress's beauty was much praised, and the Grand Duchess Konstantin worried: *"Is my hair as fine as the Empress's? Don't you think we have the same figure?"*[10]

Due to the couple's mutual efforts, the Marble Palace became the most attractive literary and musical salon, where academics and representatives of the art world met, and where intellectual interests ranked higher than the veneer of high society and vanity. Sanny reigned in her beauty, always resplendent in wonderful dresses and jewelry. For many years her husband was in love with and admired her, and the contemporaries believed that he did not notice other beauties.

The attitude of the Emperor to his second son was ambivalent: he was at once proud and extremely worried about him. At Court, against a background of general banality and boredom, Konstantin stood out, with his acerbic wit, his undiluted and passionate character, and, in particular, his burning energy and independence. Nicholas I, however, only needed efficient and dependable subordinates.

Similarly, Nicholas I was concerned about Konstantin's apparent unwillingness to subordinate himself to his brother Alexander, which remained quite a talk at Court. Well remembered was an episode when, as a young frigate captain in the Baltic, after a quarrel, Konstantin arrested his brother, the heir apparent Alexander during his visit of the vessel. Sasha was held prisoner for a few days, until the Tsar arrived and released him. Such distrust disappeared after Konstantin took an oath of allegiance to the new Tsar Alexander II in February 1855.

Konstantin, dubbed *"demi-sovereign,"* easily made enemies. Many regarded him *"a liberal, and a despot;"* more over, *"his smile caused horror"*[11] Physically, he was one of the three short Romanov men (also Paul I and Nicholas II) among dozens of tall, strapping and handsome august members, which always caused a secret inferiority complex that Kosti tried to suppress and hide. He grew a beard and wore it forked. He also sported a monocle, which was a sure sign of nihilism and extreme liberalism, according to the thinking of the time. *"The eyeglass hung from his neck by an elastic cord. When Konstantin was forced against his will into conversation, he stealthily yanked the cord and sent the monocle flying back into place in front of his eye"*[12] A dialogue ended in complete consternation of his interlocutor. Legends had it that during social events at the Marble Palace Konstantin would often single out a new servant, pin him to the wall with a gaze, and scream out his name in a sharp yell. When the victim froze, fainted, dropped his tray, or ran, Konstantin broke into hysterical laughter. These stories somehow remind us of a blood-stilling formidable gaze of Emperor Nicholas I, when Kosti's father used to employ it on his victims. *"Everything around began to pale and tremble, leib-freulines and leib-generals were scared to breathe,"* writer Alexander Herzen stated. He also named him the "winter eyes" of Nicholas I.[13]

Favorite chambers of Konstantin Nikolaevich in the Marble Palace included the Library which consisted of three rooms and contained both the books with gold monograms on the main fields of knowledge, and the Russian classics. All the Konstantinovichi were inveterate bookworms. An admirer of the talent of Nikolai Gogol, the Grand Duke regretted that his library lacked a complete collection of the great writer's works, and so he set about creating a posthumous edition of his books. Due to his assistance, the voyages of the poet Apollon Maikov and writer Dimitri Grigorovich took place. At his initiative, writer Ivan Goncharov sailed on the naval frigate *Pallada* as a secretary to Admiral Putiatin. Enormous tables here covered in green cloth and the cabinets displayed models of ships. On the walls hung marine views by the painter Ivan Aivazovsky. Being connected to the fleet from birth, the Grand Duke remained inseparable from it for twenty-eight years, and liked to say *"the fleet is my second existence."*

Together with the Grand Duchess Elena Pavlovna he established the Red Cross in the Crimean campaign of 1854-1855. During the reign of Alexander II, the Grand Duke headed both the fleet and the Marine Ministry as a full minister with the title of Admiral General. One achievement deserves particular praise: following the loss of the entire sail-driven Black Sea fleet, Konstantin Nikolaevich solved the goal of resurrecting the Russian navy. Under his management, the fleet was equipped with screw steamer craft, armor plating of ships began, and the first battleships were built. The fleet was equipped with sub water mines. In accordance with the reforms of 1855, corporal punishment was abolished among seamen, first in Russian Empire. The Maritime Collection publication commenced which included the writings of Goncharov, Pissemsky, Dal', Ostrovsky and Grigorovich. Training and education of officers improved, and the Nikolaievski Marine Academy opened in 1877. He introduced the practices of circumnavigation and the European voyages, in order *"to evaluate our own condition and backwardness."*[14]

In 1857-61, Konstantin was engaged in diplomatic delicate missions in Europe. He cruised back and forth to meet kings and queens, big dignitaries and rulers of Greece, Italy, Malta, Naples, Sardinia, and journeying to France and England. Daily correspondence between the brothers amounted to thousands of letters and most detailed reports. Konstantin's letters always mentioned his beloved *Zhinka* (Alexandra), who was a bad sailor. Her headaches, miscarriages, and other pains kept her husband worried. Alexander II never missed a chance to remind fiery-tempered Konstantin and Sanny about *"politeness, without any familiarity, to be cautious in talks and opinions."*[15]

At the spring white nights, Konstantin loved to dine in the Turkish room, where

> *there stood a divan, upholstered in Turkish material, and on a coach man's seat stood a Turkish saddle, decorated with precious stones, and there were Turkish cloth hangings. The parquet was inlaid with black wood. The floor had an opening in the middle, under which was situated a fountain,*[16]

wrote his grandson, Prince Gabriel Konstantinovich. The moldings and murals were done in the Eastern style, and on the upper sections of the walls, against a blue background, there were Arabic inscriptions in metal gilded lettering. On September 28, 1859, the Grand Duke noted in his diary,

> *At half past eleven we received Shamil*[17] *with his son Kazi Magoma in the Marble Palace. An astonishing appearance. After a short conversation I led him through the rooms. He was noticeably interested in my Museum*[18] *and the Turkish Room with its inscriptions. Then I presented him with my Koran and a bench for reading, and he was very pleased.*

The Standard Room and the Armory were located not far from the Winter Garden. There stood in special housings the banners of the Life Guards' Finnish Regiment and the Marine Guards', the head of which was the Grand Duke. When the standards were carried out after the host's death *"grandmother came to bid them farewell. They had stood there for decades."*[19] *"On Fridays, in the White Room of the palace, several musicians played, and the famous cellist Verzhbilovich attended,"* recalled Gabriel Konstantinovich.

> *Grandfather played the cello, sitting next to him. Once there was a big concert in the Marble Hall, and the orchestra of the Conservatoire played (grandfather was the President of the Russian Musical Society). Grandfather played the cello, my father played the piano with the orchestra, and Duchess Elena Georgievna of Mecklenburg-Strelitz sang.*

In the White Room (right up until 1933) there stood an excellent organ, ordered by Konstantin from abroad, and the room was often used for theatrical productions. The State Secretary A.Polovtsov, whose comments can't be regarded as objective, lists the performances of the 1880s, such as Gnedich's *Burning Letters* and fabulist Krylov's comedy *From Time to Time*. He insisted that Grand Duke Paul Alexandrovich was good in the part of a lucky lover, Dimitri Konstantinovich wasn't bad in the comic roles, that all the women were bad, and that Konstantin Konstantinovich was *"so-so, though weaker than the rest."*

Konstantin's favorite study, which Bruillov had completed in the Russian style, looked on to the Pavlovian barracks in the Field of Mars. *"Pretensions in the style of a Russian izba,"* scathed Polovtsov, who could hardly stand Grand Duke Konstantin. Apart from the portraits of the ancestors of the House of Romanov, this room was decorated with antique wooden furniture, arms, ceramics and metal utensils. The study is historic as here the reforms of serfdom were prepared. The visitors were the leading reformers who gathered around the Grand Duke in 1857-61. They represented the "Muzhikophilskaya" faction in the State Council that fought against the red-tape mongers who opposed the reform. The fiery protests of the landowners against the serf emancipation, and their rancor and hatred all aimed at the Tsar's brother Konstantin, as he chaired the Emancipation Committee and was the first to give his serfs their freedom. They openly accused him in undermining the foundations of the Empire and the property rights of the aristocracy. 'It was true that the Grand Duke was often abrupt and unpleasant, and that he made no secret of his contempt for the high aristocracy. Nor did he hesitate to show his sympathy with democratic ideas.[20] After his comment that *"it is time for some bloodletting of the aristocracy"* he became the scapegoat for each and every woe encountered by the nation. The spiteful critics accused him of being responsible for the death of the heir to the throne, Grand Duke Nicholas Alexandrovich (Nixa), the attempt on the Tsar's life by a terrorist Karakozov, and almost of the murder of Alexander II. Only a few persons considered him the head *"of the party of all thinking people, the leader of progress."* Emancipation finally became law in 1861. Later, on the twenty-fifth anniversary of his enthronement, Alexander II would name his brother his *"first assistant in the peasant reform."*

For sixteen and a half years, Grand Duke Konstantin was the Chairman of the State Council (1864-1881). The highest officials noted with respect his habit of personally studying each important issue, his forthright comments and his disagreements with the Emperor, his ability to comprehend all the subtleties of every side of any argument and to find all-encompassing solutions. He was not an ideal Chairman, as he was abrupt, quick-tempered and *"too authoritarian,"* but he could stand up for the opinion of the Council.

It was in this study that he would spend his hours of rest. In his diary (1862), Konstantin wrote: *"Evening in the study for my zhinka – Schubert, Veniavsky and Kudinger played two of Beethoven's trios. Charming, and the whole evening was a success."*[21] The host was known in the society as *"a fierce Slavophile, who speaks Russian and intends to denigrate all forms of European civilization,"*[22] Anna Tiutcheva wrote, regretting that the Grand Duke was discourteous by nature. She also mentioned in her Diary (1854) the Grand Duke's habit and impudent manner *"to gaze at people with a monocle, piercing an individual with a sharp and clever stare"* that only increased his reputation of *"a red man."*

Baroness Sophie Buxhoeveden noted that the decor of the palace was far from refined. Grand Duchess Konstantin ordered to paint redwood furniture in shocking pink and yellow, and to put on the walls the tapestries constructed out of anchors and ropes to recall the husband's nautical military service. Her boudoir was bizarre mess of photos, souvenirs, knick-knacks in pink porcelain, and her favorite stuffed pug-dog. As time passed, it became customary to dress the marble statues on the entrance stairway in green calico aprons, on the days when the Metropolitan of the Alexander-Nevsky Monastery came to wish the aging Grand Duchess a happy Christmas.

Grand Duchess Alexandra Iosifovna had an immense influence on her husband. She longed for him to be appointed the Viceroy of Poland. In the opinion of Valuev, the Minister for Internal Affairs under Alexander II, her desire for that position was even stronger than that of the Grand Duke. *"With all her will she wishes to be Queen,"* mocked Greig, Marshal of the grand ducal court. When Konstantin arrived in Warsaw in 1862, he was wounded the following day by a nationalist-terrorist Yaroshinsky, who fired at him at point blank range when he was leaving a theater. The bullet stuck in an epaulette, lightly injuring his shoulder. The terrorist had planned to carry out his assassination attempt a day before, but had been put off by the presence of the beautiful Duchess in the carriage, who was expecting a child (their last son, Viatcheslav). Konstantin embarked on a program of liberalization, reinstituted Polish as the official language, opened universities, and encouraged exiles to return. The youngest son was born in Poland, and

> *his mother decided to christen him Viatcheslav for the Russians' sake, and Waclaw for the Poles, in order to conciliate two Slav races. The result was entirely different, for as soon as a Russian mentioned the new-born baby by his name of Viatcheslav, a Pole was sure to interrupt and say aggressively, "You mean Waclaw: the child was born in Warsaw and is of course a Pole."*[23]

The Russians protested in their turn. All in vain, too late! The country was partitioned and put under martial law. An attempt to restrain the approaching squall of revolution was made by the military dictatorship of General M.N.Muraviyov. Poland soaked with blood. The grand ducal family lived under the siege. The letter of Grand Duke Michael to his brother Grand Duke Nicholas Senior, of August 13, 1862, noted: *"Yesterday my wife received a long interesting letter from Sanny: their situation is horrendous, worse than at war!.... she meets her husband for no longer than 5 minutes a day, he is exhausted"*[24] Most elite guards regiments were sent to Poland, and the *"officers was much discontented."* In August 1863 Grand Duke Konstantin was recalled to Petersburg as *"in the light of his opinions, his office and the current state of affairs in the region, his presence can not be expedient,"* and in October he was sacked from the position of Viceroy. Those days of fear and strain of life in Poland affected children health. Young Grand Duchess Vera (future Duchess Eugen of Württemberg) became wild and uncontrollable, her nerves were out of order, people regarded her as *"unbearable child."* Infant Viatcheslav, the apple of discord, was quite sick, and eventually he died early.

When the Konstantins lived in Poland, their nephew Alexander arrived, who was one day to be Alexander III.

> *Modeled on the pattern of a Hercules, or rather a moujik, he was always wrestling with someone, always knocking against something, always upsetting chairs in the way. Konstantin, himself a man of great intelligence and vast knowledge, but with a very sharp manner, treated his nephew as a nonentity. One day when the boy in his clumsy way had upset a decanter of red wine on the table cloth Konstantin called out 'such a piglet was sent to us from Petersburg!'*[25]

Alexander blushed in silence. He never forgot this insult, the revenge started stewing, and upon ascending the throne, he retaliated.

Alexandra Iosifovna could not bear any competent person being near her husband, and responded by isolating them or *"conquering them."* There is a body of opinion that holds that she brought about the breakup of their relations: being a powerful, passionate and highly sensual woman, she did not want to, or couldn't conceal her romantic intrigues with her husband's adjutants. Their long marital happiness aroused envy, evidently, a few politicians wanted to discredit Konstantin, and provoked a slander of Alexandra's unnatural tendencies. Anyway, retreating from the gossip, in 1868, her husband sent her abroad for a long period. She took her little son with her, a grand piano and the numerous retinue. Though not long before, Countess Naryshkina, one of St Petersburg's elite, recalled that *"Alexandra Iosifovna was at the summit of her extraordinary beauty. Winterhalter painted her portrait...the Grand Duke, at that stage still so much in love with her noticeably admired her, following the work of the artist."*

Another contemporary, Count S.D. Sheremetev, recalled the family scandal in a special way: *"His once beloved zhinka, admirable Josefovna as the Poles called her, a magnificent beauty, although 'a bit blind" and of a strange high-pitched voice, had strong charm of her own and realized her power. Once her destiny had been the storm and agitation."*[26] His poem commented such an opinion (author's translation)

> *Outlived and perceived,*
> *So much in a few days,*
> *A tumult of passions*
> *Burnt you in dreadful way*

When staying abroad, for short or long period, Sanny always remained in the whirl of balls, receptions, gossip and intrigues. She took with not only Viatcheslav, but also a physician, a pianist, a masseuse, a hairdresser, a keeper of her jewels, and of the purse, and so on. In addition to a mountain of luggage, her favorite grand piano arrived. For a while, famous pianist Kudinger accompanied her. She established a miniature court abroad.

In Italy, Grand Duchess Konstantin lived on a grand scale. She demanded a military ship to transfer her from port-to-port, saying that she never sailed a commercial vessel. In case the Russian administration refused, she appealed straight to Emperor Napoleon III. The latter dispatched a military boat to Villa Franche, near Nice, at the complete disposal of the spouse of the Russian Grand Admiral. At her arrival Genoa, the whole fleet greeted Grand Duchess Alexandra, however, she refused to use a small launch to get to the shore, then a special pier was built, with the prefect of Genoa in attendance.[27]

Olga wrote that Konstantin opened his eyes only twenty-five years after the marriage: he could no longer stand his wife's bigotry, her ecstatic mysticism, spiritualism, and many imaginary diseases. He indulged in work, tried to stay away from home, spent days in Kronstadt, preferred longer voyages and commitments abroad. Music became his only consolation. Into the bargain, he found himself in possession of a second family. When a discord became evident, he took a young ballet student from a choreography school as his mistress and arranged for her marriage. In time, that woman known as the ballerina Anna Kuznetsova would bear him five children, delicately dubbed "wards." A mansion for the second family was purchased in the capital on 18 English Prospect. They would spend every summer in the Crimea, at the Oreanda estate. This patch of land was bequeathed to Kosti by the late Empress Alexandra Feodorovna. The Grand Duke didn't hide his relationship with Kuznetsova, dubbing the Grand Duchess *"my government-issue wife up North,"* whilst *"his own wife"* lived in the South. To her credit Alexandra Iosifovna never tired of repeating that her husband was the most intelligent, noble and wonderful man, and that he would come back to her. Following the unexpected deaths of two of Kuznetsova's sons from scarlet fever, a telegram of condolences arrived from St Petersburg, from the Grand Duchess.[28] The illegitimate children received the name Kniazev. They had a small house in the park of Pavlovsk estate, where Konstantin preferred to stay in summer, while Alexandra Iosifovna lived at Strelna estate. According to the diary of the Grand Duke's son, Konstantin Konstantinovich, Grand Admiral had another family and children in Paris.

The archives of the second family (their descendants now live in Moscow) contain almost twenty letters that prove the real kind, caring, devoted relations among these people expelled by society. For example, Grand Duke Konstantin described in detail the coronation of Alexander III in Moscow (1883), a visit of the famous Khlebnikov's jewellery workshop, a visit of S.Tretiakov to view his celebrated picture collection and the consecration of the Church of Christ the Savior, that 'wonder of wonders'. When describing the coronation ceremony, he confidentially mentioned personal joys: *"my two darling geese Kostia and Mitia received St Vladimir Cross, 4th Class."*[29] Konstantin's letters to his daughters Marina and Anna show utmost love and tenderness.

The Marble Palace was inhabited by the large family of Konstantin Nikolaevich and Alexandra Iosifovna, including four sons and two daughters. Children rooms were located on the top floor and occupied part of the first floor. The private apartments of the sons had their own entrances from the street. Contemporaries testify that, in the 1880s, *"a seal of decay marked this gloomy edifice."*[30] Children felt offended with the extra-marital contacts of their Papa, and sided on their mother. Their son Konstantin Junior, such a Christian entered his diary that *"I can't and don't want to love Papa."* (February 5, 1883). The estrangement grew up, however, their inborn pride and vanity prevented from paving the way to hearts. Nonetheless, in September 1892, Grand Duke Konstantin Junior, read his late father's letters, and made an entry in his diary: *"Papa wrote beautifully. I came across so many tender, loving, hearty lines and expressions that I felt guilty for my cold attitude toward Papa, of which I always regretted."*[31]

The actions of Grand Duke Konstantin Nikolaevich drew little attention or suspicion right up to the enthronement of Alexander III in 1881. The young Emperor had never liked Uncle Konstantin, who teased him during his childhood, calling him "clumsy Sasha," and the uncle's liberalism and obstinacy irritated the Monarch. In private talks and letters, the young Tsar preferred to use a somehow humiliating name of Uncle Koko. This "boiler," to use the expression of one senator, with his unquenchable thirst for reform and his ability to gather the best in educated society around him, was unwanted. The reforms were shelved for the distant future and beyond. In addition, Alexander III disapproved of the support that Konstantin had given to his brother Alexander II in the troublesome issue of the Tsar's private life: the prolonged extra-marital relationship with Catherine Dolgoruky, who had four children by the Tsar. The new Tsar considered Uncle Konstantin to be a virtually amoral individual.

Konstantin's electrifying energy helped to drastically redevelop his Pavlovsk estate. The new art gallery contained fine paintings and antiques located in three halls: 225 marble statues and busts of the Roman emperors, First to Third centuries A.D. copies of the Greek originals, antique ash-cellers, bronze statuettes and antique vases. The palace museum was open for everyone from early spring to the latest autumn. A new meteorology and magnetic observatory was built in 1876, which offered a fine scientific library and up-dated technology.

In 1881, Konstantin Nikolaevich was forced to retire from all his posts *"of his own free will."* Those became hard days and years. All of a sudden, he felt forgotten, poked at, hurt with indifference, and he suffered. Occasionally he went wild and enraged. He was surely present at the coronation, May 15, 1883, when his nephew Grand Duke Alexei was appointed Grand Admiral, and retained all previous positions and ranks. On May 20, Alexis received congratulations in his Kremlin apartment, his uncle did not come. To show his protest and displeasure, on the holy day of Konstantin and Elena, Grand Duke Konstantin with his court left for a church and missed the festivities. Admiral Ivan Shestakov wrote: *"Alexis told that Alexander of Bulgaria was sitting at the Konstantin's, when the ukase was delivered about Alexis to become Grand Admiral. Enraged."*[32] The relations between uncle and nephew degraded. *"The old General-Admiral wants not to be forgotten in the Navy,"* wrote Shestakov (November 25, 1883). *"Remember me and see my superiority over my successor."*[33] A few years ago, the two brothers Sasha and Alexis liked to poke at their aging uncles and their foibles. *"Our dearest Koko lives in indescribable fear for the fate of his Dulcinea and her brood, as Fedinka Trepoff*[34] *told us, and Koko himself made a hint! Ha-ha-ha!!!"* (November 1875)[35] Note the spiteful words and disregard of *"kossolapii Sasha,"* the revenge was due. Alexander III was warned that Uncle Konstantin's resignation would much shock and upset the old Grand Admiral, but the Tsar cut it short: *'so much the better."*

Now he was seen with increasing frequency wintering abroad, spending spring and autumn in the Crimea or Pavlovsk, whilst Alexandra Iosifovna spent summers in the palace in Strelna. Konstantin's energy went on unabated. Forever holding company with academics, musicians, theologians and philosophers, he loved to talk with Ivan Turgenev; visited Greece and Schliemann's archaeological digs; attended sessions of the parliament in Paris; and proposed that the Peter and Paul Fortress be converted from a prison into a home for war invalids. The Great liberal suffered terribly: he could no longer serve his dear Russia. He was disgusted at the betrayal of those who just recently showed their adulation and devotion, and now all left him.

His last squabble with Alexander III occurred in 1886: the Konstantinovichi were expecting the first great-grandson of Nicholas I. Alexander III's new "Imperial Fundamental Law" decreed that the great-grand-children of the emperor would not be grand dukes, but only princes of imperial blood with the qualification of Highness, rather than Imperial Highness. The new law was taken by Grand Duke Konstantin as personal affront.

Fire accidentally destroyed his palace in Oreanda, and in its ruins a dining room-tent was erected; the Grand Duke lived with Kuznetsova and his children in a small house, and a second house for guests remained for the most time empty.

In 1889, Grand Duke Konstantin suffered a stroke, it made him unable to speak, and his right arm was paralyzed. In Pavlovsk he could move around only with his servants' assistance, seated in a wheel chair, and he suffered terribly that his beloved on-the-side family was not allowed to approach him. They sent them out from Pavlovsk. Instead, a much despised prude, Alexandra Iosifovna came to restore moralityin her midst. She took revenge.

> As one understands, he demands to meet them. One can guess about it by his tears, by his drives to the dacha where those people lived ... is not it cruel to ban these meetings, the only consolation and dream? ... here's a strong obstacle: Mama would never agree upon that woman to approach, wrote Konstantin Konstantinovich.[36]

The out of favour liberal and reformist died in January 1892, in Pavlovsk, in his study, the room where his grandchildren George and Vera would later live. A.Polovtsov made an entry in his diary,

> When Grand Duke Konstantin Nikolaevich was dying, during his agony his wife Alexandra ordered to let in all numerous servants to bid him goodbye. Everyone approached and kissed him, meanwhile the dying man tried hard to show his displeasure of this trouble. Countess Komarovsky, hofmeisterine of her court, tried to admonish the Grand Duchess to recall her order and stop that torture, but the Grand Duchess replied "C'est une reparation."[37]

Grand Duke Konstantin was buried in the Peter and Paul Cathedral next to his favorite sister Adini. Both daughters Olga and Vera came from abroad to the funeral. Emperor Alexander III only once attended the funeral rites.

During his life, the Grand Duke was accused of embezzlement, of being self-interested, and speculating on concessions and government contracts. After his death, it became apparent that under him the Marine Ministry had remained almost the only uncorrupted ministry of its kind. It would be impossible to deny that with his death the House of Romanov lost the most educated, independent and advanced representative, an enlightened government official and a progressive reformer of his era. Konstantin Nikolaevich possessed a renowned historical perspicacity: he recognized many of the negative features of the autocracy in Russia and outlined the problems that would confront Nicholas II.

Grand Duchess Alexandra Iosifovna carried on living in her chambers on the first floor of the southern wing of the Marble Palace until her death in 1911. She lost her sight in 1903, and never left the palace. She was buried with full ceremony: the aged Grand Duchess had lived for sixty-four years in Russia, attended three coronations, was loved by Nicholas I, and witnessed the great reforms of Alexander II. For years she kept quarreling and blaming her servants, her irritation and hysterics prevailed, and it caused much depression to her children.

However, in thememory of her children, grandchildren, their friends and guests, she remained a unique personality, a commanding old lady with snow-white hair, which was always faultlessly styled. She dressed in a beautiful black tight-fitting frock that complemented her shapely figure and bearing. Always affable and smiling, she never forgot, for a moment, her high standing and strictly followed protocol and etiquette. She could give off waves of chilling condescension by aiming her gaze and tortoiseshell lorgnette in the direction of anyone that aroused her indignation. Children would attempt to give particularly low curtseys before her. *"Even babies should have decent manners,"* was her motto.

GRAND DUKE NICHOLAS NIKOLAEVICH
(1831-1891)

By Greg King

He seemed destined for great things but, in the end, accomplished little. His legacy, which should have been one of reform and military bravery, instead became one of an infamy, submerged in the scandalous tales of his private life, his mistress, and their bastard offspring. Isolated and alienated, he spent his last two years locked away from prying eyes, suffering from insanity. Such was the life of Grand Duke Nicholas Nikolaevich Senior, one that began with such promise but instead ended as a magnificent failure.

He was born on July 27/August 7, 1831, in the Alexander Palace at Tsarskoe Selo, the third son and sixth child of Nicholas I and his wife Alexandra Feodorovna. By the time of the boy's arrival, the crown despite the fact that only six years had passed since the Decembrist Rebellion seemed secure, and the succession ensured: there were, after all, two older brothers, Alexander (the future Alexander II) and Konstantin, who could follow their father to the throne should anything unpredictable-and such things were indeed known to happen in Imperial Russia-take place.

It was an odd, almost prescient echo from the future, this happy, united Imperial Family, this Nicholas and Alexandra surrounded by their loving children in the Alexander Palace, where a similar situation would be enacted by the last of the Romanovs. Childhood, at least for young Nicholas, was comfortable, privileged, and undemanding, as these things were generally understood in the courts of Europe at that time. There was, though, no coddling, no overt indulgence: it was a Spartan regime, designed to discourage false sophistication in the imperial children, who slept on army camp beds fitted with rough wool blankets and lumpy pillows. Even if life was lived in a series of palaces-at Tsarskoe Selo, at the immense Winter Palace in St Petersburg, at the vast and austere Gatchina, or at the exquisitely situated Peterhof -it was regulated and controlled, to guard against any hauteur. A contingent of English and Russian nurses and nannies, practical to a fault, ruled the children, bathed them, fed them, clothed them, took them for walks, read to them, and prayed with them before firmly tucking them beneath their scratchy blankets for the night.

One thing, though, was encouraged: learning. Both Nicholas and Alexandra – unlike their 20th Century counterparts of the same names – valued a love of education, and a good, comprehensive education at that, an education where not just the usual social niceties of languages, dancing, painting, music, and-at least for the boys-drills took priority, but one that focused and honed the mind, that sought to create great thinkers and potential leaders for this immense and unwieldy empire. And here, at least, the young Nicholas was something of a disappointment, especially when compared to his eldest brother Alexander. But then, perhaps Nicholas could argue, with two brothers ahead of him to take the throne – Russia's heir and spare – what need was there, really, for him to become an intellectual giant? So he concentrated, and enjoyed, or endured, or plodded, through the various lessons that came his way, from Russian history to European studies, from arithmetic to science, from philosophy to religion. It was all designed to make him into a model young man, all meant to aid his brother in ruling Russia one day, the day upon which Alexander would take the throne and need the help of all of those around him-especially his trusted brothers-to steer the country on a wise course.

But the only thing that seemed to interest Nicholas Nikolaevich very much was the military. At least this was fortuitous, for his future had already been decided upon at his birth: he would enter the military and embark on a life of service. At birth, the boy thus found himself appointed Honorary Colonel in the Lancer Life Guards Regiment.[1] As a boy, he relished the play drills that had him dressed as a young cadet, carrying wooden pickets in place of rifles as he marched before the watchful and approving eye of his tutor. He was especially fascinated with forts, with ramparts, with military engineering and protective defenses, a hobby shared by more than one young boy but which Nicholas could enjoy on a grander scale.[2] He had his tin soldiers and wooden forts with which to play inside, and outside, he and his brothers practiced erecting mock forts, digging moats, and raising flags over their earthen redoubts.[3]

It was comforting and comfortable, and made for a happy young Nicholas Nikolaevich and, indeed, for a happy Imperial Family. Visiting St Petersburg in 1836, Lady Londonderry was able to meet the Emperor and his family privately. They all, she said, possessed "a peculiar charm." She found them

> *gifted by nature more than the generality: tall, handsome, graceful, well made, clever, agreeable, and different from most royal persons. They appear conscientiously good and like the late Emperor Alexander, living to fulfill 'their being's end and aim,' to be useful, to do good, and to distribute comfort and improvement on a great scale. The children seem carefully educated and in the interior appears the domestic comfort, affection, and simple privacy of a ménage in humble life, and this is singularly set off by the immense power, wealth, and great magnificence that surrounded them.*[4]

In time, Nicholas Nikolaevich grew to be a tall, thin young man, with heavily lidded blue eyes and light brown hair and mustache; in later years, he sported a closely clipped beard that ran into bushy chaos at the end of his chin. At eighteen, on completing his formal secondary academic education, he entered the Imperial Cadet Corps, where he received Infantry training and specialized study in military tactics and engineering. In 1851, on his graduation at the age of twenty, he joined the Imperial Army-as had been expected of him-serving as Brigadier Commander in the Sapper Life Guards Regiment of the Imperial Guard. He was still there when the Crimean War erupted, when at twenty-three he was sent off to the distant peninsula where the Romanovs had occasionally enjoyed the warm sunshine, to find a far different picture. Now, beneath the cypress and palm trees, as the Black Ssea sparkled in the distance, shots rang out from trenches and moldering fortifications, cannon thundered, men screamed, and chaos filled the air. He saw this all firsthand, this terrible carnage, this futility, this absurd fight over misplaced ideals of honor, at the battle of Inkerman. It left him both thrilled and repulsed.[5]

Then, in the midst of all of this uncertainty, Nicholas I died: the loss of not just the emperor, not just the country's patriarch, but of a dearly loved father. Into this void, this tragic, tumultuous fight, stepped the new emperor, Alexander II, and, as Nicholas I had hoped and expected, he quickly called upon his carefully prepared brothers to come to his aid in the service of Russia. Konstantin was entrusted with the Navy, while Nicholas was given command of the Crimean town of Nikolaiev, asked to assume responsibility for its defense. Trenches were dug and supply lines organized, but within a year the whole, this Crimean debacle that everyone insisted they hadn't wanted and yet had so eagerly embraced, had come to its ignoble end. Alexander II wanted, needed, peace, but he came away from this disastrous conflict with a new respect for his brother Nicholas and his dedication to his duties. He created him an Adjutant-General in the Imperial Suite, and asked that he preside over the necessary reorganization of the Imperial Army, particularly over the outmoded cavalry regiments and the luckless engineering corps.[6]

Nicholas threw himself into all of this when he returned to St Petersburg, and into the capital's social life as well. The privileged aristocrats who crowded the great balls at the Winter Palace called Nicholas *"the most graceful of dancers,"* someone at ease with his admiring female companions, who enjoyed this great and frivolous contrast to the horrors he had witnessed in the Crimea.[7] So successful was Nicholas at this art of the ballroom that Alexander II actually put him in charge of organizing the military guest lists for imperial balls. The men selected had to be handsome, polite, versed in etiquette, ready to drop everything to answer the imperial call, and willing-in their colorful tunics, broadcloth trousers, golden epaulets, and shining medals-to thoughtfully recede into the background to act as mere accessories for the demanding debutantes and dowagers who took their arms. Each autumn, Nicholas diligently poured over the rolls, striking the names of those whom he thought too priggish, too dull, too dubious to meet with approval, and summoning the rest to the great festive nights when the Winter Palace blazed with light and heat.[8]

And yet, for all of this apparent usefulness, this artful judgment, Nicholas-at least according to one politician-tended to be *"a noisy sort,"* someone who liked attracting attention to himself, with a difficult and obstreperous temperament and a taste for practical jokes that ran to poking unsuspecting courtiers with his walking stick.[9] He loved to dance, on that much everyone agreed on, and he loved the army, but aside from his horses, his prized and prize-winning cows, and a love of society, Nicholas seemed to have few interests, *"the dullest of men"* declared one of his critics.[10] One person grudgingly admitted that he was *"not stupid in the strict sense of the word, but ignorant, self opinionated, stubborn, and very vindictive."*[11] Many found him stringent, humorless, and prematurely serious for such a young man. Perhaps it was the military, the time spent in war, that had honed his character and sharpened his senses, but the passage of time gradually altered him from graceful dancer and practical joker to stern martinet.[12]

In 1855, Nicholas was propelled into the orbit of Alexandra of Oldenburg, his first cousin, once removed. The daughter of Konstantin of Oldenburg and his wife, the former Princess Therese of Nassau, Alexandra was born in 1838, an unimportant princess in an unimportant family on the fringes of the Romanov Dynasty. The family ties with the ruling house, though, were strong: she was the great-granddaughter of Emperor Paul; her younger brother Alexander wed Princess Eugenia Romanovsky, Duchess of Leuchtenberg, daughter of Nicholas I's daughter Maria Nikolaevna, while her younger sister Therese married another of Nicholas I's grandchildren, Prince George Romanovsky, Duke of Leuchtenberg.

It was, after all, expected of Nicholas Nikolaevich, that he would one day marry, settle down, and start a family, and it was his mother Empress Alexandra who seems to have sressed the most, thinking that the princess would make a suitable spouse for her son. Nicholas apparently went along with these plans without objection or enthusiasm.[13] But he knew what had to be done, and his engagement to Alexandra was announced on October 13, 1855.

Nicholas was a grand duke, son of one emperor, and brother of another, and possessed of a considerable fortune; according to the standards of the day, he might even have been considered vaguely handsome in a sort of raffish way. But this was all he had to offer his fiancée: the couple had absolutely nothing in common. Alexandra was a quiet, rather thoughtful young woman, whose parents had raised her with an appreciation of social responsibilities and the needs of the less fortunate. She was ill at ease at large gatherings and social events. There was nothing of her intended's conviviality, nor could she be considered-by any stretch-a beauty: Alexandra was plain, fleshy, with a wide, oval face and dowdy expression that made her the antithesis of the bevy of beauties that usually caught Nicholas Nikolaevich's eye.[14]

There was, of course, nothing at all unusual in arranged marriages, but very little about the union between Nicholas Nikolaevich and Alexandra of Oldenburg seemed to hint at any future happiness. When the couple wed on February 6, 1856, she was granted the title of Grand Duchess Alexandra Petrovna, a distinction that seemed to contrast with the rather simple tastes and demeanor of the new bride. She was a modest woman, not given to ostentatious displays, and very quickly she found her new life all too overwhelming. She disliked the public role her position forced her to play; in tight Russian court dress, forced to participate in imperial ceremonies and balls, surrounded by hundreds of younger, beautiful ladies, she seemed uneasy, uncertain of herself. And there was something else about her, a kind of peculiarity of temperament, a sense that lurking just beneath the surface lay a smoldering volcano of unpredictable emotion. *"The Grand Duchess was honorable and had a good heart,"* said Serge Witte. *'she was not stupid, but she displayed some of the abnormalities of the Russian Oldenburgs."*[15] Or at least this was what he claimed. This view-that the Grand Duchess was not quite "normal", may have stemmed from her penchant for privacy, her dislike of frivolity, or her descent from the unstable Emperor Paul, a descent she shared with her new husband – was echoed by other courtiers.[16] The only member of the Romanov Family who took a liking to her or treated her with any real kindness was another outsider, Empress Marie Alexandrovna, wife of Alexander II, who shared the Grand Duchess's mystic nature and serious inclinations.[17]

With the wedding came an impressive gift, a new country estate, Znamenka, some fifteen miles west of St Petersburg. Znamenka lay high on a bluff above the Gulf of Finland, in a line with the estates of Strelna, Alexandria, Peterhof, and Oranienbaum, a string of exquisite palaces like the pearls on a necklace that ringed the Baltic. It had passed though a number of aristocratic hands in the 18th Century, from the Golovines to Catherine the Great's favorite Alexis Razumovsky to the Shuvalov family before it was finally purchased by the Crown. At its heart lay a three-storied, baroque palace on which the great architect Rastrelli was said to have worked. Nicholas Nikolaevich commissioned architects Andrei Stackenschneider and Harold Bosse to completely renovate the structure, adding sumptuous suites of apartments that stretched out from its curved marble staircase and columned parade halls. As an enthusiastic equestrian, Nicholas Nikolaevich also added a luxurious stable with a vaulted ceiling rested on columned arcades, a bit of extravagance that allowed his beloved horses to spend their lives in suitable comfort.

And there was another palace, this one in St Petersburg, commissioned by the Grand Duke when he reached the age of twenty. Designed by architect Andrei Stackenschneider, it was a massive, neo-Italian Renaissance style building facing Annunciation Square near the English Embankment. The Nikolaevich Palace took ten years to complete, as funding was temporarily suspended on the outbreak of the Crimean War, but when finished it was one of the capital's most impressive imperial residences, with an extravagant staircase ringed by polished granite columns that rivaled anything to be found in his brother's Winter Palace. There were exquisite rococo reception rooms, and Arabian-inspired Menage, and a Byzantine chapel, the Church of Our Lady of Sorrows, the latter inspired by the Church of Our Savior of Mercy in Rostov, which Nicholas had visited in 1850. The interior, in fact, had been almost directly copied from the church by German and Russian fresco and icon painters.[18] The Grand Duke and his wife took up residence here in 1861, a regimented, militaristic life whose every detail was settled by Nicholas Nikolaevich. He was a stickler for order, and everything ran according to schedule and custom.[19] In the winter there were balls, at which Alexandra Petrovna hovered uneasily in a corner chair, visibly ill at ease as her husband moved expertly through the crowd, keeping an eye on his hand-picked officers as they partnered beautiful women-and on the beautiful women themselves.

The Grand Duke's career was in the ascendant: He served as a member of the State Council, and in 1859 was appointed Commander of the Imperial Guards Corps. He did well enough in this post to warrant further promotions. In 1864, Alexander II appointed his younger brother Commander of the St Petersburg Military District, Inspector General of the Imperial Corps of Engineers, and Inspector General of the Imperial Guard Cavalry.[20] And while he blazed with glory, his wife shrank away. Nicholas made no secret of the fact that he found his wife less than appealing: in the words of one writer, *"He loved all women except for his wife."*[21] After the births of their two sons, Nicholas in 1856 and Peter in 1864, the couple lived virtually separate lives, appearing jointly only in public at court ceremonies which dictated their presence as members of the

Imperial Family. Behind the walls of their immense palace, they went for days without seeing each other.[22] The problem, thought Serge Witte, stemmed from Nicholas Nikolaevich's *"inclination for a free and easy life,"* something that conflicted with the *"markedly sanctimonious"* and *"somewhat abnormal"* personality and religious beliefs of his wife. Alexandra's unhappiness expressed itself in increasingly poor health: at one time, when not yet thirty, she was completely confined to a bath chair, suffering from paralysis of the legs.[23] If she thought she would win her husband's sympathies, though, she was wrong: her constant complaints and lack of vivacity only alienated him, and fed his antipathy. Embittered, Alexandra increasingly retreated into the Russian Orthodox Church, spending hours in the aptly named Church of Our Lady of Sorrows at the head of the grand staircase, alone in agonized prayer.[24]

Within a decade of his marriage the Grand Duke had already taken a mistress, twenty-year-old ballerina Catherine Chislova, and he made no attempt to hide the fact, installing her in a fashionable house on Galernaya Street in the capital: this happened to be, not by accident, just across the square from his own palace.[25] The situation caused further tension and unhappiness in the Nikolaevich Palace: while the Grand Duchess was content to play the martyr, locked away in the chapel, her young sons were ignored, left to the care of their tutors. Nicholas, eight years older than his brother, was more resolute and independent, but Peter, sensitive to the open hostility that existed between his parents, began to suffer from bouts of depression and ill-health.[26]

Yet the father did nothing to improve the situation: his concern lay with Chislova, and he even once approached the Metropolitan of St Petersburg, asking for official approval to build a chapel in her house, explaining that as he was so often at his mistress's he wanted to be able to pray there. This resulted in a report directly to Alexander II, who warned his brother to restrain himself and keep private matters private. But private matters were very much public, indeed; even the Grad Duke's liaison took a public form, for Chislova used to put a lighted candle in her window as a signal to her lover across the square that she wanted him to come to her. Servants in the Nikolaevich Palace were instructed to keep a constant watch for this candle, and to fetch the Grand Duke immediately when it was spotted, no matter what he was doing. Family dinners, evenings with his sons, even balls-all were abruptly interrupted by the arrival of servants, whispering to Nicholas the agreed upon formula that a fire had erupted in the city and that his presence was requested.[27] This excuse fooled no one, least of all Alexandra Petrovna. Once, Nicholas and Alexandra were entertaining a group of young relatives at the palace when the Grand Duke's adjutant interrupted and duly reported a serious fire in the capital. Nicholas quickly rose and excused himself, but his young nephews, eager to see the conflagration themselves, begged to be allowed to follow. *"Do not distress yourselves,"* Alexandra finally told them. *"It is only a candle that is on fire."*[28]

For all of her forbearance, though, Alexandra increasingly felt humiliated – and deliberately humiliated – by her husband's behavior. One day, tiring of the gossip, the condescending looks, the whispers, she went to her brother-in-law Alexander II, complaining about her husband's actions and asking that the emperor intervene. Alexander had already privately cautioned his brother over the situation, but that was as far as he was willing to go. At the time, the emperor was involved in his own scandalous affair with Princess Catherine Dolgoruky, and was scarcely in a moral position to condemn his brother's personal life. Instead, he seems to have treated the Grand Duchess's complaints as an unwelcome intrusion. *"Your husband,"* he told Alexandra Petrovna, *"is in the prime of his life, and he needs a woman with whom he could be in love. And look at yourself! See how you are dressed! How do you expect to keep your husband's affections?"*[29]

This bit of imperial humiliation only added to the strain: Alexandra was convinced that the two brothers were conspiring together, and that neither would do anything to save her marriage. It was clear that they regarded her as an annoyance, her complaints something to be swept aside and dismissed. It was then that this meek, mild, pious woman who later became a nun apparently did the unthinkable and took her own lover in revenge. The late Jacques Ferrand found that the Grand Duchess had given birth to a son on August 9, 1867 – a son that was most definitely not her husband's, as his arrival was unacknowledged by the Imperial Family. Colonel Vikentii Zakhvatovsky, who gave the boy his surname, legally adopted him, but it is not known if he was, in fact, the father. Then, in a bold move, the Grand Duchess made her son Peter Nikolaevich the boy's godfather.[30]

At the time, there was an immense scandal over the Grad Duchess's relationship with Lebedev, her personal confessor, and it was even said that Alexander II had ordered her on an extended sea voyage – to escape the wagging tongues of court gossips or to conceal a pregnancy – and all while ignoring the similar rumors that swirled about the relationship between his brother and Chislova. Alexandra Petrovna did not returned to St Petersburg at the end of her trip, but instead took up semi-permanent residence in Kiev's Mariinsky Palace, Lebedev at her side. Serge Witte, who visited this unlikely couple in Kiev, described Lebedev as

> *an ugly, rough-hewn, boorish man who dressed as foppishly as it was possible for a priest to dress. It was evident that he exercised tremendous influence on the Grand Duchess. She felt love for him, of a psychopathological character, typical of the Oldenburg abnormality.*

He added, however, that from his own observations-admittedly gleaned during family evenings of card playing and thus scarcely liable to reveal too many intimacies – *"her relationship to this priest was platonic."*[31]

Such a turn of events might be shocking but it occurred in an era when various Romanovs were actually housing their bastards under the same palace roofs as their legitimate offspring. If the liaison seems completely out of character for the rather staid and religious Grand Duchess, it – and her semi-permanent residence in Kiev – may nevertheless have been her only way of striking back against her husband. In the end, it made no difference for the very next year, in 1868, Chislova gave birth to a girl named Olga, the first of the children she would bear Nicholas Nikolaevich.[32] She was followed by Vladimir in 1873; Catherine in 1874; and Nicholas in 1875.[33] After speaking to his brother about the situation, Alexander II agreed to the Grand Duke's request that the ballerina be raised to the nobility and their children's surname be legally changed to Nikolaiev. With this imperial approval, Nicholas Nikolaevich duly had the children christened and himself officially named as their father in ceremonies held in St Petersburg's Annunciation Cathedral.[34]

Unlike some imperial mistresses, who were content to enjoy their liaisons and the gifts that accompanied them, Chislova was quite avaricious and there are stories of her constant demands for money and jewels. Nicholas was wealthy, but between 1868 and 1875, he squandered an incredible amount of money on his paramour, to the point where he was often broke near the end of each financial year. He began to borrow money, and the promissory notes he signed mounted into a massive debt that eventually came to the attention of the Minister of the Imperial Court, who took the matter directly to Alexander II. Threats over potential lawsuits and confiscation of property eventually forced the emperor to act. In 1875 he issued an arrest order for Chislova, believing that she was systematically milking his brother out of hundreds of thousands of rubles. The man sent to arrest the former ballerina was General Peter Trepov, Chief of the Okhrana and, ironically, the man who had also shared her bed in years past. Sentiment over this previous liaison did not prevent Trepov from fulfilling his duty: he surrounded Chislova's house with a contingent of armed police and himself arrested the surprised dancer. Placed in a closed carriage and driven off to police headquarters, Chislova roared and ranted, but to no avail. After her interrogation, Alexander II had her exiled to Riga.[35]

When he learned of this Nicholas Nikolaevich was outraged. At first, he launched into a dubious plan to return his mistress to St Petersburg. He managed to bribe a young officer in the Imperial Guard named Krestovsky to marry the exiled dancer and bring her back to the capital so that he could resume his affair, assuming that the change in her marital status would prevent any further scandals. Amazingly, Krestovsky went along with this plan, but he himself was already married and when he attempted to divorce his wife in exchange for the Grand Duke's cash bribes, the whole sordid affair was spilled out in the St Petersburg Circuit Court hearing his petition, putting an end of the nefarious plan.[36]

Not content to let the matter rest, and unwilling to be parted from his mistress, Nicholas Nikolaevich confronted his brother Alexander II over Chislova's exile, accusing the emperor of hypocrisy and pointing out that he had housed his own paramour Princess Dolgoruky and their children in the Winter Palace. Whatever he said worked, for Alexander II relented and revoked his order. He did, however, advise the Grand Duke that it might be wise, in view of the publicity, to move Chislova away from the capital.[37]

Nicholas quickly snatched this capitulation and dispatched a diamond bracelet to Chislova inscribed, *"To ten years of happiness, 1865-1875."*[38] Within a few weeks, the dancer was summoned south, to the Crimea. Here, Nicholas's brother Konstantin Nikolaevich had already installed his own mistress, another ballerina named Anna Kuznetsova, and their illegitimate children in a villa near the estate of Oreanda. Nicholas purchased a small plot of land near the emperor's estate at Livadia, and built a villa to house his unofficial, second family. Throughout the late 1870s the Grand Duke spent more and more time in the Crimea. In 1877, Chislova gave birth to their fifth child, a daughter named

Galina, who died just nineteen months later.[39] But neither of his two legitimate sons, Nicholas Nikolaevich Junior. and Peter Nikolaevich, would visit him, out of respect for their mother, if Chislova or her children were present.

For a year, Nicholas Nikolaevich settled into a happy, quiet existence with his mistress and their children. The idyll was interrupted only when the Grand Duke was diagnosed with venereal disease and had to undergo painful mercury treatments. For several months, the disease was so severe that Nicholas even had to abandon his favorite pastime of riding along the Black Sea coast.[40]

Then came 1877 and the Russo-Turkish War. The Russians had long been troubled by the domination of the Ottoman Turks over the Slavic peoples of the Balkans and, perhaps more important, the empire needed unfettered access to the Bosphorus Straits. Throughout the mid-1870s, there had been riots and rebellions in Bulgaria, in Romania, and in Bosnia and Herzegovina, all ruthlessly crushed on orders from Constantinople, with violent atrocities that aroused great indignation in Europe. Although the European powers attempted a diplomatic solution, Turkey rejected demands that Constantinople recognize the autonomy of Bulgaria, Bosnia and Herzegovina, making conflict inevitable. Against this backdrop, Russia secretly funded the rebels. It had long been the Russian dream to capture Constantinople, and everyone viewed the conflict as a war between Islam and Christianity. Full of religious fervor and false pride, and egged on by a widespread public sympathy for their oppressed Slavic brothers, Russia finally declared war on the Ottoman Empire on April 12/24, 1877.[41]

With the field of battle so far away, the Russians were at a distinct disadvantage. The Ottomans had some 150,000 troops ensconced in the Balkans and held control of the Black Sea and the Danube basin; in addition, their supplies and men could be reinforced without any great effort. The Russians, on the other hand, had to dispatch their 1.2 million soldiers by train, along with their provisions, from the industrialized cities in the north; they traveled thousands of miles merely to reach the theater of war. Alexander II put his brother Nicholas Nikolaevich in charge as Commander-in-Chief of the European front, told to wrest the Balkans from Turkish domination. *"He is a far better soldier than I am,"* the emperor told his mistress.[42] Almost immediately, however, the Grand Duke encountered difficulties and had to convince the Romanians to place themselves under temporary Russian control in their common struggle.[43]

The Sultan's forces along the Danube, led by Osman Pasha, assumed that they could remain safely within their fortresses and along their fortified lines and simply wait for a Russian offensive. Nicholas Nikolaevich ordered his troops to march quickly along the Danube, but incessant rains and flooding made it a miserable campaign. Within a few months, they had reached the only significant Turkish outpost that lay between them and Constantinople, the fortress at Plevna, commanded by Osman Pasha. On July 12, 1877 (O.S.), Nicholas Nikolaevich and General Michael Skobelev launched their attack on the city, but the Turkish forces repelled their efforts and there were enormous casualties on the Russian side. With the Russians in temporary retreat, Osman Pasha could have followed and perhaps decimated his foes, but instead he remained at Plevna. A few weeks later, the Russians launched a second attack on the fortress. Nicholas Nikolaevich failed to follow up on the initial attack with a second wave of reserves, though, a lack of foresight that ultimately doomed the effort.[44] Painter Vassili Veereschagin had been dispatched to accompany the army and record its battles, and was present when the second assault took place. Once again, the Turks repulsed the Russian and Romanian troops. *"The defeat was so great,"* Vereschagin recalled, *"that it would be difficult for anyone who did not see it to imagine it. It was not a retreat, it was a disorderly flight, a complete dispersal."*[45]

The day following the disaster, Alexander II – who was visiting the field of battle – convened a war council at the Russian headquarters. Worn out and disheartened, and worried about the approach of winter and possible shortage of supplies, Nicholas Nikolaevich urged a general retreat across the Danube to the relative safety of Romania. After much discussion, all of the Russian commanders agreed, but the minister of war voiced his opposition, saying that 60,000 men had already been lost and retreat would send the wrong signal to all sides. Alexander II listened to this, then said firmly, *"Gentlemen, there will be no retreat."*[46]

Alexander II dispatched the Imperial Guard Corps to the Danube, and the Russians again prepared for an attack. Nicholas Nikolaevich directed the digging of trenches and encampments that eventually ringed Plevna, cutting off the Turkish supply lines to the fortress in an attempt to starve the Ottoman soldiers out. Early on the cold, snowy morning of November 28/December 10, 1877, the Russian and Romanian forces launched another assault against Plevna; although Nicholas Nikolaevich remained in nominal ceremonial charge of the offensive, his inability to successfully prosecute the previous campaigns meant that real responsibility lay with the Russian generals. This time, however, the Russians were not beaten back and recognizing the inevitable, the Turks – led by Osman Pasha – surrendered Plevna. Nicholas Nikolaevich wired news of this success to St Petersburg then set off in an open carriage to receive Osman Pasha's formal surrender. In this, he proved himself a man of diplomatic skill and instinct, paying tribute to his vanquished foe's tenacity and treating him with great respect.[47] It was perhaps his finest moment in the conflict.

With the victory at Plevna under his belt, Nicholas Nikolaevich continued his army's march southeast, toward Constantinople. By the end of 1877, they had reached Adrianople, less than ten miles from the Ottoman capital. The Turkish government openly talked of peace negotiations, but the Russians ignored these overtures; Constantinople was nearly within their reach, and they were loathe to abandon the centuries' old dream of taking the city. In an effort to prevent this, on January 31, 1878, the Ottoman Empire sued for peace, but the Russians continued to dismiss such talk.

Nicholas Nikolaevich wanted to march his army into Constantinople and capture the city, but Alexander II sent a number of cables warning him not to make any rash moves. With the Russians so close, Great Britain had dispatched a fleet of battleships to the Bosphorus, an ominous sign that they might forcibly prevent any occupation of the capital. England worried that the capture of Constantinople and the fall of the Ottoman Empire would affect their own regional interests, including use of the Suez Canal, and there was a possibility – a very real possibility – that England and Austria-Hungary might engage the Russians if they pressed forward and took Constantinople; as much as control of the city played into the Russian psyche and the mythological aspect with which the war had been endorsed in the papers of St Petersburg and Moscow, Alexander II could not afford to risk a general European conflict. In the Russian dictated Treaty of San Stefano on March 3, 1878, the Ottoman Empire formally recognized the independence of Romania, Montenegro, and Serbia, along with autonomy for Bulgaria and Bosnia and Herzegovina, and certain Russian rights of usage to the Bosphorus. The terms of this treaty were later modified against Russia's wishes, by the Treaty of Berlin; this left the Russians in a bad position, and there was much criticism of their losses both on the field and at the diplomatic table. In attempting to appease both Great Britain and Austria-Hungary at the expense of Russia, the Treaty of Berlin, worked out by Otto von Bismarck, left the political situation in the Balkans a tangled mess and unknowingly laid the foundations for the disaster that erupted in 1914.

In the most important test of his abilities he would ever face, Grand Duke Nicholas Nikolaevich had roved himself largely incapable of practical application of his years of military strategic training. The capture of Plevna and sweep toward Constantinople did much to erase his earlier failures in the field, however, and the Emperor awarded his brother the Order of St George, 1st Class, for bravery, and promoted him to the rank of General Field Marshal and Personal Adjutant in the Imperial Suite.[48]

The Russo-Turkish War, nonetheless, proved the dubious highlight of the Grand Duke's career. On returning to St Petersburg he found his brother frustrated over the concessions wrested from Russia in Berlin, and Alexander II laid most of the blame, quite unfairly, at the feet of Nicholas Nikolaevich. The Emperor was particularly haunted by the failure to capture Constantinople, and the issue became a sore point in his talks with the Grand Duke. On one occasion, when Alexander derided Nicholas for not having taken the Ottoman capital, Nicholas boldly pointed out, *"But Sasha, I have telegrams from you forbidding me to take it!"*

"I could never have forbidden any such things!" Alexander replied angrily, ignoring the multitude of cables he had dispatched to his brother saying just that.[49]

The Grand Duke fulfilled his duties as Inspector-General of the Imperial Cavalry, and presided over a number of government committees, including one designed to address the question of the rising tide of Nihilism in Russia, but he took little interest in the proceedings. His liberal leanings won him few friends, particularly among the more conservative elements of the country's ruling elite. Once, at a meeting to discuss the cost of army reforms, the Grand Duke angered many by suggesting sweeping changes; when one of his critics took to the floor and began to speak out against Nicholas's position, the Grand Duke seemed to drift off, playing with his fingers at the edge of the table. Finally exasperated, the elderly general fixed the Grand Duke with a stern gaze and loudly declared, *"When a person can only count on his fingers, he would do better to hold his tongue."*[50]

This disinterest finally led the Grand Duke to nearly abandon life in St Petersburg and any official duties. Instead, he fled as often as he could to the Crimea, to live with Chislova and their children. The couple were even welcomed to Livadia, spending evenings with Alexander II and his own mistress. Nicholas Nikolaevich still appeared in St Petersburg on ceremonial occasions, but all of this changed when Alexander II was assassinated in 1881 and his son took the throne as Alexander III. Alexander thoroughly disapproved of his uncle's disreputable style of life and his second, unofficial family, and gradually began to undermine Nicholas Nikolaevich's influence and position. Accusations involving military bribes and missing funds further damaged the Grand Duke, but the final straw came when Nicholas Nikolaevich asked his nephew for permission to divorce is wife and marry Chislova.[51] Alexander III was steadfast in his refusal to consider such a scandalous move – something that Nicholas Nikolaevich must certainly have known in advance. Increasingly embittered, the Grand Duke began to sell off his collection of paintings, furniture – even his wife's jewelry – and pocketed the proceeds, ignoring his debts and taking the money to the Crimea to share with his mistress. He obtained even more money by approaching several banks and private individuals, obtaining loans given to him based on property claims to items in the Grand Duke's collection that he no longer owned. This money, too, went to pay for Chislova's jewels and gowns, and to fund their illegitimate children.[52]

By 1882, though, the rumors, the debts, the and the scandal – it all became too much for Alexander III to bear. He was determined to make a clean sweep of the troublesome Nikolaevichii, not just the Grand Duke but also his peculiar wife in Kiev. He ordered Alexandra Petrovna from the Mariinsky Palace, had her beloved Lebedev returned to St Petersburg, and told the Grand Duchess not to follow him.[53] In response, Alexandra Petrovna purchased a plot of land outside of Kiev and established the Kievo-Pechersky Convent of Nursing Sisters, near the famous 11th Century Kievo-Perchersky Lavra. On November 3, 1889, she took holy orders as a nun and assumed the name of Anastasia, becoming the convent's Mother Superior, in much the same way that Grand Duchess Elisabeth Feodorovna would do after the 1905 assassination of her husband Serge Alexandrovich. Back in St Petersburg, her two sons continued to reside in the now nearly empty Nikolaevich Palace, pursuing their separate careers in the Imperial Army under the constant and critical eye of Alexander III, who distrusted them and feared that they would any day replicate the scandalous behavior of their parents.[54]

His wife's retirement into religious life did nothing to appease Nicholas Nikolaevich. Despite his nephew's warnings, he was now more than ever determined to rid himself of her, if not through divorce then through death; this was his great wish, one that he freely and openly expressed to anyone who would listen – that his wife would die and free him from his unwelcome marital burden. As things turned out, in a stroke of ironic fate, it was Chislova who fell ill and died in the Crimea on December 13, 1889. Her unexpected death drove the desolate Nicholas Nikolaevich completely insane. Suffering from delusions – possibly the result of syphilis – he began to attack every woman he met, convinced that they in turn were madly in love with him. After one ballet performance, the Grand Duke became so agitated and aroused that he went backstage and stumbled about on his walking sticks, grabbing at bodices and attempting to kiss everyone he saw. He was finally pulled from one of the young male dancers, who in his delusions he had cornered and covered with kisses. When his sons learned of this, they ordered him locked away in the former Vorontzov Palace of Alupka in the Crimea, where he was attended by an elderly manservant, the only person - it was said – who was safe from his amorous attacks.[55]

By 1890, the Grand Duke was seriously ill. *The Times* of London reported that he had *"become suddenly insane"* and as a result had been confined in the Crimea.[56] It was rumored that he was suffering from mouth cancer, from syphilis, from delusions – but in the end none of it mattered, for he quickly slipped into a haze of madness. His mania increased as the months went by until, on April 13/25, 1891, he died. He was only sixty; his hated wife would outlive him by a decade.[57]

Nicholas Nikolaevich's body was placed on a funeral train and left Alupka for burial in St Petersburg's Cathedral of the Fortress of St Peter and St Paul. When it temporarily stopped in Kiev for the customary ceremonies and prayers, Grand Duchess Alexandra Petrovna refused to leave her convent and visit the railway siding to pay the usual homage to her deceased husband. It was left to the couple's two sons to accompany the body and return it to the imperial capital.[58] Despite the years of disgrace and madness, though, Nicholas Nikolaevich was a Grand Duke, and he was given a full state funeral, attended by Alexander III, before he was interred in the crypt of the Cathedral of the Fortress of St Peter and St Paul.

Following their father's death, Nicholas and Peter Nikolaevich were forced to deal with the intricacies of his tangled and sorry estate. Nicholas Nikolaevich had borrowed heavily – and from everyone – to finance Chislova and their children, and his legitimate sons were forced to sell his St Petersburg palace to the Ministry of the Imperial Court for just over 3.8 million rubles in order to pay off their father's debts. By the time these were cleared, only a few thousand rubles remained to be divided between them.[59] It was an ironic end for the palace, which became the Grand Duchess Xenia Alexandrovna Academy for Young Women. Now, its halls resounded with laughter and life, filled with the beautiful young women the Grand Duke had so treasured in his wasted life.

GRAND DUKE MICHAEL NIKOLAEVICH
(1832-1909)

By Janet Ashton & William Lee

Michael Nikolaevich is the dark horse among the sons of Nicholas I and Alexandra Feodorovna. His career in politics, administration and the Army was a long and prominent one; he was loved and admired by generations of Romanovs who came after him, remembered by nearly all who encountered him as a man of charm and tact; and yet – perhaps precisely because he rocked few boats, did not go mad or engage in flamboyant adultery or spectacular rows with his nearest and dearest – his achievements are often overlooked or under-valued. His life coincided with that period in Russian history when the Grand Dukes proliferated in number but saw their role and influence come under attack as a result. Unable to live up to the supreme ideal set for them by both Nicholas I and nationalists at court, the Grand Dukes found themselves broadly stereotyped as *"clown, villain or non-entity."*[1] If his elder brothers – the debt-ridden Nicholas who *"loved all women except for his wife"* and the ambitious, short-tempered Konstantin – were to play the first two roles respectively, it inevitably fell to Michael to be regarded as the non-entity.

He was born in the Winter Palace on October 13, 1832 (O.S.), at 10.40 in the evening, the fourth son of the Emperor, destined to be the last child. This new baby's name might have been easily predicted. As his brothers Alexander, Konstantin and Nicholas had been given the names of the previous generation in order of age, he was duly named for his fourth and youngest uncle Michael Pavlovich. When he was christened three weeks later, his godparents included his namesake, his ten-year-old sister Olga, his aunt Anna Pavlovna (the future Queen of The Netherlands), and his maternal grandfather Friedrich Wilhelm III of Prussia. The customary English nurse, known in Russian as Maria Andreevna Yuz (her real name was probably Margaret Hughes),[2] presided over his early upbringing, every tiny detail being duly recorded in the court calendar for the relevant year. Thus we know that on June 5, 1833, Michael Nikolaevich cut his first tooth.[3] A year later, he sat at his mother's commission for his first portrait, a dual one with his elder brother Nicholas.

Nicholas Nikolaevich, just fourteen months older, was the constant companion of Michael's early years; they were raised almost as twins. Dressed in baggy peasant-style trousers and shirts, their hair in a bowl cut straight round their ears, they were sketched together time after time, and very often for publication: sitting in the gardens; standing before their tall stern father as he lectured them kindly but firmly on proper grand-ducal behaviour. *"The two little ones are very agreeable and the apples of my eye,"* Nicholas I reported to his own sister; describing them again a few months later as simply *"delightful."*[4] When the

Empress held tea parties or interviewed their elder siblings' tutors, the two little boys were with her, rolling around the floor *"very happy"* or sitting on her knee. There was nothing strained or forced about the cheerful informality: all of the imperial children adored their mother and were generally more at ease in her company than in their father's. But their infancy was nevertheless deliberately served up for public consumption as the epitome of modern family life, an example and rallying point for the whole of Russia. It was to be made clear to Russia that they enjoyed a stable home life with a father who, secure in his own position after the difficulties of his early days as Tsar, was free to guide them and who sought to prepare them for a productive adult role.

On Michael's fourth birthday he held his first "children's ball" at the Alexander Palace in Tsarskoe Selo, with fireworks for the enjoyment of the children and general public alike, and dancing for a party of young nobles. Despite the host's extreme youth, the celebrations did not even begin until six o'clock in the evening.[5] He had long since made his first public appearance. Typically, this was a visit in the company of his mother and his brother to the Cadet Corps at Tsarskoe Selo. He was then only two years old, but his career was mapped out: Michael would serve his father and nation – later his brother – in the Pauline style: he would be a soldier, unquestioning in his loyalty and obedience. Both during Nicholas I's reign and thereafter it was customary to enroll a royal boy at birth in two units. Enrolment helps define the child's future in his own eyes and the eyes of the public, and acted, at a symbolic level, as a service contract between the boy and the state. Michael was not enrolled in any unit, but had two honorary posts bestowed upon him, one of which did reflect his future in the artillery.[6] At three he was officially enrolled in the Cadets, and his training began informally while he was still in the nursery. '*so early does a military education commence in this imperial family that even the two younger Grand Dukes Michael and Nicholas of four and five years old were called up by the Emperor and made to join in the drill,*" wrote one incredulous English visitor who saw the Tsar inspecting cadets in the huge St George's Hall at the Winter Palace in 1836.[7]

Nicholas I believed that the boys' seventh birthday should mark their entry into 'service". In practice this meant that they left the care of nursemaids to pursue regular lessons under male tutelage. But emphasis was now placed upon the ideological foundation of this transformation. Thus each boy was presented with an officer's uniform and saber, to which he was certainly entitled, since his Order of St Andrew had made him a general at birth, even though this rank was now considered purely symbolic and was to have little bearing on the young Grand Duke's practical education. When Nicholas turned seven, Nicholas I wrote:

> *It is a great day for you and for us. For us, because, with this token, we dedicate our third son to the service of his brother and motherland; for you because you receive the first token of your future service…You must feel that from this moment on our whole future is no longer yours but belongs to the one in whose name you received these tokens. From this moment on you are obliged never to forget that you must ceaselessly strive through constant obedience and diligence to be worthy to bear these tokens, not in accordance with your years,*

but with the noble sentiments awakening within you, and with the object of always being worthy of your rank.[8]

That same year, 1838, a tutor duly arrived. General Alexei Ilarionovich Filosofov, assisted by V.C. Korf of the Cadet Corps, would oversee an intensive programme of studies under a veritable regiment of nineteen instructors. P.P. Gelmersen, from the School of Jurisprudence, was chosen to ensure the boys' *"intellectual development."* This choice might demonstrate the importance of law to Nicholas I, and his desire to broaden the grand ducal role to include a governmental function, but as always the emperor's progressive impulses were moderated by his traditional outlook, and he confessed to Korf that he regarded *"well-intentioned morality"* as the *"best theory of law."*[9] It would be the virtues of military practicality and obedience which would be given heaviest weight in their training, after all; and such abstractions as classical languages would not be included. In the military sphere, their studies centered upon the customary fields of fortification and artillery, with the Tsar helping to instruct them. Henceforth Nicholas and Michael rose at six and began their lessons at seven, a daily round of academic topics interspersed with rigorous exercise. They were not isolated, however: every year they followed their parents on the cheerful seasonal progress from Winter Palace to Anichkov to Tsarskoe Selo to Peterhof, interspersed with occasional visits to Moscow or to their maternal relatives in Berlin, which afforded ample opportunity for further enjoyment of military display, and which Michael first visited when he was six. At Peterhof Andrei Stackenshneider designed a little house for the two boys. Known as the Grand Ducal school, it was completed in 1841, and provided dedicated schoolrooms and living quarters not far from their mother's beloved Cottage Palace

Nicholas and Michael also grew up in close contact with their cadet contemporaries. Nicholas I wished them to establish a true working relationship with their future colleagues, since in the Decembrist revolt he had himself seen what he considered the consequences of the disloyalty and tensions arising from estrangement between Grand Dukes and Army. Thus when they were eight and nine years old, he formed a "toy" platoon for them, similar to those with which Peter the Great had been raised. The majority of the participants came from aristocratic families, but an additional ten to fifteen were summoned "in turn" from the cadet corps. The Tsar himself assumed a variety of roles, including that of drummer.[10] In 1843, having observed maneuvers there many times over, Michael spent his first active summer at Krasnoe Selo with the army, taking part in military training and the traditional summer exercises at the encampment south of St Petersburg.

The cadet activities were undoubtedly better for the boys' development than the grandiose training exercises enjoyed or endured by Grand Dukes of years past had been, since they were well-suited to their age and abilities. But the real obstacle to genuine Grand Ducal professionalism was accelerated promotion. Both boys received non commissioned officer's rank in 1846, when they were in their mid-teens, and their promotion to 2nd lieutenant followed in less than a year. They advanced to full lieutenant in 1847, captain in 1848 and colonel in 1850, though they had not yet served in a regiment, completed their education, or attained their majority. But far from receiving regimental commands (as befitted their rank), the boys continued to serve with the cadets until the summer of 1851. When Nicholas and Michael toured Russia, their father insisted that they must avoid being present at troop reviews or exercises. If obliged to attend such functions, they were to regard themselves as spectators, and in their ordinary contact with the troops they were not to supersede the bounds of their military rank. Apparently recalling his own high-handed behaviour in youth, he was determined that his sons would not perpetuate a negative image of the dynasty. They completed their education by attending three lectures at Moscow University, lending weight to the supposition that Nicholas I wished them appear well-rounded and modern.

On his twentieth birthday, October 13, 1852, Michael took his public oath of allegiance to the dynasty in the St George Hall and the Chapel at the Winter Palace, and shortly thereafter he received an inspector generalship – of the artillery. He was also named brigade commander of the Horse Guards Artillery at the same time, and this rank – unlike his basically honorary and inactive inspector generalship – was designed to act as the basis for his future career in case he never saw combat service. In the event, neither Nicholas nor Michael would face the frustrations experienced by their namesakes in the previous generation, who lacked early opportunity to prove themselves under fire. By 1853, war with Turkey loomed, and Michael accompanied his father and brother on a tour of southern fortifications. In September, six months after the Crimean war broke out, they finally joined the troops, accompanied still by their tutors and referred to as "recruits." Their father was underlining the fact that in his opinion they were still too young to function entirely independently at the elevated level expected of their rank. This was a far cry from the license given Konstantin Pavlovich, for instance, on his first foray into warfare.

Their role was mainly ceremonial at first, reviewing troops and visiting hospitals, but after they had come under fire at the Battle of Inkerman both brothers were awarded Order of St George and appointed to active roles, with Michael supervising the arming of the batteries at Sevastapol. Henceforth, he would be considered adult. Meanwhile, his political career showed signs of creeping forwards. He had already attended a state commission on the peasant question as an observer and in 1855 – the year his father died – he was appointed to the State Council.

Nicholas I's death in the jaws of likely defeat had the potential to affect Michael on far more than a merely personal level. The whole Nikolaievan system of government had been found wanting, and public perception of that fact had opened up a schism between the very dynasty and state whose unity Nicholas I had promoted, believed in and emphasized at every turn. If, in the past, officers had complained about the Grand Dukes' behaviour, they did not turn their resentment into a public issue. The Romanov service presence was one element of a system which was not only accepted but taken for granted. Ironically, it took an exiled intellectual to bring dissatisfaction to the public. Alexander Herzen, in a famous 1858 address to the Empress, advocated a practical education for Russia's Grand Dukes. Herzen wrote from London, but his publication, *Kolokol*, had a mainstream Russian readership. *"Look how unproductive the Grand Dukes' lives are,"* he wrote, *"how useless their wanderings around Russia."* His call for a re-evaluation of the Grand Ducal role – ironically along exactly the same lines that Nicholas I has envisaged in educating his sons – was only the beginning of an increasingly critical public scrutiny, and the widespread circulation of several dynastic scandals would likewise contribute to the stereotype of the useless and corrupt Grand Duke.

By these lights, Michael was the most successful product of Nicholas I and Alexandra's parenting. His passion for the artillery and his deep service ethos was bound up in a reverence for the Tsar. He possessed an unshakeable faith in autocracy and the infallibility of the Emperor. *"We have no right to criticize his decisions. A grand duke has to take orders in the same spirit a simple soldier does,"* he said of his brother Alexander II.[11] He was, in fact, a mild and tolerant man, who proved in time a very good administrator: his success sprang from his ability to act as a conciliatory and unifying force: he was too centered on the Tsar to become politicized. This was the grand ducal ideal: the passive supervisor, bringing the Tsar's majesty to people who might otherwise forget their status as imperial subjects. Physically, Michael looked the part of an impressive Grand Duke: like most of his siblings, he had grown up tall and slim; he had fashionable side whiskers and piercing blue eyes, and his fine features were more those of the Empress's family than the Romanovs. *"He has the best of personal qualities and is very good looking,"* declared a typical account from a courtier who met him at this time and observed the constant chivalrous attention with which Michael plied his beloved, frail mother.[12] Years later, another observer, his own daughter-in-law, summed up the mixture of elegant sophistication and gentleness in the Grand Duke's demeanour. *"I have rarely met so kind a man and such a perfect gentleman; a grand seigneur in every sense of the word,"* she remembered.[13] Alone among his brothers, Michael was to remain untouched by sexual scandals. On August 15, 1857, he married Princess Cecilie of Baden, the future Grand Duchess Olga Feodorovna, in the chapel at the Winter Palace. *"At one o'clock we went to the wedding,"* he wrote happily and prosaically in his dairy. *"Olga looked enchanting. Our wedding went very smoothly and I thanked God that he let me experience this day!"*[14] After a long ball in the St George Hall, they left in procession for their new home. If Michael ever after strayed from the marital bed – and it is worth noting that in that gossip-ridden court no reports or rumours ever actually named him as an adulterer – he did so discreetly, as Nicholas I had done.

Michael's successful marriage was a case of attraction of opposites: his new bride had a very different personality to his. Highly intelligent, sharp-tongued, and somewhat ambitious, she quickly made enemies in the imperial family, who gossiped that her birth was illegitimate and her real father that Romanov bugbear, a Jew.[15] The young couple took up residence in a purpose-built palace set between the Neva's Palace Embankment and Millionaia Street. Known as the New Mikhailovsky Palace, to distinguish it from the sinister Michael Castle where Tsar Paul had met his end and from the grand home of Michael Pavlovich, the new house was designed by Andrei Stackenshneider between 1857 and 1861. It differed from the houses built for Michael's brothers and sister in being terraced to the adjoining buildings, but was no less huge and imposing for that. In later years, the children of Michael and Olga used bicycles to get around it.[16] On the second floor, which was given over to the state rooms, were splendid banqueting and dancing halls with inlaid parquet floors in all shades of wood, while the third floor featured a chapel and winter garden. In the private family rooms heavy Victorian furniture predominated: Michael's study, described by contemporaries as being in the "Old English" style, featured typical fringed curtains and leather sofas, its walls adorned with family portraits. A dining room whose walls were hung with Cordoba leather afforded splendid views of the river and the Fortress of Peter and Paul: here the Grand Ducal couple dined formally with their suite every day. The exterior of the palace was a riot of columns and caryatids, a not-entirely successful fusion of Baroque and renaissance elements. It had its own landing stage on the Neva, where boats would land to bear the Grand Duke along the river to the Winter Palace or out across the Gulf of Finland to Peterhof and his own summer residence.

Michael and Olga had their summer retreat on the Peterhof Road, not far from the homes of his brothers, who visited frequently and were visited in turn. Known as Mikhailovskoe or Mikhailovka, the white Italianate house stood at the very edge of the Baltic, with heavily ornamented façades ringed by terraces, loggias, balconies and pergolas. It was probably Michael's favourite home. The interior was typical of its era, with solid furniture and a long, stuffy conservatory that smelt of lilies separating the family apartments from the dining room and ballroom.[17] But the gardens were the true glory of the palace. *"The view from our windows on the garden was very pleasant,"* recalled Mikhail's daughter-in-law years later.

> *There were masses of different kinds of trees, and a lot of lilac bushes, which are particularly lovely in Russia, and beautiful flowers everywhere all around the house as well as in the rooms. We had a wonderful fruit garden there, too, and every morning the gardener sent us small, round baskets containing every imaginable, luscious fruit.*[18]

In 1860, the Grand Duke also purchased Grushevka, a vast estate the size of Belgium in the treeless southern Ukraine. He lived off its land of 190,000 acres, which included sixteen villages and seven German-speaking colonies, but he never once set foot in it.[19]

Olga bore her husband three handsome children in quick succession, the first child – clever Nicholas - becoming his mother's favourite, and the second (Anastasia, the only girl) was her father's. The third, hapless "Misha," was however soon labeled stupid. Michael followed his own father's example in being something of a distant parent, fond but stern and aloof with all save perhaps his daughter. Olga, by contrast, was erratic: she smothered with her one favoured son with attention – by no means all of it uncritical – and was cuttingly unkind with those such as Misha whom she deemed less worthy. More wife than mother at heart, she accompanied her husband on his official engagements, sometimes replacing him when he couldn't make it, and for all their differences in temperament the two loved another sincerely and were dull when separated.

In 1861, Michael was offered the post of viceroy of Poland, that troubled borderland repressed by his father but ripe now for a period of relaxation. He struggled as firmly not to be given the job as his liberal brother Konstantin fought to be given it in his stead, and thus Konstantin Nikolaevich went to Poland where he presided over a period of political turmoil and economic consolidation before being removed from office amid unfounded rumours that he wanted to be King of Poland. His was the example of what would happen to a Grand Duke who pursued his agenda too fast to the point where he was perceived as a rival to the Tsar. Michael would not make such a mistake. A year after Konstantin, he received a vice regality of his own, that of the Caucasus, potentially even more troublesome than Poland.

Russia's colonial activity in the Caucasus had long been a part of their strategy to push into southern Asia toward an ice-free port. To this end, they made allies of the Christian peoples of the region; and encouraged rebellions against the Ottoman rulers of much of it. By the end of the eighteenth century, parts of the Caucasus had fallen under Russian rule, including the previously independent kingdom of Georgia, which was pressed to sign away its independence to its ally in 1801. Other, Islamic regions held out more determinedly for considerable periods of time, temporarily encouraged by Russia's defeat in the Crimean War and by west European interest in their plight. It was only in 1859 that Russia was finally able to defeat the Iman Shamil, who had declared a Jihad against Russia from his stronghold in the mountains of Chechnia and Dagestan. Unsurprisingly, in 1862, the region remained volatile and sensitive, with continued fighting in the northwest. Many of the native groups were at odds with each other anyway, and all were potentially hostile to the Russia conqueror. A military administrator with little governmental experience would thus hardly seem the ideal vice regal candidate, but Michael appears to have regarded the Caucasian assignment as nothing like the political death-trap represented by Poland. His status as a Grand Duke was itself invaluable. A member of the dynasty, with authority over civil government and military administration, could cement the image of the region as a votchina of the Tsar to a native population still immersed in places in a patriarchal warrior culture, and therefore responsive to such symbolism. Alexander's decision to send his brother instead of a non-royal overseer undoubtedly softened the sting of conquest. Serge Witte, himself a resident of the Caucasus in his youth, states that the news of Michael's appointment drew an enthusiastic response. *"When the news came that Grand Duke Michael Nikolaevich had been appointed viceroy, everyone was very pleased because this was the first time that a grand duke, and an emperor's brother at that, had been given the post."*[20] Michael's greatest qualification, however, was his mild and tolerant disposition. He clearly considered that a supervisor's role was to delegate authority to deserving underlings, and according to Witte, possessed *"enough good sense to rely always upon* [Caucasian] *figures."*[21] Both the Tsar and his officials were pleased to see a conformist, unambitious and dutiful Grand Duke fulfilling a role in which his royal status conferred a real benefit, far from the capital with its competitive political milieu.

This did not of course mean that Michael's period as viceroy was without its difficulties. He would never face suspicion of disloyalty, but he was dogged by accusations of financial dishonesty, much of it attributed to the stinginess of the dreaded Olga. *"On the eve of the ceremonial entry of the new viceroy and his wife into*

Tiflis," remembered Witte,

> *my uncle, who had a sharp tongue that he did not always keep in check, remarked that the Grand Duchess, being stingy, would be pleased by the fact that the vice regal carriages would be showered with flowers: she would have the flowers collected and fed to her horses, thus saving the cost of several days' feed."*[22]

Later, when the couple acquired a country estate at Borzhomi in Georgia, they were criticized for taking government lands for their own use.[23]

The house at Borzhomi, built in red-brown wood and stone and adorned with balconies and cupolas, was set in 200,000 acres of heavily wooded mountains cleaved by fast-flowing muddy rivers, stunningly beautiful and ideal for hunting. Here their sixth child Serge was born in 1869, two more boys – George and Alexander – having been born at Belyi Kluch and Tiflis respectively in 1863 and 1866. To their northern cousins in St Petersburg, the Mikhailovichi became known as "the Caucasians," Asiatic, uncivilized and dangerously radical. Those born in the Caucasus did not visit Petersburg at all until they were in their teens, and grew up surrounded by the many different nationalities who passed through their father's court, from Persians to Georgians to Tartars, all with their own languages and distinctive costume. Most ironically considering the closeness of their fathers, a nasty conflict developed in early youth between Nicholas Mikhailovich, a cynical, sharp-tongued intellectual by inclination, and his cousin Nicholas Nikolaevich, whose military temperament – excitable and *"made for violence"* – clashed fundamentally with his own. The relationship between the quiet, rather bumbling George, Michael's third son, who lived for his coin collection, and his similarly withdrawn cousin Peter Nikolaevich was a far happier one, however. George Mikhailovich cherished dreams in early youth of being an artist, but when he was so tactless as to express this wish, he was rewarded by being deprived of his dessert. All of Michael's sons were destined without question for the army, and to this end they had an upbringing as strict as his own had been, sleeping on iron beds and rising at six for a rigorous programme of academic studies and exercise that included much practice with firearms. Unlike their father, they were also isolated from cadet contemporaries and had only brothers for company. From time to time, Michael descended upon them and watched their exercises *"with a critical eye."*[24] Ultimately, "Sandro" – the fourth son Alexander – rebelled and chose the Navy for his career, much to Michael's displeasure. Nicholas, too, loathed his Army training, and once left to his devices became a historian of note. Among the sons, only Serge took enthusiastically to his father's profession, and was deeply interested in artillery and mathematics.

Michael, often accompanied by Olga and sometimes by their eldest son and heir Nicholas, traveled extensively through the Caucasus during his period as Viceroy, making his face known and dealing with sporadic local revolts. His main tasks were to preside over the abolition of serfdom and to deal with the continuing ethnic conflicts of the region. To the latter end, he encouraged members of moderate Russian religious sects to move to Transcaucasia, where *"their settlement brings great benefit to the region in economic and industrial aspects. Especially important is their settlement around our borders, both for political as well as for military goals. Each settlement strengthens the Russian element there,"* he wrote.[25] Extreme sectarians on the other hand were to be discouraged or even banished lest they foment anti-Orthodox opinions. The son of the defeated chieftain Shamil became an officer in Michael's regiment and grew thoroughly European-ized, but Shamil's followers fared less well. Many of the mountain regions, where opposition to the Russians was most intense and which were hardest to reach, were systematically cleansed of their local populations, Michael himself looking forward to the day when *"the complete cleansing of the Black Sea shoreline and the resettlement of the mountaineers to Turkey,"* had been accomplished.[26] This amounted to the expulsion of 450,000 west Caucasus mountaineers during the 1860s. Despite the Russian help ostensibly offered the poorest of these people on their journey to the Ottoman Empire, the circumstances of their removal were often brutal, with reports of people who fell from exhaustion on route and were torn apart by dogs. Late in the 1870s, following a further Chechen rebellion, Michael declared that rebellion was woven into the fabric of these mountain societies, and that the periodic removal of sections of the Chechen population should be adopted as a precautionary rather than punitive measure.[27] The Grand Dukes avoided taint by such actions partially because the overt brutality came from other people, and partially because most of the inhabitants of the areas of the Caucasus that had been Russian for some time were inclined to agree with him. In dealing with problems among the mountain peoples themselves, Michael showed more of his habitual tolerance, decreeing that mountain courts based upon local customs could be used in meting out justice, in preference to alien Russian law which would have less effect.

Michael's period as Viceroy coincided with the reform of the Russian military by the War Minister Dimitri Miliutin, the friend and fellow traveler of his brother Konstantin Nikolaevich. In the terms of the reforms, the traditional corps commands, wielding considerable autonomous power, would be replaced by several smaller divisions arranged into districts and would become largely administrative positions which accepted the guidance of the War Ministry. The initial reforms took place in 1862, when Michael's inspector-generalship of artillery and his brother Nicholas' of engineering were merged into their corresponding departments in the War Ministry, thereby forming the Supreme Engineering and Artillery Administrations. Michael initially resisted the reform, trying *"in every possible way" to delay it, and participating in "intrigues" against the war ministry. When, however, his efforts proved fruitless, he abandoned his opposition and later informed Miliutin that his reform was working "very well."*[28] It was undoubtedly the prospect of the War Minister's reach extending into his own domain which had aroused Michael's initial resentment. In the end, however, he had little to lose. After all, as Viceroy, he enjoyed a special position. The reform did not subject him to the same loss of independence and prestige experienced by ordinary commanders. He accepted it gracefully and did not attempt to overstep the boundaries of his reformed post. This was in total contrast to his more aggressive brother Nicholas, who had in any case no other post to console and occupy him.

The many antagonists of the reluctant reformer Alexander II caught up with him on March 1, 1881, on the banks of the Catherine Canal. His body torn apart by a bomb, he was carried bleeding up the steps of the Winter Palace, where he died on the camp bed in his study. On the day he died, Alexander had been on his way to ratify the existence of a consultative body composed of delegates from the town councils. It wasn't a constitution, but it was a step forward after years of re-entrenchment. It goes down in history as the "Loris-Melikov Constitution," and resembles similar plans tendered by Konstantin Nikolaevich as early as 1862.

The new Tsar Alexander III had no intention of proceeding with his father's plans. He had had a sad relationship with both his parents, over-shadowed by the memory of his more talented elder brother, who had died of cerebro-spinal meningitis as a young man. Alexander was desperate for approval and when he wrote to his parents and letter after letter neither bothered replying he was hurt and angry. *"Unfortunately, they never answer, and in response to eight letters to mother and six to Father I have received only one reply,"* he once complained.[29] This personal issue, if it did not definitely cause his political reaction against his parents, certainly left him more open to outside influence. With conservatives around him and behind him, he had come to believe that his father's affair was besmirching his patrimony, and he hated both that father and any associated with him and his reforms and his affair. His uncles were an obvious target; Konstantin Nikolaevich more than any of them. In addition to his liberal politics, Konstantin's open contempt for the younger Alexander's rough ways had been noted as early as 1862, when he laughed publicly at his nephew's table manners in Warsaw, calling him *'sasha with a bear's paws"* and a *"pig."*[30] The elder Grand Duke also - like Alexander and Nicholas – offended his nephew's morality by living openly with a mistress. Very soon after coming to the throne, Alexander wrote to his uncle, suggesting he ask to be retired from his roles as Admiral General and President of the State Council, but asking him to be present at the forthcoming difficult sessions of the State Council first. *'so I'm still useful for something, though they want to throw me away like an old, unsuitable glove,"* wrote the Grand Duke bitterly.[31] On July 13, he was dismissed from his post.

In his place, the job was given to Michael, the only one of Alexander II's brothers to thrive during the reign of Alexander III. The Grand Duke himself had no illusions as to why he was being recalled from the Caucasus and placed in this highly significant role. The State Council was the highest advisory body in the Russian Empire, jockeying for position at times with the Council of Ministers. Officially, its role was to "examine" each proposed law before it be passed to the Emperor for implementation. Although it had no formal powers to approve or block legislation, its very existence recognised two things, the first being that ruling the Russian Empire was beyond the wit or wisdom of any one autocrat unless he accepted advice, and second being that the autocrat should strive to rule by law rather than by despotism and whim. Appointing the pliant Michael to a post once occupied by Konstantin signaled a sharp change of direction in the way the throne would relate to its advisers. *"I can see what he wants: that I sit on the President's chair like a turkey, with no power of any sort,"* wrote poor Michael.[32]

Alexander's appointment of Michael had the opposite effect to the one he intended: rather than weaken the Council by placing it beneath an unambitious and unthreatening man, he actually contributed to its development as an independent body whose members turned to one another for support and ideas and could even challenge and influence the crown. Olga Feodorovna, meanwhile, was unhappy with her husband's performance – gossip charged that this was because he could not use the position to obtain favours or prominence for her personally – and she did not hesitate to tell him so. She apparently found the loss of vicereine's status hard to bear and disliked playing second fiddle in St Petersburg to the Empress Marie, who was clearly her intellectual inferior as well as being younger. Increasingly, Olga spent her time on her Crimean estate of Ai-Todor, where she laid out the gardens with devoted precision, or abroad in France or Germany taking cures of various kinds.

The Mikhailovich offspring – known in the Romanov family by the French variation the "Michels" – began to marry during these years. Anastasia's wedding to Friedrich Franz of Mecklenburg-Schwerin was a beautiful but not particularly happy affair: all of her brothers were violently jealous of the poor bridegroom for stealing the family favourite away. During one party to celebrate the engagement, the mother of the bride ordered the young Grand Duchess to her room for some minor social transgression, as if she were still a child in the nursery.[33] Alexander III's nationalistic decree of 1888 that the Grand Dukes should only marry Orthodox women if their children were to have succession rights, and his simultaneous refusal to recognise any morganatic marriages as legal, complicated things for the sons. Michael, who could see the likely difficulties this would lead to, was unhappy about it. *"My children can't marry except Orthodox and of equal stations. Where then would they find such fiancées? Or should they put a bullet to their head?"* he wondered.[34] As always, however, he accepted and supported the Tsar's decision in the end. His second son, Misha or "Miche-Miche" proved pathetically keen to marry: the friendly, rather shiftless young man began as soon as he gained control of his own finances to build a palace on the Neva to receive his intended, and he perambulated around Europe for several years, proposing to princesses who all turned him down. Eventually Miche-Miche found a bride in the person of Countess Sophie von Merenberg, a descendant of the poet Pushkin's daughter and of Prince Nikolaus of Nassau. Her unequal status placed Sophie beyond the pale, and despite his previous worries for his sons' prospects, Michael was angry at the marriage and refused to see the couple.

Within a week of receiving the news of her son's marriage Olga was dead: legend later held that she had a heart attack on receiving the telegram announcing it. Her health had been poor for some time: as her many letters complaining of her problems made clear she was aware that she was suffering from some kind of heart condition and her trips abroad were part of her search for a cure. On March 28, 1891, she was taken ill on her train on the way to the Crimea. The train returned to Kharkov where a doctor was summoned, and the Grand Duchess was attended in the Tsar's Waiting Room on the station there. She died three days later without being moved from her strange, make-shift hospital ward. For the rest of his life, the grief-stricken Michael, who blamed himself for allowing her to travel alone, kept his wife's parasol, hat and gloves beside him wherever he went.[35]

That same year Michael's closest brother Nicholas also died, apparently insane, on his estates in the Crimea. The one brother to have quarreled with Alexander II, he had fared even less well under Alexander III, who disliked his irregular personal life as much as his political activities and removed him swiftly from his posts. In 1892 Konstantin Nikolaevich died after several strokes, leaving Michael as the only surviving son of Nicholas I. Romanov men tended not to live long: they succumbed in middle age to the complications of high blood pressure and related conditions. Even the temperamentally placid Michael had his problems on similar lines: from the 1890s he complained of *"heart attacks lasting twenty hours"* that were presumably angina.[36]

His fears for his sons' marital prospects proved well-founded. Of the six Mikhailovich sons, only "Sandro" and George made suitable, equal marriages – the former to the Tsar's daughter Xenia; and George to Princess Marie of Greece, after a long engagement during which she apparently considered calling it all off. Sandro's engagement was not without its own difficulties, though not of bride or groom's making. The Empress, a notoriously possessive mother, delayed agreeing a date to the point to the point where Michael was forced to reveal how much this particular issue meant to him. Descending upon the Anichkov Palace where the imperial couple preferred to live, this most respectful of men allegedly had a full-blown row with his sovereigns, during which Marie Feodorovna accused him of *"trying to wreck her happiness"* and steal her daughter.[37] But Michael emerged triumphant, and the marriage took place in the summer of 1894.

Nicholas, the eldest of his sons, was never to marry, perhaps because he valued his freedom too highly; while Serge, the youngest surviving son (Alexis, the last-born "afterthought" of the family, died in 1895 aged twenty) became embroiled in an infamous ménage à trois with the ballerina Matilda Kschessinska and his cousin Andrei Vladimirovich. When the dancer bore a son, Sergei duly acknowledged him, but no one was ever sure who the father really was. Meanwhile, "Miche-Miche" continued to press his demands for fair treatment for his morganatic wife. *"All his behavior and activity…continues to grieve me and make me angry!"* wrote Michael to Anastasia. *"Misha insists that his wife should be recognised by their Majesties before he comes to Russia; this will not be accepted."*[38]

Alexander III's untimely death late in 1894 meant that Michael was now two generations removed from his Emperor – Nicholas II, his great-nephew, a stubborn and totally inexperienced man of twenty-six. But the long-ago indoctrination by the first Nicholas precluded his acting to advise the much younger man. *"His grand-nephew was his sovereign: as such he had to be obeyed implicitly,"* wrote his son Sandro many years later. *"Accustomed to seeing men of mature mind and iron will on the throne of Russia, he never doubted the ultimate wisdom of his grand-nephew's decisions, which nullified the potential value of his thorough understanding of the problems of the empire."*[39] In Michael's place, Nicholas II was influenced, ironically, by less scrupulous individuals, including the Grand Duke Alexander Mikhailovich himself, a man who had his family's reputation for financial irregularities and was certainly fond of a high-handed scheme.

Most of the adult Mikhailovichi sons – Misha and Alexander excepted – continued to live in their father's huge homes, and Anastasia also came often to visit with her family, taking up residence in the ground-floor rooms at Mikhailovskoe that she had lived in as a girl, with wide windows giving out onto the garden and her brother Serge living next door. Michael's grandchildren adored him. *"My childhood and the most beautiful recollections I have were influenced by this kindly man, this true nobleman,"* remembered Anastasia's daughter Cecilie of Mecklenburg-Schwerin. *"Kindness and helpfulness, chivalry and tenderness were his most profound characteristics. I have never seen him grow angry; I have never heard him say an unkind word."*[40] Childhood memories are apt to be polarized, particularly in recalling a world now gone, but Cecilie's recollections do seem to indicate some relaxation of the formerly strict household rules now the family was grown. *"Their attitude to their father was one of exemplary respect and reverence,"* she recalled of her uncles, failing perhaps to discern the core of fear still there. But she also remembered that *"they always expressed their opinions quite freely in his presence, even when they knew that he did not agree with them."*[41] In 1899, he became a great-grand-father on the birth of Prince Frederik of Denmark (the future Frederik IX), whose mother was Anastasia's elder daughter Alexandrine. Cecilie married the German Crown Prince in 1905, and Michael had the expectation that his descendants would sit on the Prussian throne too. This thought pleased him very much: the Hohenzollerns were after all his mother's family, and one for which he had always felt friendship. The growing mutual suspicions of Russia and Germany in the early twentieth century were alien to him.

In the summer of 1903, Michael had a stroke while staying at Mikhailovskoe with his family. Having gone to bed as well as normal the previous night after a game of billiards, he was found in the morning by his valet, lying by his bed paralysed down one side and unable to speak clearly.[42] In time, the Grand Duke recovered the use of his legs to the extent of being able to walk with sticks, but beginning with that winter he was to spend most of his time thereafter on the French Riviera, living in a small villa near to the home of his beloved daughter Anastasia. As was customary, large sections of his family came to join him there: George and his wife and two small daughters lived with Anastasia's family, while Sandro and Xenia acquired their own home. The resort was not without its charms for the younger generation, for as George's wife Marie was later to recall, *"all my husband's family were great gamblers."*[43] Several of them, notably Nicholas and Anastasia, won and lost vast sums in the casinos of the Riviera.

Michael Nikolaevich died in Cannes in December 1909, the last surviving child of Nicholas I by a considerable number of years. He was seventy-seven, a vast and venerable age for a Romanov male, and one which was not to be surpassed for nearly half a century.[44] His body was taken to Sevastopol aboard a Russian man-of-war, and thence to St Petersburg for interment alongside his wife and son Alexis in the Fortress of Peter and Paul. An era was over. Despite his essentially passive political role, which in its own way hastened the downfall of the dynasty through his role as President of the State Council, Michael's very existence had been a benefit to his grand-nephew's reign. Respect for this patriarch did at least hold the younger generations in check. While he lived, the Romanovs looked and acted as one family, however shiftless or discontented some of its members might be, and however withdrawn and uninspiring its head, the Emperor. But with Michael gone, every political criticism, every personal discontent, every family feud came bubbling straight to the surface. Few of them respected or obeyed the Tsar, and the Tsar's sporadic and unsuccessful attempts to hold them together undermined his own image further in the eyes of the world, at a time when his government could ill-afford this. *"The death of Michael Nicolayevitch was an irreparable loss,"* wrote one member of Nicholas II's household as epitaph for the Grand Duke. *"The unity of the dynasty no longer existed except in name; from 1910 onwards the rifts steadily widened."*[45]

3

THE SONS OF
TSAR ALEXANDER II

TSAREVICH NICHOLAS ALEXANDROVICH
(1843-1865)

By Arturo E. Beéche

*V*ery few times in the history of a dynasty has so much effort been spent on preparing an heir for the immense tasks that his future held in store. Such was the case of Tsarevich Nicholas Alexandrovich, the eldest son of Tsar Alexander II and Tsarina Maria Alexandrovna. Since early childhood, and inspired by the educational program his own father had designed for Alexander II, the Tsar designed a stringent selection of classes that his son had to undertake. Hence, by the time Nicholas Alexandrovich, known to the family as Nixa, reached his late teens, the Russian empire held him in great respect and much hope surrounded his eventual accession to the double-headed eagle throne. And yet, it was all a waste.

Nicholas Alexandrovich was born in St Petersburg on September 8/20, 1843.[1] He joined a baby sister in the imperial nursery, Alexandra Alexandrovna, whose death at the tender age of seven years left the parents devastated. Tsar Nicholas I, the proud grandfather after whom the baby was named, expressed his delight when writing to his sister Anna Pavlovna, *"it is a wonderful happiness for us and for the Empire, may God preserve this dear child for us…"*[2] In due time, six other children were to join Nicholas, five boys (Alexander, Vladimir, Alexis, Serge and Paul) and one girl (Marie). As children they formed a close-knit and rambunctious group that at times proved a challenge to the team of nannies put in charge of caring for them.

Alexander II is said to have been a loving, yet stern father to his sons. Knowing how immense Nicholas' future obligations would be, the father took particular interest in enforcing a no frills upbringing for his heir. Yet, as Tsar, Alexander had his concerns regarding Nixa. Nicholas was an artistic boy who possessed a great talent for drawing. One biographer of Tsar Alexander II argues that this aspect of Nicholas' character troubled his father much and caused him

93

to be rather severe toward the boy. *"The Tsar expressed his opinion,"* Stephen Graham argued, *"that Nicholas was trop effeminé, and then gave instructions that something be done to make his son more manly."*[3] All other recollections point to the fact that Tsarina Maria Alexandrovna more than made up for whatever her husband's emotional shortcomings were. She was far more interested in her children than in fulfilling her imperial role. In turn, all her children, Nicholas Alexandrovich included, were deeply devoted to and protective of their mother.

Alexander II's younger sons, particularly Alexander, Vladimir and Alexis, seem to have delighted in exploiting their father's lesser view of the heir, while teasing Nixa mercilessly. One time, Nicholas expressed he could be old enough to aid his father rule the empire, only to have his younger siblings deride his wishes while accusing him of being *"just too stupid"*[4] to do anything of the sort. One author also claims that Alexander II

> *did not take as much care over the upbringing of Nicholas as his father had done for Him. He did not procure another Zhukovsky to train the heir to the throne. The education of the prince was confused and ill-balanced; he was crammed with dry learning, while physical development suffered.*[5]

However, another author, the eminent Charlotte Zeepvat painted a completely different picture when she said that Nicholas,

> *was educated for the throne, whatever his brothers may have thought, and he followed a rigorous, intense programme of studies designed for himself alone. Both parents adored him, but while his father could be rather severe, his mother devoted herself singlemindedly to him, almost forgetting her other children. He developed rapidly, showing a quick mind and an interest in serious questions which impressed and, at times, even worried those responsible for his education."*[6]

As Nicholas approached his late teens, he was sent on a three-year long voyage around the Russian Empire. This voyage, which his father had also embarked on, was designed for Nicholas Alexandrovich to become both familiar and knowledgeable with the vast realm he was born to rule. His instructors were most impressed with Nicholas' uncanny and perspicacious grasp of myriad facts and issues presented to him. Professor Soloviev, one of his tutors, once recalled, *"If I succeeded in forming a student equal to Nicholas Alexandrovich once in ten years, I would think I had fulfilled my calling as a teacher."*[7] The professor was not to be disappointed and Nicholas Alexandrovich soon became the creaking empire's hope for the future.

Not everything dealing with the young man's life was centered on his studies. In fact, already there was much maneuvering among the chancelleries of Europe to provide Nicholas Alexandrovich with a future wife. A first cousin of his father's, Grand Duke Carl Alexander of Saxe-Weimar-Eisenach, hoped that the young man would choose his daughter Princess Marie (1849-1922). Nicholas Alexandrovich, however, had ideas of his own about his matrimonial prospects, while his cousin Marie ended marrying Prince Heinrich VII Reuß.

It appears that sometime in 1860 an early photo of a little-known Danish beauty was given to the young Russian heir. The girl in question was Dagmar of Denmark, the second daughter of Prince Christian and Princess Louise, herself born a Princess of Hesse-Kassel. Both Christian and Louise were descendants of Danish monarchs, her connection being more recent than her husband's. However, and as extinction of the male line became apparent, the Danish government chose Christian of Schleswig-Holstein-Sonderburg-Glücksburg as the country's future monarch. By the early 1860s it was a certainty that he would one day rule Denmark and thus his daughters gained considerable relevance in the royal marriage market. In fact, in 1863 Christian and Louise's family experienced several events that propelled them to the forefront of European royalty. Their eldest daughter, Alexandra, married the Prince of Wales in March. Three weeks later Alexandra's brother, William, was selected as the Greek monarch. He reigned under the name of George I and married Grand Duchess Olga Konstantinovna. Interestingly enough, three of their children were destined to marry into the Romanov dynasty. Lastly, later in the year, on November 16, Christian ascended the Danish throne. Consequently, marrying Dagmar would provide Nicholas Alexandrovich with excellent connections to other royal families outside the reduced sphere of Germanic dynasties the Romanovs had married into.

Princess Dagmar was born in Copenhagen's Yellow Mansion, her parents' home, on November 26, 1847.[8] To her family she was always known as "Minny." The family of Prince Christian did not have access to much money, by any means. Louise *'supervised much of their earlier education, teaching her daughters needlework and ensuring they would be proficient housekeepers."*[9] As his wife concerned herself with the education and upbringing of the children, meanwhile, Christian served in the Danish army and waited for the day when he would ascend the throne. The girls were raised in an austere, unaffected environment and *"they were always plainly dressed and as they grew older made their own clothes. Shortage of money meant that they had to change into smarter clothes immediately after outings so that nothing would be spoilt."*[10]

Christian and Louise were the parents of six children, all of whom would have an illustrious future. Their eldest son ruled Denmark as King Frederik VIII (1843-1912). Alexandra (1844-1925) followed and she would be the consort of King Edward VII of England. William (1845-1913) followed and as King George I of the Hellenes he was the founder of one of Europe's most interesting dynasties. Then came Dagmar (1847-1928) and she was followed by Thyra (1853-1933), who was described as *"sweet-tempered"*, perhaps because she was not blessed with the looks of her elder sisters. Thyra married the Duke of Cumberland, heir to the deposed King of Hanover, an unequally unattractive fellow. Last was Prince Valdemar (1858-1939), who married Princess Marie d'Orléans.

Enter thus, the Russian heir. Since obtaining the first photo of Dagmar, Nixa had continued collecting images of the blossoming, clever and dark-haired Danish beauty. By 1863 he told his mother that Dagmar consumed his attention, his heart was lost to the sixteen-year old princess. In a letter he wrote to his mother on August 3, 1863 (O.S.), Nixa expressed his feelings with much clarity,

you know dear Mama that I have not fallen in love with anyone for a long time. I'll allow others to judge whether this is a good or a bad thing. You may laugh, but the main reason for this is Dagmar, whom I fell in love with long ago, without even seeing her. I think only about her, and this holds me back from doing many things. I am not even sure if I will ever see her, but a voice within me tells me that everything will be all right. May God grant that it work out for the best; I leave it all to God, for it is a holy matter, a sacrament. I sincerely hope that my prayers will be heard.[11]

Furthermore, he reassured his mother that his mind was not lost, unlike his heart, *"It is strange to talk like this when I have not yet seen the one I love (If I can say that), but I have not lost my common sense; I am not at all infatuated or in some kind of dream state. I am writing only what I feel every moment."*[12]

Finally as summer 1864 began Nicholas' prayers were heard. Alexander II decided to send his son on a goodwill and educational voyage across Europe. Besides Germany, Nicholas Alexandrovich visited Italy, The Netherlands and France, while also spending some time at the court of King Christian IX. That Spring Denmark was at war with Prussia over the duchies of Schleswig and Holstein, a conflict that made it impossible for Nicholas to visit as he began his journey. As Nicholas prepared to bid farewell to Russia he seemed melancholy, s if knowing that he would never set his eyes on his motherland again.

On the eve of his departure, he stood taking in the view of the sea from the balcony of his Alexandria Park villa in Peterhof. In the foreground were superb clusters of tall trees, and in the distance lay Kronstadt bathed in that crystal clear summer light, so peculiar to Northern countries. He turned to one of his companions and said: "if I ever come across any site as beautiful as this abroad, I shall come content with my travels."[13]

From Russia Nixa traveled to Germany, where he met his mother at a spa and then visited his Saxe-Weimar cousins. Grand Duke Carl Alexander still hoping that Marie would snatch the Russian heir, was to be sorely disappointed. From Weimar Nixa traveled to The Netherlands, where he was the guest of the royal family, also relations as his grandfather's sister, Anna Pavlovna, had married King Willem I. The young Russian heir had enjoyed his journey tremendously, but he itched to travel to Copenhagen where his beloved awaited.

Nicholas arrived in Copenhagen in August. Crown Prince Frederik along with his uncle Prince Hans, the King's brother, welcomed him. The following day the group traveled to Fredensborg, the beautiful royal palace outside of Copenhagen. It was there that Nixa and Minny first set eyes on each other, and where the Russian heir realized that his search for a bride had come to a successful end. His impression of Dagmar was immortalized in a letter Nixa wrote to his anxious mother on August 24,

If only you knew how happy I am: I have fallen in love with Dagmar. Do not be afraid that it is so soon; I remember your advice that I shouldn't make hasty decisions. But how can I not be happy when my heart tells me that I love her, love her dearly? I came here as if in a fever, I cannot tell you what came over me when we approached Fredensborg and I finally saw sweet Dagmar. How can I describe her? She is pretty, direct, intelligent, lively yet at the same time shy. She is even prettier in real life than in the portraits that we have seen so far. Her eyes speak for her: they are so kind, intelligent, animated.[14]

After the visit, which lasted several days, Nixa lost no time in traveling back to Germany to meet his parents. Alexander II and Maria Alexandrovna awaited Nicholas at Darmstadt, where the Tsarina visited with her brothers. Back in Denmark, Nixa left a saddened future bride, for *"It was sad to leave; Dagmar's brother said…that she was sad, too."*[15] While in Darmstadt Nixa immediately approached his parents *"so that I can resolve this matter with your blessing."*[16] Alexander II had no trouble granting his son's wish to marry Dagmar, which provided the Tsarevich with untold joy.

After a brief visit to Berlin, where Alexander II's uncle Wilhelm I, had invited the Russian emperor to attend military maneuvers, Nixa returned to Denmark. He was in much discomfort, but wanted to ewaste no time in returning to Dagmar's side. Once in Copenhagen, he felt as if he had been a member of the Danish royal family and was delighted with how naturally and unaffectedly they treated him. *"I was received exceptionally well,"* he told his mother, *"like an old acquaintance, and immediately felt at home."*[17] Nicholas had a private talk with King Christian, who was delighted with the news that Nixa was planning to ask Dagmar to be his bride. The young man had hoped to ask her a few days later, but the very eager Danish monarch nixed that plan when he told Dagmar the reason behind Nicholas' second visit. Nixa wrote to his mother letting her know how the proposal transpired,

> *Her father, mother, and brother walked ahead of us, and the two of us lagged behind. I wanted the earth to swallow me up. Bit by bit I confessed my guilt: I was building up to say, "I love you" in a roundabout way but she understood clearly. A heartfelt YES was finally said and we kissed and squeezed each other's hands…I could hardly speak and although it was a cold autumn day, I was as hot as if I were in an oven. This was a wonderful moment which I will never forget.*[18]

Nicholas spent some time in Denmark getting to know his bride and her family better. To his concerned, yet joyful mother he wrote,

> *The more I talk to Dagmar and get to know her, the more I become convinced that I will find happiness through her. We talk openly about everything that interests us, everything that fills our hearts. Neither her mother nor her father had ever spoken to her about me, and it was clear that there was no external influence or preparation. It was very important for me to fin this out…*[19]

From Denmark, an increasingly exhausted Nixa continued his European tour through Germany and Italy. He visited with his parents in Darmstadt once again and from there traveled to Italy via Tyrol. By the time he reached Tuscany there were serious concerns about his health. Back in 1860 he had taken a fall from a horse and suffered an injury that would sometimes flare up and bring him much back pain. When he attended Prussian military maneuvers Nixa was already in considerable pain. Duke Nicholas of Leuchtenberg, a cousin and childhood friend, had writen to his mother and expressed his concerns *"he seems to have lost weight and a little of his looks."*[20] His parents and entourage hoped that the milder climate of Southern Europe would restore the young man's ailments. From Venice Nixa headed to Milan and Turin, where the Italian royal family hosted him. The Savoys were mightily impressed with the young man, whose knowledge of European affairs seemed to be vast and deep. After Turin, Nixa traveled to Genoa, from where he embarked on the Russian corvette *Vitiaz* and sailed to France, where he planned to visit his ailing mother.

The Tsarina was convalescing in Nice. Her tuberculosis, which would ultimately bring an untimely end to a life a suffering, had given her much trouble while in Darmstadt. Hoping to recuperate Maria Alexandrovna, withher large retinue in tow, sought the sunny skies of the French Riviera. While there Nixa spent a few days keeping his mother company, before returning to Italy.

By the time Nixa arrived in Florence, he was suffering agonizing pains. For the following six weeks he remained convalescing, unable to do much, and thus forsaking all the excursions and visits that had been planned for him. Doctors found a swelling on his back, *"an abscess, the doctors said, and while he underwent a series of painful treatments his suite did all they could to distract him."*[21] On January 1, 1865, Nixa and his entourage traveled to Livorno where they boarded the *Vitiaz* and sailed to Nice. It was to be his last voyage.

Nixa's health continued its rapid deterioration. Several medical experts were summoned, but as was the case with medicine back then, the wrong diagnosis was given. It was not until the second half of April that a Viennese doctor accurately diagnosed Nixa's ailment: cerebro-spinal meningitis. By then, however, nothing could be done to save his life.

When news of the Tsarevich's worrisome illness reached St Petersburg, Alexander II lost little time and traveled to France immediately. From Copenhagen Queen Louise and Princess Dagmar traveled post-haste to Nice, where Nixa was initially housed at the Villa Diesbach. He had become so acutely aware of noise that the sound of crashing waves kept Nixa awake at night. To counter this, he was moved to the Villa Bermond, further away from the seashore. Besides his mother, who kept constant care over Nixa, his brother Alexander Alexandrovich, who provided the imperial family with much support, accompanied them. Prince Alexander of Hesse and By Rhine and his wife Princess Julie of Battenberg were present as well. Upon seeing his brother Alexander enter the sickroom, Nixa, filled with emotion and foreboding, cried *"Sacha, Sacha, what are you doing here? Come here quickly and kiss me."*[22]

Tsar Alexander II reached Nice on April 22. The scene he found inside the Villa Bermond was devastating. The Tsarina, who had informed Nixa of his father's arrival, was heartbroken. *"Poor Ma, what will you do without your Nicky,"*[23] the invalid said, thus revealing to his mother that he was very well aware of his impending demise. Alexander II rushed to his son's bedside knelt down and kissed Nixa's hands. Tears welled aplenty and many there present were forced to leave to room as soon as they felt unable to keep theiremotions in check.

When Dagmar entered the bedroom, Nixa looked at her and said *"Isn't she just charming?"*[24] The young girl did her very best not to break down in front of her dying fiancé. It was then that some witnesses recall seeing Nixa hold the hands of Dagmar and Alexander in his own hands, as if to convey to them that he blessed their union. Much contradiction remains about this memory, but whether it actually happened or not, it only serves to point to the deep romantic figure that the dying Tsarevich cut. Dagmar shared her desolation with her father, writing to King Christian that she was glad *"to have seen, and been recognized, by Nixa before he died."* Her biographer said it it gave Dagmar much consolation *"to see the look of love on his face."*[25]

Nicholas Alexandrovich was relieved of his suffering on April 24, 1865. Consternation over his death was widespread. His parents and siblings were devastated, as were his Hessian relations, themselves reeling from the death, just eight days earlier, of Grand Duchess Anna of Mecklenburg-Schwerin, a daughter of Prince Karl, Tsarina Maria Alexandrovna's older brother, as well as a childhood playmate of the Tsarevich. Coincidentally, Anna was also born in 1843, Nixa's birth year.

Two days after Nixa's death, and in a letter to her eldest daughter, Crown Princess Victoria of Prussia, Queen Victoria shared her opinion concerning events in Nice, *"How tragic is the death of the poor Czariwitch* [sic] *only a week after his young cousin – and how terrible for poor Dagmar. What a blow for the ambitious mother! But the poor parents and bride are most deeply to be pitied."*[26]

The "ambitious mother" mentioned in Queen Victoria's sarcastic comment was none other than Queen Louise of Denmark. Ten days after Nixa's death Queen Louise wrote the English monarch a moving letter in which she shared her recollections of the sad event,

> *Your sympathy gave great pleasure to me and to my child, so severely tried so early in life...She tells me that she would not for the world have missed the past, short but happy as it was, and his look, as the Tsar led her by the hand up to his bed, I shall never forget! It was of the purest happiness, and he recognised her the whole day when he was dying! He said goodbye to her, kissed her and held her hand firmly in his until he died! We had traveled for four days and four nights and she never left his bedside, kneeling by him day and night until 1 o'clock when she kissed him and he breathed away his young life! For me it was terrible, for I loved him very much, and saw all the happiness of the poor young bride-to-be ebbing away...Minny is at Darmstadt for a day, to see the parents again. The whole dear family is so kind and loving to her that the parting is doubly painful for her.*[27]

From Rome, where she was spending holidays, Fürstin Feodora of Hohenlohe-Langenburg wrote a letter to Queen Victoria, her half-sister, in which she expressed her consternation,

> *God only knows what s best, if we poor mortals do not alone see it at present. Those two young lives also were cut short. Poor Anna and the Cezarewitch! so young, the delight of their parents and families! We stand*

speechless before out Fate! Dearest beloved sister, this life, what would it be without hope and faith and love![28]

The funeral ceremonies began two days later when Nixa's remains were transferred to the Russian Orthodox Church at rue Longchamp, which had been built under the patronage of Alexander II's mother. Throughout the painful days that followed Alexander II tried his best at keeping his composure. It was not until his son Alexander, now Russia's new Tsarevich, threw himself into his father's arms, after having kissed his dead brother farewell, that the father broke down. It was a devastating scene, and one that showed to all present that the Imperial Romanovs were, after all, human. Nixa's death not only broke his parent's hearts, but it eviscerated their marriage and changed the course of world history. The autopsy confirmed the diagnosis: *"General inflammation of the spinal marrow and brain caused by an abscess in the back muscles...The illness which proved fatal...is very rare and extremely difficult to detect. No treatment could have cured the patient."*[29] The coffin lay in state for two days. On April 28 it was taken onboard the Alexander Nevsky and the slow return to Russia began.

The imperial family traveled separately. On their way to Russia, where they expected to arrive before Nixa's coffin, Alexander II and Maria Alexandrovna repaired to Schloss Heiligenberg, the countryside estate of their Battenberg cousins. Dagmar also spent a day at Heiligenberg with Nixa's devastated family. It was not to be the last time her path crossed that of Tsar Alexander II and his family.

In Nice there remains a monument to the memory of lost hope. Alexander II purchased the Villa Bermond late in 1865. The structure was later demolished and the Tsar ordered the building of a memorial chapel on the very spot where his son had died. The cornerstone was laid on March 2, 1867. Fourteen months later Tsarevich Alexander Alexandrovich was present for the inauguration of the chapel. In 1912 Tsar Nicholas II had a large Russian Orthodox Cathedral built there.

The disappearance of Nicholas Alexandrovich changed the course of history. It guaranteed to bring an end to his parents' marriage. Within a year the Tsar began a liaison that dealt his ailing marriage a death blow. Had Nixa succeeded his father in 1881, instead of the Empire going to his brother Alexander, the course followed by Russia would have been significantly different. Nixa was prepared to be Tsar, Alexander III was not; he was groomed to carry the Empire on his shoulders, his brother was not; Nixa was imbued by the need for Russia to embrace reform, Alexander III derailed it. Perhaps, the sense of loss experienced by Nixa's contemporaries is best summed up by the thoughts of a Russian historian:

> *We are at present mourning a death which represents many others. Not only has a man died, but also youth, beauty and the stirrings of first love. This was a young man who embodied millions of good people's hopes for the future. His nobility, kindness, affability, the spirit of justice and equity in him, made him the symbol of all that is dear and sacred to us on this earth.*[30]

TSAR ALEXANDER III
(1845-1894)

By Coryne Hall

Whenhen a third child and second son was born to Tsarevich Alexander Nikolaevich and Tsarevna Maria Alexandrovna in St Petersburg on Monday, February 26, 1845, no one expected he would become Tsar. The baby was christened Alexander at 10.30am on March 17 by Their Majesties' Confessor in the Winter Palace Church, St Petersburg. He had an impressive array of godparents: his paternal grandfather Tsar Nicholas I; maternal grandfather Ludwig II of Hesse and By Rhine; two paternal great-aunts, the Grand Duchesses Elena and Maria Pavlovna; and two aunts, Grand Duchess Olga Nikolaevna and the Hereditary Grand Duchess Mathilde of Hesse and By Rhine.

Sasha, as he was known in the family, joined his sister Alexandra and brother Nicholas (Nixa) in the Imperial nurseries, presided over by their devoted English nurse Kitty Strutton. Another son, Vladimir, followed in 1847 but two years later Alexandra died at the age of seven. With the births of for more children the family was complete. The family lived either at the Winter Palace in St Petersburg, or the Catherine Palace at Tsarskoe Selo where the children had a private garden with swings, skittles and slides. There was a miniature railway, a farmhouse and climbing masts for the young Grand Dukes. As the children grew older they were encouraged to cultivate a vegetable garden.

With the death of Nicholas I in 1855, Sasha's parents became Tsar Alexander II and Empress Marie Alexandrovna. The new Tsarina lavished all her care and attention on the education of Nixa, now the Tsarevich. Sasha therefore grew up a complete contrast to his gifted elder brother. Nevertheless, the boys remained close. During the Crimean War they created their own make-believe world, the city of "Mopsopolis" ('mops' in Russian means 'pug'), which they sketched in pen and ink and kept in a special album. The pug-faces of the inhabitants were a substitute for the English Bulldog, the country with which Russia was at war.[1]

At first they studied together but, as they grew older their paths diverged. Nixa was prepared for his future as Emperor; Sasha for life in the army. Not by any means clever, his slow, ponderous brain was nevertheless equipped with sound common sense and a rigid code of morality. Although he spoke French, English and German he remained a bad linguist and his spelling, even in Russian, was poor. He had a deep horror of war and never possessed the love of military manoeuvres and parades so evident in other Romanovs.

At 6 feet 3 inches he was the tallest Romanov since Peter the Great but with this height went a heavy build and complete lack of grace. His physical strength was amazing. He could straighten horse-shoes with his bare hands, bend iron bars and smash through doors with his massive shoulders. His health was excellent and his appetite enormous. Behind his somewhat gruff exterior and rather formidable appearance was a placid, even-tempered, generous man who was devoted to his family, loved animals and children and was almost transparently honest. Responding to the formal thank-you of a German princess at a ball, Sasha replied: *"Why can't you be honest? It was just a duty neither of us could have relished. I have ruined your slippers and you have made me nearly sick with the scent you use."*[2]

As a young Guards officer Sasha was conscientious but, in contrast to other members of the family he was scared of horses and never became a really proficient rider. Outside of the regiment and his family he had few interests. Unsociable in public, the round of off-duty pleasures associated with, and expected of, a Grand Duke, did not appeal.

It was at Tsarskoe Selo some time around 1864 that Sasha met Princess Marie Mestchersky, a maid of honour to his mother. Marie, born in 1844, was described by a contemporary as *"a great beauty. There was something Oriental about her whole person, and especially about her dark velvety eyes which fascinated everyone."*[3] Soon friendship turned into love.

The following year Sasha's world was turned upside down. For some months Nixa had been unwell. After a stay in Italy he joined his mother, whose health was also poor, in Nice. Suddenly the family was informed he was dying. They were summoned to Nice, where Nixa's distraught fiancée Princess Dagmar, daughter of Christian IX of Denmark, also arrived with her mother Queen Louise. There is a story that, just before his death on April 24, Nixa called Dagmar and Sasha to his bedside and clasped their hands together, begging them to marry. The legend is uncorroborated.[4]

Sasha was devastated by Nixa's death. Not only had he lost a dear brother but he was now the Tsarevich and his carefree life as a Guards Officer was over. Gossip had also begun to circulate about his relationship with Marie Mestchersky, his *"darling Duchenka,"* and in his diary he cursed society for not leaving them in peace. The Tsar and Tsarina now made no secret of the fact that they expected him to marry Dagmar and the two mothers planned how best to bring their hopes to fruition.[5]

By June, Sasha and Marie Mestchersky had ended their affair. Sasha was confused. On the one hand he missed "M.E.", as he called her in his diary, but on the other he was hoping for a marriage with Dagmar, *"which will mean my happiness for the rest of my life."*[6]

Soon his resolve weakened and by the autumn he was seeing Marie Mestchersky regularly at Tsarskoe Selo. They continued to meet throughout the winter but, as the anniversary of Nixa's death approached, Sasha found himself torn between passion and duty. Duty, in the shape of Dagmar, was beginning to win. *"I will say goodbye to M.E., whom I have loved as I have loved no one before, he wrote on March 23, 1866... Spring and autumn of 1865 in Tsarskoe Selo will always remain in my memory..."*[7]

Then in April 1866, during a ball, Marie Mestchersky told Sasha she was engaged to Prince Karl Emil of Sayn-Wittgenstein. The shock was great and it revived all his old feelings. The engagement was broken and Sasha decided to renounce his rights to the throne to marry her. *"I want to refuse to marry Dagmar, whom I cannot love and don't want..."*, he wrote. *"I don't want any wife but M.E."*[8]

There was an angry scene when Sasha told his father. The Tsar replied that Marie would be sent away. He ordered his son to go to Copenhagen and pro-pose to Dagmar. Sasha noted sadly that he and Marie said goodbye in a side room at Tsarskoe Selo.[9] *"Oh God, what a life, is it worthwhile after everything that has happened? Why was I born and why aren't I already dead?"* Sasha wrote in anguish.[10]

On June 2, the Tsarevich arrived in Denmark. Three weeks later he pro-posed to Princess Dagmar and was accepted. Neither had wanted to marry the other, but it is clear from diaries and letters that both thought this was Nixa's wish.

They were married on October 28 in the Great Church of the Winter Palace. After conversion to Orthodoxy, Dagmar became Grand Duchess Maria (Marie) Feodorovna. The young couple made their home at the Anichkov Palace on St Petersburg's Nevsky Prospekt but their life was not easy at first. Although fond of one another, both remembered the love they had lost. They had little in common. Sasha liked to spend the evenings quietly at home. His wife preferred parties and dancing. Although she tried to improve his boorish manners, Sasha remained awkward in society and tolerated social occasions only to please her. Yet by the end of the year Sasha was recording their new-found happiness.

Under her influence he began to study, observe and broaden his limited interests, reading literature, history and economic science. Alexander II showed little inclination to initiate his heir into the business of government but in 1866 Sasha became a Member of the State Council and, two years later, of the Committee of Ministers. Konstantin Pobedonostsev, Nixa's former tutor, became a regular visitor to the Anichkov and his creed of "Autocracy, Orthodoxy and Nationality" soon found a willing disciple in the Tsarevich. A reactionary to his fin-gertips, Pobedonostsev encouraged him to believe that his father's reforms were a threat to the autocracy, a view in which Sasha needed very little prompting.

The Tsarevich had great trouble in adjusting to his new position and all the public duties attached to it. On a trip to the Caucasus in 1869 relations between Sasha and his wife were increasingly strained. At one point he refused point blank to leave their boat, insisting that the deputation of welcome come on board instead. After the presentation of the traditional bread and salt he retired to his cabin, leaving her to cope alone. Later he began to shout and throw things. The following year things were no better and again there were tensions apparent during an official journey.

Their eldest son Nicholas was born in 1868. Alexander followed in 1869 but died within a year. The birth of George in 1871 was followed by Xenia (1875) and Michael (1878). Sasha delighted in his young family. He liked nothing more than a good romp and insisted they be brought up as normal healthy youngsters. In 1877, on the outbreak of the Russo-Turkish war, the Tsarevich was given an army command, earning the Order of St George for bravery. It was the first time he had been separated from his wife and children and he missed them dreadfully.

As his family grew, Sasha's relations with his own father became more distant. Firstly, because of a complete difference in outlook between father and son, the Tsarevich had no involvement with affairs of state. Sasha soon became the leader of a strong reactionary opposition party. A prominent member of this group was Pobedonostsev and, as the Tsarevich grew more receptive to his ideas it became obvious that once he came to the throne all reforms would stop.

The second reason was the Tsar's involvement with the young Princess Catherine Dolgoruky, by whom he had four children. Sasha saw this as an insult both to his mother and to the dignity of the throne. When, just forty days after the death of Empress Marie Alexandrovna in 1880, Alexander II married his mistress and created her Princess Yourievsky, relations between father and son deteriorated further.

On March 1, 1881, Alexander II was assassinated by a terrorist's bomb as he returned to the Winter Palace. Ironically, he had just signed a Manifesto for the reform of the Council of State, paving the way for full franchise in the future.

The Tsarevich and his family were having lunch at the Anichkov Palace when news reached them that a bomb had been thrown. They hurried to the Winter Palace, where the mangled body of the Tsar met their eyes. There was nothing the doctors could do. A priest was summoned to administer the Last Rites as the Tsarevich and Princess Yourievsky held the dying man's hands. By 3.35pm it was all over.

In these dramatic circumstances, Sasha succeeded to the throne as Tsar Alexander III. The reaction to his father's murder was swift. Alexander II's manifesto was torn up and most of those involved in his assassination were hanged. All the liberal ministers resigned and in their place were appointed the reactionaries favoured by the new Tsar. Terrorists were hunted down and imprisoned; newspapers, books and magazines were heavily censored, university studies were curtailed and student organisations suppressed. Civil liberties were suspended at will. Alexander III would reign as an autocrat and those who did not share this view soon began the long trek to Siberia.

Soon after his father's funeral, warned that his family's lives were at risk, Alexander III moved his family to Gatchina, a magnificently isolated palace about 30 miles from the capital which had once belonged to the Emperor Paul. From the outside the massive building looked like a barracks, with towers, battlements, high walls, octagonal towers and a moat. The palace had to be hastily renovated for occupation and workmen were still busy when the Imperial family took up residence in April.

Alexander III shunned the luxurious state rooms in the central block, instead living in a series of low, vaulted rooms on the mezzanine floor of the Arsenal block which had formerly been occupied by members of Emperor Paul's court. On the ground floor was the Arsenal Hall, where the principal part of family life took place. In this large, vaulted room were sofas, a dining-table, a billiard table and many toys. A staircase connected this hall directly to the Emperor's study. Security at the palace was tight. Visitors were carefully scrutinized and each security pass carried the bearer's photograph. Cavalry patrolled the park boundaries and at night Cossacks paced up and down outside the Imperial family's rooms.[11]

Every morning the Emperor rose at seven, washed in cold water and dressed in the costume of the Russian peasant, or *Moujik* – a long cotton blouse which hung below his belt, with baggy trousers. He was the first ruler since the seventeenth century to grow a beard and soon earned the nickname of *The Moujik Tsar*. After making a pot of coffee he sat down at his desk and began work. Later the Empress joined him for a simple breakfast of rye bread and boiled eggs. In 1882 the birth of Olga, their only child to be "born in the purple," completed the family.

Throughout his reign, Alexander III lived in a state of siege. At his coronation in 1883 there were very real fears for the Imperial family's safety. In 1887, when the family returned to St Petersburg for a commemoration service for Alexander II, some students carrying crude bombs concealed in hollowed-out books were arrested in one of the capital's main streets. Among the five students tried and hanged for this attempt was Alexander Ulyanov. His younger brother was later known to the world as Lenin.

Cut off from any liberal thought, Sasha became increasingly unenlightened, suspicious, distrustful and obstinate. The Tsar was his own Prime Minister. There was no parliament and no elections. The State Council was purely an advisory body and ministers reported directly to him. He was not obliged to take their advice and could dismiss any of them at his pleasure. They were not permitted to resign. *'shut up!'* he bellowed at one unfortunate minister, shaking him by the collar. *"When I choose to kick you out you will hear of it in no uncertain terms!"*[12] He worked through mountains of state papers, scrawling blunt comments, not always polite, in the margins. The country had become a police state and corruption was rife. A new police division, the Okhrana, was established. Their undercover agents intercepted letters, infiltrated organisations and collected evidence against those suspected of subversion. Pobedonostsev now spent half of every year at Gatchina in the dual role of adviser to the Emperor and tutor to the Tsarevich.

As a family man the Tsar was in his element. When the children grew older he took them into the woods around Gatchina to teach them the secrets of nature. They cleared the gardens, made bonfires and baked potatoes over the hot cinders. There were picnics in the woods, the Tsar driving the children in a wagonette. When the snow came they went sleighing, or tobogganing down a hill. Every year the Tsar tested the ice on the newly-frozen pond. Treading carefully until it gave way, he landed up to his knees in water.

They moved in a regular pattern between the Imperial residences. The New Year found them at the Anichkov for the Season, which Sasha hated. During the summer they moved to The Cottage at Peterhof and in August attended the army manoeuvres at Krasnoe Selo. They then moved to Poland for the hunting, on to the Crimea or back to Gatchina after the autumn trip to visit the Empress' family in Denmark. Sasha disliked change and this timetable was seldom altered. All the family looked forward to holidays in Denmark, which Alexander III compared to being "out of prison." King Christian and Queen Louise had a large, united family who liked nothing more than to be together at Fredensborg or Bernstorff, where practical jokes were very much a part of their way of life. Sasha joined in the fun wholeheartedly. One day, spotting the top-hatted figures of King Christian and King Oscar of Sweden, he could not resist squirting water at them from a garden hose. The family stole apples from the orchard and threw them at the attic windows to see who could smash most lights; Sasha carved his monogram on the tree-trunks, a past-time strictly forbidden to the old King's grandchildren. He was *"just like a schoolboy up to all kinds of pranks,"* leading the children into mischief, recalled his nephew.[13] The Emperor felt so at home in Denmark that he bought a house there. The Kejservilla, situated just outside the gates of Fredensborg, proved to be the perfect place for the Emperor to work on state papers and perform his physical exercises in private. Sometimes he even held tea-parties.

In the autumn of 1888 the Imperial family paid an official visit to the Caucasus. On October 17 their train was rattling back across the Russian countryside on the return journey. Security was tight. Every bridge, every culvert and every level crossing was guarded and the Tsar's destination was never announced in advance. As they approached Borki the train suddenly gave a violent lurch. Then there was a mighty bang, followed by the sound of clanging iron as the rear coaches crashed against those in front and the train was derailed.

One by one the family emerged, bruised, shaken but luckily unhurt. Sasha's leg was badly trapped and it took some minutes to free him. His leg was coal-black from the thigh to the knee and he limped for several days afterward. According to the Empress' letters, there is no truth in the story that the Emperor held up the roof so that his family could escape. In fact the roof of their carriage had been almost completely ripped off. Sasha was reputed to have joked that his ambitious brother Vladimir, who envied him the throne, would be disappointed that they had all survived and he would not be Tsar.

Having satisfied themselves that their children were safe, the Tsar and Tsarina attended to the wounded. As the Emperor pulled people from the wreckage the Empress helped to bandage the injured. Finally, a relief train arrived but the Imperial couple still refused to rest until all the wounded were comfortable and the bodies had been taken on board. Twenty-one people were killed, and thirty-five wounded. The Emperor's favourite dog, *Kamchatka*, was crushed.

Although the official enquiry blamed the excessive speed of a train that was too heavy, on rails that were light and sleepers that were old, rumours persisted that a terrorist had smuggled a bomb aboard. Undoubtedly the events at Borki increased the nervous tension of the Emperor and, especially, the Empress. Sasha became more moody and unsociable, shunning public functions to an unprecedented degree. He began to drink more heavily and the effects of terrorism, together with worry over his wife, took their toll on his own health but he was determined to preserve the autocracy.

Politically, Alexander III remained a reactionary. Probably influenced by his wife's family, who remained rabidly anti-German, the traditional ties that bound the Russian and German empires were loosened. In 1887 Sasha refused to renew the "Three Emperors' League" between Russia, Germany and Austria and began to look toward France. In 1891, when some French warships paid an official visit to Kronstadt, Sasha stood bareheaded while the Marsellaise (previously banned in the Russian empire) was played. Two years later France and Russia signed a secret military alliance, which ensured that Russia would not have to confront the mighty German army (or the combined forces of Germany and Austria) without an ally. Europe was now splitting into the battle lines of 1914 – the triple Alliance of Germany, Austria and Italy on one side; France and Russia on the other. Only England remained undecided.

In 1893 Serge Witte was appointed Minister of Finance. Huge foreign loans were negotiated to finance the construction of the Trans-Siberian Railway, which opened up the route to the Far East. Coal and iron ore were exploited, the engineering industry flourished and the textile industry thrived.

Sasha also supported the arts. He patronised *The Wanderers*, a group of Moscow artists who organized traveling exhibitions, and was a keen collector of paintings and Russian decorative art. After his death The Russian Museum of Alexander III was opened in St Petersburg to house his collections.

Despite drastic economies introduced in the Imperial Palaces, Sasha was concerned at the increasing size of the Imperial family and the consequent drain on his purse. In 1886 he introduced a new statute limiting the title of Grand Duke (with an allowance of £20,000 a year) and Grand Duchess (with a dowry of £100,000) and the predicate of Imperial Highness, to the sovereign's children and grandchildren in the male line only. The next generation would become princes and princesses with the title of "Highness" and a lump sum of £100,000 at birth. Great-great-grandchildren would be "Serene Highness." Sasha kept the family firmly in place and, unless summoned, they had to request an audience. They were all expected to attend weddings, christenings and the Emperor's family dinners. The autocratic Tsar never let them forget that they owed him allegiance as subjects. *"stop playing the Tsar!"* he told his brother Serge, who overstepped the mark.[14]

Under Alexander III the Court became more nationalistic and all the palace staff were required to be Russian. A new "Russianised" army uniform was introduced, those with German names were removed from government and high commands in the army and the German language was forbidden at Court. Meetings with foreign monarchs were kept to a minimum.

Alexander III believed that all the peoples of the Empire should observe Russian customs and the Orthodox religion. His most violent hatred was directed against the Jews. They were forbidden to live outside the Pale of Settlement and their rights were restricted further. He also wanted the total Russification of Finland (a part of the empire which the Tsar ruled as Grand Duke), with the Russian language used in all Finnish institutions.

The Tsar's Russification policy did not prevent him from enjoying his annual cruise in the Finnish skerries. Sasha was a keen fisherman, who once famously said that Europe can wait while the Tsar goes fishing. He had heard about the good salmon fishing in the Langinkoski Rapids near Kotka, east of Helsinki. In the summer of 1880 the Imperial yacht anchored for the first time in the sheltered bay which still bears the name of the Emperor's Harbour. The Imperial family fell in love with this beautiful place with its swiftly foaming rapids and Sasha said he would like to have a fishing lodge built on the river bank. Shortly afterward the fishing rights were signed over to him and the Finnish architect Magnus Schjerfbeck set to work on the plans.

In 1888 Sasha took his wife and children to see how work was progressing. It is said that he personally carved the steps from a large stone found on the beach. The Tsar met the local fishermen and fetched vodka for the Guards Musicians who played on board the Imperial yacht. Noticing that the fishing lodge had no flagpole he immediately ordered that one be erected. The following day deputations from Helsinki and Kotka arrived for an official welcoming ceremony. The Tsar's Standard was hoisted, the Imperial Hymn was played and the boats in the mouth of the river fired a salute. The Tsar proposed a toast to Finland, local choirs sang and the Finnish National March was played.

Langinkoski was presented to the Imperial couple by the State and the people of Finland. On July 15, 1889, the Tsar and Tsarina gave a house-warming party. Choirs and bands came from Helsinki and Vyborg and later that night the Imperial Family watched from their yacht as bonfires were lit all along the coast. The fishing lodge was small and very simple, with all the furnishings, porcelain and glassware made by Scandinavian craftsmen. The newspapers reported with some surprise that the Imperial couple led a very simple life. The Tsar chopped firewood with a locally-made axe. The Tsarina and her children peeled potatoes on the kitchen porch for the salmon soup she cooked in a copper kettle on the kitchen stove. However, she did not like to do the washing up. The amenities were very basic. There was no running water, the Tsar carried buckets from the river to the kitchen; no sewage disposal system and no electricity but there was a telephone (the number was Kotka 33). In all, they made about ten visits to these peaceful surroundings.

Like his father before him, Alexander III did not encourage his heir to become involved in affairs of State. Confident that there was plenty of time, he allowed Nicholas to settle into the easy-going life of an army officer and a play-boy. This was probably Sasha's biggest mistake as, unknown to him, time was running out.

In the autumn of 1893 Sasha was ill with fever and bronchitis. Now, at the beginning of 1894, he was weakened further by influenza. He suffered from frequent headaches and insomnia and complained that his shoes did not fit. Nobody noticed his feet were swelling. Professor Zakharine found signs of nephritis, an inflammation of the kidneys, and for several days medical bulletins were issued. The first Court ball of the season, at which Grand Duchess Xenia would make her debut, was postponed for a fortnight.

Sasha's condition was not helped by his love of drink. In an age of heavy drinkers the Tsar was no exception but, once the doctors diagnosed kidney problems, drinking was forbidden. Empress Marie kept a stern eye on him but, undeterred, Sasha had a special pair of boots made with a secret compartment for a flask. General Tcheverin, one of his closest companions, did the same. As soon as the Empress had left the room they played a game called 'Necessity is the Mother of Invention.' The Tsar looked at Tcheverin and said, *"Necessity, Tcheverin?" "Invention, Your Majesty,"* replied Tcheverin, as on the count of three the flasks came out and they both took a swig.[15]

The Tsar recovered sufficiently to carry out his duties but the doctors advised him to cut down his workload. Although a month short of his forty-ninth birthday, the after-effects of Borki, the strain of his position, worry over the health of his son George and the constant fear of assassination had taken their toll. Sasha looked and felt many years older and the doctors, deceived by his powerful frame, failed to see that he was very ill. Out walking with eleven-year-old Olga, he could hardly keep up with her. Alarmed for the future, the Emperor and Empress finally gave the Tsarevich permission to propose to Princess Alix of Hesse and By Rhine, whose choice as his bride they had previously opposed.

By the time the Imperial family left for their summer cruise in June the Tsar had lost a considerable amount of weight, suffered from insomnia and was badly in need of a change of air. As his health continued to deteriorate a young doctor diagnosed an acute case of nephritis, for which there was no cure.

They returned to Peterhof for the wedding of Grand Duchess Xenia and the Tsar's cousin Grand Duke Alexander Mikhailovich on July 25. All the splendour of the wedding could not hide the Tsar's illness. He looked old and tired, his clothes hung off him and his mighty frame sagged. Nevertheless, he was happy and able to enter into the celebrations. His younger daughter recalled that she never saw him like that again.

At the army review that August the Tsar fainted. A few days later he carried out his last public engagement, the launching of the battleship *Admiral Seniavia*. The doctors advised him to travel south for a complete rest and change of air but the Tsar insisted on going to Poland for the shooting. At first he went out with the guns, but soon became restless, lost his appetite and ate alone in his study with Olga. The Berlin specialist, Dr. Leyden, was summoned. He confirmed the earlier diagnosis of nephritis. There was little in the way of treatment but a chance that a warmer climate might help. The Imperial family moved south to Livadia in the Crimea.

They settled into the Maly Palace and were at first able to go on excursions into the countryside. Soon the Tsar became restless and refused to stick to the strict diet prescribed. Sometimes he sent secretly to the guardroom for a plate of rich cabbage soup and rye bread but this deviation from the diet showed in his deteriorating health. *"It was like seeing a magnificent building crumble,"* wrote his nephew Prince Nicholas of Greece.[16]

The family began to congregate as, day by day, the Tsar became weaker. Soon no one dared stray far from the house. On October 20 Sasha's breathing became laboured and his heart was weakening rapidly. As respiration became more and more difficult he was moved into an arm chair. The end was evidently near. The Empress sat with her arm around him, the family knelt in his room and prayers for the dying were intoned. Outside a late autumn fog grew thicker. *"Then, without pain, at the very moment* [Dr] *Hirsch was presenting him with a glass of wine,"*[17] the Tsar gave a big sigh and his head dropped onto his wife's breast. Everybody was stunned.

The mighty Alexander III was dead and the star-crossed reign of Nicholas II had begun.

GRAND DUKE VLADIMIR ALEXANDROVICH
(1847-1909)

By John Van der Kiste

G rand Duke Vladimir Alexandrovich was born on April 9/22, 1847, the fourth child of Tsarevich Alexander Nikolaevich and the Tsarevna, born Princess Marie of Hesse and By Rhine. He was a lively baby, and according to his maternal uncle Alexander, he *'squawked like a rook.'*[1] As he was the third son, it was unlikely that he would ever ascend the throne. Although many a grand duke or prince would probably have been relieved, Vladimir seemed mildly resentful of the fact. His eldest brother Nicholas was a delicate youth, while the second-born, Alexander, was strong but rather slow-witted and clumsy. Vladimir sometimes felt that he would make a better tsar than either of them.

When the ailing Tsarevich Nicholas fell ill at Nice and died in April 1865 at the age of twenty-one, it was rumoured that Tsar Alexander II thought his second son unworthy to take his brother's place and, therefore, would nominate Vladimir as successor instead. This would have had its precedent in the choice of Grand Duke Nicholas, the future Nicholas I, in preference to his elder brother Konstantin in 1825. However, the grief-stricken tsar quickly dispelled any doubts by confirming Alexander as his heir. Soon after returning to Russia from his son's deathbed, Tsar Alexander called upon his subjects to take an oath of allegiance to the new Tsarevich. Sadly, there would always be rivalry between the brothers. Alexander's self-confidence was not helped by the knowledge that Vladimir was more intelligent, more cultured, more articulate, and had the social graces which he lacked. In the spring of 1867, the Tsarevich and Vladimir both accompanied their father to the International Exhibition in Paris, and not surprisingly, Vladimir made the better impression of the two.

In the spring of 1874, Vladimir was betrothed to Princess Marie of Mecklenburg-Schwerin. Marie was the daughter of Grand Duke Friedrich Franz II and of his first wife, the former Princess Augusta Reuß-Köstritz. Born at Schloß Ludwisglust, outside of Schwerin, Marie was to develop an immense capacity to propel herself to the stratosphere of the royal circles. Initially, she was expected to wed the Prince of Schwarzburg. However, when the possibility of marrying her Russian cousin Vladimir became apparent, adieu went the Schwarzburger. Vladimir and Marie's wedding took place at the Winter Palace in August of the same year. The young couple were ideally suited to each other, and they made their home in the Vladimir Palace on the Neva River embankment.

The Vladimirs were the be the parents of five children. Their firstborn, Alexander, arrived in 1875, a year after his parents' wedding. He died at St Petersburg in 1877 months before his second birthday. A second son, Kirill, followed in 1876. One year later the nursery was joined by Boris Vladimirovich. The year 1879 saw the arrival and Andrei. Three years later Marie gave birth to her yongest child, Elena (Helen), who in later years would marry Prince Nicholas of Greece. The Vladimirovichi were a close-knit family group, whith Vladimir and Marie becoming exceedingly doting parents, which would cause them more than a few headaches as their children entered adulthood.

Having joined the army as a young man and enjoying the usual rapid promotion of a Romanov, Vladimir accompanied his father and his brothers Alexander and Serge to the front in the Russo-Turkish War of 1877–8, fighting against the Turkish armies as the commanding officer of the XII Corps of the Russian army.

In 1881 after the assasination of Alexander II, the new sovereign, now Alexander III, was temporarily numb with shock at the horror of his father's violent death. Though equally affected, Vladimir regained his composure more quickly and it fell to him to leave their father's deathbed at the Winter Palace and announce the news to the crowds outside. As it was considered ominous for the new reign if the imperial messenger used the words "death" or "die," he called out in his loud booming voice: *"Godusar Imperator Van Prikazal Dolga Jit!"* (The emperor has bidden you to live long!).[2]

Like his younger brother, the lifelong bachelor Alexis, Vladimir disliked the Spartan regime of Alexander III's court, and he regarded the Tsar's homely establishment at Gatchina as no better than a provincial manor. He and Marie had always reveled in the good life and were now effectively the leaders of Russian society. Clever and artistic, they loved entertaining and their balls eclipsed the splendour of those held at the Winter Palace. Less straitlaced than the Tsar and Tsarina, they never excluded divorced persons from their functions. While gambling was frowned on in certain quarters, the Vladimir Palace positively encouraged it and had its own roulette wheel.

During Alexander III's reign the Vladimirs and Alexis were regular visitors to Paris, spending so freely that coaches advertised sightseeing trips around nightclubs, known as *la tournée des grandes ducs*. According to his cousin Grand Duke Alexander, Vladimir's appearances in the capital *"meant a red-letter day for the chefs and maitres-d'hôtel of the Ville Lumière, for after making a terrific row about the "inadequacy" of the menu, he would invariably finish the evening by putting a lavish tip in every hand capable of being stretched out."*[3]

As the next eldest brother, it was clear that Vladimir would occupy a prominent role in the empire. From 1886 to 1905, he held the post of commander of the St Petersburg military district, and for a time he was governor general of the Caucasus. Despite his military interests, but unlike his Prussian counterparts, he was no philistine. In fact Prince Wilhelm of Prussia, the future Emperor Wilhelm II, had his doubts as to Vladimir's love of all things military. On a visit to Russia in May 1884, Wilhelm reported back to his grandfather, Emperor Wilhelm I, that while the grand duke took a great deal of interest in the troops under him and was well acquainted in everything concerning the regulations and military organisation, he had heard *"that he does all this from a feeling of duty, not for love of it, as indeed, do most of the other grand dukes in the services."*[4] Vladimir was more renowned for his artistic patronage, as an accomplished amateur painter, an enthusiastic patron of the ballet, and a collector of ancient icons. When appointed president of the Imperial Academy of Arts, he filled the position with great enthusiasm. The younger grand dukes felt he treated them with ill-concealed contempt, and they had little time for him, thinking they could never engage him in conversation unless they were prepared to discuss the fine arts or the superiority of French cooking.

The long-simmering rivalry between Vladimir and the tsar only intensified during the Alexander's reign. Apart from their hatred of England, the brothers had little in common. Alexander called Queen Victoria *"a pampered, sentimental, selfish old woman,"*[5] while Vladimir felt their sister Marie, married to the Queen's second son Alfred, Duke of Edinburgh, had always been treated unfairly in Britain, largely because she was not given precedence at court over the Danish-born Princess of Wales. Such a state of affairs was hardly unreasonable as the wife of the heir to the throne was surely the second lady in the kingdom after the Queen herself; but the senior Russian grand dukes chose to regard it as a grave affront, not to say insult, to Romanov dignity.

The broad-shouldered, thickset yet spry Vladimir had always had the more forceful personality, and he was slightly envious that his bovine, slow-witted elder brother should be heir to the throne. As a bachelor he had been prepared to accept what divine providence had ordered. Yet after his marriage, his sharp-witted German wife only widened the fraternal breach. Grand Duchess Vladimir looked down on Tsarevna Marie Feodorovna, herself a forceful personality. The Tsarina was a Danish-born princess and a lifelong foe of all things German ever since the kingdom of her father, King Christian IX, had suffered severely at Prussian hands during the war of 1864.

Alexander would always remain slightly in awe of the clever, more decisive Vladimir and his equally intelligent, not to say scheming, sister-in-law. It was harder for Alexander to ask for loyalty and obedience from a brother only two years younger than himself than from a son. As an example, the grand dukes were generally forbidden to enter the Tsar's study without an appointment, but Vladimir refused to comply; thus, he often managed to get his own way with the Tsar who found it difficult to argue, particularly if caught off his guard. Although the Tsar said nothing, he was often left fuming at Vladimir's lack of respect.

Despite his love of hospitality and frequent generosity, Vladimir was unpopular in St Petersburg. While he had his friends and admirers, others disliked him for his coarseness, drunkenness, and his unashamedly partisan German wife. It was wise of the couple to spend more time in Paris where there were fewer opportunities for family friction.

Though the Vladimirs were always glad to visit Paris on their own volition, at least twice the Tsar had to order them from court. Grand Duchess Vladimir wrote regularly to Princess Bismarck in Berlin, describing people and matters at the St Petersburg court from a somewhat jaundiced view. One day she was careless enough to leave a rather vitriolic letter on her writing table, and one of her husband's aides, Count Paul Shuvalov, feeling that his duty to his sovereign was greater than to his master's troublesome wife, showed it to the tsar. The latter sent for his brother, told him that his wife must cease forthwith, and that it would be politic for them to remove themselves for a while. Vladimir was outraged and feared his wife would be misrepresented as a German agent, yet he had no alternative but to obey.

This episode paled in significance in comparison to another scandal. The Vladimirs were regular visitors to the St Petersburg opera and supper afterward at Cubat, a fashionable restaurant noted for its excellent cuisine. One evening while they were there, the grand duchess heard voices among which she recognised that of the French actor Lucien Guitry, then appearing in a play in the city. She summoned a waiter and asked that Guitry be presented to her. He was entertaining a group of Bohemian friends including his lover Mademoiselle Angèle, but the Grand Duchess insisted that his party join hers. Guitry feared his friends' standards of behaviour might not be compatible with imperial decorum and tried to decline the invitation, but she brushed his objections aside. The enlarged party became increasingly merry until a drunken Vladimir seized Mademoiselle Angèle and kissed her. Encouraged by the Grand Duchess, an angry Guitry reciprocated by putting his arm round her and giving her an equally unashamed kiss. This was too much for Vladimir who took the actor by the throat and threatened to kill him. The restaurant soon descended into uproar with other patrons either fleeing for safety or eagerly joining in the mayhem. Unable to restore order, the management had to send for the prefect of St Petersburg.

When the Tsar was told what had occurred at the restaurant, no one had ever seen him in such a rage before, and even the Tsarina did not dare speak to him for three days. Once he had calmed down, he ordered Guitry to leave Russia by the next train – as must his brother and sister-in-law. If they refused to comply, they would be sent somewhere considerably less accommodating than Paris. When they were forgiven and allowed to return, it seemed that they had learnt their lesson at last, and there were no more similar incidents.

Vladimir was always the most Anglophobic of his brothers and held that the British were *"at the bottom of every trouble in the world."* When his younger brother Serge was betrothed to Princess Elisabeth (Ella) of Hesse and By Rhine, he objected on the grounds that she was far too English. Her mother Alice, Queen Victoria's second daughter, died of diphtheria at the age of thirty-five, and the Queen had taken a major hand in Ella's upbringing. Nevertheless, Ella soon endeared herself to her in-laws and any resentment was only temporary. However, Vladimir's suspicions surfaced again when the Tsarevich Nicholas became betrothed to Ella's younger sister Alix, whom he considered even more under the spell of her grandmother in England.

In October 1888, the Tsar, Tsarina, and their sons were involved in a serious accident when their train was derailed near Borki en route from the Caucasus. Whether this was due to terrorist sabotage or mechanical failure was never established, but twenty-one people were killed and many were injured, some maimed for life. Though still suffering from shock as they climbed from the wreckage, the Ttsar commented wryly, *"Imagine Vladimir's disappointment when he hears that we all escaped alive."*[6]

By this time Tsar Alexander III and Vladimir agreed on one thing: they were both disillusioned with the oppressive security and privacy their positions required. Vladimir complained of this state of affairs to Alexander Polovtsov, a member of the state council. His reply:

> *Both the emperor and you live in conditions which make it very difficult
> if not impossible to know people...You live your lives under lock and key, see peo
> ple at official receptions, and speak to two or three whom fate or intrigue have
> brought close to you and who find in you a means to the attainment of their
> goals.[7]*

In the autumn of 1894, Tsar Alexander became seriously ill. Full of con-
cern for his brother, Vladimir told him to consult a German specialist, Dr Ernest
Leyden. Though virulently anti-German, by now the Tsar was too weak to argue.
Leyden examined him, diagnosed a severe case of nephritis, and sadly admitted
that there was no hope of a cure. When Alexander's death placed the unprepared
Tsarevich on the throne as Tsar Nicholas II, for the second time in thirteen years
Vladimir was ready to play a supportive role to a new monarch. At his brother's
funeral he took the Duke of York round St Petersburg on sightseeing tours. He
suspected that the young Grand Duke shared the anti-German prejudices of his
mother (the Princess of Wales) and aunt (the Dowager Tsarina) and Vladimir was
keen to try and enlist some Russian support as well as sympathy for Germany
from the next king of England but one.

Tsar Nicholas II always remained in awe of his uncle Vladimir, looking
up to him as the senior representative of his late father's generation. Early in the
new reign, he confided in Vladimir how hard it was for him to rule, as he had
been kept so ignorant of government affairs while he was Tsarevich. Vladimir had
little affection or respect for his nephew and had never concealed the view that he
regarded himself just as good if not better than his elder brother. As a result, he
was disinclined to start being deferential to a nephew twenty-one years his junior. However, he proved a useful ally of the tsar at his wedding, insisting force-
fully to the Dowager Empress that it was only right for the bride to be driven to
the ceremony in a golden coach and that as future empress certain imperial diamonds should be presented to Alix.[8] As the recently widowed but indomitable
Marie Feodorovna still regarded herself as the first lady in the empire and the
family, there were few men brave enough to tell her what she did not wish to hear.

During one of their times together, Vladimir told the Tsar he remembered
clearly the accessions of the last two tsars. On each occasion, in 1855 and 1881,
Russia had been in a far worse state than now (1894) when she had enjoyed peace
for thirteen years. This state of affairs, he assured him, was a legacy of Tsar
Alexander III's policy of "Russia for the Russians." Changes would be required,
but there was no need to hurry.

> *One should not give anyone grounds to think that the son condemns the
> order created by his father or the choice of people whom the latter had summoned
> to work with him. Initially, one should suspend changes and should follow the
> main line of his father's policy.[9]*

Uncle and nephew might have established a better relationship had it not
been for the presence of the Tsarina. While her husband's two youngest uncles,
Serge (married to the Tsarina's sister Ella) and Paul, were friendly with her, Grand
Duke and Duchess Vladimir constantly criticized her behind her back for her lack

of humour, chilly nature, dull clothes, and above all, her poor Russian. Moreover, the Vladimirs' attitude and behaviour, once mellowed under Alexander III's reign, was now back in full force and they behaved just as they wished with a blatant disregard for decorum. Court mourning for the late tsar was meant to last for one year but it did not prevent them from giving a lavish, riotous wedding anniversary party during the mourning period in which, it was said, each member of the gypsy orchestra (and maybe the imperial host himself) became riotously drunk.

In May 1896, the Tsar and Tsarina were crowned. Tragically, the coronation festivities were marred by the accident at Khodynka Field in which at least a thousand spectators, trying to obtain gifts being distributed freely among the crowd, were trampled to death. Tsar Nicholas II wanted to cancel the ball that evening as a mark of respect to the dead and injured, but Vladimir and his brothers persuaded them to continue with the festivities as if nothing had happened on the grounds that the French government and embassy, who had paid for the ball, would be grossly offended. There was no question of the sovereign and his wife not staying for supper; to leave the ball early would appear *'sentimental.'*[10]

Less than a year later, Vladimir fell out with his youngest brother Paul. The latter, who had lost his wife in childbirth, had an affair with Olga von Pistolkors, wife of a captain in his regiment and aide-de-camp to Vladimir. In 1897, Olga gave birth to his son. For once Vladimir and Tsar Nicholas II were in agreement; Vladimir was outraged with Paul for having let down the family and stealing the wife of his aide-de-camp. Paul paid the price by being banished from the Russian empire for several years. Madame von Pistolkors was divorced by her husband, and when she married Paul, Vladimir was *"quite undone,"* claiming that Paul had gone back on his word.[11]

During his nephew's reign, Vladimir and his wife continued to dominate Russian society. As president of the Academy of Arts, he took a special interest in the ballet and befriended the impresario Diaghilev who found the management of the Maryinsky Theatre too conservative. Diaghilev wanted to form a troupe of artists from the Maryinsky and take them abroad – where he could introduce them to new dances and new music – when the Russian theatre was closed. Vladimir provided him with the finances needed to realise his ambition of dazzling the capitals of Western Europe.

In January 1905, Russia was shocked by the "Bloody Sunday" massacre. A peaceful procession of workers went to take a petition to the Ttsar at the Winter Palace but was fired on by the army, acting on orders of the St Petersburg police. Over two thousand were killed or wounded. It was thought that Vladimir was responsible for the order as the senior imperial military figure in charge, but he was innocent and deeply saddened that people should believe he was the cause of the massacre. Firm and dictatorial he might be, he would never have been so foolish as to authorise such an inflammatory act. Nevertheless, revenge on the imperial family came swiftly. Less than a month later, Grand Duke Serge was assassinated in broad daylight in the Kremlin. Vladimir begged the tsar to be allowed to attend the funeral but this was denied him as he would undoubtedly be another terrorist target, and his safety could not be guaranteed if he appeared in public. Moreover, he could not go to Moscow as he was officially responsible for the security of the capital.[12]

Vladimir's distress at the murder of his brother soon gave way to fury at the treatment of his eldest surviving son Kirill, who, in October 1905, married his cousin Victoria Melita, the divorced former wife of the Tsarina's brother Ernst Ludwig, Grand Duke of Hesse and By Rhine. Vladimir stormed into the Tsar's study demanding that his son be allowed to return home forthwith. When his imperial nephew said nothing, remained calm, and gave the impression he was trying not to listen, Vladimir tore the decorations from his uniform, threw them to the floor, stormed out of the room, slammed the door loudly behind him, and subsequently resigned all his administrative posts. However, less than two years later, the tsar, having made his point, relented and agreed to recognise the wedding officially.

This act of forgiveness came just in time for by now Vladimir was in poor health. When his younger brother Alexis died in Paris in November 1908, he knew he would be the next to go. On February 4/17, he had a major cerebral hemorrhage at his residence at Tsarskoe Selo and within minutes he had passed away.

His wife, Grand Duchess Maria Pavlovna remained a force to be reckoned with in the last days of Imperial Russia. Defiant, even insolent at times, she was a thorn on the side of Nicholas II and Alix. Her criticism of the Tsar and Tsarina was well-known and she made no secret of her utter disgust concerning how Russia was governed. She survived the revolution and after a harrowing, but bold, escape, Maria Pavlovna, along with a significant portion of her fabulous jewelry collection, reached Europe only to die soon after at a French spa. The stress suffered during the revolutionary nightmare was far too much for her weakened heart to survive. Grand Duchess Maria Pavlovna died at Contrexéville, France, on September 6, 1920.

GRAND DUKE ALEXIS ALEXANDROVICH
(1850-1908)

By Zoia Belyakova

G rand Duke Alexis Alexandrovich, the fourth son of Emperor Alexander II, received from the kings of heaven and earth everything that one could wish for a lifetime: health, power, good looks, immense wealth, female love, a responsible social position, and the top ranks. Alexis was the tallest, the sturdiest and most good-looking man among the Tsar's elder handsome, tall, and strapping sons. Like his brothers, he had a tendency to put on weight, not helped by his epicurean tastes, verging on gluttony. He was always elegantly dressed, grew sideburns and frequently changed his hairstyle. The Grand Duke's womanizing made him excitingly scandalous. Among all the Romanovs, passionate admirers of female beauty, he was the undisputable champion in love matters. Relatives and other contemporaries give similar opinions of Alexis *"Man of the World; bon vivant, spoilt by women; Very handsome, all women fell in love with him."* Professionally, he became known as the man of *"fast women and slow ships."*

Alexis was born in St Petersburg on January 2/14, 1850. This birth was a happy consolation for his parents after two deaths in the Imperial family, those of young Grand Duchess Alexandra (Lina) in June 1849, and of Grand Duke Michael Pavlovich in September 1849. Alexis' birth put an end to the prolonged deep mourning at Court. On January 2, 1850, a special order of Nicholas I announced its complete end. At birth, a tiny unaware infant was appointed honorary Colonel of the Life-Guard Moskovsky regiment, was enlisted into Life-Guard Preobrajensky and Chasseurs regiments, and was enlisted into the Marine Guards. Thus, the baby boy was designated to have a career in the navy. The order for the State Treasury had to pay 50,000 roubles a year for his upkeep and upbringing. On January 22, his baptism took place at the Grand Winter Palace church, his godparents being his three uncles Konstantin, Nicholas and Michael, his uncle Prince Karl of Hesse and By Rhine (brother of Grand Duchess Maria Alexandrovna), Prince Peter of Oldenburg and his aunts Maria and Olga. The Emperor himself brought the baby to the baptism font, and presented him with the order of St Andrew. Traditionally, an icon with the image of the patron saint St Alexis was pained by Academician Maikov at the cost of 115 roubles in silver. Its dimensions were the size of the baby boy.

Alexis grew in the numerous merry company of his brothers and cousins. His father, the Tsarevich Alexander Nikolaevich, came to see his *"adorable little ones"* a few times a day, although being much indulged into learning his future *"tsar's crafts."* In the early 1850s, children remained the centre of their parents' interests and attention. At that time, they looked like an admirable beautiful and very happy couple. Father conceived all pet names for his offspring: the eldest Nicholas was called Nixa, Bulldog for Sasha, Tubby for Vladimir, Seichik was a gentle abbreviation of Alexis, they named Maria a Duck for her awkward gait, and the younger boys were Gega (Serge), and Pitz (Paul). Alexis was a sincere, kind and attractive child, and sincerity, openness and friendliness remained his individuality.

His childhood companion was his cousin Nikola, Grand Duke Nicholas Konstantinovich, who was often left to the care of Alexander II and his wife, as his own father Admiral-General Konstantin Nikolaevich was on a permanent voyage. Nikola was exactly four weeks younger and destined to the navy as swell. Initially they had classes together.

Traditionally, at seven, the august sons changed their customary boy's Russian style shirt with a belt for their first officer dress uniform such as hussars', lancers', etc., depending on the regiment that they remained enlisted or appointed an honorary colonel since their birth. On January 2, 1857, happy Alexis was given his naval officer dress uniform, supplemented with a midshipman rank. The Tsar wrote to his brother Konstantin who was then at sea that Nikola *"...soon he too will be favored. It will be nice to see both our little sailors in identical dress uniforms."*[1] Cousin Nicholas (Kolia), Duke of Leuchtenberg wrote his mother Grand Duchess Maria that Alexis was given *"officer's dress uniform in the presence of Uncle and Aunt, and that Moskowsky Life Guards presented him with a saber."*[2]

At nine, Alexis received his new tutor, Captain First Class, Konstantin N. Possiet (later Vice-Admiral), a famous traveler, an experienced seaman, the scion of the French noble family that had moved to Russia in the days of Louis XIV. In winter, his duty was to provide teachers with the programs, to specify daily classes and introduce strict discipline for their two wards. Possiet appeared in the Winter Palace in January 1859, as noted in his diary (written in three languages, the Dutch being one of them): *"13 January...introduced to the Emperor. January 14...introduced to the Heir. January 15. First time at Alexis Alexandrovich."* Classes began in March, 1859. The tutor did not see much diligence in studies, neither discipline was satisfactory. Quite soon Possiet noted: *"Alexis Alexandrovich is least of all to be allowed to deviate from a task, nor to be allowed to chat with Nikolai Konstantinovich. They must be forced to rewrite all that has been written badly."*[3] Laziness, misbehavior, and minimal diligence and inattention remained the tutor's concern. Soon classes for the two fellows were arranged separately. Their daily books in instruction were *The Naval Cadet's Guide and Seaman's Companion.* Occasionally, Possiet complained to the Emperor, and once the latter threatened: *"I will whip you."*

Accompanied by the tutor, the young sailors' summer voyages were restricted to the Gulf of Finland. In 1864, Alexis's training on board the screw frigate *Svetlana* was still confined to the Baltic Sea, but two years later on the frigate *Osliabia* he visited Copenhagen, Lisbon, the Madeira Islands and the Azores. In 1866, he was promoted to lieutenant. In 1867, he sailed in the capacity of officer of the watch aboard the frigate *Alexander Nevsky* in the Mediterranean Sea.

The standard of education for Alexander II's children obviously declined in comparison with the times of Nicholas I, who chose "governors by God" like Vassily Zhukovsky and Karl Merder for his children. The Empress Maria now decided to personally hire the teaching staff, giving preference to men of

Germanic background with tough, strict and hardy character. She, nevertheless, was aware of the weaknesses of these tutors and would say, *"Name me just one individual in the whole of Russia, who would combine a natural wit, an excellent educa-tion, a strong will with stern principles, faith, and pure morals, then I will vouch to over-come all impediments and engage such a man for my sons' tutelage."*[4] Starting with his twelfth year, only Tsarevich Nicholas Alexandrovich had private classes with the best professors. *"Not a single teacher of the younger grand dukes had a Russian name, except for a priest and a music teacher, and only one of them, Sperer by name, was a uni-versity professor, the others taught at high schools."*[5] The teachers squabbled, intrigued, and fawned upon the Empress, as they tried to induce her disfavor to the Russian tutors. When the royal boys were in their teens, they did not care for learning. There was neither trust, nor goodwill between instructors and their stu-dents. The Germanic teachers never mastered the Russian language nor were they versed in Russian history. Classes in history and geography were carried out in German, and reading German books was compulsory. Conversing in Russian with strangers was prohibited. Little wonder that Sasha, Vladimir and Alexis had a tendency to laziness and resisted indoctrination, they called their adolescence *"most disgusting memories"*(A.Polovtsov). There was little friendliness and mutual affection between Alexis and Possiet. Their relationship was compared with *'scratching a knife on glass.'*[6]

At ten, Alexis received a birthday gift from Uncle Konstantin: a naval yacht *Zabava* modeled after the *America* yacht. It was specially commissioned at Abo shipyards in Finland at the cost of 23.500 roubles in silver. In summer 1860, the boys took part in their first naval practice in the Baltic, slept aboard yachts and stood watch. Their first nautical life experience made a different impression. Possiet noted: *"Alexis said it became interesting. His satisfaction when we went ahead of Volna, his discontent when later Niksa, at a ruff sea, went ahead of Zabava. Nikolai Konstantinovich became a little sick, and he fell asleep. Alexis remarked "Nikola is so strange. Now when it became so interesting, he is asleep."*[7]

He sent letters to his parents, in full detail, about his naval experiences, and what he saw ashore: a factory, lighthouses, a fishermen's village (s), the little house of Peter the Great on the Catherine Canal, Lutheran churches in Revel, etc. In a letter to his mother dated October 22, 1863, he shares his thoughts about an art exhibition:

> *One of the best pictures is the so called Last Supper painted by N. Gey. Yet, the name given to the picture is completely wrong because it shows the departure of Judas and the awe on the faces of the disciples who are witnessing the exodus of a traitor. The face of the Savior does not have the usual divine expression, something disapproved of by many viewers, especially the clergy men...Also forgot to say, that Doctor Zdekauer examined me and found that my bones and the body construction are like those of a prehistoric man and, apart from that, there is a good half an inch of fat, which I should lose with age. My brothers laughed at his comments.*[8]

He also mentioned reading two clever comedies by famous writer Denis Fonvizin *The Brigadier* and *The Young Ignoramus*, and the *Government Inspector* by Nikolai

Gogol. In 1865, during a summer visit to Novgorod, Alexis bought the picture *"God's Mother Fainting,"* may be on the impression of the Empress-Mother grievance and the shock at Nixa's death in Nice, 1865.

The following year Alexis went to Copenhagen with his brother Vladimir to participate in the engagement of Alexander and Princess Dagmar. It was a delicate mission. At that time, Sasha was madly in love with Marie Mestchersky, a lady-in-waiting of the Empress. He was prepared even to renounce his right to the throne so that he could marry her. Enraged, Alexander II sent Marie abroad and ordered his son to go immediately to Copenhagen and ask for Dagmar's hand. Two sad fates joined – of Dagmar, still mourning the death of her ill-fated fiancé, and of Alexander, suffering and humiliated. Alexis, cheerful and kind-hearted, was then irreplaceable. The young couple tried hard to make their marriage work, but the wounds from losing their beloved had not healed. Alexander found it hard to adjust to his new position as tsarevich, his introduction to the state affairs, tedious receptions and ceremonies. On the contrary, Dagmar, who became the Tsarevna, Grand Duchess Maria (Marie) Feodorovna (Minny), took at once to the splendor of court life. She troubled only about her husband's temperamental, violent and sulky mood. For Minny, Alexis became a true friend, always ready to diffuse the tension between her and Alexander with a joke or small talk, or just with his ability to listen and understand. He accompanied the young couple on their summer journey to the Caspian Sea in 1869 where his mere presence acted as a cure. Later as the Empress, Maria Feodorovna would protect Alexis up until his death, more than once redeeming his bruised reputation.

In the 1870s, the sea voyages became a real escape and salvation. The family atmosphere at the Winter Palace seemed strained and gloomy. Alexander II's children never allowed, even between themselves, any discussion of their father's private life. Such was the upbringing in the spirit of absolute respect to the will of the autocrat anointed by our Lord. The family succeeded in hiding the Emperor's secret liaison with Princess Catherine Dolgoruky from the youngest sons, Serge and Paul. Later the Grand Duchess Marie remembered that: *"It seemed particularly unbearable to me at that time that Papa prohibited us to be admitted to his rooms without prior announcement."*[9] Courtiers noted that in those trying, critical times Alexis, who was usually so jolly, cheerful, and loving to tease, rarely ever smiled. He was unhappy to live in the Winter Palace, unable to avoid the family of the Emperor's lover. His brothers had left; Alexander and Dagmar settled in the Anichkov Palace on Nevsky Prospect, and, since 1872, Vladimir lived at 26 Palace Embankment in his own residence.

In 1870, Alexis took the oath to the Throne and his military oath to the Motherland. At 20, his education was completed. He received a yearly allowance of 142.857 roubles 14 kopecks from the Appanage Department. The august children were supposed to become acquainted with realities and requirements of life. Not an easy objective if we recollect the notes of General N.A. Yepanchin.

Alexis Alexandrovich was a good hearted person, but he showed little seriousness in life and work and his education had strange gaps. During the voyage on the frigate Svetlana, Grand Duke Alexis, upon arriving in New York, was playing cards with his fellow officers...after the game the Grand Duke pointed out at one of the coins and asked what it was. They answered: "Piatachok, five kopeck copper coin."

The Grand Duke studied it with great curiosity and said: *"I see it for the first time in my life."* Undoubtedly, it was not a joke, but evidence of how far away from life he was really kept.[10]

In June/July 1870, he made his next trip to the Northern Seas. Alexis arrived at Archangel, where his duties as a member of the Imperial Family included visits to children's educational establishments, orphanages, foundling houses, secondary schools, theological seminaries, and colleges and also inspections of publishing houses, courts and the fire brigade. It is unknown how deeply the Tsar's son understood the issues, but he donated generously and studied in detail the work of the local Admiralty. The important guest attended the contest of private rowing boats, a traditional favorite entertainment of the townsfolk. In the last race, *pomor* women (seaside dwellers) participated and created great enthusiasm amongst spectators. The winners were generously awarded with silver watches to the helmsmen and gold earrings to the helmswomen.

In the late 1860s, Alexis had problems of his own. He fell in love with Alexandra (Sashenka) Zhukovsky, the daughter of the famous poet Vassily Zhukovsky. Her father had spent twenty-four years at the Imperial court, teaching Russian to the Prussian-born wife of Nicholas I and then tutoring their son, the Tsarevich Alexander. After resigning in 1841, Zhukovsky went to Germany for medical treatment where he married Elisabeth von Reutern, daughter of a painter friend. A baby girl called Alexandra was born in November 1842. At ten, Sashenka was described as a beauty by her admiring father, who raised his daughter himself. She was blessed with intellect, broad mind, open heart and kind nature. Zhukovsky died in Baden-Baden in 1852, in two years his wife followed him to a grave, and siblings Alexandra and Pavel became orphans. The Imperial family looked after the children and much cared about them. Alexandra often visited Court, where she played with the Emperor's children. At the age of sixteen, she became a maid-of-honor to the Empress Maria Alexandrovna.

Out of five maids-of-honor of the Empress, the youngest two, Marie Elimovna Mestchersky and Alexandra Zhukovsky, were regarded by the elite of St Petersburg as the most beautiful. Dark-eyed Marie exuded a sense of oriental languor, while Alexandra had fair hair, blue eyes and a fine complexion. Despite their two-year age difference, these orphan girls became close friends and confessed little heart secrets to each other. Countess Kleinmichel noted Maria's fiery temperament and Alexandra's Germanic romanticism in *Memories of a Shipwrecked World*. For the sake of the adorable "M.E." as he often mentioned in his diary, the Tsarevich was ready to abdicate his rights to the throne. Finally he had to enter his diary: *"Farewell, dear Dusen'ka."*[11] Luckily, he never regretted the occasion.

Grand Duke Alexis fell in love with Alexandra Zhukovsky when he was nineteen and she was twenty-seven. They kept their affair carefully hidden and met mostly at the Anichkov Palace, home of Alexander and Minny, where they enjoyed performing in amateur theatricals. Alexis seemed blinded with his love.

Nothing could teach him wisdom or a good lesson, neither Sasha's failure, nor the Emperor's decision to strip his cousin Duke Nicholas of Leuchtenberg of his rank and force him into exile when he concluded a morganatic marriage to Nadezhda S. Akinfieva (neé Annenkova). The wedding took place on 9/21 September 1868 in the Russian Orthodox Church in Geneva.

Duke Nicholas' bold move possibly captured the heart and imagination of his cousin Alexis. On July 23, 1868, the Duke of Leuchtenberg illegally crossed the Russian border in a naval vessel disguised as a sailor. He sailed from Liepaja to the Prussian port of Memel, before traveling to Rome through Königsberg and Berlin. In Rome, he reunited with Nadine, who was already expecting their first child. In an attempt to cover up the scandal, Alexander II gave the Duke, who served under him as a Major General, backdated foreign leave. Nicholas was warned that if he failed to return to service in Russia after six months, he would lose his rank, titles and Russian citizenship. Love, honor and a sense of duty to his wife and child, however, prevailed. If the child had been born in Russia, it would have been regarded the offspring of Nadine's first husband Akinfov, to whom she was still legally married and was fighting for a divorce.[12]

Alexis was well aware of a scandalous marital chaos in the Romanov family, which his favorite aunt, Grand Duchess Maria, had started after a morganatic marriage to Count Grigory Stroganov. The second families of the two Alexis's uncles, Grand Dukes Konstantin and Nicholas, and even the marital sins of Tsar Alexander II gave rise to gossips, and destroyed the remains of prestige of the Imperial household.

Hearing about the extramarital affairs and second families of his various relatives, Alexis could not help wondering why his great love should be forbidden. Weren't his relatives as human as he was? What do pointless formalities mean in comparison with life and happiness, matters of honor and conscience, and one's vow to God? Alexis and Sashenka decided to flee abroad and marry there. The legend has it that they concluded a secret and hopeless illegal marriage in Switzerland in 1870. Lack of money and the need to continue in service, however, forced Alexis and Alexandra to return to Russia. The marriage was annulled, while the Orthodox priest who married them was said to have been defrocked. Alexandra was then found to be carrying Alexis's child. Although the couple begged the Empress for permission to marry, they were refused. As a result, Alexandra Zhukovsky was forced to leave the Imperial court.

Alexis's tutor Vice Admiral Konstantin Possiet began to notice his ward's strange indifference to everything around him. Torn between duty and conscience, he often pleaded sickness or hit the bottle. His parents reasonably worried about their son's way of spending the time. Who was she to ask for help? Alexis turned to his sister-in-law Minny, there was nothing she could do to help the lovers. Meanwhile Alexis continued to regard Alexandra as his lawfully wedded wife. A photograph to her is signed *"To my dear little wife from her faithful husband."* This probably explains the reason why Alexis decided to remain a bachelor, unable to promise God to love and honor another woman while his first wife's fate was still uncertain.

At Sashenka's advice, Alexis began writing a diary during a cruise on the River Volga in 1869. Desiring to *"do something to please my dear little wife every day,"* the Grand Duke poured out his love on the pages, which he then gave to Alexandra to read. The passages reflected the depths of Alexis's feelings. In June 1869, he noted that when reading a letter from her, his feelings

> *spoke so strongly that I feared I would lose my mind. I wrote You the whole truth, because I do not know how to write banal phrases. I wrote down all my innermost thoughts, which I never thought I would tell anyone. I found it painful and terrible to think that I should go away from You without knowing whether I will see You again. I repeat that you are my <u>pride</u> and <u>sacred thing</u>.*[13]

Throughout the entire river cruise, Alexis remembered their walks together in Pavlovsk and their final meetings, words and promises. He complained of loneliness without his "angel." *"I could not sleep for a long time, I wanted to see You and to forget the whole world with You. I want only You, You alone and they have taken You away from me, I curse all people and everyone in this world."*[14] All this may have been the reason why Alexander II decided to send his increasingly desperate son on an official visit to the United States in 1871 – a trip unexpectedly extended into a round-the-world voyage lasting almost two years. In 1880, the Tsar received an official invitation from President Ulysses S. Grant to send a member of his family on a state visit, in gratitude for Russian support for the Union cause in the American Civil War. No better choice than Alexis, serving as a lieutenant on board the *Svetlana*, far away from his lover Alexandra.

On the eve of his departure on August 20, 1871, the Emperor and all the available grand dukes in St Petersburg came to bid Alexis farewell. Vice Admiral Possiet commanded the squadron and the flagship was the frigate *Svetlana*. The following day, under a clear sky with a low wind, they lifted anchor and left St Petersburg for two years. Grand Duke Alexis, commander of the foremast and lieutenant of the Imperial Russian navy, took the first watch on the *Svetlana*, from six o'clock to midnight. Possiet noted in his diary: *"Grand Duke Alexis appeared to be extremely sad on the first night. This soon passed, however, and by the time we arrived in Copenhagen, he had begun to return to his normal state, which I recently find to be far more serious than before."*[15] On August 26, they called in at Copenhagen, where Alexis performed his official and family duties by visiting Crown Prince Federik and his wife Louisa. The squadron left the Danish capital on September 1, 1871.

At the port of Marseilles, they say, inconsolable Alexis and a company of Russian sailors went on a wild spree in a merry dames' house. The local police instituted proceedings against Alexis, but another naval officer Eugene Alexeiev by name went in his place, paid the fine and easily passed as His Imperial Highness. Alexeiev was later richly rewarded with a series of rapid promotions. Vice Admiral Possiet's travel log describes the large quantities of strong Madeira wine purchased by Alexis when they called in at the Portuguese island on September 24. They were not slow to begin its consumption and Alexis *"could not always be called entirely sober."*

From every port, Alexis wrote emotional bitter letters home to his mother. This convinced the Tsar that the voyage should be extended. On 31 August, Alexis sent an impassioned plea from Copenhagen:

I do not feel that I belong to myself or can abandon them [Zhukovsky and the expected child]. *There is a feeling in this world, which nothing can overcome. This feeling is love....For God's sake, Mother, do not destroy me, do not sacrifice your son. Forgive me, love me, do not cast me into an abyss from which there is no way out.*

On September 12, Alexis wrote again to his mother:

The more I pray, the more I feel that God will only forgive me when I fulfill my duty to Him with my conscience. Otherwise, He will not forgive me. You know that. This is not the voice of youth or passion, but a clear, honest and implacable feeling...I am too proud and honest to withstand this feeling. I do not want to be a shame and disgrace to my family...For God's sake, do not destroy me. Do not sacrifice me for the sake of some prejudices that will fall apart in a few years. You understand how it feels like to have a wife and child and to abandon them. To love this woman more than anything else in the world and to know that she is alone, forgotten, abandoned by everyone, suffering, about to give birth at any moment...while I remain a beast called a grand duke, who can and ought, by his position, to be a vile and nasty person, and no one dares say to his face. Offer me a ray of hope, I cannot live like this, I swear to you by God...Help me, give me back my honor and life, it is in your hands.[16]

Alexis also wrote to his lover Zhukovsky, who had been banished from Russia to give birth abroad. He asked dear Minny and his elder brother Sasha to offer her support: "*What a terrible feeling it is to be far away from her! Minny, you yourself have children, you must understand what it means to have a wife and child and to leave them. It is too awful!*"

Alexis's brothers tried to help him. They reported his sufferings to their august parents, who refused to change their mind or to legalize the relationship. Grand Duke Vladimir finally wrote to Alexandra Zhukovsky:

Dear Alexandra Vasilyevna! I have spoken at length with the Empress about everything that has happened. Neither she nor the Emperor agree to a marriage. That is their final decision, which neither time nor circumstances will change, believe me. Now, dear Alexandra Vasilyevna, please allow me, in view of our long friendship and your long-standing affection for me, to speak straight to your heart. Do you remember when I visited you after seeing off my brother? When we parted, I took both your hands and, looking straight into your eyes, asked you if you really loved my brother. You replied that you did. I believed you, how could I not believe you? You now know the situation he is in. You also know the firm will of my parents. If you really do love my brother, this makes me pray to you on my knees not to destroy him, but to give him up, voluntarily and unequivocally."[17] Alexandra heeded the request.

On November 14, 1871, Alexandra Zhukovsky gave birth to a son in Salzburg. The baby was christened Baron Alexis Seggiano. In March 1884, Alexander III gave the boy the official name and title of Count Alexis Alexeievich

Belevsky-Zhukovsky (after the estate of Belev, the favorite place of the poet Vassily Zhukovsky). On November 13/25, 1875, in Munich Alexandra married a guards officer from Saxony – Baron Christian Henri von Wöhrmann (1849-1932), thus becoming Baroness Alexandrine de Wöhrmann, née Zhukovsky, Seggiano. By this time, she already possessed a handsome dowry.

Previously unpublished archival documents show that Alexis did not abandon his wife and son. After her marriage, Alexandra Zhukovsky received a large check and a lifetime pension. Alexis was appointed by the Tsar the personal controller of her finances. The following order, marked *confidentielle*, appears in the correspondence of the Ministry of the Imperial Court: "*Award Baroness Alexandra Vassilyevna von Wöhrmann, née Zhukovsky, owing to the services of her late father, an annual lifetime pension of twenty-five thousand roubles, from one part of His Majesty's own capital, as of 13 November this year, to be paid in three installments, the first payment to be made on 13 March 1876.*" Alexandra received a handsome check for 27,083 francs, which she signed in her own hand: "*Receipt given that I have received, from the Ministry of the Imperial Court, via the Imperial Mission in Rome, a check for twenty-seven thousand and eighty-three francs (27,083). Rome, 16 (28) December 1875. Baroness Alexandrine de Wöhrmann, née Zhukovsky, Seggiano.*"[18] A telegraph from Rome to the Ministry of the Imperial Court in St Petersburg confirmed that the check had been delivered. The money was transferred to Alexis's bank account. Perhaps due to a foreboding that his own lifetime was coming to an end, the Emperor instructed Alexis to pay Alexandra the annual sum of twenty-five thousand roubles, in three installments, for the rest of her life.

Such a wrecked private life destroyed Alexis's hopes in justice and human dignity, and enforced his skepticism and disappointment in people. However, it didn't stop him from being sociable and good hearted. His Imperial Highness officially remained a bachelor (incidentally the only unmarried son of an Emperor in the House of Romanov). For the number of romances and love affairs both in Russia and abroad he was an undoubted champion. Yet, God never again blessed him with true and fulfilling love.

The Svetlana sailed west, and on November 19, five days after baby Alexis was born, they entered New York harbor. The American steamer *Mary Powell* sailed out to meet them.

The pilot who guided the *Svetlana* into the North River was disappointed to see an ordinary looking lieutenant standing watch and seeming "*no more royal than I am, and why all that mess about?*" The enthusiastic reception included appropriate speeches, a procession up Broadway with bands and national guardsmen, the bells of Trinity Church chiming "God save the Tsar" on the way to Clarendon Hotel. Cannons fired, New York yelled its head off. Possiet noted that all regiments ceremonially marched by Alexis, standing on the hotel balcony, and at night, a local money-bag sent musicians who serenaded for an hour under the balcony.

Alexis was a celebrity of some magnitude and was treated as such – feted and acclaimed – wherever he went. Each city tried to outdo the rest in giving him a lavish welcome, and he listened to flowery speeches made by public officials. In Boston, for example, he was treated to a "brief address" by James Russell Lowell that included quotations from Swift, Madame de Stael, d'Alembert, and

Cervantes. Alexis was greatly surprised that the youngest Democracy was so crazy about royalty and titles. Nonetheless, he enjoyed his visits to major cities including Washington, Philadelphia, Boston and Chicago, with invitations to grand receptions, universities, factories, shipyards, naval academies, and local landmarks.

Public curiosity was intense. The myth of Alexis the lady-killer spread around. Young women were most interested in His Imperial Highness. In addition to being young, aristocratic, and handsome (six feet two inches tall, 'light golden hair', 'very large hands' and 'immense' feet"), he was a romantic figure, *'sent from Russia to break up an affair with someone not acceptable at court."* All whetted feminine admiration. From New York to New Orleans, with interim stops in nearly twenty cities, he survived a whirlwind of galas, balls, dinners, operas, inspections of factories and shipyards, and official reception by President Grant and the Cabinet of the United States. He was the first Romanov to be ever received by an American President, and he remarked thereafter that the American males probably lacked good manners judging by President Ulysses S. Grant.

His Imperial Highness then embarked upon a grand tour of America and of Canada. He went to Boston, Toronto, Montreal, and Ottawa. He visited Niagara Falls, where the sight made *"his imperial blood curdle."* In Cleveland and Detroit he was literally besieged by admiring women. In Chicago he was taken to the stockyards, and gave the mayor $5000 for those persons still in need after a recent conflagration.

As a climax to the visit, the Americans had organized a buffalo hunt to meet the request of the august guest. Over 1300 people were involved, under the patronage of General Sheridan, Lieutenant Colonel George Custer, 'Buffalo' Bill Cody, soldiers, and a whole Dakota tribe. The party traveled to "Camp Alexis" on Red Willow Creek by army ambulance. Hospital tents had been set up, Alexis's tent was carpeted and furnished with his own bed since it was difficult to find one adequate to his large frame. Champagne was offered all around whenever he brought down a buffalo, and his high-ranking officers wore uniforms resplendent with gold and lace.

Alexis learned the techniques of shooting a moving buffalo. While in Colorado, he was once almost hit by an angry bull charging straight for Alexis' horse, but he kept his nerve, and shot cleanly. The companions were genuinely impressed. Alexis cabled his father that he killed three bison. The cablegram recalled the time two years before when the Tsar had watched Alexis kill his first bear. The first buffalo was clearly another such milestone. Next night in camp, the Indians performed their traditional war dance and hunting skills. Alexis generously presented gifts to everyone.

During Alexis's encounters with an enthusiastic democratic public, there were trying occasions when people insisted on telling him ambivalent jokes, but he never lost his royal self-control and perfect manners. Worst of all, they clapped his imperial back or pressed his ribs. His Imperial Highness always remained affable, although it was unimaginable that a commoner in his own country would have been able to approach him as Americans constantly did, let alone touch his august person.

At New Orleans Alexis and his entourage met the Russian fleet and sailed away. The expedition visited Havana, Brazil, went around the Cape of Good Hope, and entered the Chinese and Japanese seas. In Japan, the Grand Duke paid a visit to His Majesty the Mikado in his castle, the host took him around and arranged a falcon hunt for the guest. A day later, the Mikado reciprocated with a visit to the Russian ship, something unheard of before: His Imperial Majesty had never put his foot on deck of a European ship. Having visited China, Philippines, the bays and posts of the Seaside Russia's Province, Alexis returned overland to Tsarskoe Selo on July 16, 1873. However, the correspondence between Alexander II and Possiet proves that the Sovereign wanted to delay his son's return until 1874. During the round-the-world trip Alexis Alexandrovich was promoted to Captain First Class, and in 1874, he became Commander of the *Svetlana*.

Starting his seaman's career at ten, the Grand Duke spent 21 years on it, and for 1,772 long days remained sailing away from home. At the age of just over twenty, Alexis had already cruised a lot. He crossed the seas by sail ships, frigates, and corvettes. The second Russian voyage to the US in 1877, with His Imperial Highness in command of the *Svetlana*, was interrupted because the Russo-Turkish war broke out.

The tragic death of Alexander II was the cause of a drastic change in Alexis's career. In 1881, the new sovereign Alexander III dismissed the gifted and capable Grand Admiral Konstantin Nikolaevich and appointed his infinitely handsome, dedicated and hedonistic brother Alexis as both Head of the Navy and of the Naval Department. In 1888, he became full admiral. Time and history would regard this appointment as one of the worst mistakes Alexander III made in his thirteen-year reign.

Alexis had to settle down. He had waited for a residence of his own longer than many other grand dukes, and hardly started receiving "at home" before the age of forty. His palace was under construction in 1884-85, when His Imperial Highness had already been promoted to the top office and the top rank in the Russian Navy. The site for his palace was chosen far from the centre, in the traditional marine part of St. Petersburg, downstream the river Moika. In the best tradition of Peter the Great's era, it became a spacious estate, an entire palace-and-garden unit, probably the last newly built estate in the capital. The customer wished to live in a mansion resembling an old romantic castle as if brought over from medieval France, but with all possible comfort of the late-19th century. Work was entrusted to the Academician of architecture Maximilian E. Mesmakher. The interiors were perfectly consistent with the owner's way of life, who followed his motto *"to experience everything in life"* with enviable inexorability.

As Grand Admiral (1883) in the time of Alexander III, Alexis contrasted drastically to his distinguished predecessor, his uncle and godfather Konstantin Nikolaevich. Alexis was no longer attracted by the sea and preferred terra firma. His life mainly consisted of gourmet meals and beautiful women. Moreover, in 1897, the Russian Grand Admiral *"bought himself a house in Paris and stays there, rather than at a hotel, every time he travels. One cannot but be amazed by such expenditure…"*[19] Alexis's years in office, which he reluctantly took in his stride, were an undisputable disaster. He never motivated improvements and resisted reasonable reforms. His knowledge of nautical affairs was limited to the days of sail ships, and the golden days of his voyages aboard the *Svetlana*. The fighting qualities of the Russian Marine remained as they were, which was not due to, but rather despite the Grand Admiral's efforts. Grand Duke Kirill had to admit that *"in the late nineties, our fleet was in poor condition, most units being out of date and of no practical use whatever..."*[20] The Naval Minister Ivan Shestakov, an honorable and uncompromising personality and administrator, referred to his chief as a vagabond in his diary and described the latter's "activities" so unfavorably that the diary was banned from publication. Shestakov's entries in his diaries (1882-88) testify a grave irresponsibility on the part of the Grand Duke and many high officials. *"The Grand Duke seems indifferent not only toward the Navy, but also to all matters, and it is not his concern whether Russia is coping"* (1882); *"Not a bit of support from the Grand Duke. Does not think of necessities. Most difficult to make him decide"* (1883); *"Received by the Grand Duke. He drives me mad with his laziness and indifference. He reminds that he was a responsible seaman officer, and is laughing lightly"* (1884); *"...hard to cope with Grand Duke's partiality and memories of his youth, although his life was much tougher than that of his brothers."*(1887)[21]

Corruption utterly demoralized the Naval department, once considered the best competent and efficient under Konstantin Nikolaevich. Alexis was accused of embezzlement; a sad joke has circulated about the women of Paris costing Russia at least a battleship a year. *"The pockets of honorable Alexis,"* a contemporary wrote, *have room enough for a few battleships and several Red Cross millions. He was smart enough to present his mistress, a ballerina, with a wonderful red cross of rubies; which she wore on the exact same day as when the deficit of two millions was announced."*

In Nicholas II's reign, attempts were made to replace Alexis and his deputy Nicholas Chikhachev who practically controlled the department. The intrigue against them was inspired by Alexis' cousin, Grand Duke Alexander Mikhailovich, but the powerful protection of the Dowager Empress reliably defended that partisan of *"slow ships and fast women."*

In 1881, Grand Duke Alexis was also appointed the member of the State Council. His diligence in this new office was caustically described by A. Polovtsov: *"Alexis Alexandrovich can think only about how, without infringement of decency, he could escape to Zina's bed. His face is expressing nothing but extreme boredom."* According to Serge Witte, he had no personal ideas of the state affairs, nor could he entertain a serious thought.[22] However, Alexander III overlooked his favorite brother's laziness and inactivity demanding solely that he would never interfere with politics. As a bachelor, His Imperial Highness was usually under an influence of a woman that he had an affair with. He always remained a striking personality, well-groomed, and full of irresistible charm. Queen Marie of Romania mentioned in her Memoirs her first meeting with Uncle Alexis on the Peterhof lawn: as a little girl, she was visiting her Russian relations when *"that giant, blue eyed Lohengrin, had paid me my first compliment."* The memory of his greeting warmed her like sunshine: *"Ah! Here's the pretty one!,"* he exclaimed. That night, she peered into a mirror at her face, realizing that she was pretty and could charm men. She was five then.

Along with his brothers Vladimir and Serge, he used to pound his fists and bellow at his nephew Nicholas II for whatever he wanted. The young Tsar was much intimidated by his uncles and tried to meet their requests. Alexis demanded benefits for his lover Eliza Baletta. She was a mediocrity, a negligible actress who wanted the richest contracts and best roles. Teliakovsky, the Director of the Imperial theatres, used to refer to her as *"a worthless wench that ruins the repertoire"*[23]

Grand Duke Kirill Alexandrovich wrote,

> *How well I remember Uncle Alexis with his handsome figure accoutered in a strange garb of his own choosing and invention, which gave him the appearance of a real showman. It was a kind of red-striped flannel suit – a Mephistophelian affair – of which he, alone, among all men on earth, was a proud possessor. He was pleased with it and liked to be seen about in this fantastic get-up. 'I am better dressed than any of you fellows', he would say to us.*[24]

It is easy to imagine the hunt for Grand Duke Alexis. *"Night after night, he is visited by ladies from the high society, whoever he would honor with an invitation,"* wrote a contemporary. Drinking at the gypsies' together with his brother Vladimir, fancy 'stag parties" with guests finally plastered in the Lower Dining-room of his palace, parties and routs filled his pastime in Russia. However, the life in Europe offered more pleasure, far from the notoriously investigative domestic media, where he showed himself to the best advantage. Five-star hotels like the "Ritz", or "Continental", where his retinue occupied whole floors, chic restaurants with everybody standing at attention, with crowds of waiters and no other public admitted. The police blocked streets when the Russian grand duke was to pass. Casinos were locked, when he appeared there with a charming woman beside him and his entourage, the stakes skyrocketed to half-million. That easy kind of existence suited him. Brothers Alexis and Vladimir made conversational the expression "the grand duke style." The European elders kept telling legends about them still in the 1930s.

Both Paris and St Petersburg knew about Alexis's passionate love toward his relative, Countess Zinaida de Beauharnais, Duchess of Leuchtenberg. They gossiped about *menage royal a trois*, the cuckold of a husband Eugene of Leuchtenberg, Nicholas I's grandson and Napoleon's great-grandson.[25] Duke Eugene was repeatedly beaten by the giant Alexis on the threshold of his own bedroom in his house at 44, English Embankment, in vain trying to complain to Alexander III about his promiscuous august brother. The Tsar quietly replied that if the Duke of Leuchtenberg was incapable of managing his life himself he could not expect others to assist him to do so. To avoid scandals, Eugene preferred silently go to sleep on a sofa in his study. Zinaida Dimitrievna rode in an open carriage together with Alexis, showed around the diamonds given to her by her lover. Alexis paid Zina's bills and those of her drunkard husband in Europe and Russia. The Countess presided during parties at the Alexeievsky Palace, made lists of invitations, and *"it was just for her sake that the Grand Duke opened the doors of his palace to St Petersburg beau-monde,"* thought A.A.Mossolov. The infernal beautiful Zina reigned there, ignoring envy and gossip with truly royal dignity. According to Alexander Mikhailovich, the Grand Admiral was ready to sacrifice the entire Russian Navy for marvelous Zina, and kept showering her with unimaginable gifts. Zinaida was a favorite company also for the future Emperor

Nicholas II, who had recorded in his diary on January 4, 1892, while he still remained a grand duke: *"At 6 3/4 went to the dress rehearsal of Massena's opera Esclarmonda. Was over at 11 1/2, then at Uncle Alexis' for a supper. Zina amused us with singing."* Her unexpected death in 1899 when she was only 44 years old became a heavy blow for Alexis.

Grand Duke Alexis could account for two wars. In 1877-78, as a Rear Admiral in His Majesty's entourage, as Head of the Guard Marine, he was in command of the Danube flotilla: they built bridges, ferries, and protected them. That first war brought Alexis Alexandrovich the Order of St George, 4th Class. The second war, 1904-05, against Japan was shamefully lost both by the Grand Duke and Russia, for which his personal responsibility cannot be denied. He presided over all conferences at the Naval Department in 1904. Serge Witte related: *"The Grand Duke had shown an extreme weakness in the matter of preventing that war, though he realized that war would bring more harm than advantages."* He disapproved the idea that Admiral Rozhestvensky's squadron be dispatched from the Baltic Sea, around Africa, to a real disaster – but abstained from decision. In the Japanese Sea, at Port Arthur and in the Tsushima Straights, the Russian Navy was heavily defeated. Alexis received a derogatory nickname "Tsushimsky." A populous legend had it, that the enraged Emperor Nicholas II, had told him: *"You'd better, Uncle, steal twice more, but make the armor twice stronger."* This story was concocted by those crowds who came to smash windows in the Alexeievsky Palace in the days of national disaster in December, 1904. St Petersburg was enraged at Grand Duke Alexis for his ineptitude resulting in the sorrowful condition of the Navy; there started a mass movement demanding his resignation. Nicholas II was strongly against Alexis's wish to go to Moscow in order to attend the funeral of his brother Serge. Security chiefs reported that *"terrorists were hunting after Alexis as a wild beast."* Alexis sobbed like a child: *"What a disgrace!,"* but obeyed, and lost the chance to meet his illegitimate son. After the Tsushima defeat, Alexis and the Naval Minister Avelan requested resignation. Indeed, still in the rank of the General-Admiral and Member of the State Council, Grand Duke Alexis resigned. It is probable that he suffered and felt guilty. However, that did not interfere with his hurrying to Paris to follow his French mistress Eliza Baletta.

Such was Grand Duke Alexis Alexandrovich, reportedly a nice noble fellow never doing any harm, incapable of intrigue or murky deeds. The Marshal of St Petersburg Nobility, Count A.A.Bobrinsky, related about him as following: *"A good fellow, but all with a tint of Peter the Great at the court of Louis XV. Rough laughter, boisterous jokes..."* The Grand Duke's death of pneumonia in Paris on November 1, 1908, caused sorrow not only to his relatives, but also to those who had known him intimately. Nicholas II noted in his diary: *"My favorite uncle is dead, a noble, honorable, courageous sole! May the kingdom of Heaven be his!"*[26] Another contemporary A. Bogdanovich noted in her diary:

> *Alexis Alexandrovich died in Paris. As General-Admiral he was no good, all disturbances in the Naval Departments began in his day. Under him embezzlement flourished. He burned his life in revelry, the autopsy revealed that his liver began to deteriorate when he was still alive, his heart doubled in size, and his lungs looked like a sieve.*[27]

His Imperial Highness Grand Duke Alexis Alexandrovich was buried in the Peter and Paul Fortress, at the grand ducal mausoleum. He had left no will. His heirs were appointed by a special imperial decree of January 10, 1909.

The property was shared by his brothers Vladimir and Paul, and his nephew Michael Alexandrovich. The inventory of the building and its interiors was done by architect P. Siuzor. The valuables to be shared included, as listed in dozens of pages, not only thousands of bottles of wines vodka, liquors from various countries, but hundreds of silver bowls, flasks, vessels, trays, sparkling wine buckets. The lists mentioned hundreds of paintings, infinite number of Oriental and European porcelain, silverware, more than ten silver dinner and dessert table sets, and furniture. A secrete paper in the Court Interior Department revealed Alexis's wish to pay E. Baletta a pension, and to grant pensions to all servants that he had once paid them.

Later, a co-heiress Grand Duchess Maria Pavlovna, widow of Vladimir Alexandrovich, did the evaluation of the property and land at two million roubles. On her order, in 1909, over 500 paintings and objects of decorative art were auctioned thrice. A lot was purchased by A.K. Faberge & Co. Private individuals gradually bought the land. Finally, in 1911, the German embassy leased the palace and garden for 18 months. During the First World War, a gray-haired valet who had served Alexis for thirty-five years whined when showing tourists around the Grand Duke's bedroom: *"Alas, a German slept in my master's bed."* Nicholas II did not allow to sell the palace in parts. In 1914, a certain A.K.Reshko from Simferopol bought the palace, outbuildings, and the garden at 2.5 million roubles.

Between 1917 and 1941, the palace was occupied by various offices, and its beauty could not save it from being looted and desecrated. Particular damages occurred in the 1960-90s. At present, this formerly dilapidated palace has been restored to some of its former glory.

In regard of Grand Duke Alexis's issue, in 1896, at the age of twenty-five, Baron Alexis de Seggiano came into his capital of 100,000 roubles and the accumulated interest. Before then, he had lived in Wiesbaden, Germany, where he was taught by a Russian Orthodox priest, Alexander Smirnopulo. The boy's uncle Pavel Zhukovsky also contributed to his education. His mother Alexandra lived in Germany, until she died in Wiesbaden on August 26, 1899. Alexis Belevsky attended military academy in Russia, and served as an aide-de-camp to his uncle, Grand Duke Serge. In 1894, he married Princess Maria Petrovna Trubetskoi (1872--1954), the daughter of Prince Peter Trubetskoi and Princess Elisabeth Belosselsky-Belozersky. Maria was a lady-in-waiting to Grand Duke Serge's wife Grand Duchess Elisabeth (Ella). The couple had three daughters and one son – Elisabeth (Ella), Alexandra (Sandra), Maria (Marie) and Serge. Tsarina Alexandra Feodorovna was godmother to Ella (1896-1975), while the Dowager Empress Marie (Dagmar) and Grand Duchess Elisabeth were godmothers to Sandra (1899-1994) and Maria (1901-1996). The godfather of Serge (1904-1953) was his uncle, Grand Duke Serge, who attended the christening shortly before he was murdered in Moscow in 1905.

After the death of Grand Duke Alexis in 1908, the Belevskys continued to keep a stable financial position. In 1910, six members of the Romanov family – Grand Duchess Maria Pavlovna (Miechen), her three sons (Kirill, Boris and

Andrei), Grand Duke Paul and Grand Duke Michael – became the legatees and trustees of the late Grand Duke Alexis. They awarded a sum of 1,008,125 roubles to Count Belevsky and his family, who renounced all claims of inheritance.

After the 1917 revolution, Maria (née Trubetskoi) fled from Russia with her children. They settled near Baden-Baden, where the Trubetskoi family had a villa called Zelech. The children grew up in Baden, where there was a large colony of Russian émigrés.

Alexis was unable to escape from Russia with his family. After qualifying as a biologist, he disappeared in the purges in 1932 or 1933. Staffan Skott claims that he was killed in Tbilisi. His only son Serge married Nina Botkina and died in Los Angeles in 1953. Their daughter now lives in France.

The three girls all married Russian émigrés. A few descendants of Grand Duke Alexis now live in New York and France. A direct descendant of Tsar Alexander II, Alexis Teissier from New York City holds the title of Count Belevsky-Zhukovsky. His mother, Maria Gika Perevoshchikov, is Grand Admiral's Alexis great-granddaughter.

GRAND DUKE SERGE ALEXANDROVICH
(1857-1905)

By Ilana Miller

As a child, the young Princess Marie of Edinburgh adored her Uncle Serge, Grand Duke Serge Alexandrovich, a younger brother of her mother, Grand Duchess Maria Alexandrovna. She sensed what so many others did - that he, the fifth son of Tsar Alexander II and the Empress Marie Alexandrovna, deeply loved children. She grasped, instinctively, that though severe when the occasion demanded, he would also come *"to see us in our bath...or to tuck us up in our beds and to kiss us good night."*[1] The future Queen of Romania, who chronicled her life so beautifully, wrote nostalgically about a figure whom the world hardly saw as sympathetic. She, who was a well-known worshiper of beauty, thought him handsome, tall and upright with a magnificent figure. She did reluctantly concede that *"no doubt there was in his face something of the fanatic that he was at heart."*[2] Nevertheless, she finished her portrait of the Grand Duke stating *"[f]ew perhaps cherish his memory, but I do."*[3]

This profile of a tender, yet sternly solicitous uncle, who was also such a puzzling and enigmatic figure, confounds facile understanding. Grand Duke Serge Alexandrovich was a contradictory character, at once cruel and kind, tender and harsh. History portrays him as a brutal and unpopular figure full of unattractive vices and oddities. Despite the general agreement that he might well have been a homosexual, there were also suggestions that he had been sexually coercive, or conversely, sexually indifferent toward his wife. Yet, on the other side of the broad ledger, he was a deeply religious man who loved children, was a good friend, and was, as Governor-General of the ancient capital of Moscow, in a position of great responsibility.[4] His nephew, Grand Duke Kirill Vladimirovich said that he had *"the loftiest principles coupled with a character of the rarest nobility. Such he will always remain in my memory."* Perhaps in this he is the most Russian of the Grand Dukes, for Churchill, himself, described the Motherland as *"a riddle wrapped in a mystery inside an enigma."*[5]

Grand Duke Serge was born May 11, 1857, at Tsarskoe Selo. Christened in the palace chapel, he grew up with his closest sibling, his younger brother Grand Duke Paul and with his cousins, Dimitri and Konstantin Konstantinovich. While still a child himself, he loved children and was a favorite with younger children.[6] He was devoted to his mother and in the company of Paul and his older sister, Marie, he traveled with her as she made her rounds of visits on the Continent. Oftentimes, the Empress Maria Alexandrovna was looking for pleasant weather and agreeable places that would improve her declining health. At other times it was just to get away from her untenable marriage.

Serge's parents were more or less estranged as the little boy grew up, since the Tsar Alexander II had eventually installed his mistress and her small children on the floors above the family rooms. Perhaps the young boy was not mature enough to understand the situation. Nevertheless, he must have sensed his mother's anguish at so blatant a betrayal. To distance herself from this unpleasantness, the Tsarina, accompanied by her sons and daughter, traveled frequently to the Heiligenberg, near Darmstadt in Hesse. Here, at this relatively simple palace, the home of her brother Prince Alexander of Hesse and By Rhine, and his morganatic wife, Princess Julia of Battenberg, the unhappy Empress was able to escape her cruel situation. At the Heiligenberg, Marie had no need to concern herself with the nearly unimaginable grandeur of the Russian Imperial Court since life at the palace was very much a middle-class existence.

These annual visits which started in 1863, gave the three youngest Imperial children, Marie, Serge and Paul, an opportunity to play with and know their Hessian and Battenberg cousins. The Tsarina's older children, Nicholas, Alexander, Vladimir, and Alexis, were uninterested in the youngest children of the family. Marie Alexandrovna, however, the only daughter, developed a close friendship with Princess Marie of Battenberg. Nevertheless, unlike his older brothers, Serge was very patient and kind to his younger relatives. Princess Alice of Hesse and By Rhine told her mother, Queen Victoria, with evident amusement, that seven year old Serge had quite a passion for her eldest daughter, Victoria, who was only seven months old at the time.[7]

While the children hiked in the hills, played in the faux-ruins of a monastery, walked up and down precarious donkey trails and climbed trees, Serge was the one who would pick up a smaller child when he or she stumbled. It was particularly noticed that he frequently held out his hand to Princess Elisabeth, Victoria's little sister, known to her family as Ella. *'serge had often left his games with the other boys, to lead* [Ella] *gently by the hand, guiding her uncertain footsteps down the steep garden paths.'*[8]

It seems logical that Serge felt more comfortable with the younger children since he was shy, self-conscious, somewhat inarticulate and nervous. Never easy-going and garrulous as his older brothers, he was easily embarrassed. At such times *"he drew himself up very straight and eyes grew hard. [I]t often gave people the wrong impression of him, taking him for arrogant and cold."*[9] As he grew; he was as quiet as his brothers were boisterous, and most certainly sensitive and insecure. The insecurity could be explained by events in his early life. The death of his eldest brother, Nicholas, when he was but eight years old, was a tragedy that affected him deeply. In addition, the illness and withdrawal of his mother had its obvious impact. Perhaps the most profound and frightening event in his young life was the first attempt on his father's life when he was only nine years old. Undoubtedly, this contributed to his reactionary character as an adult.

Serge was educated and groomed for a military career. Nevertheless, he enjoyed the humanities: history, painting, art, and especially archeology, as well as music and acting. He was well read, and with his brother Paul he enjoyed meeting many great figures of Russian literature including Dostoevsky.[10] His detractors, including the Ambassador from France, Maurice Paléologue, have said that he was ill-educated, however, this does not coincide with the curriculum that his tutor Admiral Arseniev created for both Paul and Serge. Certainly, the fact that he learned Italian to read Dante shows some love of learning.[11] His brother-in-law, Grand Duke Ernst Ludwig of Hesse and By Rhine, also contradicted this statement saying that he was *"very well read and a man of high culture."*[12] Both Ernst Ludwig and his sister, Victoria, Princess Louis Battenberg, who thought him very refined, commented that Serge often recommended books to them.

A love of Russian Orthodoxy emerged in his early life. He *'strictly observed all the canons and rites of the Church; he prayed often, respected fast days and frequently attended church services."*[13] He would later travel to Palestine in order to found the Russian Society of Palestine. This was a group devoted to the conservation of Orthodox shrines with Serge as its president. The society was also responsible for building schools in the Levantine area which would teach Russian Orthodoxy.

In 1877, during the Russo-Turkish war, Serge, and his older brothers, Alexander and Vladimir, accompanied their father to the front. The young man, who had entered the military two years before, was awarded the Order of St George for bravery in the field. In February 1880, yet another failed attempt was made on the life of Alexander II. However, on March 13, 1881, the nihilists finally succeeded in murdering the great Tsar Liberator. This tragedy along with the death of his beloved mother in June of 1880, less than a year before, was devastatingly traumatic to the young Grand Duke. To add further anguish to his young life, his father, only a little over a month after the death of his mother, married the mistress whom he had installed on the floor above the Imperial apartments. Tsar Alexander II married Catherine Dolgorouky, who was later created Princess Yourievsky. This pleased no one in the Imperial family, and was felt to be another betrayal by the young man. The grief and anger that Serge experienced with these events was probably mitigated somewhat by his mother's bequest – the lovely summer home of Illinskoe.

Illinskoe would always be a refuge, a place to which Serge could retreat. Here he could live the simple country life that he loved. The two story house, situated by the Moskva River, was just sixty kilometers outside of Moscow. A wooded country estate, it was surrounded by a park, cottages, farm and villages. The entrance of the large oaken structure was a pillared portico, with the approaching drive bordered by two rows of lime trees. The rear of the building faced the river with a broad terrace where they might eat breakfast, or have tea. There they could always enjoy boating, fishing and bathing.

Unlike his ursine older brothers, Serge grew tall and slim. By his mid twenties, he had a close-clipped beard and wore his hair very short. In the many penned descriptions of the young man can be seen the reflections of the authors' opinions of their subject. Queen Marie thought him handsome, with a mouth that was often closed in a thin, cruel line. *"His eyes were steely grey and his pupils could narrow like those of a cat...and then there was something almost menacing about him."*[14] His brother-in-law, Grand Duke Ernst Ludwig described him as *"tall and very blond, with a handsome face and nice light green eyes."* The Grand Duchess George Mikhailovich described him as *"tall, fair and good-looking, but inclined to be a bit unbending; this gave the impression that he was grand and stuck-up."*[15] The Baroness von Buxhoeveden wrote, similarly, that Serge was *"a real seigneur, of high culture, artistic temperament and intellectual pursuits...a certain shyness made him seem outwardly stiff and unresponsive.*"[16] Curiously, most of the positive writing about Serge, from relatives and friends, had qualifiers which somehow nullified the positive descriptions. Paléologue, the French Ambassador, needed no such rationalizations, and described him as having *"a good figure but a disagreeable face, distinguished by grayish-white eyebrows and a hard look. He continued that Serge was quarrelsome, despotic, and unintelligent."*[17]

After the harrowing deaths of his parents, Serge began, in earnest, his courtship of Princess Elisabeth of Hesse and By Rhine. They had been playfellows during those long ago childhood times when Serge and his family visited the Heiligenberg, and now their regard for one another deepened. Ella was pressured against the match. Not, however, because her Grandmother, Queen Victoria, thought Serge, himself, an unworthy suitor. The Queen had a deeply held dislike for Russia, its society and the depraved debauchery of the Grand Dukes, which as far as she was concerned, was common knowledge. Though, she pointed out, Serge and Paul were the exceptions, the Queen was sure that *"the former is not improved of late."*[18]

There were constant discussions of the match between Queen Victoria and her granddaughter, Ella's older sister, Victoria. Most of the letters from the Queen lamented the idea, while Princess Victoria tried her best to placate her grandmother about what seemed inevitable. The best defense being an offense, the Queen tried to throw other worthy and eligible men in her granddaughter's path. In addition to Crown Prince Wilhelm of Prussia, who had early on, tried his suit with Ella, and was positively rebuffed, there were several others. One such fellow was Prince Friedrich of Baden, known as Fritz in the family. Ella, however, would have none of him. *"Oh! dear! How very unfortunate it is of Ella to refuse good Fritz of Baden so good & steady, with such a safe, happy position, & <u>for a Russian</u>. I do deeply regret it."*[19] Beside all the other negatives, she was convinced that the climate of Russia had killed nearly all the German princesses who went to live there.

Eventually Ella made a final decision to accept Serge. Although the Queen was most unhappy about it, Ella's Grand Ducal family was pleased. His future brother-in-law, Prince Ernst Ludwig, was happy to welcome him into the family and joined a letter writing campaign, along with another sister, Irene, and Ella, herself, to tell the Queen what a nice and kind man Serge was. *"I'm so glad you will see Serge"* Ella wrote, *"and hope he will make a favorable impression on you. All who know him like him and say he has such a true and noble character."*[20] Their father confirmed the issue when in September 1883, the Grand Duke Ludwig wrote to Serge's brother, Tsar Alexander III: *"I did not hesitate to consent because I have known Sergei since he was a child. I see his nice, pleasant manners and I am sure he will make my daughter happy."*[21]

By November, the engagement was officially announced, and the pundits were now free to offer their various opinions. Ella, wrote Sir Henry Ponsonby, the Private Secretary to Queen Victoria, *"has got her fine bold Russian. He isn't handsome, but she likes him and prefers him to the gentle but rather dull Baden prince who was told off for her."*[22] Queen Victoria's daughter the Crown Princess of Prussia, was on the side of those who saw something they liked in Serge. She told her mother *"there is something quiet and gentle, in fact rather melancholy about him, and his appearance and manners have something high bred and distingué which one misses in*

Tsar Peter III
(né Duke Karl Peter of Holstein-Gottorp).

Empress Catherine II, The Great
(née Anhalt-Zerbst).

Tsar Paul I.

Empress Maria Feodorovna
(née Sophie Dorothea of Württemberg).

Tsar Alexander I.

Grand Duke Konstantin Pavlovich.

Tsar Nicholas I.

Grand Duke Michael Pavlovich.

Tsar Alexander II.

Tsar Alexander II and Empress Maria Alexandrovna.

Left to right: Grand Duchess Maria Alexandrovna, Tsar Alexander II holding Grand Duke Serge Alexandrovich, Grand Duke Vladimir Alexandrovich, Grand Duke Alexander Alexandrovich, Grand Duke Alexis Alexandrovich and Tsarevich Nicholas Alexandrovich.

Empress Marie Alexandrovna with her two youngest sons, Grand Dukes Serge and Paul Alexandrovich.

Empress Maria Alexandrovna
(née Marie of Hesse and By Rhine).

Empress Maria Alexandrovna with two of her children, Maria Alexandrovna and Paul Alexandrovich.

Empress Maria Alexandrovna holding her grandson Prince Alfred of Edinburgh (c. 1875).

Grand Duke Konstantin Nikolaevich, a talented musician, enjoyed playing the cello.

Grand Duke Konstantin Nikolaevich with his eldest son Grand Duke Nicholas Konstantinovich.

Grand Duke Konstantin Nikolaevich with five of his children. In front: Grand Dukes Dimitri, Konstantin and Viatcheslav Konstantinovich. Middle row: Grand Duke Nicholas Konstantinovich and Grand Duchess Olga Konstantinovna. At back, their father, Grand Duke Konstantin Nikolaevich (c. 1865).

Grand Duchess Alexandra Iosifovna with her eldest children, Grand Duke Nicholas Konstantinovich and Grand Duchess Olga Konstantinovna.

Grand Duchess Alexandra Iosifovna in the early 1860s.

Grand Duchess Alexandra Iosifovna.

Grand Duke Nicholas Nikolaevich Sr.

Grand Duchess Alexandra Petrovna
(née Alexandra of Oldenburg).

Grand Duke Nicholas Nikolaevich Sr.

Grand Duke Michael Nikolaevich.

Grand Duchess Olga Feodorovna, wife of Grand Duke Michael Nikolaevich. Olga Feodorovna was born Princess Cecilie of Baden.

Four generations: Grand Duke Michael Mikhailovich, Grand Duchess Anastasia of Mecklenburg-Schwerin, Princess Alexandrine and Prince Frederik of Denmark.

Grand Duke Michael Nikolaevich.

Tsarevich Nicholas Alexandrovich.

Tsarevich Nicholas Alexandrovich (c. 1861).

*Tsarevich Nicholas Alexandrovich with his sister
Grand Duchess Maria Alexandrovna (c. 1864).*

Tsarevich Nicholas Alexandrovich and his fiancée
Princess Dagmar of Denmark.

The Russian Orthodox Chapel built on the spot where
Tsarevich Nicholas Alexandrovich died.

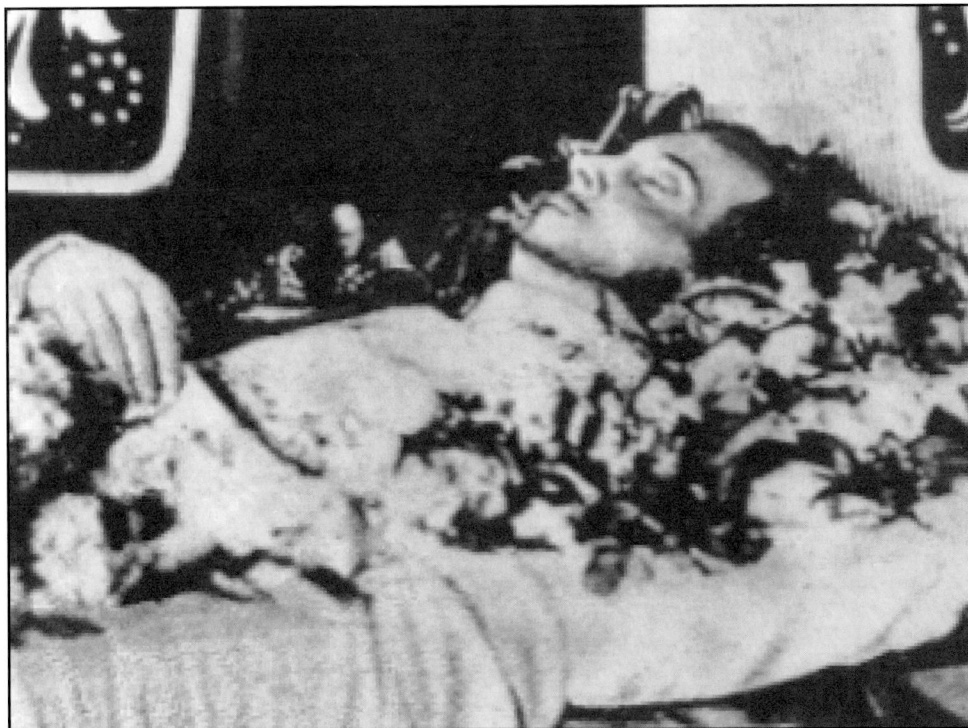
Deathbed of Tsarevich Nicholas Alexandrovich of Russia, Villa Bermond, Cannes – April 25, 1865.

Tsarevich Alexander Alexandrovich and his brother Grand Duke Vladimir Alexandrovich.

Tsarevich Alexander Alexandrovich in the 1870s.

A composite image showing Tsar Alexander III and Empress Maria Alexandrovna with Tsarevich Alexander Alexandrovich and Tsarevna Maria Feodorovna.

Tsar Alexander III and Empress Maria Feodorovna.

The Imperial Family at Krasnoe Selo, 1892. Seated, left to right: Grand Duchess Xenia Alexandrovna, Grand Duchess Marie Pavlovna, Grand Duchess Helen Vladimirovna, Grand Duchess Alexandra Iosifovna, Empress Marie Feodorovna, Tsar Alexander III, Grand Duke Michael Mikhailovich, Grand Duke Paul Alexandrovich. Row behind: Dukes Karl-Michael and Georg of Mecklenburg-Strelitz, Grand Duke Konstantin Konstantinovich, Queen Olga of Greece, Tsarevich Nicholas Alexandrovich, Grand Duke Serge Mikhailovich (behind Nicholas Alexandrovich), Grand Duke Vladimir Alexandrovich, Grand Duke Nicholas Nikolaevich, the Younger (behind Vladimir Alexandrovich), Duke Alexander Petrovich of Oldenburg, Grand Duke Dimitri Konstantinovich, Duke Peter Alexandrovich of Oldenburg and Duke George of Leuchtenberg. Seated at front: Grand Duke Alexis Mikhailovich, Grand Duke Michael Alexandrovich, Grand Duke Andrei Vladimirovich and Grand Duke Boris Vladimirovich.

*Empress Maria Feodorovna
(née Dagmar of Denmark).*

Tsarevna Maria Feodorovna with her two eldest sons,
Grand Dukes Nicholas and George Alexandrovich.

Grand Dukes Nicholas and George Alexandrovich
(c. 1876).

Empress Maria Feodorovna and her sister
Alexandra, Princess of Wales.

The Imperial Family at Gatchina. Left to right: Tsar Alexander III, Tsarevich Nicholas, Empress Maria Feodorovna, Grand Duke Michael, Grand Duke George and Grand Duchess Xenia.

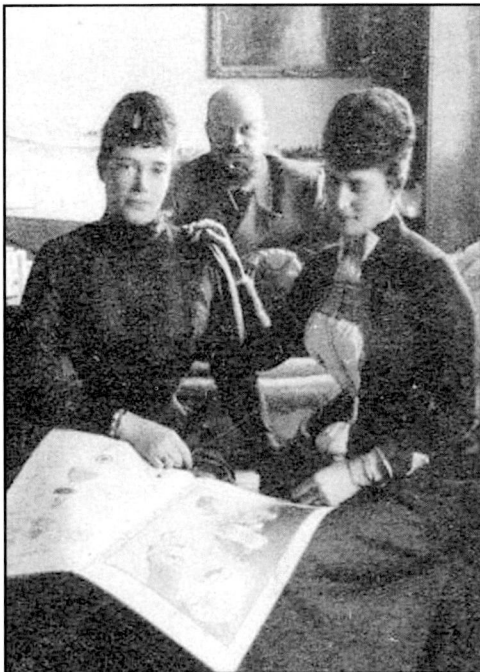

Tsar Alexander III and Empress Maria Feodorovna visiting Denmark. With them is her sister Alexandra, Princess of Wales.

The Imperial Family at Gatchina. Left to right: Tsarevich Nicholas Alexandrovich, Grand Duchess Xenia Alexandrovna, Empress Maria Feodorovna, Tsar Alexander III, Grand Duke George Alexandrovich. Grand Duke Michael Alexandrovich can be see at the bottom of the imagine.

A royal gathering in Denmark. In back, from left to right: The Duke of Chartres, Prince Henri d'Orléans, Prince Valdemar of Denmark, the Duchess of Chartres, Princess Marie of Denmark, Princess Louise of Wales, Prince Christian of Denmark, Princess Louise of Denmark, Crown Princess Victoria of Wales. Second row: Prince Carl of Denmark, Princess Louise of Denmark, Empress Marie Feodorovna, Grand Duchess Xenia Alexandrovna. In front: King Christian IX and Queen Louise of Denmark, The Princess of Wales holding the hand of Grand Duchess Olga Alexandrovna, Grand Duke George Alexandrovich, Tsarevich Nicholas Alexandrovich and Grand Duke Michael Alexandrovich.

Grand Duke Vladimir Alexandrovich.

Grand Duke Vladimir Alexandrovich and his wife Grand Duchess Maria Pavlovna.

The Vladimirovichi. Left to right: Grand Duke Boris Vladimirovich, Grand Duke Vladimir Alexandrovich, Grand Duchess Elena Vladimirovna, Grand Duchess Maria Pavlovna, Grand Dukes Kirill and Andrei Vladimirovich (c. 1884).

*The Vladimirovichi.
From top: Grand Duke
Kirill Vladimirovich, Grand
Duke Andrei Vladimirovic,
Grand Duchess Helen
Vladimirovna and Grand Duke
Boris Kirillovich, c. 1888.*

*From left: Prince Nicholas of Greece, Grand Duke Boris Vladimirovich, Grand Duchess Helen Vladimirovna,
Grand Duke Andrei Vladimirovich, Grand Duchess Maria Pavlovna and Grand Duke Kirill Vladimirovich.*

Grand Duke Vladimir Alexandrovich (c. 1908).

*Grand Dukes Alexander, Vladimir and
Alexis Alexandrovich.*

Grand Duke Alexis Alexandrovich.

Grand Duke Alexis Alexandrovich in Boyar costume.

Grand Dukes Paul and Serge Alexandrovich.

Grand Duke Serge Alexandrovich in the mid-1860s.

Grand Duke Serge Alexandrovich in 1883.

Grand Duke Serge Alexandrovich c. 1870.

Grand Duke Serge Alexandrovich and his wife,
Grand Duchess Elisabeth Feodorovna (Ella).

Grand Duchess Elisabeth Feodorovna and Grand Dukes
Serge and Paul Alexandrovich.

Grand Duchess Elisabeth Feodorovna reading at home.

Grand Duke Serge Alexandrovich and his wife, Ella.

Grand Duke Paul Alexandrovich.

Grand Duke Paul Alexandrovich and
Grand Duchess Alexandra Georgievna.

Grand Duchess Alexandra Georgievna
(née Alexandra of Greece and Denmark)

Grand Duke Paul Alexandrovich and his daughter Grand
Duchess Maria Pavlovna Jr.

Grand Duke Paul Alexandrovich visits with the children from his marriage to Princess Alexandra of Greece. Left to
right: Grand Duke Dimitri Pavlovich, Grand Duke Paul Alexandrovich and Grand Duchess Maria Pavlovna Jr.

Grand Duke Serge Alexandrovich in later years.

Grand Duke Paul Alexandrovich and his second wife Olga, Princess Paley.

Grand Duke Paul with his second family. Left to right: Princess Olga Paley, Princess Irene Pavlovna Paley, Prince Vladimir Pavlovich Paley, Princess Natalia Pavlovna Paley and Grand Duke Paul Alexandrovich.

Grand Duke Nicholas Alexandrovich c. 1871.

Tsarevich Nicholas Alexandrovich and his fiancée Princess Alix of Hesse and by Rhine, Coburg 1894.

Tsarevich Nicholas Alexandrovich in England, 1894.

Empress Alexandra Feodorovna and her two oldest daughters: Olga and Tatiana c. 1897.

Empress Alexandra Feodorovna
(née Alix of Hesse and By Rhine).

Empress Alexandra in a pensive mood at the
Alexander Palace, Tsarskoe Selo.

Tsar Nicholas II's Coronation – The Kremlin, Moscow, 1896.

A Romanov gathering. Standing, left to right: Grand Duke Paul Alexandrovich, Prince Nicholas of Greece, Grand Duke Michael Alexandrovich, Tsar Nicholas II, Grand Duke Vladimir Alexandrovich and Duke Peter Nikolaevich. On the window, same order: Grand Duchess Helen Vladimirovna, Grand Duke Michael Nikolaevich and Grand Duchess Marie Pavlovna the Elder.

Tsar Nicholas II relaxing in his study at the Alexander Palace, Tsarskoe Selo.

A Romanov Gathering.
From left: Grand Duke Paul Alexandrovich, Prince Adolph of Schaumburg-Lippe, Empress Alexandra Feodorovna, Grand Duke Serge Mikhailovich, Tsar Nicholas II, Duke George Maximilianovich of Leuchtenberg, Grand Duchess Marie Pavlovna the Elder, Duchess Eugenia Maximilianovna of Oldenburg, Grand Duchess Anastasia Nikolaevna of Leuchtenberg, Grand Duke Serge Alexandrovich and Grand Duke Vladimir Alexandrovich.

The Imperial Children. Left to right: Grand Duchess Anastasia Nikolaevna, Tsarevich Alexis Nikolaevich, Grand Duchess Olga Nikolaevna, Grand Duchess Maria Nikolaevna and Grand Duchess Tatiana Nikolaevna.

Tsarevich Alexis Nikolaevich and his Spaniel, Joy.

Tsarevich Alexis Nikolaevich in Cossack uniform.

Tsar Nicholas II visits troops in the company of his son and heir, Tsarevich Alexis Nikolaevich.

Grand Duke George Alexandrovich.

Tsarevich George Alexandrovich.

Left to right: Grand Duchess Olga Alexandrovna, Grand Duke Michael Alexandrovich, Grand Duke George Alexandrovich and the Dowager Empress Maria Feodorovna.

Seated from left: Prince Nicholas of Greece, Tsar Nicholas II and Grand Duke Michael Alexandrovich.

Grand Duke Michael Alexandrovich.

Count George Mikhailovich Brassov.

some of his brothers."[23]

Others, however, were horrified because they saw Ella as a sacrificial lamb. In particular, the Grand Duke Alexander Mikhailovich, who made no secret of his dislike for Serge, wrote in his memoirs: *"As though to accentuate his repugnant personality on a background of virtue, he married Grand Duchess Elizabeth, the elder sister of the young Czarina. No two human beings could have offered such a contrast."*[24] This memoir was written, of course, much later, and it is not certain that rumors of Serge's vices and cruelty were circulating at that time.

The couple was married June 15, 1884. Following a lengthy Orthodox service, they were married a second time in a Lutheran service, since Ella had not converted to Russian Orthodoxy. After the services, a banquet was held in the Concert Hall of the Winter Palace. Serge's brother, Tsar Alexander III and his wife, the Empress Marie Feodorovna, had to act in *loco parentis*, and according to the tradition, greeted the newly wedded couple with bread and salt at their St Petersburg home. Afterward, Serge and Ella spent their honeymoon at Illinskoe, which Ella grew to love as much as did Serge. After the frantic and exhausting ceremonies, the rustic peace of Illinskoe was a relief. There, the newlyweds could walk, read, relax on the broad balconies and drive in a leisurely manner around the neighborhood. Out in the country, Ella cooked over a fire. Teas and lunches were taken al fresco. They occupied their time sketching, and visiting the village near the house. Though the village was poor, they did make some improvements. Serge seemed to believe that everyone had their place in life and though the peasant's life was hard, due, he felt, in no small part, to alcoholism, that was their portion. It was a medieval attitude at best.

Serge, himself was very exacting. His life ran according to schedules, plans and outlines. He had very definite ideas about how his wife should dress and what jewelry she should wear with each ensemble. Ella often designed her own dresses, or painted designs on them, and Serge would make sure that she had the right pieces to wear with each costume, usually selecting them himself. In other ways, however, he treated Ella very strictly, like a child or perhaps a student, who if she erred, was scolded. According to Queen Marie, on such occasions when the Grand Duchess was put in her place, Ella would bow her head, and say softly, *"Mais, Serge."* While Marie saw him as a strict but loving schoolmaster, others saw something quite different. Grand Duke Alexander Mikhailovich positively resented the tyrannical way in which Serge treated his wife. Paléologue agreed and went further. The Grand Duke, he wrote, treated Ella rudely, was suspicious, jealous and found fault with everything she did. Though he loved her, it was in a covetous, incomplete and wayward fashion. This is an interesting statement as it may go along with what others would soon be saying about Serge – that he was a homosexual and that their marriage was, in fact, never consummated.

After the marriage and honeymoon, the couple returned to the Belosselsky-Belozersky Palace in St Petersburg. Serge and his new wife entered into the social whirl of St Petersburg society. That society loved Ella, and, unlike her younger sister, Alix, thought her extremely glamorous as well as beautiful. Also, unlike Alix, Ella loved society, parties and dancing. Serge's brother Paul spent a great time with them in the city, and was often Ella's dance partner. Serge, according to some historians, not only did not display jealousy, but also encouraged his wife to pick her dance partners from amongst his officers. This contradiction of Serge's actions and motives seems the rule rather than the exception. However, it appears that it was at this time that much of the negative rumors and gossip about the Grand Duke began to emerge and widely circulate. His new brother-in-law, Hereditary Grand Duke Ernst Ludwig wrote in his defense

> *From that day forth* [Crown Prince] *William* [of Prussia] *hated him and went after him in every possible way. Anything bad about his career that could be said was said. Anything which could harm him was spread all over. Every little piece of gossip, everything his representatives reported to him, was repeated. So it came about that everyone in Germany had a totally false picture of Serge. People still can't believe that the Kaiser lied and through jealousy tried to ruin the man.*[25]

Though there were obviously some that believed that the calumnies about Serge originated in Berlin, the home of Ella's spurned suitor,[26] there were others who felt that Wilhelm was not incorrect in his assessment of Serge and that there *"must be a streak of cruelty and meanness in the Grand Duke."*[27]

In addition to rumors about their marriage that one might expect from Berlin, there was also many comments about the fact that the Grand Duke *"appeared to be a bit effeminate,"*[28] and was a *"well-known homosexual."*[29] It was said that though Ella and Serge slept in the same bed for the duration of their marriage, he *"left* [his wife] *untouched on account of his curious tastes."*[30] Someone else noted for his odd tastes and his dislike for Serge, Felix Yussoupov, said that he adored the Grand Duchess but thought that Serge had strange manners, but most of all *"hated the way he stared at me."*[31] Finally, even the fairly sympathetic Count Witte, who stated quite positively, that though he did not agree with Serge's views, he respected them, noted that Serge was *"always surrounded by comparatively young men, who were excessively affectionate toward him. I do not mean that he had unnatural instincts, but there was evidently some psychological abnormality, which expressed itself in a marked liking for young men."*[32]

If the rumors were true and Serge was, in fact, a homosexual, it might follow that such a predilection was in constant conflict with his deeply religious nature. Indeed, those natures were probably warring against one another resulting in a man who was severely repressed. This might account for the cruelty he exhibited, his stern thin-lipped visage, and his martinet-like attitude even toward the people he loved and who loved him. There was never a point in his adult life when he may have felt free to be himself, where he was not in absolute control of himself and trying to control those nearest to him.

In the first years of their marriage the Grand Ducal couple forged their relationships within the Imperial Family. Paul, who had been Serge's closest brother and companion growing up, became a dear companion to the couple as well, and spent a great deal of time as a guest in their various houses. He also traveled with them abroad. They were very close to Tsar Alexander III and his wife, the Empress Marie, who, had, against the wishes of Queen Victoria, promoted the marriage of the young couple. As the years went by, Serge and Ella became extremely close to the Imperial children as well.

In those early years, Serge was appointed commander of the Preobrajensky Guard, which had previously been under the command of his elder brother, the Tsar. He had, according to Mossolov, head of the Court Chancellery, *"been adored by his officers."*[33] However, apropos to the rumors, Mossolov also called his private life a scandal that was the talk of the town.

In 1887, Ella and Serge were the official representatives of the Tsar and Tsarina, when they attended the Golden Jubilee of Queen Victoria. They were the ideal choice since Ella was, of course, the Queen's granddaughter. During the proceedings, Serge was awarded Knight Grand Cross of the Order of the Bath. Certainly Ella continued to promote Serge to her relatives and let her grandmother know, in no uncertain terms, that she was indeed, very content in her marriage. However, Queen Victoria was suspicious of all the positive endorsements her granddaughter was writing and remarked to Ella's sister, Princess Louis Battenberg, *"Ella's constantly speaking of her happiness I don't quite like. When people are very happy they don't require to tell others of it."*[34] When they returned home, Ella's letters to her grandmother continued to be filled with reassurances, as though she were persuading herself as well as others.

The following year, however, they made a trip accompanied by Paul, which undoubtedly filled Ella, as well as Serge, with a great deal of spiritual happiness and contentment. In September of 1888, they embarked from Odessa to make the journey to Jerusalem and the Holy Land. There, they dedicated the Church of St Mary Magdalen, in memory of Serge's mother, the Empress Marie Alexandrovna. The church was a beautiful onion-domed structure that seemed almost incongruous in the Levant, but somehow, blended in with the other churches, synagogues, and mosques of the ancient city. They were deeply impressed with the Church of the Nativity in Bethlehem and the Church of the Holy Sepulcher in Jerusalem. As the three of them walked the Stations of the Cross in the Christian quarter, they were profoundly moved. Some say that it was in Jerusalem that Ella acquired her propensity for religion. However, it was observed that it started well before that time. When she was a little girl, Ella told her sister, Victoria, that she wanted to be a nun when she grew up. While she was in the Holy City, it is said that Ella prayed for a child, but indeed, she may have been looking for guidance for other reasons.

Ella had not been converted to Russian Orthodoxy upon her marriage to the Grand Duke, and had, for several years been considering doing just that. She probably began to think seriously about her conversion at the time she was in Jerusalem. However, she would decide to do so several years later. Meanwhile, after touring the region, the three stopped in Athens on their way home to join the celebration for the official engagement of Grand Duke Paul and Princess Alexandra of Greece. In 1889, when the young people married, they became the particular friends of Serge and Ella. The two couples spent happy times together.

In January of 1889, Princess Alix, Ella's little sister, and her father, Grand Duke Ludwig IV, traveled to St Petersburg to stay with Ella and Serge as guests in their town residence, the Belosselsky-Belozersky Palace. Alix would attend her first ball there, and her sister and her cousins, the children of the Tsar, made sure that Alix's days were filled with pleasurable activities. She went skating, sledding, dancing, to parties, theater evenings, and cotillions – all accompanied

by her cousin Nicholas and his sister Xenia. The Tsarevich was particularly attentive. On January 29, as a culmination of all the fun and festivities, Alix had her
"coming out" ball – an opulent and glittering affair.

Serge and Alix's liking for one another blossomed during this visit and
lasted their lives. Serge, uncharacteristically, was able to tease Alix saying that he
had known her so long he had seen her bathed. Alix, also, uncharacteristically,
was able to take the teasing in good humor. Naturally, when she returned to
Darmstadt, besides the inevitable let-down that the end of such wonderful times
would always have, there was no doubt that she left her heart with her cousin
Nicky, and with Russia. Ella and Serge were extremely aware of the attraction and
would now do all they could to promote the match.

The following April of 1890, Serge's new sister-in-law, the Grand Duchess
Paul, gave birth to her first child, a little girl called Marie. Serge was asked to be
the godfather of the little girl, and because of his great love for his brother and
children in general, he was delighted to accept. He and Ella visited England again
at the end of 1890 and, thereafter, Serge accepted the most important post of his
career – his brother, the Tsar, appointed him Governor-General of Moscow. Even
though he expressed reluctance to leave his command of the Preobrajensky
Guard and his younger brother, Paul, he was also very excited at the prospect of
living in the ancient capital of Moscow.

At the end of this same year, an extremely important event in the couple's
lives took place. Ella, after a great deal of thought and self-examination made the
decision to convert to Russian Orthodoxy. She told her father and grandmother at
the end of that year as well as her siblings. The major point she stressed to one
and all was that Serge in no way influenced her decision. She told them, that
although she knew in her heart that he longed for the moment of her conversion,
he had never pushed her toward it. Indeed, she said, when she told him there
were tears in his eyes. Interestingly enough, her grandmother, the Queen, was
most supportive, simply saying that Ella really understood what she was doing.

Others, however, were not so persuaded that this was a purely independent move. Her sister, Irene, convinced that Ella was too impressionable, was
very upset about the conversion. *"The Times"* of London also expressed its doubts:

> *I repeat most positively my assertion that Princess Elizabeth of Hesse
> is not changing her religion willingly, but is only yielding to moral coercion of a
> very brutal kind, and such as ought to be taken into consideration by all those
> reigning families of Europe who, in giving away their daughters to Russian
> Grand Dukes, have treated Russia as a civilized State acting as other civilized
> States do in respecting marriage contracts.*[35]

Ambassador Paléologue was also skeptical and wrote in his memoirs that
Serge had forced his wife to convert. However, this is simply not borne out by the
fact of her many letters about her decision to her family – it is clear that she
arrived at the conversion on her own, and that, *"her religion was a private enclosure
where even* [Serge] *might not trespass."*[36]

Meanwhile, the couple moved to Moscow and Serge took up his duties as
Governor-General. It was here that the public and extremely reactionary face of

the Grand Duke became more and more apparent. It seemed that "[g]*reat power under his hand brought out all the negative qualities.*"[37] of his complex and paradoxical character. The atmosphere in Moscow was one of political dissent, and the Tsar felt that his brother, whose ideas were very much like his own, could deal with workers, students and others who were dissatisfied with their lot. It was here that his profound anti-Semitism and possible paranoia were given full reign and repressive policies, especially toward Jews were enacted.[38] Indeed, he had a "[m]*istrust of ideas beyond his horizon, loathing of the Jews, proneness to suspect subversive activities on the strength of a flickering light seen through a chink of a basement shutter.*"[39]

Edicts were put forth that year saying that either Jews must leave Moscow or convert to Orthodoxy. Under this proclamation, approximately 30,000 people were forced to leave the city. Of those that remained, young women were permitted to do so, only as long as they registered as prostitutes. Businessmen, who were allowed to stay under certain quotas, were permitted to operate their business only on the proviso that the signs on their buildings clearly stated that they were Jewish-owned businesses. In addition, he ordered that the Great Synagogue, which had just completed construction, and was scheduled to open for worship on Passover, be closed. The following year, Serge had the Jewish quarter torn apart by Cossacks and the residents thrown out. His brother, Tsar Alexander III, approved since he considered the Jews enemies of Christianity. But it is clear that Serge's devout religiosity, at times, bordered on the maniacal.

Apart from these cruel and tyrannical edits, Serge had a great love for the city he administered. He was painstaking with every detail of governing and a man

> *who was undoubtedly anxious to act conscientiously in the performance of his duty, and manifested, as Governor-General of Moscow, a Haroun al-Ratschid kind of activity in going about amongst the people, personally inspecting the bread and other food subject to official examination, and inquiring into and righting abuses. He would spy out fraudulent weights and the measures, and generally ferret out grievances, going about the town disguised as a private individual.*[40]

This style of governance was one he no doubt handed down to his nephew, Nicholas, who was renowned for spending endless hours on minutia.

Oddly enough, even as the authoritarian despot of the city, the Grand Duke was misunderstood. "*Although he was a staunch, uncompromising monarchist, conservatives took him for a liberal, while true liberals saw him as an obstacle to the reforms they thirsted for.*"[41] Mossolov felt that Serge would have been ideal for the job one hundred years earlier, and perhaps that was true, but the world was changing and the creaky Imperial Family was simply not changing with it.

Outside of his love for the city, there were other reasons that Serge treasured being the virtual Viceroy of Moscow. As a young man, one of his favorite subjects during his studies had been archeology. Indeed, as an ardent archaeologist, "*he had always desired to be Governor-General of the ancient and historic original capital of Russia, a wish shared by his wife, who greatly admired the picturesque surroundings of Moscow.*"[42] So Serge and Ella were content to spend their time studying the capital, its buildings and its long and fascinating history.

They spent the summer of 1891 at Illinskoe with their close companions, Paul and Alexandra. It was a halcyon summer that ended in tragedy. In September, Grand Duchess Paul, at only seven months pregnant, gave birth to a son, Dimitri. Alexandra fell into a coma from which she never emerged. The young woman died after six days. Naturally, the baby was undersized, and even appeared to be dead when he was born, however, a midwife noticed faint signs of life and the child survived.

Paul was inconsolable at his wife's sudden and shocking death, and his brothers, Serge and Tsar Alexander seemed to be the young husband's only comfort. The entire household went into mourning and at Alexandra's funeral Paul had to be physically restrained from falling on the coffin as it was being buried. Serge, too, was very attached to the Greek Princess and highly distressed, he locked the door to the room at Illinskoe in which she had died. He alone kept the key to the lock, and the room was left untouched.

Serge was also instrumental in coaxing the premature Dimitri to life, taking the small bundle and warming it himself and making sure that the baby received the care crucial to its survival. Serge and Ella became the guardians of little Dimitri and his older sister Marie Pavlovna, as Paul threw himself into his army duties. He was, during the first few years, unhappy and restless and became, for the most part, an absent parent. Serge enjoyed his role as a strict yet loving guardian. However, even in this, loving him was a difficult proposition. Indeed, Marie Pavlovna did love her uncle, but she wrote that "[t]*hose few who knew him well were deeply devoted to him, but even his intimates feared him, and Dimitri and I feared him too.*"[43]

About four years after Alexandra's death, Paul embarked upon an affair with Olga von Pistolkors, the wife of a captain in his regiment and aide-de-camp to his brother, Grand Duke Vladimir. The Imperial Family closed its eyes to the affair, and in 1897, the couple produced a son, Vladimir. Against the objections and strong disapproval of his family, the couple eventually married in Italy. Consequently, the family rejected Paul and his new wife, who went to live in Paris, having two more children.

Serge and Ella, who had tried to dissuade Paul from the marriage, became the legal guardians of Dimitri and Marie. Marie's memoirs certainly conveyed the feeling that her brother and she felt abandoned by their father. She was also bitter that Ella did not seem to reciprocate the worshipful feelings she had for the Aunt with whom she lived. As a matter of fact, she portrayed the Grand Duchess as cool and unfeeling toward her. Knowing the Grand Duke's outwardly cold disposition, perhaps a clue to understanding Ella's treatment of Marie was a result of her own jealousy of Serge's tenderness toward the two motherless children. Later, Marie reconciled with her father, though the two children never permanently lived with Paul again. There is also some evidence that Serge was jealous of the love that Marie and Dimitri had for their father. According to Marie, "*in spite of the great sorrow that my uncle felt at his brother's misalliance, he could not conceal the joy he felt at the fact that from now on he would be able to keep us entirely to himself.*"[44] So in their household, there was a convolution of conflicting emotions, leading to misunderstandings and jealousies.

During this time, Serge and Ella had also been involved in another enterprise. They promoted the promising attachment between Ella's sister, Princess Alix of Hesse and By Rhine and Serge's nephew, the Tsarevich Nicholas Alexandrovich. Their budding acquaintance which had began at Alix's "coming out" party now seemed about to flower. Though Queen Victoria was very set against the match, and was much annoyed at their interference, writing, *"Ella and Serge do all they can to bring it about, encouraging and even urging the Boy to do it?"*[45], the battle would soon be effectively lost. Though Alix was extremely reluctant to change her religion to Orthodoxy, with Ella's help and encouragement, especially in view of her own conversion, Alix was eventually made to see that the change was quite possible. In April of 1894, at the wedding of her brother, Ernst Ludwig to Princess Victoria Melita of Edinburgh, and after a good deal of soul searching, Alix finally consented to the conversion that would enable her to become Nicholas' wife.

The engagement was announced during the wedding festivities. Though not all were happy about it, Serge was obviously enthusiastic about this development since he had always been good friends with his youngest sister-in-law. He also recognized that Alix had already conceived a great love for Russia. After the engagement, he lectured the young princess on the principles of autocracy and the divine and *"mystical nature of the tsar's office."*[46] As events evolved, this can hardly be seen to Serge's credit.

After the announcement, Alix traveled to England to spend the last months before her wedding with her grandmother. This was, no doubt, to reconcile the Queen to the loss of yet another granddaughter to Russia. It was also a custom that Queen Victoria had with her Hessian granddaughters.

Unhappily, Nicholas' father, Alexander III, was ill with kidney trouble and began to worsen as summer turned into fall. Staying at Livadia for a more temperate and healthful climate, it was here that Paul and Serge were quickly summoned as their brother's illness became critical. Soon, Alix, too, was summoned to the Crimea to be at Nicholas' side at the Tsar's deathbed. He died at the beginning of November. The new young Tsar Nicholas faced a future of which he was uncertain and, unfortunately, ill-prepared.

His uncles were ready and willing to influence the young man as he tentatively took the reigns of the government. Some thought that the influence provided, especially by Serge, was particularly reactionary. Their constant presence around someone who felt as unsure and indecisive as Nicholas was seen as bullying by some, though not by all. Some actually thought this was the first instruction of any kind the Tsar had received in statesmanship – instruction that his father had tragically neglected to give him. Count Witte, for example, wrote that *"[a]t the time three of his uncles, Grand Dukes Vladimir Alexandrovich, Alexis Alexandrovich, and Serge Alexandrovich, who occupied fairly important posts, exercised considerable influence and continued to do so for many years. They were all first men and quite suitable as grand dukes."*[47]

Alix's (now Alexandra's) marriage to the new Tsar was brought forward, now taking place just a few weeks after the death of Tsar Alexander III. It was a quiet celebration just as the coronation in 1896, almost a year and a half later, would be an occasion of fabled splendor. The crowning of the last tsar and tsarina was also an occasion of unparallel tragedy, and for the superstitious that tragedy became an ominous portent of the future.

The tragedy of Khodynka Field is well-known for the disastrous consequences it had on the image of the Romanov Family and particularly as an inauspicious beginning to the reign of Tsar Nicholas II. On May 30, as part of the coronation festivities, commemorative mugs, free beer, food and souvenirs were to be passed out to the people. By dawn of that day, there were nearly two million people gathered on the great field, just outside of Moscow, and waiting for the distribution. According to some accounts, a rumor began circulating throughout the crowd that there would not be enough for everyone. Impatience, along with the fact that many in the crowd were already drunk, contributed to what happened next. The crowd pressed forward, there was a stampede, and as many as 1,429 people were crushed, trampled and suffocated to death, as well as thousands seriously wounded.

The Imperial couple were severely shaken and saddened and spent the day visiting hospitals. That night, a ball was held in their honor by French Ambassador. They had refused to go, however, Nicholas's uncles, including Serge, insisted that it would be an insult to the French if they did not, and Nicholas was no match for their persuasions. That night, as they attended the ball, many other parties also took place, and the contrast was horrible, and worse - noted. Many were stunned and angry at the callousness of this decision, including members of Imperial Family.

As Governor-General, Serge, who was ultimately responsible, was, indeed, blamed. Many were justifiably critical of Serge over this horrific episode and he offered to resign. However, Nicholas, heavily influenced by Alexandra, refused to accept his resignation. Serge's nephew, Grand Duke Alexander Mikhailovich, who, as has been said, had no love for his uncle, wrote that he was a complete ignoramus entrusted with a job far beyond his capabilities. *"Uncle Sergei...played a fatal part in the downfall of the empire, having been partially responsible for the Khodynka catastrophe during the coronation...The Czar should never have allowed* [him] *to retain his post in Moscow after the storm of indignation caused by the Khodynka catastrophe."*[48] Further, he wrote, he and his brothers had demanded Serge's dismissal after the tragedy. The younger man was amazed to see his uncle attending the balls and parties that evening wearing, he said, a big smile. Alexander was positive that the foreign legations would think that Serge had completely lost his mind.[49] Another member of the family, Olga Alexandrovna, the new Tsar's sister, saw the situation differently. She felt that the demands of resignation actually incriminated the entire family instead of laying the blame at the door of one member, and that the Tsar was correct not to accept Serge's resignation.[50]

Not surprisingly, the disaster of Khodynka field was a direct result of the usual bureaucratic infighting over local jurisdiction between Count Vorontsov-Dashkov, of the Ministry of the Imperial Court, and the office of the Governor-General. During the controversy, some accused Serge of being given free reign, solely because he was the Uncle and brother-in-law of the Emperor. Certainly, in the case of young Nicholas, he *'simply listened to the last voice he heard"*[51], and that was often one of his Uncles. Petty power struggles, tangled lines of authority, lack of planning and plain incompetence resulted in Serge's being rightly criticized and taunted as "Prince Khodynskii" by ridiculing crowds.[52]

Serge's relatives reacted strongly to the Grand Duke's obvious unpopularity with the people of the city, and the attendant waves of discontent. Grand Duke Konstantin Konstantinovich wrote in his diary, *"Sergei does not like anyone to disagree with him, he gets annoyed and loses his capacity to think coolly and logically."*[53] Alexander Mikhailovich continued his censure, saying, Serge *"flaunted his many peculiarities in the face of the entire nation, providing the enemies of the regime with inexhaustible material for calumnies and libels."*[54] Someone far more objective and shrewd, Queen Victoria, wrote: *"But oh! How awful & dreadful is that fearful catastrophe of that Fete! It is simply ghastly. – Would it have not been better to have stopped the Balls etc. for it looks so unfeeling to go on just the same."*[55]

After this lamentable beginning to the Emperor's reign, Serge and Ella once again withstood the rumors and gossip that had continually plagued their marriage. Ella reacted right away, saying that *"the abominable lies told about us...are not edifying...People, I suppose, could not believe that we were harmless and happy, so began trying to prove the contrary...We are very happy."*[56] Many besides the rumor mongers, including Felix Yussoupov and Alexander Mikhailovich, wondered at the marital relationship between the two. It would be a constant source of speculation, even to the present day. Perhaps Ella saw Serge as her own personal crusade, someone she could save from himself and shield from others. Maybe she sensed the inner torment of conflicting aspects of his nature and personality – the devoutly religious and the repressed homosexual, and it aroused her compassion. Or, perhaps, she was simply a loyal wife who kept her complaints and unhappiness strictly to herself. It was not unheard of, especially in those times and in those circles, to suffer in silence. She evidently did not confide even in her own family.

Marital and personality issues aside, Serge and his brothers, constantly pressed advice and tried to advance personal agendas on their tentative, vacillating nephew. Dissatisfaction continued to smolder and sometimes burn brightly in the capital. In 1899, there was widespread student rioting. Serge advised severe repressive measures, making him even more unpopular and, even, vehemently hated by many. That he became such a detested figure may explain all the rumors about his personal life and the questions of his competency as a public administrator during his tenure as Governor-General. According to Count Witte, the city's dislike of Serge and his policies went far to explain why Moscow now existed in a state of opposition to the government.

Civil strife continued into the new century and Serge, rightly, feared for his life. No doubt, he realized that he might very well suffer the same fate as had his father before him. It is also not difficult to think that very likely he had carried these dark thoughts with him since the dreadful day his father was assassinated. As a result, he took many precautions, eventually traveling in separate conveyances and making separate appearances from his wife and family.

In February of 1904, Russia declared war on Japan and new troubles began. Grand Duchess Serge, however, was in her element organizing hospitals and caring for the wounded and sick. But even these humanitarian projects did little to add luster to Serge's reputation. There was always another way to see such altruism. *"During the war with Japan* [the Grand Duchess] *collected funds to equip a hospital train, but this humane projected never materialized, because someone embezzled the large sums subscribed in response to Ella's appeal, and it was said in some quarters that Serge himself was implicated in the fraud."*[57]

Russia could not conceive of Japan having the power to defeat her and was shocked when news of Japanese victories began to arrive, and to make matters worse, the Russian navy was destroyed. As the year wore on, the war incited more domestic unrest. In December 1904, Port Arthur in Manchuria fell to the Japanese. During that month, there were also meetings and conferences as the government tried to plan what to do about the war and the local unrest. At a conference, taking place on December 4, reforms were proposed to try to subdue the crowds. Serge wrote in his diary, *"I very much dislike a certain project about elections."*[58] Of all the reforms proposed, this one was Serge's least favorite. He was not moved by the idea of the people having representatives with a voice in legislative affairs. These reforms were completely at odds with Serge's policies since he had taken the office of governor. He could not believe that Russia was ready for such a transformation. His brother-in-law, Grand Duke Ernst Ludwig wrote, *"Many of the things* [the Liberals] *wanted seemed impractical to him, or to have come before their time...Many the time when I went through my thoughts with him, always to have him say, That's fine for Hesse – but for Russia, not yet."* I learnt as much from him as from a great many books.[59] Sadly, it is more likely that anyone learning from Serge, would have learned to be without foresight or ingenuity.

Serge was implacable about reforms, an immovable object meeting an irresistible force. He chose to resign as Governor General of Moscow after thirteen years in office, rather than acquiesce. This time there was no opposition from Nicholas, or Alix, and the retirement was *'settled in principle"*[60] during Christmas at Tsarskoe Selo. Further, according to Baroness Buxhoeveden, he virtually admitted his lack of vision to his nephew, saying: *"New ideas require new men...I am unable to change my views, and if you want to start on a new policy, you must do so with the help of men who are whole-heartedly in support of it."* Even after this admission, there were those who continued to think well of Serge. Count Witte thought him good at heart, but limited, stubborn and reactionary, who, not surprisingly, was surrounded by like-minded people.[61] It was later given out to the press that the Grand Duke's resignation was for reasons of health.[62] After his resignation, and because he was worried about his family's security, he moved them into the safety of the Kremlin. Serge officially gave up his post on January 1, 1905.

Whatever reluctant reforms the Tsar put forward, were not enough to quell the continuing turmoil. Sporadic strikes which took place in St Petersburg began to spread rapidly elsewhere. Oddly enough, these strikes were sponsored by the police union and one of them, the Assembly of Russian Workmen was led by an Orthodox priest, Father Gapon. On Sunday, January 22, a large crowd carrying icons and portraits of the Tsar marched slowly and in an orderly fashion to the Winter Palace. They had with them a petition on which they stated the workers' grievances and called for a constituent assembly. As the crowds neared the Palace, the authorities panicked and began firing on the amassed demonstrators, killing many. What resulted was the infamous events of "Bloody Sunday". After this horrific event, the Tsar was no longer seen by the peasants and workers as their "Little Father" but as "Nicholas the Bloody". Naturally, Serge characteristically recommended that the severest measures be taken to put down the disturbances.

One contemporary historian said that Serge had the look of someone with the foreknowledge of what was to come. *"He wore a haggard, haunted, frightened look which seemed to betray a premonition of the tragic fate in store for him."*[63] With the lack of wisdom in which so many of these incidents of discontent were handled, it is hardly surprising that the human face of repression, the Grand Duke Serge Alexandrovich, would become a primary target of assassination.

As in his father's case, there was more than one attempt made on Serge's life. On February 13, 1905, the attempt was successful. At three o'clock in the afternoon, when his carriage was inside the Kremlin walls, a bomb was thrown and Serge was blown to bits. Ella had heard the explosion from her rooms and rushed out to see what had happened. She numbly began to gather the parts of the body strewed everywhere saying *"Hurry, hurry, Serge hates blood and mess."*[64] Though little remained, the pieces of her husband were placed on a stretcher, covered by a cloak, and taken to the Nicholas Palace. Ella wrote telegrams informing the family, though Alexandra and Nicholas were advised not to attend the funeral, and did not.

Her sister, Victoria, rushed from London to be at her side. When she reached Moscow, she found Ella very brave, calm, and collected, though she noted that she could neither eat nor sleep. Thirty-seven years later, Victoria wrote in her memoirs that,

> [c]ontrary to the general belief [,] she and Serge had led a happy married life, tho it was he who was completely the head and master of the house. Ella was very willing that he should be it and he was full of affectionate attentions to her. As to bringing up Paul's children, she left it entirely to him, who was a devoted uncle to them. Both Ella and Serge were very fond of children and it was sad that they never had had any of their own.[65]

One would hardly think that Victoria need cover-up for her sister so many years after the events, and with so many of the players dead.

After Serge's death, contemporary historians continued to disparage his memory. An obvious propagandist delighted in repeating the most outrageous rumors concerning the Grand Duke saying,

> One of the leaders...has ceased to exercise his dire influence and his criminal activity, in consequence of a terrorist outrage in February, 1905...He was sapped by the tuberculosis which in its latent period had manifested the entire psychosis characteristic of this disease, intermittent euphoria and megalomania, a total absence of moral sense, exaggerated erotomania and various superstitions.

This particular writer also accused him of extortion, blackmail, defiling orphans, being a sadist and forcing a dance teacher to procure for him – women, not men.[66]

A more reasonable critic calmly stated that

he was the least popular of the Grand Dukes, and that the general feeling toward his charming and amiable consort, the sister of the present Empress, was one of pity that she should be married to such a man, who had been singled out from among all the other Grand Dukes by the scandal-mongers of St Petersburg for general execration, and reputed, by universal consent, to be the victim of unmentionable vices.[67]

It is hardly necessary to say that Serge was a man who aroused very strong emotions in the people who knew him best as well as the people who suffered under his rule. From his relatives, the memories were fond: his cousin, Princess Marie of Erbach-Schönberg, wrote in her memoirs: *"How fond I had been of* [Serge] *from a child, and how frightful was this reminder of the 18th March, 1881, when my beloved Kaiser Alexander* [Alexander II] *likewise met with just such a fearful end!"*[68] The Grand Duchess George Mikhailovich said what many others who knew him had often said, *"I speak of the Grand Duke Serge as I knew and liked him, and not the stern disciplinarian who was feared by all who came under his authority. The public Grand Duke Serge – the autocrat feared and hated by the revolutionaries - was not the Serge I knew."*

Still a paradox, Serge remains as we found him. Perhaps not so much mysterious in who he was and how he acted, but in the end, why he was so loved by those who knew him, and so hated by those who did not.

GRAND DUKE PAUL ALEXANDROVICH
(1860-1919)

By William Lee & Lisa Davidson

Grand Duke Paul entered the world on September 21/October 3, 1860, the eighth and youngest child of Emperor Alexander II and his consort, Empress Maria Alexandrovna. Paul's entrance came midway through a grand ducal 'baby boom' unprecedented in the history of the Romanov dynasty. It had begun modestly with the birth of five boys between 1843 and 1850, four of them sons of the future emperor.[1] There was then a lull until 1856, broken by the birth of Nicholas Nikolaevich, after which an astonishing eight more boys appeared in as many years, the fourth being Paul himself.[2] In all, Nicholas I's four sons would bestow a total of sixteen Grand Dukes upon Russia, more than had existed in the previous two centuries of Romanov rule combined! Not a single one of them would die in infancy, and only three died before reaching full maturity.[3] How could Russia possibly support so many grand dukes, each of whom would eventually receive a large appanage allowance and a service position in keeping with his imperial dignity? The problems associated with this embarrassment of riches could not but impact the smallest member of Alexander II's nursery.

These issues were greatly complicated by the fact that the Empire's greatest period of reform since the reign of Peter the Great coincided almost exactly with this baby boom. The emancipation of the serfs in 1861, though it did little to relieve the misery of the enormous peasant class, nonetheless marked a real turning point for the country – one which touched every single Russian in some way. The military reforms, meanwhile, prompted by Russia's disastrous Crimean defeat in 1855, would have a direct and profound effect upon the Grand Dukes themselves, as would the growing role of public opinion.

Alexander II's immediate predecessors, Paul I and Nicholas I, each had four sons, and those sons in turn had either been specifically pre-designated for the grandest of future military roles or knew without doubt that they would receive them upon attaining their majority. These were not mere honorary colonelcies, which even women, or foreign royalty, could hold. They were general inspectorates and corps-level commands which would permit the Grand Dukes to make as significant a mark upon the Empire as their own drive and abilities would allow. Of course, unless the designated holder of such a post proved to be utterly incapable of living up to it on even a symbolic level, he need have no great fear of losing it over issues of indifference or incompetency. There was certainly no question of competition from within the family. However, in spite of this "job security" Grand Dukes still faced rigid requirements which stifled nearly all individual aspirations save the military ones and proscribed a personal life which included mandatory marriage to a foreign wife. Is it any wonder that one Grand

Duke in this period referred to his devoted spouse as his "government issue" wife?

Once the Grand Ducal baby boom occurred, the specter of competition loomed. No sons except the immediate heirs received a pre-designated grand future role during Alexander II's or Alexander III's reigns, and none but the Emperor's own sons could expect to receive one as an adult without, to some extent, earning it – if only in competition with his own relatives. This presented challenge which were all but unknown to prior generations, and some if not all of the grand dukes so impacted were able to effectively meet these sudden changes, let alone the coming changes that the Revolution would bring to them. Into this wake fell Paul, but that would be years in the future.

Baby Paul, in contrast, was in a relatively strong position. With five older brothers he could not reasonably expect to ascend the throne, but he still held automatic 'seniority' over his ten male cousins from the three junior branches of the family. If there was a disadvantage to being one of the Emperor's sons, it lay, surprisingly, in the sphere of education. Prior to Alexander II's reign, no Grand Duke had ever attended a military college (though Nicholas and Michael Nikolaevich were members of Cadet Corps), but the Crimean defeat had ushered in a new, more professional military ethos in Russia, raising the bar for Grand Ducal performance. It would, from now on, be crucial that they not appear as mere amateurs to their military colleagues, men who prided themselves on their professionalism.

In any event, it was not just the service milieu that was changing – becoming more invested in the idea of professional qualifications, practicality, and the importance of the state relative to the dynasty – but also public opinion. As with most politicians, Alexander III needed partners in reforming the military, emancipating the serfs, and radically changing how his country was governed. His greatest ally in the implementing the Great Reforms was his younger brother, Konstantin. So, when Grand Duke Konstantin Nikolaevich's conservative foes and political rivals began to foment public opinion against him, one should also view this as a veiled attack on the Emperor and his attempts to liberalize Russia. Most immediately, however, they were able to public opinion brilliantly as a weapon to sabotage Konstantin's efforts as Viceroy of Poland in 1863. Several years later, when every eligible grand Grand Duke joined in the Russo-Turkish War of 1878, public scrutiny and criticism of their role as meddling amateurs, whether fair or unfair, made it perfectly clear that the days of the grand military seigneur were over, and what was wanted was a sense that Russia's fate lay securely in the hands of highly capable professionals[4] and not a bunch of profligates masquerading as officers.

At any even more personal level, preceding these two events, came an attack aimed directly at the Empress, specifically in her capacity as the mother of five (at that time) sons who would grow up to occupy positions of importance in Russia. Alexander Herzen, the expatriate publisher of "The Bell" (*Kolokol*), wrote her an open letter which appeared in the November 1, 1858, issue of that progressive journal. The fact that "The Bell" had been banned in Russia certainly did not prevent it from reaching her. The letter was not overtly hostile to the Romanovs per se, but made it clear that the time had come for the Grand Dukes to prove their worth – a thing which they could do only by returning to the ideal of service pioneered by Peter I, and the only way they would be able to realize that ideal was by receiving a truly practical education – one that allowed them close contact with ordinary Russians. Otherwise, Herzen warned, their lives would be *"unproductive"* and *"useless."* Marie was devastated. She wept. She considered Herzen himself a scoundrel, but found much truth in what he said on this occasion, and insisted that if only a man could be found who somehow combined intellectual brilliance with "a strong will, firm principles, faith and uncorrupted morality," she would gladly strike down "all obstacles" to bring him to her sons.[5]

Such a woman – one who could see the merit in an adversary's criticism of herself, who idolized the strength and practicality of the previous Emperor, who was genuinely horrified at the thought that any of her sons might grow up to be superfluous, a burden upon their nation – might be expected to have taken decisive action to counter such a possibility, and Marie did try: it was she who pressed Alexander, for instance, to allow the Tsarevich to attend an algebra class at the Pages Corps, where he was to be treated like all the other boys.[6] And she had another valuable quality as well – she was able to perceive the proverbial 'writing on the wall' – to grasp that Russia's modernization, though necessary and desirable, made the dynasty's position genuinely precarious. Indeed, the greatest single danger in reform rather than revolution is that often reform accelerates expectations to a point that cannot be met. With this brilliant insight, Empress Maria Alexandrovna was neither blind nor defiant as her future granddaughter-in-law, Alexandra Feodorovna, would be.

Marie's fragile state was already noticeable in 1857 when the time came for the baptism of her seventh child, Serge. She was consumed by a premonition that the baby would drown, and also feared that dynasty itself was on the verge of some great catastrophe. Her foreboding is more understandable when viewed in the context of the mood surrounding the baptism – a lavish affair which included a banquet for eight hundred guests, each of whom received an expensive gift. Given the poor state of Russia's finances at the time, such extravagance provoked *"great dissatisfaction"* among the public.[7] Serge, after all, was not a tsarevich but a fifth son, and it is not unreasonable to assume that some members of the public were already alarmed at the proliferation of grand dukes.

But her insights did not, unfortunately, make Maria Alexandrovna a popular Empress or a strong and steady source of guidance to her children. She had a morbid tendency that would go beyond perceptiveness to fear, pessimism, and anxiety, and lead her to cling to her three youngest children and impart those characteristics to at least two of them – sons Serge and Paul, the former of whom would be a forceful but reserved and acutely sensitive and prickly man, while the latter frail and largely passive (thus arguably the most like his mother of all the *Alexandrovichi*). These youngest two would stand in striking contrast to the three robust and boisterous middle boys, Alexander, Vladimir and Alexis. Eldest son Nicholas was perhaps more like the youngest two – refined and sensitive – but without the disadvantage of having been raised in the shadow of his mother's fear and sorrow. He was reputedly – and not surprisingly – her favorite, so much so that the middle children were said to be "neglected". Dimitri Miliutin writes: *"All care, all parental tenderness, was concentrated on the first-born heir to the throne."*

Thus Nicholas's sudden death, though a tragedy, might conceivably have opened the way for the younger children to have a better relationship with their mother than the middle three had had. It certainly seems to have made that relationship a closer one. But, in the event, the shattering blow Marie suffered from Nicholas's death (and the previous death of her daughter Alexandra) undoubtedly contributed greatly to the breakdown of her own health and nerves.

Marie, of course, need not have worried. Both Serge and the dynasty would outlive her, albeit only briefly. Her husband, despite her nervous state, nonetheless entrusted her with the supervision of their children's education, and she tried to maintain a dutiful severity with the boys, but she was not up to the job. Many of the men chosen to be tutors and preceptors in the Imperial household were mediocre at best. The heir and Grand Duke Alexis were educated separately from their brothers, in the latter case because of the special preparation deemed necessary for a naval career, but the remaining four were paired up, Alexander and Vladimir sharing one preceptor, and Serge and Paul another. In the latter case, the man in question was Admiral D.S. Arseniev, who did indeed possess a strong pedagogical background, and must have been chosen for that reason since neither Serge nor Paul had been designated for a naval career. One could thus argue that Arseniev's appointment, good as it might otherwise have been, showed a measure of indifference to the younger boys' military training and their individual talents and capabilities. One might hazard a guess that the pursuit of reforms in Russia made both of Paul Alexandrovich's parents rather indifferent to him.

Tiutcheva, a lady-in-waiting who had become governess to Alexander and Marie's only surviving daughter, Grand Duchess Marie, genuinely loved the Empress, but was not satisfied with the boys' upbringing. She was an ardent Slavophile and a nationalist, and fought to cement Konstantin Pobedonostev's position in the imperial household. Pobedonostsev, who began his tenure at the Winter Palace as law tutor to the Tsarevich, has been described as an *"unyielding reactionary."*[8] Tiutcheva does not deserve such a label herself, but the two of them shared a reverence for indigenous Russian culture, a cherished vision of the ideal autocrat, and an unwavering devotion to the state. After the heir's untimely death, he was attached to the new Tsarevich, Alexander, but neither he nor even Tiutcheva herself could resist trying to imbue Serge and Paul with their vision of Russia's glorious past and future. They clearly hoped that the younger boys would not be superfluous Grand Dukes, but active shapers of that future. Tiutcheva's role as one of the boys' tutors was a break from Romanov tradition, since boys past seven were supposed to be instructed and supervised only by men, and the two youngest would, overall, preserve a closer connection to the feminine realm than their brothers, being close in age and frequent playmates of their sister Marie and kept near by their anxious mother. Tiutcheva's access to, and particular influence upon them is thus not surprising. Even after they were grown and Tiutcheva herself had left the Winter Palace she remained close to them through correspondence, endeavoring consciously to act upon them *"in the spirit of Slavophilism."*[9]

How, then, did these two young men come to see Russia and their own roles within it? Pobedonostsev and Tiutcheva were both great believers in 'spirit' – in the mystical link between the Romanovs and their people, in the idea of 'Holy

Mother Rus'. They were certainly thereby in keeping with one of the great movements of the second half of the 19th century in Russia – the one that produced the silver age of Russian literature, the blossoming within academia of a new appreciation and attempt to collect and preserve Russia's indigenous folk tales and lore, and the general ideal of a Slav future distinct from Western Europe and its influences. The effects of their influence would be very clear in Serge, as in his nephew Nicholas II – less so in Paul, who seems to have absorbed something of the other spirit – the practical, modernizing spirit of the age – the spirit desired but so feared by his mother, anathema to Pobedonostsev, but not entirely out of place in Tiutcheva's philosophy. Thus we can assert that, of all the Grand Dukes, Paul Alexandrovich was truly the child of the Great Reforms.

So, with his Empress mother being entirely in charge of the young Grand Duke's education, and with her often morbid outlook on life, who was available to give Paul the nurturing that most people crave and indeed require for a well adjusted adulthood? Unfortunately, neither parent was at a place in their lives where they could give their youngest child what was so desperately needed. This alone would later explain all of the scandal that was ever associated with his name. For, what had once been a happy marriage between the Imperial couple crumbled into an unhappy circumstance for them both. Maria Alexandrovna was told that she could no longer have marital relations with her husband after Paul's birth. While some marriages could weather such a storm that enforced celibacy brings, the death of their heir, Nixa, was a death knell to their marriage. Maria Alexandrovna was unable to bear the grief of the loss of her oldest son and never recovered from it. Her husband was also devastated but instead of breaking down, he began an adulterous alliance with Prince Catherine Dolgoruky which would eventually result in a second family for the Tsar of all the Russias.

To be fair to the Emperor, the Russian terrorist organization Narodnaya Volya (People's Will) also sentenced their sovereign to death during this time. The first attempt against Alexander II's life came in 1866, when Paul was six years old, and it is doubtful that he heard anything about it, though it surely increased his mother's anxiety. More attempts followed over the course of the next fourteen years, and Paul could not have been kept entirely unaware of them. Did he see them as isolated incidents, with no real bearing on the relationship between the Russian people and the dynasty? Did he share anything of his mother's presentiment of doom? Whatever the case may have been, those incidents, representing the external aspect of his existence, were to some degree paralleled by the internal drama – the slow, inexorable decline of his mother's health. Marie seems to have suffered from a chronic form of pulmonary tuberculosis – something she could live with for years, but never conquer, something that would force her and her loved ones to watch death approaching by degrees. Was Alexander's fate any less inevitable than hers? Perhaps not, but at least he could face the challenge with vigor, whereas his wife's world was one of ever shrinking borders, ever dimming lights.

The climate of her native Darmstadt was thought better for the Empress's health than that of Petersburg, so she traveled there often, taking her youngest children with her. It is possible that Paul was influenced by the relatively modern attitudes he encountered there, though Serge certainly wasn't.

Back home, a movement was afoot to ease Russia toward a modern constitutional monarchy. Paul's uncle, the brilliant Grand Duke Konstantin Nikolaevich, was one of the leading proponents of such a move, and the Emperor seemed inclined to favor it. In a strange way, however, this 'liberalizing' of the autocracy may have gotten jumbled up in some minds with the idea of moral corruption within the imperial family. If some of the younger Grand Dukes, like Vladimir and Alexis Alexandrovich, were sowing their wild oats with a vengeance (they were accused of conducting "wild orgies" in Paris)[10], then that could have been viewed as a distasteful but natural aspect of high-spirited youth (though it certainly did diminish the dynasty's prestige at a time when it was not high to begin with). But the same could not be said for mature men such as the Emperor's two brothers, Nicholas and Konstantin, both of whom had separated from their wives and taken up openly with mistresses, and what was a hundred – a million – times worse, the Emperor himself had formed a serious bond with his mistress, to the extent of moving her (and the children they shared) into the Winter Palace! It was believed by some that Alexander's impropriety may have contributed materially to the reactionary inclinations of the Tsarevich (Alexander III) and his brother Serge.[11] The latter, though only three years older than Paul, tried his best to shield his sensitive younger brother from what he himself had discovered about their father's infidelity, and apparently he succeeded, perhaps allowing Paul a measure of admiration for their father that he himself now lacked, but such artificially supported illusion certainly could not last forever.

Marie at last succumbed to tuberculosis in 1880, and Alexander lost no time in marrying his mistress only weeks later, with the reported intention of making her Empress-Consort and legitimizing their children in due course. Rather than telling his youngest sons about the marriage himself, Alexander passed that task on to Arseniev, the preceptor who had been with them since childhood. Serge's disgust can be imagined. Paul, his mother's own fragile son, was so shocked that he suffered a physical breakdown and had to be sent away to Greece for complete repose among the loving warmth of his cousin Olga's happy, close-knit family.[12] Incredibly, this was probably the very best thing that could have been done for young Grand Duke Paul. Away from the stiff, cold formality of the Romanov court, he basked in the love he saw with his Athenian cousins.

One member of that family was, of course, his future wife, who was then a girl of twelve – Princess Alexandra of Greece. Was it her girlish perception of heroic suffering in Paul that turned her heart toward him? Perhaps so, but that would have to wait since even he, though twenty, was really still a boy and she still a girl. While his brothers and cousins had been gaining in responsibility and experience, participating, for instance, in the Russo-Turkish War (Alexander, Vladimir, and Alexis Alexandrovich all received important commands. Serge was attached to his elder brothers), Paul had done little but travel and learn the hard way how cruel life could be, and how cynically people could behave.

Paul's travels included a visit to the Vatican and an audience with Pope Leo XIII in 1881. It was there in Italy that he and Serge learned of their father's death at the hand of bomb-wielding terrorists on March 1/13, an event that does not seem on the surface to have impacted Paul as deeply as news of Alexander's remarriage had less than a year previously. Surely, the Emperor bears much of the responsibility for this, for he could have been much more sensitive to the feelings of the children from his first family, especially young Paul. Clearly, the Emperor spent his time with those he wished, such as Sasha's son, Nicky, who he saw every day, and his second family, now having named them the Yurievskis. But regardless of what he showed others, the death of even an indifferent and in his estimation, immoral parent, must still have been devastating to a man as sensitive as Paul was proving to be.

Thus power passed into the hands of the Tsarevich, now Alexander III, and dreams of a constitutional monarchy were squelched. The age of the Great Reforms had come to an ignominious end. Paul, for whom Alexander, fifteen years his senior, was more a surrogate father than merely an older brother (he even called Alexander's wife, Marie Feodorovna, "Mama"), does not seem to have sought any political or advisory role, whether in defense of his father's modernizing legacy (as Vladimir initially did), or in support of Alexander's more conservative inclinations. But, ironically, the reactionary Tsar Alexander III had much more personal warmth toward his youngest brothers as did Dagmar, than did their father the reforming Tsar Liberator Alexander II.

Less than three months after the assassination he and Serge were again abroad, this time touring Jerusalem with their cousin, Grand Duke Konstantin Konstantinovich. It is certainly possible that the three young men discussed Russia's future and that of the dynasty. They could hardly have failed to realize that the time had come for their generation of Grand Dukes to step up and assume whatever roles they were destined to play in Russia's history. And, indeed, within ten years of the Jerusalem trip, the intense, serious, and very conservative Serge would become Governor General of Moscow, one of Russia's most powerful political offices and, after Alexander III's death in 1894, a close advisor to the young Emperor Nicholas II. Konstantin would have a relatively modest role as the head of military education in Russia, but would establish himself as a distinguished writer and important patron of the arts, in close touch with many of Russia's most brilliant novelists, playwrights, poets and painters. Paul, on the other hand, would not show a great deal of interest in either government or the arts (though his youngest son, Vladimir, would show great talent as a poet).

Serge and Konstantin, on this particular trip in 1881, both cemented their status as men passionate about their Orthodox Christian faith. Serge was a founding member of the Orthodox Palestine Society, and thus took a special interest in all that he saw. Konstantin would later write a play about Christ's passion and resurrection, which undoubtedly drew upon, and benefitted greatly, from his memories and impressions of Jerusalem. Paul might have been taken for the younger brother/cousin tagging along, the more so since, back in Russia, he earned a reputation as a "carefree" young man. David Chavchavadze writes: *"He was charming, elegant, humorous, a good dancer and a great favorite among the ladies,"* different from Serge *"in every way."*[13] Such lightheartedness might seem odd from the young man who had grown up in the shadow of his mother's sorrow, and shown such acute sensitivity himself. After all, he had lost both parents in the space of less than a year, and can hardly have had a chance to make his peace with his father before the man was violently torn from his life. Was there guilt attached to this state of affairs, and did he remember anything of his mother's gloomy premonition of the dynasty's inevitable demise? It is hard to believe that he was, indeed, as blithe as he seemed to St Petersburg's socialites. His son Dimitri, not yet born, would project a similarly carefree and frivolous attitude as a young man – seemingly the very type, like his father, of the *bon vivant* Grand Duke – even while he struggled privately with depression and feelings of inadequacy, and cultivated a passion for politics and an amazingly astute understanding of the forces shaping his motherland.[14]

Paul may not have been a born leader like his cousin Nicholas Nikolaevich (Jr.), who would rise to the position of Supreme Commander of the Russian Army during the First World War, but he had a genuine love of military service – especially cavalry – and began his service career with the Grodno Hussars. That he was not, at heart a playboy, and was demonstrated by his marriage to Princess Alexandra of Greece on June 17, 1889. He might have remained a bachelor like his brother Alexis and met with little opposition from the family, because after all, the Emperor had three sons. So did Grand Duke Vladimir, so the succession still seemed absolutely secure, and the surfeit of Grand Dukes had already prompted Alexander to change the 1797 Statute on the Imperial family so that Emperors' sons like Paul could pass their Grand Ducal title only to their own children, not to their grandchildren. But a settled family life was precisely what Paul wanted, and the match with Alexandra, enthusiastically championed by Marie Feodorovna, seems to have been imbued with genuine love.

Still, one wonders if the bond between the two brothers, Serge and Paul, was stronger than that of either man with his wife. Serge and Elisabeth's marriage, which produced no children, was known to be a peculiar one. Paul, meanwhile, was rumored to be infatuated with his sister-and-law. This connection was the source of the first scandal associated with Paul. Gossip at the time implied an unhealthy connection between Paul and his brother's wife. Doubtless the truth was probably much more mundane. Paul was very attached to his brother as are many siblings who have faced trauma without much parental support and Paul doubtless was drawn to Ella's warmth and beauty just as were most men she encountered. The two couples were extremely close, though it is difficult to say whether the wives would have chosen one another's companionship under other circumstances. Paul and "Alix" lived in St Petersburg, Serge and "Ella" in Moscow, but they all came together for holidays at Illinskoe, Serge's country estate on the Moscow River.

When Paul and Alexandra had their first child, Marie, in April 1890, it was a cause of rejoicing for both couples, and the newborn seemed to possess the happy prospect of growing up in the midst of not just two doting parents, but four. But tragedy struck the following year when Alexandra died giving birth to the couple's second child, a boy, Dimitri. That event occurred in early September, while Paul and Alexandra were still on a late summer visit to Illinskoe. The baby had not been due for another two months, and there were no doctors at hand. Alexandra was only twenty-one years old. Paul, at thirty, had become a widower with two children, and must have been in a state of shock. It was his brother, Serge, who showed the most active concern for the newborn, bathing the little boy himself, and Serge, too, who instructed that the room in which Alexandra had died should be locked forever.

Yet, one must ask – why did the lovely young Grand Duchess receive no pre-natal care? And, if no care, what in the world was a very pregnant young bride doing going for a boat ride at a place with no available medical care, as indeed Alix was doing when she had her stroke? These are very difficult questions to pose. But, one must look to her husband at least for part of the responsibility for this death. In the aftermath, her children were half orphaned and a hospital in Athens was founded in her name which still stands.

Paul, meanwhile, returned to St Petersburg without his newborn son, the baby being judged too fragile to travel, and a precedent was thus set very early on for a kind of joint parenting between the two brothers. The children would take up permanent residence in the nursery of their father's palace in St Petersburg, but would also spend a great deal of time at Ilyinskoe with their uncle and aunt. A photo taken in 1892 shows Paul, looking thin and haggard, with both children on his knees, their round, plump-cheeked faces in sharp contrast to their father's long and weary-looking visage. A companion photo taken at the same time depicts what at first glance seems an odd family group – two adult men and one woman with two children, the adults, of course, being Serge, Paul and Ella. Dimitri sits on Paul's lap, and Ella is holding Marie. An 1899 cabinet photo shows the two children alone with their uncle, his arms around them both.

So far as his career was concerned, Paul's ascent within the military was quite gradual. He become Commander of the Horse Guards in 1891, a *very* modest post for a 31-year-old Grand Duke, and remained there until 1896, at which time he advanced to a divisional command, still modest.[15] At some point before 1902 he obtained command of the 1st Guards Corps, which was finally what one might call a genuinely Grand Ducal position.

Meanwhile, Alexander III's death in 1894 had led to what some viewed as a rapid degeneration of the Imperial Family, with the young Nicholas II quite unable to impose his will upon his uncles and cousins and ensure the kind of cohesiveness and discipline upon which Alexander III had insisted[16] Paul, who lived quietly with his children, was, indeed, one of those who voiced disapprobation, complaining openly to his military colleagues that family squabbles had become endemic because no one feared Nicholas.[17] Paul was certainly not a bully or a playboy himself, but he showed himself capable of joining forces with his brothers to thwart Nicholas when, in 1896, it was thought that the young Emperor might levy some kind of punishment upon Serge for having allowed the Khodynka Field disaster. He (Paul) joined Vladimir and Alexis Alexandrovich in threatening to resign from Russia's service if Serge were penalized in any way.[18] Whether or not this stance had anything to do with his decision, Nicholas declined to take action against Serge, but, of course, a generational line had been drawn in the sand, with Nicholas cast in the unlikely role of potential upholder of dynastic accountability in the face of outdated Grand Ducal privilege.

Aside from his willingness, in that one instance, to back his brother against the Tsar if need be, Paul probably gave Nicholas little cause for worry relative to the other Grand Dukes. In the event, however, it was he, of all people, who turned out to be the first Grand Duke to push Nicholas to the brink, and bring down severe punishment upon himself. This was the second of Paul's scandals, and one must look to his lack of nurturing to fully comprehend what he did and why he did it.

Paul first met and fell in love with Olga von Pistolkors (nee Karnovich), the woman who became first his mistress, then his wife, in 1895. Olga's husband, with whom she had three children, was an officer in the Horse Guards and an aide-de-camp to Paul's brother Vladimir. In 1897 she gave birth to Paul's son, Vladimir (called "Bodya" by his parents and siblings because as a small child he could not pronounce "Volodya", the diminutive form of Vladimir). It was understandably too much for Olga's husband, Eric von Pistolkors, who demanded a divorce. The affair nonetheless remained covert for the next five years while Paul pursued his military career and raised his children. He was a distant, but affectionate father to Dimitri and Marie. He enjoyed reading to them, and was not above romping with them from time to time. But, they simply didn't see enough of him to satisfy their deep need for parental love, and certainly didn't know he had another child to care for (though they once caught sight of Bodya's photograph on his desk). Paul spent increasing amounts of time with Olga abroad, and on one such trip, on October 10, 1902, he married her, against Nicholas's orders, and was stripped of his service and dynastic rights (including his 200,000 ruble annual appanage income), exiled, and deprived of the custody of his eldest two children, who would now go to Moscow to live full time with Serge and Ella.

The great irony, of course, is that Paul, who was so devastated by his father's re-marriage in 1880, had now done the same thing to his own children, and in a much more damaging way given their young ages and the predictable consequence that they would be torn from their home and their one surviving parent. Indeed, if he had been a playboy, flitting from mistress to mistress and fathering numerous 'natural' children, his behavior might have been shrugged off as that of just another high-living Grand Duke. Nicholas might well have tolerated it as he did in the case of his favorite uncle, Grand Duke Alexis. But, as things stood, to contract a morganatic marriage was both to defy the Emperor and to renege on one's dynastic duty. A precedent had been set by Alexander III, who refused to allow Grand Duke Michael Mikhailovich return to Russia with the morganatic bride he had married abroad. Nicholas surely felt he could do no less, and probably hoped that a loud and clear message would be sent to the rest of the bachelors in the family. It was, of course, to no avail. Grand Duke Kirill married a divorcee in 1905, and suffered the same punishment, albeit for a shorter term (he was allowed to return to Russia and resume his status and duties in 1909, perhaps because his marriage did not have the added outrage of being morganatic). Grand Duke Michael Alexandrovich was the next to contract a morganatic marriage to a divorcee in 1910 and suffer the by now familiar penalties. He, like Paul, was allowed to return in 1914. It should be noted that both Michael Alexandrovich and Paul's morganatic marriages caused particular outrage in the officer corps, because 'stealing" a brother officer's wife is something that is still highly objectionable in any country. All three of these 'renegade' marriages proved to be very loving ones, but the damage done was not negligible, either to the prestige and cohesion of the dynasty, or, on a more personal level, to Paul's children.

Paul and Olga settled in St Cloud, just outside Paris, in a house (No. 2

Avenue Victor Hugo) that was palatial if not an actual palace. Paul had inherited three million rubles from his father, and that sum had more than doubled by 1902, giving him a capital of seven million, but he was only allowed to transfer three million of the total abroad, and money would be an issue in future.[19] In 1906 he passed a message along to the Emperor through Baron Fredericks, begging for the restoration of part of his appanage income (and received a positive reply).[20] Of course, it undoubtedly helped that he and Olga, with their son and two daughters, born in 1903 (Irene Pavlovna) and 1905 (Natalia Pavlovna) lived quietly. A portion of Paul's diaries remained outside Russia during the revolution, and eventually passed into the hands of his eldest child, Grand Duchess Marie, who deposited them at Mainau, her son's private island in Lake Constance. These volumes do not make for exciting reading! They depict Paul as a gentle, home-loving man, religiously observant, and a creature of habit, keeping to a schedule of meals, walks, and naps that scarcely varied from one day to the next, and might, indeed, have been a sanatorium regimen. He loved to read out loud to his wife and children in the evening, a habit that drove the teenaged Dimitri mad with boredom on those occasions when he was allowed to visit his father abroad.[21] But *what* he read he never mentions in the diaries, which leads one to believe that the subject matter itself really didn't matter much. It was, perhaps, more the family togetherness that he enjoyed – seeing his wife and children gathered closely round him, safe from all outside harm. He wrote often to Dimitri, and was clearly greatly concerned with his son's upbringing. A request to Nicholas (made sometime in 1906) that the teenaged boy should be sent to live with his father in France was turned down by the Emperor, despite Paul's insistence that it was Dimitri's *own* "passionate" wish as well as his (Paul's).[22] As for his eldest daughter, in a letter of May 12, 1907, Paul informed Nicholas of his belief that seventeen was too young for a girl to marry, and expressed great satisfaction that that decision had been made without his input or approval, and that he had not had a chance to get to know the prospective groom. He complained bitterly that the guardianship established over his eldest children had *"ripped my children away from me as much as it possibly could."*[23] The real subject of the letter, however, was Nicholas's refusal to allow *both* Paul and Olga to come to Russia for Marie's wedding, and the continued state of exile and official disgrace, no matter how cozy and pleasant his life in Paris, clearly cut Paul to the quick.

Serge's death on February 17, 1905 at the hands of a bomb wielding terrorist was a major catastrophe both for the Imperial Family in general and for Paul in particular. It was the first time a member of the family had been killed since Alexander II's assassination almost twenty-four years prior ago, and was a glaring demonstration of the fact that no real resolution or state of security had been achieved. There remained a volatile and violent undercurrent within the dynasty's relationship to its subjects. For Paul, the fact that he had had such painful, unresolved issues with his father in 1881 must have been echoed with his brother in 1905. After all, Serge had co-opted his paternal role, and though that could be looked upon as a brotherly favor, it is hard to imagine that there was not some deep-seated resentment as well. Returning to Russia for the first time since 1902 (and without his wife and younger children for support, since they were still considered unwelcome by the rest of the family) he had to confront both the

Emperor who had banished him and the son and daughter who had been betrayed by him – all against the backdrop of his beloved older brother's murder.

Grand Duke Konstantin Konstantinovich paints a very moving picture of Paul's first meeting with his children at the train station in Moscow – all three were so overjoyed to see one another, and yet so grief-stricken, and the tears flowed.[24] Konstantin found it painful even to look at Paul. He (Paul) was *"lost,"* *"beaten down,"* and *"leaned on"* Konstantin for support during the entire funeral.[25] There was, however, one ray of hope, as Paul saw it, amidst the tragedy of Serge's death, and that was a rapprochement between himself and Nicholas. The two men met at Tsarskoe Selo before Paul proceeded on to Moscow, and, looking back upon that meeting when he had returned to France, Paul felt certain that his situation would now undoubtedly improve. He wrote Nicholas a gushing letter on February 24, expressing his relief at the knowledge *"that you are no longer angry at me, that you understand me and have forgiven me, that you yourself told me that I behaved honorably – that's a wonderful feeling, and my heart is so light! If any comfort can be taken from poor Serge's terrible end, it's the thought that his death has given me your forgiveness."*[26]

As it turned out, however, forgiveness did not equate to restoration of rights and privileges, to acceptance of Olga (who now bore the German title Countess Hohenfelsen) and her children, or to the lifting of the shadow that overhung Paul's own reputation. Paul's struggle for control of his eldest children continued, as we have seen, and was imbued with bitterness on his part. In the years that followed he would often resort to his brother Alexis as a go-between between himself and the Emperor, though he continued to write Nicholas directly, especially when he was particularly hurt or incensed. Nicholas's unwillingness to allow Olga to accompany Paul to Marie's wedding to Prince William of Sweden in 1908 led Paul to write an angry letter, announcing that he himself would not be attendance. He explained that he had borne his punishment meekly, but that, having proved his love for Olga and his honor through *"five years of exemplary family life"* he now had *"a right to expect different treatment."*[27] In the event, Olga was allowed to visit Russia with Paul in November 1907 (Nicholas sent his permission not directly, but through Alexis), which overjoyed Paul, and she was also allowed to accompany him to the wedding the following April.[28]

Olga did everything she could, in the years that followed, to gain Alexandra's approval, even sending the Empress (through Paul) some watercolors of the little Tsarevich that she herself had commissioned from a French artist (Mme Mantovani Gutti).[29] She also paid for a French edition of Elchaninov's laudatory book on the Romanov Jubilee in 1913, and Paul very proudly pointed that good deed out to Nicholas in a letter of May 29, 1913.[30]

Paul's exile was, in the end, lifted in 1912, and he was restored to all his Grand Ducal rights and privileges. He commissioned the building of a new residence in Tsarskoe Selo, modeled after his home in France, and utilizing the labor of imported French workers and artisans.[31] He and Olga remained in St Cloud with their daughters while the home was being constructed, not returning permanently to Russia until the spring of 1914.

In an undated "memorandum" [zapiska] to Nicholas, written in late 1914 or early 1915, Paul made six requests with regard to the status of his wife and their three children: that they should receive princely titles, that these titles (along with the marriage itself) should be publicly acknowledged in an official "ukase", that Olga and the girls should be allowed to follow the Imperial Family in official processions, that Paul should be able to present his wife to members of the family without recourse to a "hofmeisterin", that Olga should not have to register in the guest books of the Grand Duchesses when she visited, but be able to leave her visiting card, and that Paul and Olga should be given boxes next to the Imperial Box at various theaters.[32] Nicholas refused only the last of these requests, and Olga and her children received the title of Princesses and Prince Paley. Paul, meanwhile, resumed his post as commander of the 1st Guards Corps.

These requests, quite trivial sounding when one considers that they were made while Russia was at war, should by no means be taken to sum up who Paul really was. As unimpressive as his early career had been, it is impossible to say absolutely that he would not have matured and become a servitor of consequence in Russia if he had not been banished in 1902. His behavior during the war showed, at least, that he very much wished to play an important role and to contribute to his country's well-being. He begged to be given a military position of any kind, even a humble one, and was overjoyed when the Emperor made him Commander of the 1st Guard Corps. Nicholas described the scene to Alexandra: *"When I informed Paul of this intention of mine, he wept, and nearly suffocated me – he is so keen on taking part in the war!"*[33] But, for all practical purposes, it was already too late. Even as the elated Paul prepared to return to Tsarskoe Selo from Stavka with the sole intention of packing for a longer stay away from home, he was beset by illness severe enough to prevent him from traveling. On November 8 Alexandra wrote Nicholas: *"What now about poor Paul? I doubt his ever being able to take up his service, to my mind* [he's] *a finished man, that does not mean that he may not continue living with care, but not at the war, & I pity him deeply."*[34] Two days later she reported that Paul was losing weight daily and, in fact, weighed less than Anastasia. *"He receives nobody, not wishing them to see how he's changed... am so awfully sorry for him – at last all his wishes achieved – & nothing of any avail."* Rasputin was, moreover, predicting that he would "certainly" die.[35] The crisis, at that moment, had been caused by his malfunctioning gall bladder, though cancer was suspected.[36] Paul himself wrote Nicholas on the 24th:

> *Unfortunately I am still not allowed out, and, because of that, I cannot tell you personally how devastated I am that the doctors will not allow me to go to the front. I was so elated with, and proud of, the command with which I have been entrusted. But about that, I beg you: don't count me out yet. God grant that, by the end of this winter I will be so much stronger that I will be able to serve you and the motherland once more as part of our splendid army, which I love ardently.*[37]

Of course, Rasputin was wrong in this instance, and Paul did not die. The crisis passed, and, after a delay of several months, was able to assume his command post in May 1916. David Chavchavadze writes: *"He spent most of World War I at Tsarskoe Selo, but when his health permitted, he commanded the First Imperial Guards Corps at the front, ranking as a full general of cavalry."*[38]

Meanwhile, an interesting phenomenon was taking place: Alexandra had embraced Paul, her husband's last surviving uncle and her neighbor in Tsarskoe Selo, as a special friend and confidant. This would hardly seem like a particularly noteworthy event were it not for the existence of an ever-widening schism between Nicholas and Alexandra on the one hand, and the rest of the Imperial Family on the other, the most insurmountable obstacle between them being the role of Grigory Rasputin as a self-appointed advisor to the Emperor. Paul was clearly someone Alexandra felt she could trust. He was a gentle, good-tempered man, a family man and semi-invalid, without any ambitions that might be taken by her as a threat to her husband or son. It was she who urged Nicholas in repeated letters to give him a military role in the first place, and she who kept Nicholas appraised of his health. The two of them spoke frequently about their mutual concern for Paul's eldest son, Grand Duke Dimitri Pavlovich, and Alexandra insisted to Nicholas that Paul, like herself, though the young man should be sent to serve with his regiment and not be allowed to remain with Nicholas at Headquarters where he formed grandiose ideas about his own importance and became convinced that Nicholas wanted and valued his advice.[39] Through all this, Paul, who had shown unconditional support for Grand Duchess Marie at the time of her divorce in 1913 (insisting to Nicholas that divorce was the only recourse, and defending her to the Emperor against the *"unjust attacks"* of the Swedish King),[40] seems to have taken Alexandra's side against Dimitri – at least that is what she herself perceived and reported to Nicholas. Was it true? It's scarcely hard to believe that Paul would be concerned about his son's behavior and at times dissatisfied. Dimitri was known to move in 'fast' circles, with lots of lady friends – among them ballerina Vera Karalli, actress E.I. Time, and Grand Duke Michael's morganatic wife, Countess Brassova. But there is nonetheless reason to believe that either Alexandra (in relation to Nicholas) or Paul (in relation to Alexandra) was guilty of misrepresentation. In late August 1915, at the time of one of Alexandra's most critical letters to the Emperor about Dimitri, something very important was going on – more than important – critical to the dynasty and Russia. Nicholas had all but decided to take over the supreme command of the war effort from his cousin, Grand Duke Nicholas Nikolaevich. Alexandra, who had come to dislike "Nikolasha" strongly and considered him threat to her husband's popularity, if not his throne, and so asked Paul to have dinner with the French Ambassador, Maurice Paléologue, and sound him about the proposed change. In her letter to Nicholas of 22 August she noted Paul's *"personal dislike"* for Nikolasha, and distaste for the man's *"mixing into everything"* and presenting himself as *"a sort of second Emperor."* On this particular subject, she noted, Paul and Rasputin said *"the same thing."*[41]

But Maurice Paléologue's account of his dinner with Paul and Dimitri makes it clear that father and son alike were horrified at the prospect of Nicholas taking over the supreme command, and that they considered Nikolasha (in Dimitri's words) *"a paragon of patriotism and selflessness."* Dimitri had been trying since early that morning to arrange a meeting with Nicholas for the sole purpose of dissuading him, but the Emperor refused to see him. It may very well be that Alexandra, who did not appear to be mentally stable during this period, felt that Paul agreed with her, even if he did not. He clearly had Paul's full support, at least in this instance, and both men were acting in a manner very far removed indeed from Alexandra's depictions.[42]

In the event, nothing could dissuade Nicholas from his decision. In the words of Anna Vyrubova (cited by Paléologue), he viewed himself as the *'sacrificial victim"* whose life was needed *"to save Russia."*[43] If he'd known that his life would literally be taken from him, as would those of so many other members of the family, he might yet have been willing to accept that fate – so long as Russia was, indeed, 'saved." That, alas, was not to be.

One could view Paul's not entirely forthright friendship with Alexandra as self-serving. After all, he obtained several concessions from Nicholas during the course of 1915, amongst them a title for his wife and younger children and a highly-coveted military position for himself. On the other hand, it is hard not to see a degree of admirable wisdom and restraint in his behavior vis a vis Alexandra. He maintained close ties to her while so many of the other Grand Dukes burned their bridges one by one, and might have hoped to maintain some influence for the good, however slight.

In 1916 he was finally awarded something almost all his brothers and cousins (and even his son Dimitri) had already achieved – a St George's Cross (4th class), Russia's most coveted military decoration. But he had precious little time to enjoy it before he himself was thrust into the forefront of the conflict between Nicholas and Alexandra on the one hand, and the rest of the family on the other. On December 16, 1916, Dimitri participated in the assassination of Rasputin. Paul, who was at Stavka when Nicholas received word of that event, though the Emperor seemed relieved.[44] He, for his part, was horrified that Dimitri had been involved (though he took solace in the fact that his son had not been the actual killer), but supported his son. He drafted a letter to the Emperor, asking that Dimitri, who suffered from ill-health, not be sent into Persian exile, and fifteen other members of the Imperial Family added their signatures to his. The request was indignantly refused, and anyone might have thought that the final chapter had been written on Paul's close involvement with the Imperial couple. But the Grand Duke remained a quiet, unthreatening presence in Tsarskoe Selo, not given to explosive pronouncements or shrill and futile warnings of doom.

Though not one of the family members who had rushed to the Sergei Palace in Petrograd to stand beside Dimitri and his co-conspirator, Prince Felix Yussoupov during their period of house arrest, Paul at least wanted to see his son before the latter's departure for exile in Persia, but Dimitri himself, in a tearful telephone conversation, asked his father not to come. Such a painful farewell would be beyond his ability to bear.[45] Neither, of course, could know that they would never have another chance to see one another again.

One last act remained in Paul's belated career as the voice of the Romanovs. On February 28, 1917, (O.S.), four days after general revolutionary disorder had begun, Alexandra summoned Paul and bid him to go to the front and gather what loyal troops he could to *'save the throne"* at all cost. He declined to do so, being already convinced that any such effort would be hopeless. Alexandra summoned him again the next day, but this time he did not even bother to go. He was busy drafting a constitutional manifesto. Thirty-six years to the day after the assassination of his father, Alexander II, Paul was prepared to finish what the late 'Tsar Liberator's' untimely death had interrupted so disastrously – the transformation of the Russian Empire into a modern, democratic, constitutional monarchy. He signed the document, as did Grand Dukes Michael Alexandrovich and Kirill Vladimirovich.[46] It was then delivered to the Duma, and accomplished absolutely nothing. It was, quite simply, too late. The Great Reforms could not be revived in 1917, and Paul, who might have become one of the most important of the Grand Dukes in the end, instead remained superfluous. It was he who finally told Alexandra on March 3 that her husband had abdicated. Romanov rule in Russia had come to an end.

Paul and his family remained united at their home in Tsarskoe Selo as long as they could. Louis de Robien attended Paul's birthday party on July 12, 1917, and noted that Irene and Natalie Paley performed in a little play written by their brother, Bodya, in which Natalie played *"a boy king"* and Irene *"a young nihilist dressed in black!"*[47] Indeed, it was the outspoken scorn of Olga Paley and Bodya, directed at the Provisional Government, that reputedly led Alexander Kerensky to place Paul under house arrest in August, 1917. He was persuaded to relent and remove the guards from the Grand Duke's home, however, after a conciliatory visit he received from Paul's eldest daughter, Marie.

A much greater ordeal was his arrest by the newly triumphant Bolsheviks in October of that same year. This time he was taken from home and held for two weeks at the Bolsheviks' headquarters in the Smolny Institute. De Robien wrote:

> *It seems the Bolsheviks were rather embarrassed by their prisoner. They wanted to move him to the Fortress, then to Kronstadt, which could have had tragic results. The Grand Duke was very insistent, and protested so strongly that the tovariches allowed themselves to be persuaded. He heard them saying, 'He's a nuisance, that man, he doesn't want to go anywhere.' Finally, after a great deal of palaver, they decided to leave him at Smolny, where they shut him up in a room guarded by a quad of sailors. The Grand Duke, moreover, has no complaints about his guards: some of them even addressed him as 'Comrade Highness'! They found an armchair for him and settled him into it; one of them begged him to read the newspaper to them and explain it, and they asked his permission to smoke while listening. The Grand Duke naturally agreed, and it must have been strange to see this Romanov in general's uniform and wearing the order of St George, with his majestic look and superb presence, reading Pravda to a group of disheveled sailors.*[48]

His release this time was due to his ill health, and he was allowed to remain in Tsarskoe Selo for the same reason after all the other male Romanovs had been deported to the provinces on March 18, 1918, his son Bodya included. In August 1918 he was arrested a third time, and this time imprisoned in Petrograd along with Grand Dukes Dimitri Konstantinovich and Nicholas and George Mikhailovich. Olga visited him as often as she could, bringing extra food, which he shared with his three cousins. According to Grand Duke George, who wrote frequent letters to his daughters in England, Paul held up well despite his frailness, better, indeed, than the robust Nicholas Mikhailovich who sunk into a deep depression and would sometimes not even join the other three for their walks in the prison yard. In December 1918 Paul was transferred to a prison hospital. A few weeks later, when his wife went to visit him, he was gone, having been transferred to Cheka headquarters.[49] She would never see him again.

Yet, efforts were under way to save the last four Grand Dukes in Petrograd. Maxim Gorky went directly to Lenin and obtained a pardon for them – a pardon that was unfortunately received too late. Paul himself was under no illusions about what remained before him. His daughter Marie relates that he had a pre-sentiment that the end was near. While stories vary, what most likely happened to the four is as follows.

The three grand dukes who remained imprisoned at the Fortress of Peter and Paul were awakened in the middle of the night as the date changed to January 27, 1919. They were eventually joined by Paul who was driven to the Fortress from the Cheka. The four Grand Dukes were ordered to strip to the waist. Some reports have Paul unable to stand and lying on a stretcher. It would have been very cold – about 20 degrees below zero. They were led from the Trubetskoy bastion to the center of the Fortress and in front of the Cathedral whose height dominated the skyline of Petrograd. In front of the Cathedral was a ditch, and inside the ditch were the corpses of thirteen other unfortunates. The Grand Dukes were next told to stand in line. One by one they were led to the edge of ditch so that after they were shot, their bodies would fall into the ditch, meaning that the Bolshevik firing squad had little clean up to do. Thus perished "Uncle Bimbo', the renowned historian Nicholas Mikhailovich who took his pet cat to his execution; his brother, Grand Duke George Mikhailovich whose children were safely in the West; Grand Duke Dimitri Konstantinovich, son of the Great Reformer Grand Duke Konstantin Nikolaevich; and Grand Duke Paul Alexandrovich. All perished quickly but knowing in advance they were to die.

Paul left the House in St Cloud and some money in a Berlin bank, but the latter, due to inflation, amounted to very little by the time Princess Paley could retrieve it and divide it between herself, Dimitri and Marie (the latter two were living together in London at that time, along with Marie's second husband, Prince Sergei Putiatin). Sophia "Mimi" Polovtsov, the wife of one of Paul's former aides, tried to contact the late Grand Duke at a Paris séance in 1920, and claimed success, informing Dimitri that he could rest assured that his father was well and happy on the other side. Dimitri was not entirely convinced that his father had truly spoken, but was also not prepared to dismiss the idea out of hand.[50] He decided not to inform his sister, fearing it would only serve to upset her. It was he, on the other hand, who was overcome by sorrow when Olga sent him a trunk of Paul's clothes, hoping he could make use of them. He just couldn't bring himself to wear them, but Marie took a more practical approach, passing them on to her husband.[51] Times were tough, after all!

And if, indeed, Paul was watching from the other side, he could surely take some solace from the fact that four of his five children had survived the revolution and would succeed in making new lives for themselves outside Russia, as would their children and grandchildren. His three grandsons, Count Lennart Bernadotte, Prince Paul Ilyinsky, and Prince Michel Romanoff, would all live to see the fall of the Soviet regime, and Prince Ilyinsky would attend the burial of Nicholas and Alexandra in St Petersburg. More's the pity that Paul's own remains, and those of the other three Grand Dukes killed with him, have never been found. Although recent press reports suggest that the remains of the four Grand Dukes have at last been located.

The need to reform Russia did not die with Paul and his cousin Konstantin that cold January night. The country would undergo over seventy years of governance by a party who relied on lies and violence to remain in power. As the 100th anniversary of the death of the child of the great reforms approaches, it has been proven that for Russia, reform is the only option for meaningful change.

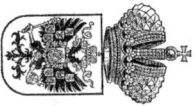

TABLE #3: DESCENDANTS OF ALEXANDER II

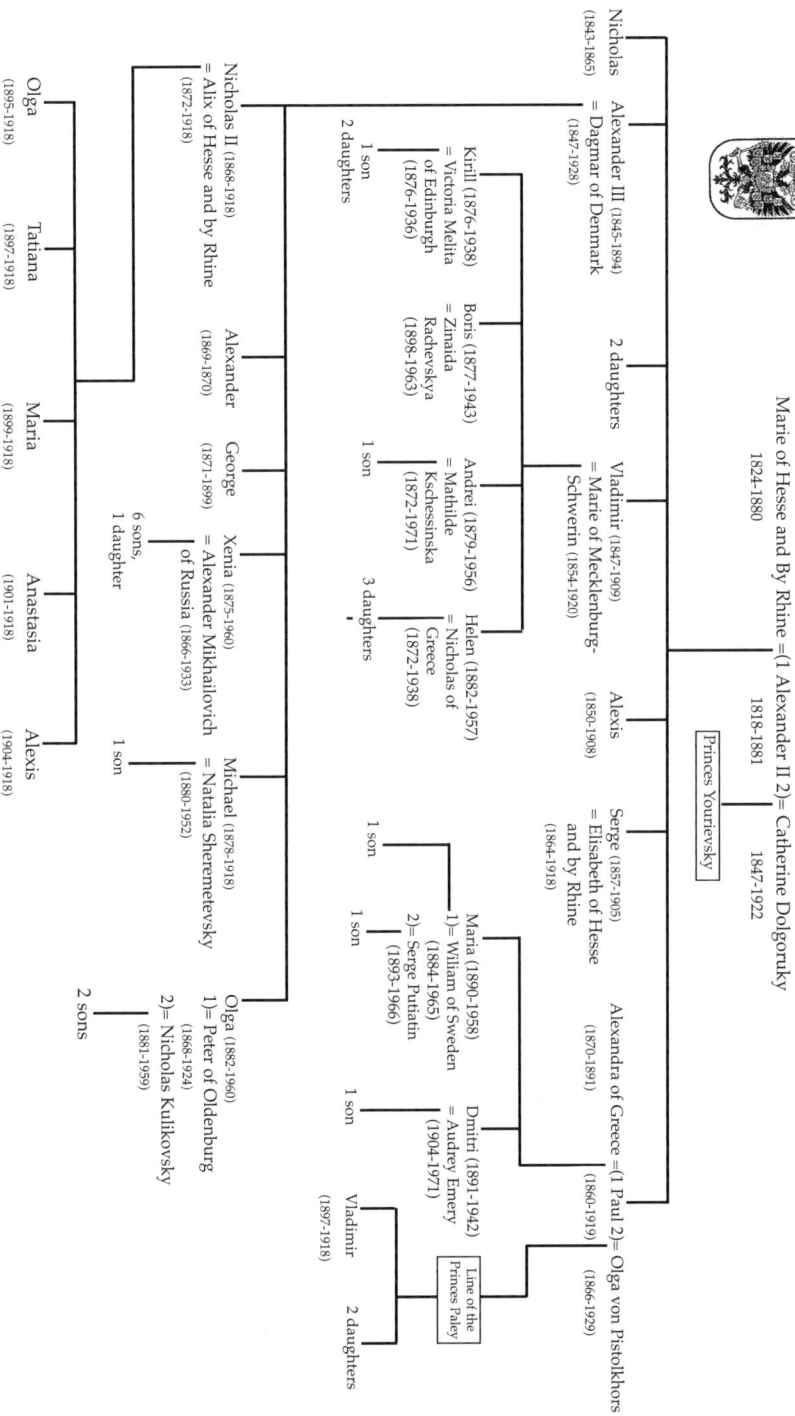

Marie of Hesse and By Rhine =(1 Alexander II 2)= Catherine Dolgoruky
1824-1880   1818-1881   1847-1922

Princes Yourievsky

Nicholas (1843-1865)

Alexander III (1845-1894)
= Dagmar of Denmark (1847-1928)

Vladimir (1847-1909)
= Marie of Mecklenburg-Schwerin (1854-1920)

Alexis (1850-1908)

Serge (1857-1905)
= Elisabeth of Hesse and by Rhine (1864-1918)

Alexandra of Greece =(1 Paul 2)= Olga von Pistolkhors
(1870-1891)   (1860-1919)   (1866-1929)

Children of Alexander III
- **Nicholas II** (1868-1918) = Alix of Hesse and by Rhine (1872-1918)
  - **Olga** (1895-1918)
  - **Tatiana** (1897-1918)
  - **Maria** (1899-1918)
  - **Anastasia** (1901-1918)
  - **Alexis** (1904-1918)
- **Alexander** (1869-1870)
- **George** (1871-1899)
- **Xenia** (1875-1960) = Alexander Mikhailovich of Russia (1866-1933)
  - 6 sons, 1 daughter
- **Michael** (1878-1918) = Natalia Sheremetevsky (1880-1952)
  - 1 son
- **Olga** (1882-1960)
  1)= Peter of Oldenburg (1868-1924)
  2)= Nicholas Kulikovsky (1881-1959)
  - 2 sons

Children of Vladimir
- **Kirill** (1876-1938) = Victoria Melita of Edinburgh (1876-1936)
  - 1 son
  - 2 daughters
- **Boris** (1877-1943) = Zinaida Rachevskya (1898-1963)
- **Andrei** (1879-1956) = Mathilde Kschessinska (1872-1971)
  - 1 son
- **Helen** (1882-1957) = Nicholas of Greece (1872-1938)
  - 3 daughters

Children of Paul
- **Maria** (1890-1958)
  1)= William of Sweden (1884-1965)
  2)= Serge Puttatin (1893-1966)
  - 1 son
- **Dmitri** (1891-1942) = Audrey Emery (1904-1971)
  - 1 son
- **Vladimir** (1897-1918)

Line of the Princes Paley

Olga (1882-1960)
1)= Peter of Oldenburg (1868-1924)
2)= Nicholas Kulikovsky (1881-1959)

2 daughters

TABLE #4: THE GRAND DUKES OF HESSE AND BY RHINE

Ludwig II = Wilhelmine of Baden
1777-1848   1788-1836

Ludwig III (1806-1877)
= Mathilde of Bavaria
(1813-1862)

Karl (1809-1877)
= Elisabeth of Prussia
(1815-1885)

Alexander (1823-1888)
= Julia von Hauke (1825-1895)

Marie (1824-1880)
= Alexander II of Russia
(1818-1881)

Ludwig IV (1837-1892)
= Alice of Great Britain
(1843-1878)

2 sons / 1 daughter

Princes of Battenberg

3 sons &
1 daughter

Dagmar of Denmark = Alexander III
1847-1928   1845-1894

Ernst Ludwig (1868-1937)
1)= Victoria Melita of Edinburgh
(1876-1936)
2)= Eleonore of Solms
(1871-1937)

Friedrich
1870-1873

Victoria = Louis
1863-1950   1854-1921

Marie
1874-1878

Elisabeth = Serge
1864-1918   1857-1905

Alix = Nicholas II
1872-1918   1868-1918

Irene (1866-1953)
= Heinrich of Prussia
(1862-1929)

Alice
(1885-1969)
= Andrew of
Greece
(1882-1944)

Louise
(1889-1965)
= Gustaf VI of
Sweden
(1882-1973)

George
(1892-1938)
= Nadja de
Torby
(1896-1963)

Louis
(1900-1979)
= Edwina Ashley
(1901-1960)

1. Olga (1895-1918)
2. Tatiana (1897-1918)
3. Maria (1899-1918)
4. Anastasia (1901-1918)
5. Alexis (1904-1918)

Waldemar (1889-1945)
= Calixta of Lippe
(1895-1982)

1 son / 3 daughters

1 son / 1 daughter

2 daughters

Elisabeth
1895-1903

Sigismund (1896-1978)
= Charlotte of Saxe
Altenburg (1899-1989)

Heinrich
1900-1904

George Donatus = Cecilie
1906-1937   1911-1937

Ludwig = Margaret Geddes
1908-1968   1913-1997

1 son / 1 daughter

Ludwig   Alexander   Johanna
1931-1937   1933-1937   1936-1939

4 THE SONS OF TSAR ALEXANDER III

TSAR NICHOLAS II
(1868-1918)

By Lisa Davidson

Nicholas II, the last tsar of Russia, has been the subject of numerous books, films, articles, and documentaries. The amount of material available on him is truly staggering. And yet, a balanced portrait of the man remains elusive. There are apologists who explain away every failing and critics who brand him weak willed and lacking character with few redeeming qualities. The middle ground is nowhere in sight, and everyone, including his contemporaries, seems to have an opinion about him. And yet, how many of these opinions are based upon Nicholas himself and how many on the dramatic circumstances of his life? After careful study of his life and times, it is immediately apparent that the challenges he faced might have been too overwhelming for all but the most skillful of politicians. As an individual, he was full of contradictions and inconsistencies, but he was a fundamentally decent man burdened with a difficult wife and a seriously ill son. He is ultimately a tragic figure, as he neither understood nor deserved his horrible fate.

For all that is known of him as Emperor, fully more than half of his life would be spent in the shadows as a Grand Duke, with thirteen of these fateful years also as Tsarevich of Imperial Russia. It seems that for all that many who know something of Imperial Russia think that they know Nicholas II, as a human being, he is certainly lesser known than many would imagine. In this chapter on the life of the last tsar, hopefully several lesser known aspects of Nicholas II will emerge. Writing about someone who has a tragic end is made more difficult if one does not anticipate the tragedy to come. Even more difficult perhaps is writing about someone who is regarded as a saint in the Russian Orthodox Church. If such a thing must be considered, then it is difficult to write an honest history. So, for the purposes of this chapter his status as a Passion Bearer will be ignored and his death will not be anticipated until it is actually upon him. To not do this would be to miss vital information about Nicholas II, who is very much as Churchill described Russia, the personification of being a *"riddle wrapped in a mystery inside an enigma."*

There is absolutely nothing enigmatic about Nicholas' birth. He was born some 18 months after his parents' marriage. In the summer of 1864, Tsarevich Nicholas Alexandrovich became engaged to the charming Princess Dagmar of Denmark. While not as classically beautiful as her sister Alexandra, the Princess of Wales, young Princess Dagmar glowed with her first love for the Russian heir. But, tragedy struck when Nixa, as Nicholas was known, died only months later, on April 24, 1865.[1] Nixa was just 21 years old.[2] Both Dagmar and Nixa's brother, Sasha, grieved heavily for him, but it was clearly expected that these two who survived him would marry one another, and so they did, on November 9, 1866[3], about 18 months after Nixa's death. Three years after the death of one Nicholas Alexandrovich, the young couple departed from the Orthodox tradition of naming their first son after the husband's father, and named their baby son in honor of the unfortunate Nixa. Thus, the man who became the last tsar of Russia began his life as a living symbol of a life lost prematurely, becoming the second Grand Duke Nicholas Alexandrovich. Being a symbol of matters that had little to do with him personally would always be part of Nicholas' existence.

The Russia that Nicholas was born into seethed with turmoil. Nicholas' grandfather, Tsar Alexander II by all accounts was a ruler committed to reform, his most famous being the emancipation of the serfs in 1861. This was just the first of many reforms which began a total transformation of Russian society. However, reform comes with a price. With every reform and liberalization, expectations grow, and there were always those for who changes from above moved far too slowly. Alexander II was a gentle and sensitive man with much the same demeanor as his grandson, Nicholas. A critical difference between the two emperors, who both had overbearing fathers, was that the best and the brightest subjects wanted to work with the Tsar-Liberator. By the end of Nicholas II's reign, few of the most politically minded Russians wanted anything at all to do with his government. This 'brain drain" in turn exacerbated the difficulties Nicholas had in effectively responding to challenges after 1914. The job of governing the Russian Empire had always been a complex one – but without able ministers, that is precisely what happened to Nicholas – it became an impossible one. So, even though Nicholas Alexandrovich was endowed with many of the qualities which lead his predecessors down the road to success, his circumstances were so vastly different, that they instead lead him down the road to ruin.

For someone with such a difficult life ahead of him, Nicholas had a remarkably happy childhood. He spent a great deal of time with his Imperial grandfather, usually seeing him every day, and grew to admire and emulate his calm and confident grandsire. His mother, who in Russia was known as Maria Feodorovna, also delighted in her baby Nicky. And, unlike many fathers of his class and circumstances, young Nicky's father was very much involved in his daily life. Alexander III's nieces and nephews, many of whom would become crowned heads of Europe, uniformly adored their playful "Uncle Sasha". Nicholas' closest companion of his childhood was his brother George, who was possessed of a wily wit. But, he was not as sheltered from his rambunctious Romanov cousins as his own children would be. Nicholas particularly enjoyed his cousin Grand Duke Serge Mikhailovich while a young boy, and as Serge's elder brother Alexander Mikhailovich was falling in love with Nicky's sister,

Xenia, 'sandro' joined the mix. By all accounts, Nicholas Alexandrovich was devoted to his family and would remain so throughout his life. Would that his dynastic family have been as devoted to him as he was to them, but it wasn't always that way. He was always his grandfather's "Sunbeam", a nickname that would be echoed when his own son was small.

Alexander II was firmly in control of Russia at the start of his reign. By the time he was assassinated in 1881, Russia had started onto the path of becoming ungovernable. The People's Will – the Narodnaya Volya – sentenced the reform minded autocrat to death. They made a total of eight attempts on his life both because they despaired of change coming too slowly but also because they wanted to prevent Russia from becoming more democratic and as a result, avoid revolution. Thus, the domestic terrorism they practiced was largely responsible for the end of reform from above in Imperial Russia. But by killing Alexander II, they were further responsible for the replacement with a liberal tsar with a reactionary one. In fact, since Alexander II had a relatively long lived brother,[4] it is even possible that, had he not been assassinated, the long years of reaction under his son Alexander III might have been avoided all together. We know that Alexander III died prematurely of nephritis at age 49. It is not inconceivable that Alexander II, if allowed to live out his natural life to perhaps the age of 80, could have easily outlived Nicholas' father. It is of course impossible to know what this would have meant to Russian history, but it is entirely possible that there would have been no revolution at all had this happened. Imagine what a conservative Nicholas would have done had he inherited a Russia that had been governed constitutionally for seventeen years. While Alexander II was an autocrat, he governed far more in the style of a constitutional monarch.

One of the marked characteristics of Nicholas II was his desire to bring people into agreement. While not a useful quality in an autocrat, it has been frequently pointed out by others, including Massie,[5] that it would have made Nicholas an excellent constitutional monarch. Unfortunately, his inherent conservatism did not help him at all in creating an effective constitutional system, but had he inherited one, he would have perhaps made refinements on it and at the very least, preserved it. When one examines the first ten years of Nicholas' reign, it appears this is precisely what he did with inheriting the reactionary regime of his father. He made refinements and improved upon what his father had created. For example, while Nicholas II was clearly an anti-Semite, he nonetheless listened to what educated Jewish subjects had to contribute, as we shall see with a man who predicted the end of the Russian monarchy due to an unsuccessful war. This is something Alexander III would never have done. We can thus conclude that, while the Narodnaya Volya was unsuccessful in promoting its own agenda, its terrorist members were perhaps the most successful of all the revolutionaries of Russia, in that their murder of Alexander II virtually ensured the failure of the reign of his grandson, Nicholas II.

In reviewing the life and times of Nicholas II, we therefore view him as a man who had the deck solidly stacked against him from at least the age of twelve. Had he been a "great man", he could have perhaps actualized a different outcome, but even that is doubtful. We can only present several scenes from his very eventful life, but in choosing the impact of his grandfather's assassination, the canonization of his favorite saint, the death of his father, the birth of his son, his own vision of "a great Russia", the genesis of the World Court, his abdication, and his own assassination, it is hoped that the truly enigmatic nature of the last of the tsars will emerge for the reader.

One tremendous misunderstanding about Nicholas II is the idea that he did not want to be tsar at all. The source of this bit of misinformation is Nicholas' brother-in-law, Grand Duke Alexander Mikhailovich, who was also his cousin. Sandro, as he was known, survived the Revolution and wrote *Once a Grand Duke* in exile. In a famous quote from that book, he reports Nicholas saying to him, on the death of his father:

> *Sandro, what am I going to do? What is going to happen to me, to you, to Xenia, to Alix, to mother, to all of Russia? I am not prepared to be a Tsar. I never wanted to become one. I know nothing of the business of ruling. I have no idea of even how to talk to the ministers. Will you help me, Sandro?*[6]

On the surface, this is a rather damning quotation. And, coming from his own brother in law, its accuracy has never been questioned. However, how can we be absolutely certain that Alexander actually heard Nicholas say this? There were no tape recorders in 1894, and we very much doubt he could remember word for word what his cousin said on that fateful day. What we can be certain about is that the principals involved in this little vignette were all dead by the time *Once A Grand Duke* was published, save for Nicholas' sister Xenia. For someone as sensitive and passionate as Nicholas, the death of his father before his fiftieth birthday must have been utterly devastating. For anyone, the loss of one's father at least initially can leave one feeling much less secure in the world. Most of us dealing with the emotional fallout that losing a parent creates don't have to worry about turning around and governing an empire teetering on the brink of ruin and revolution. It is entirely possible that Nicholas said something like this to Sandro, but, since much of what the Grand Duke wrote about his other relatives is quite self serving, it is more likely that he didn't. If we examine one of the sentences, for example, the one about Nicky not knowing how to talk to ministers, we know for a fact that this was untrue. Nicholas sat on many committees as Tsarevich, and in this capacity, he got to know many of his father's ministers, some of them, quite well, in fact. So, clearly, he knew how to talk to ministers. And, he knew Sandro did not know how to do this, so why is the Grand Duke giving us the impression that Nicholas would come to Sandro for help? We also know as a faithful Orthodox Christian, Nicholas, conservative that he was, would not have said he never wanted to become Tsar. The actual Nicholas accepted his lot throughout his life, he did not rail against it. And, if he confided his actual feelings to anyone at this particular time in his life, it is far more likely that he would have said something like this to his fiancée, Princess Alix, who had recently arrived in the Crimea from Darmstadt. So, it appears that there is a reasonable chance that Nicholas did not say one of the most well known statements attributed to him.

What is unquestionable is that a grieving Nicholas quickly filled the voids left in his life due to the illness of his brother George and the death of his beloved father with his marriage to Alix, who became known as Alexandra Feodorovna upon her conversion to Orthodoxy, on November 26, 1894.[7] During their early marriage, the couple were eager to establish their own household, and the Alexander Palace, the smaller of the two Tsarskoe Selo Imperial palaces, soon became their favorite home. There seems to have always been some tension between the younger Empress, Alexandra, and her mother-in-law, the Dowager Empress. Maria Feodorovna was certainly more socially poised than her daughter-in-law, who in all fairness spent a good amount of time in her early marriage pregnant and raising small children. But, the schism between Nicholas and Alexandra and the glittering world of St Petersburg's elite, which would prove to be so pivotal at the time of the Revolution, really began as two shy young royals, grieving for the loss of their fathers, began to isolate themselves in suburban Tsarskoe Selo. Alexandra, rather than embracing that society, generally thought its members immoral and not worth knowing. Perhaps they were both, but a savvier bride might have kept these opinions to herself and at least tried to develop some sincere friendships among the women of the rich and powerful. This would have been highly useful to her husband, which is after all, the "job" of a royal consort. Alexandra's women friends, on the other hand, seemed to have always been, not bright and interesting people, but those who would defer to her and admire her, women such as Anna Vyrubova and the Montenegrin sisters, Grand Duchesses Miltza and Anastasia. The characteristics of these friendships are such that it is obvious that Alexandra was insecure in her friendships with women. This, in turn, very likely made her depend more heavily on her husband for companionship than is now considered emotionally healthy. Nonetheless, the early years of their marriage seem to have been fairly happy and there is little evidence that Alexandra was at all interested in politics at this time.

A pivotal year for the couple was 1896, the year of their coronation as Emperor and Empress of Russia, an event held, as tradition demanded it, in Moscow. Their first child, their daughter Olga had been born on November 15, 1895, nearly a year to the day of their marriage. The planning of the coronation of a Russian Tsar was a massive undertaking that took over a year of planning. There is plenty of evidence from Nicholas and others that he relished this consummation of his "marriage" to Mother Russia, finally refuting his cousin's misstatement about Nicky not wanting to rule his country. Indeed, he would remember his coronation as one of the happiest days of his life, and always try to honor the trust he believed the Almighty had placed in him by making him Tsar of all the Russias. Nicholas' pronounced modesty was very much in evidence as he rode into Moscow in a plain tunic on horseback.[8] Instead of the massive Imperial Crown, he had wanted to use the ancient Cap of Monomak, the crown used by the Kievan Princes of the Rus. This, however, was not permitted as the rituals of Imperial Russia must be followed by everyone, especially the Emperor. Unfortunately, the joy he felt at his coronation was quickly dashed by the deaths of hundreds of his subjects at Khodynka field[9] due to poor planning by Governor-General of Moscow Serge Alexandrovich, Nicholas' uncle and brother-in-law. It was a tragedy he would never live down, and the couple retired to Serge and Ella's country estate to recover from the strain.

Perhaps one of the most perplexing matters in Nicholas' life occurred in the period between 1898 and 1901. History tells us that Nicholas was a weak tsar, personally indecisive, and an ineffective ruler. His support of pogroms in the early 20th century is unquestionable, so we can easily add "anti-Semite" to the long list of his failings. It is quite disconcerting, then, to discover that in 1898, the Emperor met with Ivan Bliokh, a wealthy Jewish railroad magnate, who was author of a six volume work, *Le Guerre Future*. From this meeting, Nicholas became familiar with Bliokh's work and his ideas that technology would make land based wars a matter of attrition and economic prowess.[10] For those who believed Nicholas stupid, it is difficult to reconcile that idea with the knowledge that he not only studied Bliokh, but grasped the importance of his work. Indeed, he sought to apply it by calling a Peace Conference which convened in The Hague on the Emperor's 31st birthday, May 18, 1899, and concluded July 29, 1899, scant days after the burial of Nicholas' brother, George.[11]

The purpose of this conference was to urge worldwide disarmament. In this, Nicholas II is rightly credited with being one of the founders of the modern movement for worldwide peace. The stated goals of the conference were: *"With the object of seeking the most effective means of ensuring all peoples the benefits of a real and lasting peace, and, above all, of limiting the progressive development of existing armaments."*

While not all of Bliokh's ideas ultimately proved correct, he was accurate in predicting that both the Russian and German monarchies would not survive a world war. Hence, remarkably, Nicholas knew exactly what he was walking into when war was declared in the summer of 1914. Of more enduring value were the protocols agreed to at the Conference. They became the basis for the International Court of Justice, now part of the United Nations, and the means by which nations can settle differences through arbitration and adjudication rather than warfare. Much of the basis of international law began with this conference called by Nicholas II. For this work, Nicholas was nominated for the very first Nobel Peace Prize in 1901. While it was ultimately won by the founder of the International Red Cross and a French pacifist, his was certainly the more enduring contribution to world peace. As a final irony, Nicholas begged his cousin Kaiser Wilhelm II to submit his grievances in August 1914 to the Court for arbitration. Yet, "Willy" held the Emperor in such low esteem, he refused. Clearly, his contemporaries had nearly as much difficulty as we in unraveling the enigmatic Tsar. Would that the Kaiser had listened to the Tsar, many lives, including Nicholas' might have been saved.

While the enduring triumph of Nicholas' life was the founding of the International Court of Justice and other international institutions, arguably his worst mistake was his choice for a wife, Princess Alix of Hesse and By Rhine. As with his grandfather, Nicholas tended to fall in love quite easily. He was also in love for a time as young man with the prima ballerina Mathilde Kschessinska who survived the Revolution and married Nicholas' cousin, Grand Duke Andrei Vladimirovich while living in exile. When he was younger still, he was reportedly smitten with his cousin, Princess Victoria of Great Britain. Doubtless, the history of Russia would have been far different had Nicholas simply married his cousin Toria. While the marital love of Nicholas and Alexandra has long been celebrated, especially in Robert K. Massie's Pulitzer Prize winning *Nicholas and Alexandra*, and even romanticized by others, this was not, in the writer's opinion, a healthy relationship. Undoubtedly, Nicholas and his wife loved one another very much, and they seem to have had a pleasant enough home life. But, there were always underlying tensions which kept their everyday existence from being less than harmonious. And, as she became older, much of this stemmed from Alexandra being such a difficult personality.

It was often remarked that Nicholas was a shy person. Yet, he was always able to rise to any occasion and most of those who met him found him to be personally charming. Alexandra, as Princess Alix was known in Russia, was also shy, but she lacked her husband's charm. He was born into a prestigious position in life and thus had few insecurities about his place in society. With Alexandra, it was a different story. She became haughtier, more regal, and more arrogant than any of her in laws. She did very little to make friends in Russia. Rather, she expected to be admired. Yet, children in general loved this empress and her own children seem to have adored her. The main problem with Alexandra is that she rejected the advice of everyone who knew her circumstances better than she did. Her grandmother, Queen Victoria, actually tried to warn her about the difficulties of being the Empress of Russia, to no avail. Alexandra thought she knew better. She was evidently a person who just could not be told anything, and as a result, her very presence seemed to make matters for everyone around her much more difficult than they needed to be. This was true while she was an empress and it remained the case when she was a prisoner of two revolutionary governments.

The common belief is that Nicholas II was a bad tsar. The truth is, absent of World War I and its various scandals, Nicholas II could be considered a reasonably competent monarch who demonstrated some outstanding leadership qualities. At times he was a visionary, as we saw with the founding of the Institutional Court of Justice, and at times he was a mystical religious leader, as we will see with the canonization of St Seraphim of Sarov. It is impossible to fully consider the life of Nicholas without touching on his deep and abiding religious faith. In very many ways, it was his defining characteristic.

In spite of his royal heritage, Nicholas Alexandrovich was a humble man, even refusing to ever advance his military rank beyond that of Colonel, the rank he held at the time his father died. During a period when many of the upper classes considered Orthodox Christianity to be hopelessly out of date, Nicholas was devout to a fault and entirely sincere in his religious beliefs. Prayer and religious observances, such as fasts and church services, were essential parts of everyday life for him and his family. To be as committed to his faith while at the same time a ruler with absolute power was a dichotomy that only he and perhaps a few others could understand. Nicholas seems to have always been aware of a dire destiny that he would face. The story of a Japanese wise man that met with him and foretold his future during his world tour in 1890 perhaps illustrates the reason why:

> ... *Danger is hovering over your head, but death will pass you by and the shoot will be stronger than the sword and the shoot will shine brilliantly. Two crowns are destined for you - an earthly and a heavenly. Gems play on your crown, O master of a mighty realm. But the glory of the world passes and will dim the gems on your earthly crown, while the glittering of your heavenly crown*

will last forever. Great sorrows and upheavals await you and your country. You will fight for everyone, and everyone will be against you. Beautiful flowers bloom on the edge of the abyss, and children rush up to the flowers and fall into the abyss if they do not listen to the warnings of their father. You will offer a sacrifice for your whole people, as the redeemer of its recklessness. I see fiery tongues above your head. This is the consecration. I see innumerable fires on altars in front of you. This is the fulfillment. Here is wisdom and part of the mystery of the Creator. Death and immortality, a split-second and eternity. Blessed be the day and hour on which you came to old Terakuto.'

A few days after this, there was an attempt on the life of the heir. A Japanese fanatic struck him on the head with a sabre, which gave him a minor wound since Prince George, who was all the time with the heir, parried the blow with a bamboo shoot. By command of Alexander III, the shoot which had played this role was encrusted with diamonds and returned to Prince George. Thus did the shoot prove stronger than the sword, and the shoot shone. The records witness that after his visit to the hermit Terakuto the heir was for a long time thoughtful and sad.[12]

Nicholas was often described as being overly accepting of his faith to the point of being fatalistic. This, however, seems to have been more a part of his character as he aged.

Certainly one matter of great concern to Nicholas and Alexandra during the first decade of marriage was their lack of a direct male heir. By all reports, their four daughters, Olga, born in 1895, Tatiana (1897), Marie (1899), and the most famous of his children, Anastasia (1901), were lovely, intelligent, and charming. All would doubtless have gone on to satisfactory marriages had they only managed to survive the Revolution. But, the Fundamental Law of the Russian Empire stipulated a male only system of primogeniture unless the male line became extinct. Thus, from the death of Alexander III in 1894 through 1899, the heir to the throne was Nicholas' brother, George, who was living the life of an invalid in Abbas Tuman. After George's death, Nicholas' youngest brother, Michael was heir, something that reportedly irritated Alexandra greatly, and perhaps explaining why she made no effort to find her handsome brother in law a wife. Given their tremendous faith, it is perhaps not so surprising that the Imperial couple sought a spiritual solution for their lack of sons. For many years, there had been talk amongst the Orthodox faithful about a man who became known as Seraphim of Sarov, who died in 1833.[13] On July 16, 1903, the couple arrived in Sarov for the consecration of Seraphim as a saint in the Russian Orthodox Church. For three days they prayed, with Alexandra bathing in a pond thought to be holy. During this time, a letter entrusted by Seraphim to the faithful of the area, and addressed to the Tsar who would consecrate him, was delivered to Nicholas. It was said that this letter told him of the troubles to come, for he was quoted afterward as saying he feared nothing until 1918.

Nonetheless, the couple left Sarov with the certainty that they would conceive a son, and we know, of course, that they did, for Tsarevich Alexis Nikolaevich was born August 12, 1904, at Peterhof. In his photos, their son looks handsome and healthy. But, looks can be deceiving. It quickly became apparent that the young heir suffered from a blood disease that was genetically present in the Empress' family, hemophilia. At the turn of the last century, those afflicted with this disease, primarily males, did not lead long lives. A simple bump could cause often massive internal bleeding and for this reason, most young hemophiliacs of the time did not survive childhood. Of course, the Tsar of Russia could afford the very best of medical care for his children, and his son received it. Alexis was ultimately able to survive his younger childhood and arrive at adolescence, only to have his young life cut short with the murders at Ekaterinburg.

The year 1904 would prove to be a watershed year in the reign of Nicholas II. For close to 10 years, he was able to continue his father's policy of staying out of wars. In order to develop economically, Russia desperately needed peace. Nonetheless, the desire for an ice-free port on the Pacific Coast and a lack of respect for the aspirations of Japan and of Asian countries in general caused Russia to not operate in her best interests. In a tactic that would be repeated at Pearl Harbor, the Japanese launched a sneak attack on Port Arthur on February 8, 1904. It was a move that electrified the world. Up until that point, European powers expanded their borders without fear of reprisals. That was all about to change. The responsibility for the disastrous Russo-Japanese War lies entirely with Nicholas II as Emperor and Autocrat. In less than five years, he would go from visionary peacemaker to unsuccessful war wager. It was a decision that would ultimately lead to the loss of his throne.

In a little over a year's time, the war nearly bankrupted both countries, although the Japanese were able to inflict significant losses on the Russian Navy and even greater losses in Russian prestige within the world community. Fortunately for Russia, the peace treaty brokered by American president Theodore Roosevelt was highly favorable to the Russian Empire considering the many losses inflicted on her by Japan. In fact, the terms were so favorable that there were riots in Japan protesting them. But, the damage had been done to Russia's status and to Nicholas' reputation. Looking back, we can clearly see that prior to that trip to Sarov, there was a certain balance in his life, with certain amounts of fortune and misfortune. Once the die was cast and the couple birthed their son, they would never know true happiness again. For Alexandra, while her prestige increased by being the mother of the heir, her health declined, likely due to the stress of knowing she had unintentionally caused her son's illness. She may have been difficult and prudish before Alexis' birth, but afterward, most people outside her family and many within it found her to be absolutely impossible. And, this is the point at which we can clearly emphasize once again that Nicholas' greatest error of his life was his choice of a wife. While many choose to focus on their enduring passionate relationship, the fact is, that relationship seemed to become increasingly unhealthy and lacking in balance and mutual support from that point on. And, Alexandra continued to not do her job as Empress, because she clearly did not understand it. Instead, she judged the upper class Russians harshly and with little Christian compassion.

For Nicholas, his thirties started with enormous promise and ended in a stalemate. The illness of his son fractured his happy home. Never again would home be the refuge from the outside world for him. Physical exercise increasingly got him out of the house and probably decreased his stress. As his children matured, he devoted more time to them and his official duties. As a father, Nicholas Alexandrovich excelled and shone. While we don't think he was always a good husband, he was the best of fathers. Truly his finest work can be shown in the amazing characters of Olga, Tatiana, Marie, Anastasia, and Alexis. What would make Ekaterinburg so heartbreaking is that Nicholas very likely expected death for himself but probably never saw it coming for his five much loved children. In addition to his private sorrows, the military embarrassments of 1904/1905 led to the first of the Russian Revolutions, the Revolution of 1905.

Much of the history of the Revolution of 1905 has been forgotten. It's to be expected if the Revolution does not result in a permanent change in government. In a nutshell, the popular uprisings during 1905 included more domestic terrorism by revolutionary groups, numerous assassinations of government officials, general strikes, and most memorably, Bloody Sunday. The result of all of these events is that the Tsar was forced to call a Duma which created a very limited form of constitutional government. Once all of the turmoil was over, and the state had brutally subdued the opposition, matters seemed to return to the status quo that had existed in 1904. But, of course, things were never the same again. At January's traditional Blessing of the Waters, cannon at the Fortress of Peter and Paul that was supposed to be shooting blanks was loaded with live ammunition, and the Emperor very narrowly avoided injury. Because of this action, Nicholas was advised, along with other members of the Imperial Family, to leave St Petersburg. So, when workers lead by secret police informant Father Gapon marched on the Winter Palace days later on January 22, 1905 along with several thousand workers, a tragedy occurred. Troops guarding the Palace fired on the crowd of thousands, and at least hundreds of people were killed. In Moscow, revolutionaries assassinated Grand Duke Serge Alexandrovich, son of the Tsar Liberator and husband of Alexandra's sister, the Grand Duchess Elisabeth Feodorovna, that same February. Conditions had deteriorated so badly by then that the entire Imperial Family was advised not attend Serge's funeral in Moscow. This was something that could not have been imagined even five years before this. The destruction of much of the remaining naval fleet at Tsushima that May seemed to many to be a final indignity, and it fueled even more unrest and strikes. And, all of this leads to calling the Duma.

With hindsight, it is completely obvious now that the dynasty finished losing control of the country in 1905. This had been started in 1881 when the Narodnaya Volya succeeded in assassinating the Tsar Liberator. The only thing is, no one realized this until many years later. But, the Imperial Family wasn't ever safe again after 1905. They existed in a kind of shadow world, apart from the society over which they governed, and yet were never again a part of that society. The big problem with this was, they never realized it until it was far too late. Bloody Sunday was a human tragedy of great proportions, but it also once again damaged Nicholas' reputation on the international stage just when he needed a result that was much the opposite. Since he followed advice to not be in the capital when the marchers came, and never issued any orders to fire on the crowds, he cannot be directly blamed for Bloody Sunday. Here is what he wrote in his diary about it: *'serious disorders took place in Petersburg when the workers tried to come to the*

Winter Palace. The troops have been forced to fire in several parts of the city and there are many killed and wounded. Lord, how painful and sad this is!"[14]

Since revolutionaries referred to Nicholas as "Nicholas the Bloody" after this incident, it is important to analyze this event in terms of his personal responsibility. Politically, it would have served him far better had he issued a statement blaming the troops for firing on the crowd and stating he didn't order that action. Nicholas was not enough of a politician to do this, and it hurt him enormously, both at home and abroad. Clearly, he did care deeply about what happened to the workers, but all of that was lost in translation with a public that was becoming deeply disenchanted with the autocracy. It was his goodness as a human being which caused this course of action, not a weakness of character or any amount of indecisiveness. Thus we find at yet another critical juncture of his life that Nicholas' own words and actual behaviors do not match the descriptions we have received about him from contemporaries.

It should also be noted that Grand Duke Alexander Mikhailovich's claim about Nicholas not wanting the crown is rather soundly disproved by his cousin's actions in 1905. After all, had Nicholas really not wanted to rule Russia, 1905 offered him a perfect exit opportunity. Instead of abdicating or turning the country over to the revolutionaries, Nicholas made only the concessions he needed and as soon as he could he reversed the concessions he could. This does not sound like someone who does not want to be a Tsar. In the aftermath of the Revolution of 1905, Nicholas was able to find his best prime minister and his best chance to hold on to the throne.

Peter Arkedevich Stolypin (1862 -1911) would prove to be the ablest of all ministers to serve under Nicholas II. He was a law and order kind of man, and his willingness to suppress peasant uprisings lead to summary executions, which were called 'stolypin Neckties" because they involved hanging those convicted. Stolypin proved talented in working with the Duma, and he initiated agrarian reform built around small family farms. By stimulating the economy, he brought much needed economic recovery. Indeed, in 1910, the Ukraine supplied 10% of the world's grain exports. Naturally, the reforms from above, which had not been seriously pursued since Alexander II's time, made both conservative monarchists and revolutionaries alike nervous. His response to the revolutionaries was famous: *"You want great upheavals, but we want a Great Russia!"*[15]

But, it was most likely the conservative monarchists, and not the revolutionaries, who put an end to Stolypin, as he was assassinated in Kiev on September 18, 1911. The investigation into his murder was halted by the Tsar before anything conclusive was discovered. The Okhrama agent who killed him was executed, but it was never proven who was behind his death.

Between Stolypin's death and the outbreak of World War I was the Romanov Tercentenary. This was actually a series of events which celebrated the 300 years of Romanov rule from 1613, at the end of The Time of Troubles, through 1913. Among the most significant of the celebrations was Nicholas II commissioning a copy of the famous Feodorovskya icon, because St Feodor was the patron saint of the Romanovs. It was said that the new icon turned dark, which was said to be a bad omen for the Romanov Dynasty. Amazingly, the Feodorovskya survived the Revolution and is still kept in the Kostroma area today. There are many name coincidences associated with the dynasty. For example, the first Romanov tsar was named Michael, or Mikhail, Romanov, and the last tsar by some reckonings was Nicholas' brother, Michael, who deferred accepting the throne. The first Romanov woman associated with the Russian throne was named Anastasia and the last grand duchess born into the dynasty was also named Anastasia. When he accepted the throne from the Zemsky Sobor, Michael Romanov was virtually a prisoner in the Ipatiev Monastery. The last place the family of Nicholas II lived was also their last place of confinement, the Ipatiev House. And so it went, was it all coincidence?

There are many theories as to why the February Revolution of 1917 happened. The writer is of the opinion that, absent World War I, the gradual reforms of Nicholas II had a good chance of reclaiming the hearts and minds of the Russian people that had been lost in the previous generations. Economic recovery was well underway when Russia was dragged into the First World War as Bliokh had predicted, the Russian monarchy was not capable of surviving a modern global war. Certainly Alexandra being oblivious to the importance the public opinion had proved disastrous to her husband's throne, especially in the years 1915 -1916. When Nicholas took direct command of his armies in 1915, he was warned that the move was mistaken, as it kept him away from his capital and would too closely tie him to the success or failure of the war. Many have wondered why he made this decision which proved so very pivotal when Revolution came. Regardless of his reasons, this was yet another great mistake by Nicholas II, and one for which he is totally to blame.

It was during this period that rumors about Rasputin and Alexandra reached a crescendo. The Siberian healer had been a part of the life of the Imperial Family for over seven years when the Tsar left to assume command at Stavka. The relationship between Rasputin and the Empress was one bound to be misinterpreted, as nothing had been made public about the Tsarevich's illness. Without knowing that Alexis Nikolaevich was often gravely ill, the public had no means of understanding why their Empress would be spending extended periods of time with a man not her husband. In addition, Russia was and is a highly xenophobic nation, and they were at war with Germany. Thus, Nicholas seemed to be leaving his empire in the hands of a "mad Monk" and "The German Woman". The fact that Alexandra was more English than German in outlook, that Rasputin was neither mad nor a monk, none of it mattered in those months in 1915 and 1916. The war was not going well, and supplies were as scarce as hope for the future. When Prince Felix Yussoupov and Grand Duke Dimitri Pavlovich conspired to murder Rasputin to rid the dynasty of such a great threat to its prestige, the murder itself further damaged the good name of Romanov throughout the world. Lurid tales circulated, none of them true, but most believed.

When Nicholas II's government finally collapsed in the early months of 1917, there were so many causes that it seemed a miracle that it hadn't happened sooner. After finding no support from his generals, Nicholas abdicated his throne on March 15, 1917, while in a railroad car in Pskov.[16] Interestingly, he abdicated on behalf of both himself and Alexis, after conferring with Dr. Fedorov about the possibilities of Alexis' long term survival. While much has been written about how much Nicholas II seemed to enjoy himself once he was relieved of his responsibilities, his own words about his abdication tell a much different story:

> *March 15, Thursday: In the morning Ruzski came and read his very long direct-wire talk with Rodzianko. According to this, the situation in Petrograd is such that a Ministry of the Duma would now be powerless to do anything, for it has to contend with the Social-Democratic Party, represented by the workers' committee. My abdication is required. Ruzski transmitted this talk to Headquarters, and Alexeev sent it on to all the commanders-in-chief. By 2 o'clock replies were received from them. The gist of them is that in order to save Russia and keep the army at the front quiet, such a step must be taken. I have agreed. From Headquarters has been sent a draft of a manifesto. In the evening Guchkov and Shulgin arrived from Petrograd, with whom I discussed the matter, and I handed them the signed and altered manifesto. At 1 o'clock in the morning [16th] I left Pskov, with a heavy heart because of the things gone through. All around me there is treachery, cowardice, and deceit.*

Those words would echo. All around him, Nicholas felt treachery, cowardice, and deceit. Those who had given oath to support him would not, leading to treachery. Royal family members are likely accustomed to a certain amount of falsehood from those around them, but to be so utterly abandoned, Nicholas must have felt quite deceived. And, fearing the revolutionaries, those attached to the former Emperor began abandoning their service to him almost immediately, which must have seemed to him to be cowardly at the very least. In utter devastation, he began making his way home to Tsarskoe Selo. While many criticize Nicholas for placing his family above his duty as a ruler, he finally lost the Russian throne not due to indifference to his subjects but due to his subjects' indifference to him.

So began siteen months of imprisonment for Nicholas, Alexandra, and their five children. At first, they were confined at their home in Tsarskoe Selo. It must have been very strange to be prisoner in a home where they had lived so happily. In July 1917, came the Kornilov Rebellion, probably the Right's last play for power. In order to suppress this rebellion, Prime Minister Alexander Kerensky decided to arm the Bolsheviks. It was a fateful mistake. The following month, Kerensky sent the Imperial Family into exile in Tobolsk, a city through which Nicholas had passed while he was Tsarevich. And there the Family remained, relatively safe and comfortable, for a period of months until the new Bolshevik government, who had seized power in November 1917, became aware of the Imperial Family once again. The Ural Regional Soviet managed to seize Nicholas, Alexandra, and Marie as they were being transported to Moscow. Their train finally stopped in Ekaterinburg, the capital of the Red Urals, where Nicholas said, *"They hate me here."*

The family would not survive the Ural Bolsheviks' tender mercies for long. As the Czech Legion became increasingly more powerful, they made their way into the Urals and were days away from taking control of the city, when the Ural Bolsheviks, prior to evacuating the city, decided to murder the entire Imperial Family and their remaining retinue. It was a decision that would transform Nicholas, just as the Japanese wise man had told him during his World Tour.

"Death and immortality, a split-second and eternity."

There are those who hypothesize that Nicholas knew his end was coming by the fact that he stopped making diary entries the Saturday before they were all killed. Perhaps Alexandra, too, knowing Marie Antoinette's fate, also anticipated that Yurovsky's squad were not jailers, but executioners. But, likely no one was entirely sure what would happen to everyone. There are various quotes of Nicholas' last words after Yurovsky read his death sentence in that half basement room nearly 100 years ago. Those that seem most probable are these: *"Lord, oh, my God! Oh my God! What is this? Oh, my God! No! I can't understand you. Read it again, please. What? What?"*

It was for him, as the wise man told him, a split second before he died. The entire execution squad turned on him at once, anxious to kill the man known as "Nicholas the Bloody". The people he loved best, his wife, his son, and his daughters, watched helplessly as their husband and father was pierced with bullets and fell to the ground. His was the most merciful death in that room, because at least it was fast. Of all the intended victims in the room, the shooters most wanted to hit him. Unfortunately, his daughters were wearing fortunes of jewels, sewn into their undergarments to avoid pilfering by their guards. This would make their deaths slow, and possibly agonizing.

For years, the Ural Bolsheviks were able to keep secret the grave where Nicholas and three of their children and their remaining suite and servants had been hastily buried. In 1979, Alexander Avdonin and Geli Ryabov found the remains. The gravesite was excavated in 1991, and for another seven years, the remains resided at the Ekaterinburg Morgue. On July 17, 1998, eighty years after their deaths, the bodies were buried at the Fortress of Peter and Paul in St Petersburg the traditional burial place for Russian Tsars and Grand Dukes.

Nine years later, in July 2007, the remains of their son and a fourth daughter were finally located by amateur archaeologists. While not buried as of this writing, the mysterious disappearance of Nicholas and his family has now been unquestionably explained.

As we have seen Nicholas II, he was a man who had a very short but happy childhood. He was the most adored grandson of the Tsar Liberator, Alexander II. In character and demeanor, Nicholas was very much like his grandfather, but the two men ruled under vastly different circumstances. Nicholas Alexandrovich, like many of his ancestors, was well suited to military life and would have doubtless enjoyed an extended military career while serving as heir to the throne. Fate, however, had different plans for him. His grandfather died a premature death due to his assassination. His father died a premature death due to illness, and Nicholas himself died shortly after his 50th birthday. We know that Nicholas had a sense of destiny, and sensed that his fate would not be a happy one. And yet, he didn't live his life that way at all. A tragic life is what he had, but he didn't live it tragically.

There are those who will make excuses for his many mistakes both as a man and as a ruler. We shall not join them. As a man, he did not like standing up to his wife, who erroneously believed he needed her to *"pour her will into his veins."* And, he certainly chose the wrong wife for the job he had to do. Nicholas would have done well with someone with more charm and who was less judgmental. He would have been better served, perhaps, being a religious man, a patriarch or bishop, rather than a more secular leader, and avoided the wife situation all together. But, that would have meant no children, and Nicholas was a man who loved his children and was an excellent father. As a man, his desire to see everyone in accord would have been fine at a dinner party, but it worked against him in the autocracy that was Imperial Russia.

As a ruler, Nicholas II has a complex legacy. After the Revolution, it was popular to blame him and label him weak. Those who have lost everything are very anxious to blame someone, and an unsuccessful ruler is an excellent target. Yet, if we carefully examine the years of his reign, we discover that that he was not always a bad tsar. Sometimes he was excellent, as with starting the International Court of Justice and the impetus for the United Nations, and sometimes he was disastrous, as with involving his country in two wars they could not win. Most of the time, he was neither excellent nor disastrous. He was reasonably competent. However, Russia at the time needed a great tsar, not merely a competent one. And, even the most skillful of politicians would have had a real struggle in the years 1894 through 1917, Nicholas clearly was not that highly skilled. So, we are left with these echoes in time. No Romanov, be it tsar, grand duke or duchess, has left such an enduring legacy. We can truly say of Nicholas II that he is much better loved and appreciated in death than he ever was in life. As a deeply devout Orthodox Christian, perhaps this fate was ultimately kinder to him than it seems.

TSAREVICH GEORGE ALEXANDROVICH
(1871-1899)

By Lisa Davidson

George Alexandrovich was perhaps the strongest and least known of all the influences on his brother, Emperor Nicholas II. Always in the shadow of his older brother, and yet integral to the family he left behind in Russia, His Imperial Highness Grand Duke George Alexandrovich died a premature death at age twenty-eight from complications of tuberculosis, alone, but never forgotten. In the four years since Nicholas' accession to the Imperial Throne, George had been his Heir and Tsarevich. And yet, the Imperial court knew little of him, as he made his home on the East side of the Black Sea, in the spa town of Abbas Tuman in the Caucasus. In his short life, Grand Duke George brought joy and laughter to his family and in death, he gave his brother the one thing no one else could – the ability to be buried with their ancestors in the Fortress of Peter and Paul. Who was this shadowy figure about who so little is known? Most intriguingly, would history have told a different tale had he been able to survive until 1917? And would the intervening years have been so very different with George instead of without him?

His Imperial Highness Grand Duke George Alexandrovich was the third born son of Grand Duke and Tsarevich Alexander Alexandrovich and his wife Grand Duchess Maria Feodorovna in her native Denmark, of Russia. Sasha and Dagmar made a most unlikely couple. He – a gruff giant who could be a big teddy bear – was paired with the somewhat frivolous ex-fiancée of his late older brother. However, the couple surprised everyone, maybe even themselves, by achieving a highly successful royal marriage. Their first son, who was named after the late Tsarevich Nicholas Alexandrovich, was to become the last Tsar of Russia, Nicholas II. In 1869, the couple's second son, Alexander, was born, the strongest and healthiest of the four boys they were to bring into the world. Ironically, Alexander died of meningitis before he was a year old. In the days before antibiotics, this was often the fate of children afflicted with bacterial meningitis.

Grieving over the tragic loss of their baby son, the couple was undoubtedly delighted when Dagmar gave birth one year after baby Alexander's death, on Tuesday, May 9, 1871,[1] to George. He was unfortunately not as strong as Nicholas was and certainly less healthy than the late Alexander had been, but unlike the unfortunate brother Alexander, he survived and to an extent, thrived. George did have *'severe respiratory problems"* from birth on,[2] and according to Dagmar's biographer, Coryne Hall *"was the cause of much future worry to Dagmar."*[3] Nonetheless, plans for George's christening proceeded at a normal pace.

It is likely that George was named for Dagmar's brother who, although he was the second son of the King of Denmark, and named William at birth, became His Majesty King George I of the Hellenes. This is a possibility, as baby George's two godfathers were his paternal grandfather, Tsar Alexander II, and The King of the Hellenes, his maternal uncle. At the christening held on Monday, May 29, 1871[4], the two godfathers were joined by his godmothers. Selected by the couple for these positions were The Dowager Queen Caroline-Amalie of Denmark and Grand Duchess Alexandra Petrovna. And so, life began in the strange combination of circumstances that all of the later Romanov children experienced. On one hand, their family was the richest in the world and the Romanovs were known for their extravagance. Conversely, however, the children of this family were brought up in nearly Spartan simplicity with plain food, uncomfortable furniture, and very little in the way of pomp or circumstance.

George's childhood experiences were very similar to his older brother's, as they spent nearly every day together for the first nineteen years of his life. They shared a bedroom, a living room, a study, and they had many of the same tutors. There was no one closer to Nicky than his brother George until Nicholas' marriage to Princess Alix in 1894. They shared every day together, and Nicky enjoyed his brother's wit most of all. According to his sister, Olga, he wrote down every funny thing that he heard George say. When Nicholas II became tsar years later, he could be heard laughing uproariously over his brother's jokes, long after the latter's death.[5]

Many people thought that George was the most intelligent of the six children born to Alexander III and Maria Feodorovna. Of course, this acumen was a decidedly mixed blessing as Olga related to her biographer:

> To make matters worse, Georgie had a colorful accomplice in his green parrot Popka, who for reasons unknown to me hated Mr. Heath. Every time the poor English master entered Georgie's room, the bird would fly into a rage and then imitate Mr. Heath with the most exaggerated British accent. Mr. Heath would become so exasperated that he refused to enter Georgie's room until Popka had been removed.[6]

The family was joined by Xenia and Michael and lived in the Anichkov Palace among other homes in the years while their family was growing. Like other Romanovs, they made annual sojourns to homes in Livadia, Peterhof, and Tsarskoe Selo. In addition, they also joined Dagmar's large family for get togethers in Denmark. It was a full and happy family life that George Alexandrovich was born to. Unfortunately, it was not to last.

Their domestic idyll was shattered in 1879 when "The People's Will", known in Russia as Narodnaya Volya, a domestic terrorist group, sentenced Alexander's father, His Imperial Majesty Tsar Alexander II to death. Several unsuccessful attempts were made on the Tsar's life. The stress of being human target practice took its toll on the Tsar. At one point he remarked, *"Am I such a wild beast that they must hound me to death?"*[7] He treated his dying wife, the former Marie of Hesse and By Rhine, badly, by bringing his mistress and their children to live with his legitimate family in the Winter Palace. The unfortunate empress died on June 3, 1880, completely alone. The Tsar, terrified for the safety of his mistress, Catherine Dolgoruky, married her morganatically on July 18, 1880, scant weeks after his first wife's death. Alexander II's despicable treatment of his late wife and his insistence on marrying his mistress rent the fabric of the Imperial Family's unity. It would never be repaired, and in fact, internal divisions severely undermined the dynasty then and throughout the reigns of the next two emperors. Never again would there be unity in the Imperial Family of Russia.

Tsarevich Alexander and his family tried to maintain good relations with his father in the months following this unfortunate marriage. In this, Alexander was more successful than his wife was. Dagmar, grateful to her mother in law for her support, was much more conflicted about her new in-law. On the morning of March 13, 1881, the Tsar attended Mass with the couple after signing a manifesto that would create a more liberal government. Next, Alexander II attended a parade and visited his cousin, Grand Duchess Catherine Mikhailovna. While returning to the Winter Palace, his entourage encountered bomb-carrying terrorists. The Tsar was unharmed in the initial attack, but stopped to look after those who had been injured. It was the golden opportunity for which Narodnaya Volya had been waiting – the backup bomber did his dirty work and the Tsar's lower body was virtually obliterated in the blast. He was not, however, dead, at least not yet. He asked to immediately be taken to the Palace.

It was this ghastly and bloody scene that Alexander, Dagmar, and their two sons, Nicholas and George, entered at the Winter Palace. At the time, Nicholas was twelve years old and George, nine. Their grandfather, the Tsar of all the Russias, was supposed to be the most powerful person on the face of the earth. Yet, the fallacy of this notion was shown to them in the horrific relief of this flawed man, as he spent his last hour of life bleeding to death in incredible pain, with his young wife in a blood soaked nightgown at his side. In a very real sense, the Russian Revolution began, not as it is often said, with the Decemberist uprising of 1825, but with the murder by domestic terrorists of a man who was supposed to be an autocrat. Ironically, Alexander II was the last Romanov tsar genuinely committed to reform. His son, Alexander III was a true reactionary, and his son, Nicholas II, was a true conservative. Neither embraced reform as a solution to Russia's ills. But, at least part of the blame for this must be left at the terrorists' door. And, George and Nicky must have found the whole scene in the Winter Palace to be a living horror that they would remember as long as they lived. After March 13, 1881, the Winter Palace was never again inhabited as a regular home of the Imperial Family. Under the later tsars, the Winter Palace was used as a temporary residence, and also was used for ceremonies. And today, it is part of The Hermitage.

In spite of the efforts of his parents to create an atmosphere of domestic tranquility, by the time his academic studies began in earnest, "Georgie", as he was known in the family, was thrust into a much different world, as the second son of the Tsar of Russia. The murder of their grandfather caused the Imperial Family to literally and forever more pull back both literally and philosophically from their subjects. Never again would they walk carefree down the streets of St Petersburg, at least not without the secret police following them. In doing this, they lost touch, to a great extent, with the lives of ordinary Russians. While the perpetrators of Alexander II's murder were themselves executed, his surviving family became virtual prisoners. Alexander III moved his family to Gatchina, in the suburbs of St. Petersburg, where he and his family could be better guarded. Gatchina had been the milieu of Tsar Paul, and his great grandson virtually fled there with his young family.

Thus began the isolation of the Romanovs which would find its full flower under Nicholas II and his virtual retirement to the cozy domesticity of Tsarskoe Selo. For this, Nicholas' wife, Alexandra Feodorovna, is generally blamed. However, this was very much the life that Nicholas had lived as Tsarevich under his father for the thirteen years following the death of Alexander III. And so, the two brothers, Nicholas and George, became even closer than most royal siblings of their time, sharing living quarters, tutors, meals, and every aspect of life together. They were also to share the experience of fleeing Gatchina when their father would become drunk and violent. Because of this upbringing, in a very real sense, there were only two people in his life that Nicholas II completely trusted and with whom he shared the majority of his life. Most of us know the story of Nicholas and Alexandra, but before his wife, there was his brother George, and they were very devoted to one another.

While Nicholas loved the life of a young Imperial Hussar officer, George aspired to a career in the Imperial Navy. The Romanovs were a family devoted to military service, as had Empress Marie Feodorovna's father. According to their cousin, Grand Duke Alexander Mikhailovich, Georgie left on a "practice cruise" in the summer of 1889, when the he was 18 years old.[8] George loved the Navy, and his intelligence and charm would doubtless have made it possible for him to have a most successful naval career, even without his Imperial connection. Unfortunately, the weak state of his physical health made this impossible, and his naval experience was limited to studies as a Naval cadet.

It was during this period that the two brothers renewed their acquaintance with their cousin, Princess Alix of Hesse and By Rhine. During the winter of 1889, Alix arrived in St Petersburg for six weeks to visit her sister, who was married to Grand Duke Serge. It was Alix, the future Russian Empress, who christened George, "Weeping Willow", and her letters to "Nicky" contain references to "The Weeping Willow" and "Willow". Nicholas states in his diaries that his serious feelings for Alix began with this particular visit.[9]

Royal parents frequently use tours to distract their offspring from interest in those they consider unsuitable. It was in that spirit that Alexander III arranged for his heir and George to visit the Middle East and Asia in 1890. Alexander wanted to get Nicholas to stop thinking about marrying Alix, and the Tsarevich had just finished his studies. Nicky and Georgie departed for Athens to visit their cousins who ruled there and to be joined by the third traveler in their party, Prince George of Greece (1869-1957). Prince George was a paternal uncle of Prince Philip, the Duke of Edinburgh, and the King of Greece's second son. There is a rather interesting photo of the three princes in *The Romanovs: Love Power & Tragedy* smoking from a Turkish pipe while in Egypt as the guests of the Khedive, the ruler of the country. As the three travelers made their way to India, George Alexandrovich became increasingly ill. His fever became persistent, and in spite of wanting to continue on to the Far East, his Imperial parents demanded that Georgie come home. There is a particularly poignant letter from his mother to

Nicky, which describes her feelings at the time:

> *My dear Nicky – you can't imagine in what anguish I have passed these last few days on account of my poor Georgie's condition;...for I know that Georgie will listen to no one and believes that it is shameful to look after oneself a little... I have already had two telegrams from Georgie who is still asking to be allowed to go to Columbo...is still more tropical and therefore not desirable for him...In any case Alishevsky will be sent by us to meet him in Greece and after having examined him he will decide what is best to do.*[10]

The prevailing medical thought at the time was to provide tubercular patients with a lot of fresh air and good food in hopes that their health would improve. Shortly after his return to Greece, Grand Duke George was sent to the Imperial hunting lodge of Abbas Tuman in high in the Caucasus Mountains in hope that a change in climate would benefit his health. Abbas Tuman is now located in the Republic of Georgia, about seventy miles from the Black Sea, and a very short distance from the Turkish border. In terms of distance from the capital and his family, only the far reaches of Central Asia and Siberia were farther away. The Caucasus was considered to be a very wild country indeed, although Georgia itself is a most ancient country.

The move to Abbas Tuman can be seen from several different perspectives. On the one hand, a clever, intelligent young man such as George must have chafed under the overly protective watch of his mother. Living so far away from his family gave George the opportunity to have his own household, out of the reach of his very concerned, but very controlling, mother. His letters from the time he moved there in 1891 reflect a more adult perspective than was shown by any of his siblings, regardless of age, for many years to come. However, he was also very far away from the many important events that would transpire over the final eight years of his life, and so his potential influence over his powerful relatives was muted. From 1891 on, he was truly "The Willow of Abbas Tuman", visible, present, of interest, and yet just part of the Russian Imperial landscape.

In the first year of his "exile", George's parents celebrated their silver wedding anniversary, primarily in Livadia and Yalta.[11] Grand Duke Alexander Mikhailovich, who wrote in his memoirs that he considered Georgie a brother due to their mutual admiration for Xenia and their love of the navy, accompanied George from Abbas Tuman to Livadia to meet the gathering royals.[12] The anniversary represented a kind of apogee of sorts for Alexander III and his consort. They had been reigning for ten years, their three eldest children were grown and getting ready to leave the nest, and they were as recovered as they were going to be from the horrors of the previous decade. As Tsar of Russia, Alexander III actively suppressed dissent and those he felt responsible for his father's murder. He pursued active Russification within the Empire, causing resentments and bitterness in non-Russian areas that would erupt and boil over onto his eldest son and grandchildren. While his reign is viewed by some as "holding the line" against domestic terrorists, since he did not address the sources of their discontent, he did nothing to remedy the situation. And, in many ways, his reactionary policies actually damaged relations with his Imperial subjects, though it is doubtful he knew this, or was even remotely aware of it.

In the meantime, George's residence became a vacation destination of sorts for many of the Russian Imperial family. One of Faberge's beautiful Easter eggs, the Caucasus Egg, created in 1893 for Empress Maria Feodorovna as a gift from her husband shows the estate of Abbas Tuman and a portrait of George in his Naval uniform. The egg is currently displayed at the New Orleans Museum of Art in New Orleans, Louisiana USA.[13] The Empress made it a point to visit her son as often as she could, often visiting several times per year. Grand Duke Alexander Mikhailovich relates a story that in 1892, he had but two weeks off from his naval service, and spent his entire leave with Georgie at his mountain home. He recalled, *"The doctors thought that plenty of cool air would heal his affected lungs, and we slept under warm blankets with wide open windows, in a temperature of 10 below zero."*[14] According to Sandro, both hoped that George's father would live a long life because Alexander III had not prepared his brother Nicky to rule. Of course, this was not to be.

In the mean time, George's close friendship with his cousin Grand Duke Alexander Mikhailovich underwent a severe strain while Sandro visited George with his fiancée and Georgie's sister, Xenia and Maria Feodorovna. In a very funny letter to Nicholas dated June 9, George says:

> *Remember how you wrote me about the appalling behavior of Xenia and Sandro...They almost broke the ottoman and generally behaved in a most improper way; for instance, they would lie down on top of each other, even in my presence, in what you might call an attempt to play Papa and Mama. To the point where I got angry at such impudence.*[15]

This conduct was thankfully corrected by the marriage of Xenia and Sandro on July 25, 1894.

While George was establishing his independent life in the Caucasus, his Titan-like father was in declining health. He had a bad case of bronchitis in 1893, and by 1894, the Imperial doctors had diagnosed a kidney ailment that ultimately took his life before the age of fifty. Alexander III must have been a very vital man because no one around him could seem to fathom that he was mortal. George was able to see his larger-than-life father before he died. However, Alexander III proved to be all too human, succumbing to nephritis on November 1, 1894, at the age of forty-nine, at his estate at Livadia in the Crimea. While most know that this untimely death made Nicholas II Tsar, it also made George "The Grand Duke George Alexandrovich the Tsarevich", although he was more frequently referred to as the Thronfolger, or Heir to the Throne. While this was indeed an exalted rank, it was not one he expected to hold for long. Within days of their father's death, his brother Nicholas was to marry the woman he loved, Princess Alix of Hesse and By Rhine. Being young, healthy, and very much in love, it was expected that George would hold his new title a very short time, indeed. However, as is well known, Alexandra produced four daughters in succession, three of who were born before George's death. So, the Grand Duke was Tsarevich for the remainder of his life, from November 1, 1894 through July 10, 1899.

It was a title, however, that he seemed to wear lightly. Of greater concern to him was that he was missing important family events. He missed his sister Xenia's wedding in 1894 and he wrote to Nicky on November 9 of his regret at missing the new Tsar's wedding to Alix. *"I congratulate you and Alix with all my heart; may you be happy and may God bless you. I am so sad not to be at your wedding; I am in despair that this is the second one in the family that is taking place without me."*[16]

Nonetheless, George still traveled on occasion with his family. In August 1895, Xenia and Sandro left their baby, Irina with Nicky and Alix and accompanied the Dowager Empress Maria Feodorovna and George to the Empress' homeland, Denmark. Unfortunately, George spent the entire time in Denmark in bed. He was coughing up blood.[17] In April 1896, he accompanied his mother to the South of France. In a letter to Nicholas, Maria Feodorovna reports, *"Georgie is better again and spent some time sitting on the balcony this morning."* Yet clearly, poor health increasingly left George alone except for family visits to his mountain retreat.

After the birth of Grand Duchess Tatiana in June 1897, George wrote to his brother Nicholas the following tender missive:

> *I congratulate you and Alix with all my heart on the birth of your daughter. Of course I was overjoyed when I received your telegram announcing the event but forgive me if I was a little disappointed to learn that it was a daughter, not a son. I was already preparing to go into retirement, but it was not to be....it's already seven years how terrifying the way time flies. I become sad when I start to remember those happy times.*[19]

Yet clearly, as one reads the letters, there is an increasing despair from George. His family clearly wants him to be healthy. It is a wish he cannot fulfill. While blessed with wealth, intelligence, good looks, and charm, it is obvious that he is aware he will not live a long time. It is quite easy to pity him as he begins his final descent into the oblivion of his earthly life.

However, in many ways, George Alexandrovich was the most fortunate of the five children of Alexander and Dagmar who reached adulthood. His two sisters, Xenia and Olga, would survive the Revolution and yet lose the majority of their material wealth and die in exile, often dependent on the kindness, not of strangers, but of family and friends. A far more chilling end was ahead of his two surviving brothers, Nicky and Misha, who would both die as victims of murder by the orders of the Ural Regional Soviet. In contrast, George Alexandrovich died a rather quick and relatively painless death due to complications from his disease after an accident in July 1899. Of the five, he was the only one to be buried at the Fortress of Peter and Paul until the burial of Nicholas II and part of his family in 1998. They were finally joined by their mother in 2006, as the Danish Royal Family at last permitted the reburial of Maria Feodorovna according to her final wishes to join her husband.

In the final years of his life, George took advantage of the beautiful view of the skies to build Russia's first high altitude observatory, on the grounds of his home.[20] The observatory still stands, and with its modern telescopes, it is possible to see the surface of the moon from the former estate of Grand Duke George. He was able to spend his winters in Algiers, but his health quickly deteriorated during the spring of 1899. He anxiously awaited the birth of Alix's third child, hoping against hope to at long last be relieved of the burdens of his Imperial inheritance as Heir. Most disturbingly, because he was no longer able to walk, he had taken to using a motorcycle to move about Abbas Tuman, in spite of orders from his doctors to the contrary.[21]

Motorcycles at the turn of the twentieth century were a largely primitive affair. They were usually repurposed bicycles, with their motors carried either behind the handlebars and or around the knee area of the rider's body. They were doubtless far more dangerous to ride than bicycles as they moved at a much faster speed. On the morning of July 10, 1899, George left his estate on such a con-veyance. When he had not returned several hours later, his staff mounted a search. They learned a Malakani woman had found him at the side of the road with blood coming out of his mouth.[22] Without an eyewitness or an autopsy, it is difficult to precisely determine how this tubercular son of Tsar Alexander III died. According to a physician the writer consulted, it is most likely that George began bleeding into his lungs, as evidenced by the blood coming out his mouth. This alone could have caused him to lose control of his motorcycle. However, it's also possible, though not as probable, that he simply had a motorcycle accident, and that the injuries he sustained in that contributed to his death due to his extreme-ly poor health. Regardless of the circumstances, he was just 28 years old. The offi-cial cause of death was *'severe throat hemorrhage."*[23]

His last letter to his beloved brother Nicky is particularly poignant with all that would follow.

> *My dear Nicky – I congratulate you and Alix with all my heart on this new happiness for your family – the birth of your third daughter…I am terribly sad and upset that I have not yet been able to see your daughters and get to know them; but what can I do! It means it's not my fate and everything is the will of God.*[24]

One can also detect in this the fatalism that was thought to be so unique to Nicholas II. Clearly, in the case of George, he had an abiding religious faith and also an acceptance of what was to come.

There was widespread mourning for Grand Duke George. He had been away from the capital for nearly eight years when he died and had not been able to help his brother with his duties for many years. It has been suggested that as the most clever and intelligent of his siblings that the outcome of events in 1917 would have been different had George, and not Michael, been offered the throne of Russia after the abdication of Nicholas II. While there is every possibility the ultimate outcome would have been different, it is likely most that, had George not died and been so far away during his brother's reign, that perhaps the crises that gripped Russia in early 1917 would not have occurred at all. Nicholas spent near-ly every day of his fifty years of life with just two people. For the first half of his life, that person was his brother George, and for the second part, as we know, it was Alexandra. Perhaps the loss of George lead in part to the extreme influence his wife wielded with Nicholas. What seems sure is that few people could be totally candid with the last Tsar of Russia. The one person who could have talked to Nicholas about how badly Rasputin had damaged the dynasty, and how bad an idea assuming command of his armies in 1915 was, and not offended him in the process likely was the person whose death Nicholas so grievously mourned after the birth of his daughter Maria. So, the death of Grand Duke George should be viewed as an event that, if altered, could have changed the course of history. The hows and the whys of this change are, of course, a matter of complete speculation that we will leave to the writers of fiction.

History, however, was not done yet with George Alexandrovich. After Nicky met his horrific end with Alix and their children in that half basement room in Ekaterinburg in 1918, it would be many decades before his remains were discovered. After this discovery was announced to the world, Nicholas' remains were subjected to testing, comparing his mtDNA to two of his maternal line relatives for purposes of confirming his identification. And, so, the Duke of Fife, a maternal descendant of Nicholas' aunt Alexandra, and Madame Xenia Sfiris, Felix Yussoupov's granddaughter, provided blood samples for this purpose. While there appeared to be a match in mtDNA with the two live donors, there was an abnormality noticed in the Tsar's mtDNA. While scientists concluded they could be 98% certain that the remains were those of Nicholas II[25], the purported Nicholas remains had what is known as a hetroplasmy, which made the scientists less than 100% certain that the remains were those of the tsar. The best donor source to help test the abnormality was Tikhon Kulikovsky, the son of the brother's youngest sister, Grand Duchess Olga. For reasons of his own, Tikhon declined to help the Russians working on his uncle's identification. It is likely that a small degree of uncertainty about the tsar's remains would have continued had the investigators not resolved to exhume the remains of Grand Duke George Alexandrovich to do the job that their nephew refused to do.

George had been interred at the Fortress of Peter and Paul on July 26, 1899. Almost 95 years to the day, between July 6 and July 13, 1994, the remains of the late grand duke were exhumed. A portion of his skull and his leg were removed for testing in the United States. In 1995, the results of the test were announced. Grand Duke George's mtDNA exactly matched that of the purported remains of his brother, Tsar Nicholas II, down to the very hetroplasmy that had led to the exhumation in the first place. It was a final service from the Grand Duke known as Willow that allowed his brother to at long last join him and their Romanov relations and to be buried at the Fortress of Peter and Paul in St. Petersburg. It was an act which, albeit involuntary on the part of George, nonetheless, was a most fitting ending for the two brothers who were so incredibly devoted as they were to one another in life.

Abbas Tuman is still remarkably the same as when the Grand Duke George lived there for nearly eight years. Now known as Abastumani and located in the Republic of Georgia, it escaped the environmental devastation that characterized the Soviet period. George's estate provided the land for the world renowned Abastumani Astrophysical Observatory and his house, once abandoned is now the home of local nuns. And young men likely continue to ride their motorcycles down the mountainous roads where the life of Tsar Alexander III's most promising son came to such an abrupt close. Very likely, the outcomes of their rides will prove to be far less devastating for the world.

GRAND DUKE MICHAEL ALEXANDROVICH
(1878-1918)

By Lisa Davidson

O f all the sons of Tsar Alexander III, none so looked the part or appeared more classically Imperial Russian, than did his last son, Michael Alexandrovich. While Nicholas II strongly resembled his mother, and their brother George looked a great deal like their Greek royal cousins, it was Michael who looked just the way one imagined a tsar or grand duke was supposed to look. And yet, appearances can be deceiving. Because he was both his parent's favorite child, they often spoiled him. At it's worst this unfortunate conditioning made Michael seem like, in the words of one observer, *"a very large child in an adult's body."*[1] There were definite reasons underlying Michael's behavior, but no one in his lifetime was apparently interested in discovering them. For, Michael was not a bad person, but could be a very immature individual as an adult. This in turn ill suited him for the trials that would confront him in adulthood. However, even had he been less spoiled, more mature, and in the opinion of some, stronger of character, it is very doubtful that his life would have had a different outcome. The life and death of Michael served to punctuate the trials and promise of the last Tsar's reign, as well as the horror and brutality of the regimes that followed. His ancestor, Peter the Great, made history. Misha, as his family knew him, was swept into a political tidal wave over which he had little control. In the end, his blood would be shed as a sort of ghastly trial balloon to gauge public opinion about murdering more prominent Romanovs, including his brother, Nicholas.

Grand Duke Michael Alexandrovich was born in St Petersburg on December 4, 1878, the fifth child, and fourth son, of the Tsarevich Alexander Alexandrovich, and his wife Marie Feodorovna. As previously mentioned, one brother, Alexander, died as a baby. His two older brothers, Nicholas and George were very close to one another. Michael, a middle child to a T, was sandwiched into the family after the birth of sister Xenia and before the baby, Olga. In a family full of Nicholases and Alexanders, this grand duke was named after his great uncle, Grand Duke Michael Nikolaevich, who served as one of his three godfathers.[2] Other godfathers guiding the young Michael were his grandfather, Tsar Alexander II, and his mother's brother, Prince Valdemar of Denmark. Michael's godmothers included his maternal grandmother, Queen Louise of Denmark, and his great aunt, Grand Duchess Alexandra Iosifovna. His christening was celebrated just before Christmas on December 22 at the Winter Palace.

Michael's father became Tsar in 1881, upon the tragic assassination of his father, Tsar Alexander II. It is therefore likely that the young grand duke had no memories of his paternal grandfather or of his father before he became tsar. Also, the relatively peaceful life the family had enjoyed prior to this time was forever shattered. Instead of the urbane Anichkov Palace, Michael's childhood was spent primarily at the suburban palace of Gatchina. It was Gatchina, located outside St Petersburg, and the former home of his great-great grandfather, Tsar Paul I, that Michael would forever regard as home. Descriptions we have of his family's life at Gatchina speak of a relaxed, countrified existence stressing modesty and simplicity over pomp and circumstance. These, of course, were relative terms when one's father was the Tsar of Russia. While Alexander III could be fierce and domineering with other members of the large Imperial Family, he could also be a doting and lenient parent, especially with his favorite son, Misha. Nicholas II was known to be insecure and was shy as a child. In contrast, little Michael appeared to be friendly and confident as befits a favored offspring.

According to Trotsky, had Alexander III drank less, history could have been forever changed.[3] While doubtless Alexander III would not have died a premature death had he not drank so excessively, there were other, subtler results from his alcohol consumption. Looking past the surface of the apparently confident child, one can nonetheless detect the unmistakable presence of a chronic alcoholic prominent in young Michael's life. In point of fact, Michael was just as hungry for approval as was his older brother Nicky. Both were sharply self-critical and as adults had difficulty dealing with angry people or in accepting personal criticism. As a result of having an alcoholic father, Michael and to a great extent, Nicholas, were regarded as weak or lacking character. In the early 20th century, few who observed them would bother to discern the difference. Hence, with this enormous impediment, the young grand duke began his education.

History was Misha's favorite subject, and he regarded Russian history as a "chronicle of his family."[4] Educating their children was very important to the Imperial couple, and Michael exhibited the intelligence shown by his other siblings in pursuing his studies, as well as the free spirit fostered by his relatively liberal upbringing. However, the Romanovs were not a particularly intellectual family, and thus one should regard his education as rather superficial, although it was doubtless broad in scope. Ultimately, the career intended for Misha, as for all other Romanov males, was that of a military officer. While his brother Nicky served in the elite Cavalier guards and brother George in the Imperial Navy, Michael became an artillery officer, with a particular emphasis on tactical warfare. It is very easy to see that as Michael's life unfolded, how very well suited he would have been to a simple life as a military officer, devoted to home and country. It was a life denied to him by circumstance and history

Not surprisingly, Michael was closest to his younger sister, Olga, who called her older brother "Floppy".[5] They enjoyed a bit more than a decade together at Gatchina before their father's premature death from nephritis in 1894. His father's death brought Michael's youth to a similarly premature end. Because his brother, the new tsar, Nicky, married only weeks later, little thought was given to Michael becoming second in the Romanov succession after their brother George. Apparently, little thought was given to the marriage of either of the remaining Alexandrovich brothers. This was easy to understand in the case of the tubercular George, but much less so with Michael. It is apparent from reviewing the marital choices made by all of Empress Maria Feodorovna's children that she was happy with none of them with the possible exception of the one marriage she arranged herself: the unhappy union of Olga Alexandrovna to Prince Peter of Oldenburg. However, when it came to Michael, her efforts proved to be too little and too late.

In July 1899, Grand Duke George died of tuberculosis at his estate in Abbas Tuman in the Caucasus. With George's death came Michael's inheritance of his brother's estate at Brasovo[6] and more significantly, the title of Tsarevich, or heir to the throne. For, in spite of Nicholas' happy marriage, by this time, the Imperial couple were parents of three daughters and no Romanov heirs. The role of a young adult heir to the Romanovs was similar in some respects to that of a United States Vice-President. He attended numerous weddings and funerals. Michael represented Nicholas at the funerals of both Queen Victoria in 1901 and Edward VII of England in 1910. The Tsar's reluctance to leave his young family greatly increased the traveling required of his heir, both at home and abroad.

As a result of his foreign travels, Michael became something of an Anglophile. Many of his tastes and preferences shaped during those years reflect those of the English aristocracy of the period. He was an accomplished equestrian, an avid automobile driver, and loved animals and country living. During most of his adult life, he lived at his childhood home, the Gatchina Palace.

One would have thought that given the shortage of Alexandrovich heirs that more effort would have been made to find Michael a wife. It is even more curious when one considers that the Heir was a strapping six feet tall, immensely handsome, intelligent, rich, and charming. It is hard to imagine who would not have wanted him. And, yet, he remained unmarried for many years.

Michael remained unattached into the new century and after Nicholas' health crisis in 1900 and the birth of his niece Anastasia in 1901. While traveling in the summer of 1902, he fell in love with the beautiful Princess Beatrice of Edinburgh, reportedly at first sight and she with him.[7] In retrospect, a marriage between this granddaughter of Alexander II and his grandson Michael may have increased the prestige of the failing dynasty. Unfortunately, neither the tsar nor the Russian Orthodox Church would permit a marriage between the two first cousins. While such marriages were fairly common between European royals, for reasons unknown, Nicholas prevented his brother from marrying his first love. Stunningly, both delayed their marriages. Beatrice did not marry Infante Alfonso until 1909, and Michael's marriage would be another three years beyond Beatrice's, in 1912. Doubtless, Michael was resentful from that point on about the subject of being free to marry a partner of his choice.

This resentment may in fact explain in part his second attachment, this time to a woman no one but her own family would have considered being suitable for him. Michael's second love was named Alexandra Kossikovskaya, but she is known in history as "Dina". She was older than Michael by three years and was not considered to be a great beauty. A lady in waiting to Michael's sister Olga Alexandrovna, who at the time was the wife of Prince Peter of Oldenburg, Dina and Michael were friends for some time before a romance blossomed between the two of them. A second reason for this relationship, at least in Michael's mind, was the birth in 1904 of his nephew, and Nicholas' new heir, Alexis. Like their brother, George, Michael had not relished the "job" of being heir to the throne and by all reports was genuinely thrilled for this brother and his wife and their new addition. While Michael doubtless knew of his nephew's hemophilia, the fact that Alexandra had at long last given birth to a son probably made him feel that the whole subject of his being an heir was permanently shelved. With that out of his life, Michael felt that he could marry as he pleased.

His choice of the brilliant but unspectacular Dina as a prospective bride is an interesting one. While he was certainly attracted to Kossikovskaya, he probably would not have considered marriage to her had she not been convinced that Michael owed it to her as an honorable man and had her ambitious lawyer father not been backing her up. All of this seems to indicate that there was a sexual relationship between the two, and given his sense of honor, which differed significantly from that of other grand dukes of his time, he may have indeed felt compelled to offer her marriage. However, Michael was also aware of the Fundamental Law of the Russian Empire that required him to make an equal marriage and at that, only with the permission of the tsar. Dina, armed with her lawyer father, tried to get Michael to make a case to marry her, but the father's legal nitpicking persuaded no one. The Dowager Empress got wind of what was afoot and immediately fired Dina as Olga's lady in waiting and arranged with Nicholas to have her exiled from Russia.

It was at this highly belated point that the Dowager Empress made her one meager attempt to find a bride for Michael. While it would be said in the future that Nicholas II stubbornly refused to act until the act had lost all meaning, the same could be said of Maria Feodorovna with respect to arranging Michael's marriage. Her choice of partners was excellent in Princess Patricia of Connaught, but her timing and execution were beyond endurance. In order to diffuse the rumors about Michael and Dina, the Dowager and her sister, Queen Alexandra, arranged in September 1906 for a seemingly credible rumor to be spread in the media that Princess Patricia and Grand Duke Michael were going to marry. Of course, since the two principals had absolutely no knowledge of these impending nuptials, the "news" proved most embarrassing to them both.

And yet, all of this seems especially in hindsight so very unnecessary. Clearly, the dynasty should have placed much greater emphasis on finding good brides for their grand dukes. While it should always have been a priority, some urgency should have come into play regarding Michael first while Alexandra was pregnant with Anastasia. Nicholas came very near to death from typhus. During the health crisis, Alexandra learned the implications of the law that precluded any realistic chance for her daughters inheriting the throne. Many trace her obsession with having a son to this time. But, clearly, there were many opportunities for a suitable bride to have been found for Michael prior to the abortive "engagement" in 1906. And, afterward, it is beyond understanding why no efforts were made to find him a suitable wife. While Michael bears a good share of responsibility for what ultimately happened in his private life, his family, most especially his mother and Nicholas, also must share in it, because after 1906, there were no discernable efforts made by anyone in his family to find Michael a mate.

The consequences of this inaction would ultimately prove disastrous for the dynasty. While Michael ceased to be first in the succession in August 1904 with the birth of the Tsarevich Alexis Nikolaevich, the boy's very fragile health still made Michael's marriage and family important to the Romanov dynasty. As fate would have it, Michael met his future wife through his military career. Michael had been an officer in his mother's regiment, popularly called the Blue Cuirassiers, and more formally, Her Majesty's Life Guard Cuirassier Regiment, serving as a squadron commander, headquartered at Gatchina. There, the Grand Duke first met the wife of one of his officers, Natalia Sergievna Wulfert, in December 1907. As related by Rosemary and Donald Crawford in their 1997 biography, *Michael and Natasha*, this meeting resulted in love at first sight, at least for Michael.

It was by falling in love with and ultimately marrying a woman who had two divorces to her name that caused yet another scandal for Michael and the Romanov dynasty. Making matters worse, it was the second affair of its type to hit the Imperial Family in recent years. In 1902, Grand Duke Paul Alexandrovich, Misha's uncle, had married the estranged wife of Grand Duke Vladimir Alexandrovich's adjunct. The officer corps was understandably upset with the dynasty over these liaisons, and while Michael may have felt justified in his actions, the society in which these occurred could not and would not forgive this otherwise blameless young man for this conduct. This, in turn, diminished the prestige of the House of Romanov just when it needed the opposite result. While Michael's affair with Natasha Wulfert did not destroy the dynasty, it left him in a much-diminished position when his brother abdicated the throne a scant 12 years later. This, however, was in the future from the time of their first meeting. Just who was this Jezebel, this temptress who so utterly transformed Misha's life?

As described by her contemporaries, Natalia Wulfert was a beautiful girl of eighteen years with an independent demeanor when she met Grand Duke Michael. Of course, this was only partially correct. Natalia Sheremetevsky lied about her age constantly. The Crawfords give her date of birth as June 27, 1880, which would have made her a young woman of twenty seven, not eighteen, when the fateful meeting took place. Daughter of a Moscow lawyer, she first married at twenty-one, to the music director of the Bolshoi, Serge Mamontov. Her marriage allowed her an entrée into society that would have been denied to a single middle class woman. However, the Mamontovs proved to be incompatible. While they became parents to young Natalia, always known as "Tata", Serge Mamontov preferred to remain at home when not working, while his young wife was more of a social butterfly. By the time of her first meeting with Grand Duke Michael, she had been married to husband number two, one Lieutenant Vladimir Wulfert, only for a very short time. And, she had married Wulfert after she told Serge Mamontov that she was in love with Wulfert!

Thus began a love triangle that involved an initially clueless Lieutenant Wulfert, who felt honored that Grand Duke Michael wanted to be friends with him and his wife, and Michael and Natasha. While Olga Alexandrovna's memoirs are silent on the subject, it is evident from surviving photographs that she was involved in her own love triangle at the time, with her husband, Prince Peter of Oldenburg, and the man who would become her second husband in 1916, Colonel Nicholas Kulikovsky. Apparently the Michael/Natasha/Wulfert triangle was unconsummated between the first two for some time. Yet, this changed at least by the fall of 1909, when Michael and Natasha conceived their child, and very likely, before this. What is recorded is that Natasha left Wulfert before becoming Misha's lover. While Mamontov had been accommodating when Natasha moved on once she decided she loved someone else, Lieutenant Wulfert was not. He insisted on raising a scandal, which caused much difficulty in the Imperial Family. And, because Natasha became pregnant and actually gave birth to Michael's child while married to the unfortunate Lieutenant Wulfert, it further complicated how her future brother-in-law Nicholas and others perceived her and Michael and the legitimacy of their whole relationship.

While many are familiar with the British royal family's disdain of divorced persons as spouses for their members, the Romanov standards are different, and more complex. Under the Pauline law, members of the Imperial Family are prohibited from entering into "unequal marriages." This standard was interpreted by reigning tsars as requiring marriage into other royal or aristocratic houses with the approval of the Tsar. Interestingly enough, most of the matrimonial scandals of Nicholas II's reign involved marriages of members of the Imperial Family to Russian subjects outside of the aristocracy. For example, their sister Olga Alexandrovna married for the second time a perfectly respectable, but unaristocratic colonel. So, part of the family's objection to Natasha stemmed not so much from her divorcee status, but from her lack of aristocratic ancestry. She was, as has been pointed out, merely a middle class woman. However, it was known in the family that Olga had never been happy in her first marriage, so many in the family were actually happy for her finding fulfillment in her second marriage to a commoner. Contrast this with Michael, who after two unsuccessful love affairs was in the clutches, for this is how his family saw it, of a woman who would stop at nothing to entrap him. Because he was normally such a good person, the blame for the affair was perhaps unfairly placed primarily on Madame Wulfert. While Michael had many admirable traits, it appears he was just as culpable as Natasha in the matter of their love affair and likely more so. For, he certainly owed his junior officer enough loyalty to not poach his new bride. Unfortunately for all, including the Emperor, this is precisely what Misha did.

On July 24, 1910, Natalia gave birth to their only child, George, named for Michael's late brother. In order for his only child to legally not be the child of Lieutenant Wulfert, Michael had to promise never to marry Natasha, even though he plainly wanted to. The young family, consisting of Michael, Natasha, Tata, and George remained together from 1910 until the stalemate between the brothers was broken. Interestingly, Nicholas continued to present himself to his family as the totally injured party throughout what would come to be known as the "Brassova affair". However, he never mentions to his mother and others the provocative actions he took which precipitated other actions by his brother. For example, Nicholas had to approve Natasha's second divorce and allow for his nephew's birth certificate to be "adjusted". It is very doubtful if he would have done this had Misha not assured him that he intended to keep Natasha as his mistress only. Nicholas also never mentions how the Okhrana became a virtual fixture in their lives, reading their mail and following them whenever they went abroad.

Nicholas was embarrassed by the scandal of Michael's love affair and had his brother resign from their mother's regiment and arranged for Michael's reassignment to a remote command in Orel. From 1909 until October 1912, the couple enjoyed a clandestine relationship. They spent most of this period living at Michael's estate at Brasovo while Michael was based in Orel. They may have been happy to remain there, but fate and the Tsar had different plans. Nicholas ordered Michael to return to the capital to serve with the Chevalier Gardes in the fall of 1911.[8] As the Dowager Empress also sponsored this regiment, this once again brought much unhappiness to the couple, especially when compared to the relative tranquility of their life at Brasovo. Maria Feodorovna made it known that Natasha was not to be welcomed into regimental homes or events. In Petersburg, Natalia was thus subjected to many petty humiliations from Michael's brother officers and it was more difficult for her and Michael to live together when he was not on duty. It is also doubtful that Misha would have overlooked the woman he regarded as his wife in all but name being treated so shabbily as a result of his family's action. Thus, the fragile cocoon, which had contained this scandalous relationship to an extent, began to unravel. Once completed, the unraveling would forever cement Michael and Natasha's relationship.

Two events, Alexis' medical crisis at Spala in 1912 and the start of World War I in 1914, were further catalysts to this change. When Michael heard of the gravity of Alexis' illness at the hunting lodge in Spala, Poland, in 1912, he panicked. It finally became clear to him that if Alexis died, Michael would again become heir to the throne. At this time in his life, he was worried that this change in his status would cause him to be separated from his new family. And, he was completely unwilling for this to happen. With his nephew's frail health and the apparent end to Alexandra's childbearing, Misha feared his bachelorhood would be sacrificed to a dynastic marriage. It is difficult to imagine what made him have this particular fear, as his family's utter indifference to finding him a wife must have been obvious to everyone. Nonetheless, during the crisis, he married Natalia in Vienna on October 29, 1912 in a Serbian Orthodox Church. The couple were able to achieve this feat in spite of the Okhrana's following them everywhere. In this, they were aided by their own cunning and by the secret police's incompetence. The later failed to detect the required reading of the banns over three successive weeks at the Viennese church. By humiliating Natasha in St. Petersburg and making it impossible for them to live comfortably any more, this combined with the fragility of the Heir's health, the Imperial Family suddenly found their least favorite couple legally married. It was a masterful execution of Michael's will, as the Serbian Orthodox Church was beyond the reach of its Russian counterpart, and the marriage could not be annulled by the Tsar's word.

Misha's defiance of his family in matters matrimonial foreshadowed his cousin's, Edward VIII's refusal to go on without the support of the *"woman that he loved."* Romantics may thrill at the depth of the Grand Duke's love for Natalia, but, for Nicholas II, the act was one of crass betrayal. It left the Tsar angry and devastated, particularly over the timing, so close to his own son's near death. It was an act with no defense whatever from the Imperial Family's point of view, as clearly Michael's first loyalty should have been to his brother and the dynasty. The breach between the two brothers was not mended until World War I, with Michael's return to Russia, and the relationship between the two was probably never fully repaired. Indeed, as Nicholas wrote to his mother[9] on

November 7, 1912,

> *Between him and me everything is now, alas at an end, because he has broken his pledged word. How many times he promised of his own free will, not because I pressed him, not to marry her! What revolts me more than anything is his reference to poor Alexei's illness which, he says made him speed things up.*

While it was insensitive of Michael to in effect blame his nephew's weak health for his marriage, it was not his only motivation, as shown in his letter to their mother:

> *Tt is now five years* [it was actually closer to 4] *since I met Nathalie S. and I love and respect her more each year. But, morally it was always very hard on me and in particular the last year in St. Petersburg convinced me the only way out of this painful and false situation was marriage. But I never wanted to distress you and might never have had decided on this step, were it not for little Alexis's illness and the thought that as Heir I could be separated from Nathalie, but now that can no longer happen.*[9]

While we have read Nicholas' condemnation of this marriage, it is rather ironic that Nicholas himself did nearly the same thing as Michael did five years later. Faced with an opportunity to save the monarchy by abdicating the throne and permitting this same Alexis to rule Russia with Michael as Regent, Nicholas instead abdicated on behalf of his son because he couldn't bear to be separated from him. So, we have two brothers in two critical situations, and neither one was able to set aside his personal considerations and do what was best for the country they both loved so dearly. Both these actions contributed to the eventual fall of the dynasty, and both ultimately lead to their own deaths.

For the next two years, Michael and Natasha were exiled from Russia. Nicholas quickly removed Michael from the Regency to which he had been named after Alexis' birth – a regency that would have taken effect in the event of Nicholas' death or incapacity. Most observers saw this as Alexandra's first major play for power. By removing Michael from the Regency, Alexandra ensured that she would be the defacto regent. Alexandra also supposedly was behind demands that Michael divorce his wife, and that all of his assets be frozen and kept beyond his reach. While it is likely that Alexandra had opinions about Michael's marriage, all of the foregoing overlooks the fact that Nicholas was hurt, devastated, and very angry with Michael. Unfortunately, the depth of the anger of the Emperor and Empress had the effect of creating enormous sympathy for Michael and Natasha while they made their home in France and England until the outbreak of World War I in August 1914.

Nicholas did not immediately request his brother's return home when hostilities broke out in August 1914. Michael's best friend, General Ivan Ivanovich Vorontzov-Dashkov, interceded between the two brothers, suggesting that Misha be recalled to command the "Wild Division." The Wild Division was an all-volunteer irregular division of the Russian Army, composed of six regiments of Muslims from the Caucasus region. Michael was a wildly popular choice as commander among the division's fighters, and photos exist of the tall, handsome Grand Duke attired one of their colorful uniforms. While the uniform looks rather chic to the modern eye, Natasha preferred his more polished Guards uniform and regarded his appointment as further retribution for their marriage.

Natalia established several hospitals around Petrograd, as St Petersburg was now called, even turning their property in Gatchina into a Danish Red Cross hospital. The later proved to be a fortuitous move after the Revolution. A Petrograd mansion Michael inherited from Grand Duke Alexis Alexandrovich was converted into yet another hospital.[10] While he never received Natalia, Nicholas at last granted his sister in law the title of Countess Brassova, with her son also to be called Count Brassov. Nor is there any record of the Imperial couple or their children ever meeting Michael and Natasha's son. However, by all accounts, she was quite content to be the *"grand duke's woman,"* and bore the disdain of her Imperial in-laws with dignity. Most importantly to the scandalous couple, their son was at last legitimized. On this one point everyone from the Tsar to Natalia agreed: that George Mikhailovich Brassov was in no way responsible for the unfortunate circumstances of his birth. As to Natasha, so long as Misha lived, she was content. As a hostess, she frequently entertained members of the Imperial Duma, an activity of which her in-laws highly disapproved.

Michael proved to be a brave commander of his "Wild Division." It is interesting to note that, while much of the Army mutinied after the Revolution, these fierce men remained a disciplined fighting force. They only disbanded in 1920 after having continued to fight in the White Army, when they were evacuated to Constantinople with General Wrangel. Some of their descendants may be the present day rebel fighters in Chechnya, as many Chechens fought in the Wild Division. Michael's own service with the division was highly commendable. On the orders of Brusilov, a tough commander who never pandered to the Imperial Family, Michael was awarded the Order of St George 4th Class, Russia's highest award for gallantry. It is evident from reading about this honor that Michael was highly courageous in battle. Due to this honor, it would be very difficult to believe two years later the claims of Alexander Kerensky that Michael refused the throne of Russia *"because his life could not be guaranteed."* Michael Alexandrovich had documented evidence of being brave while under enemy fire. Kerensky's claim then, was highly dubious at best, if not an outright fabrication.

There is no evidence that Michael took part in the Grand Ducal plots of 1916-1917, and it is believed he remained loyal to his brother to the last. The animosity between the two couples – Nicholas and Alexandra and Michael and Natasha – seems to have been confined to the two women by the end of the war. Alexandra was patronizing and hostile – referring to her sister in law never by name but as "Her". In Alexandra's world, there was only room for good and bad, and Natalia knew exactly where she stood when it came to her sister-in-law. For her part, Natasha had sympathy from the many that hated Alexandra, but she was no peacemaker herself. In fact, there is some evidence that 'she" tried to get "Him" involved in the plots, but he refused, contradicting the notion his wife ruled him. He was stunned, along with the rest of the world, by Nicholas' abdication for himself and Alexis, in March 1917. The Romanov dynasty, which began in 1613 with Tsar Michael I, would now end with Michael Alexandrovich. But, was he, as many say, the last tsar?

Some historians do consider Michael to be the last Tsar of Russia. What is beyond doubt is that he was named Nicholas' successor. Had things been different, he may have become Tsar. However, he inherited a situation that, by the hour, careened out of his or anyone's control. As his brother wasted time making and unmaking decisions, as he tried to return to Tsarskoe Selo and then had to turn back, the time remaining for the dynasty was slipping away as sands in an hourglass. As events unfolded, Michael expected to be named regent on behalf of Alexis. He and many others felt that sympathy for his nephew would help diffuse some of the furor of the Revolution. With Nicholas' second abdication, in addition to being surprised by his brother's placing personal considerations before the good of their country, Michael realized that his many absences from the capital and the scandal over his marriage left him with precious little political capital. How different might the situation have been had he had Princess Beatrice and legitimate heirs at his side? Now, he would be a tsar without a court, or a following. It is interesting to note that while many, including Nicholas, criticized Michael's handling of events in the February Revolution, there was no visible support for Michael beyond a few announcements in churches throughout the empire forthcoming after Nicholas' abdication. To answer the question about Michael's status beyond these practical considerations, one must refer to the Fundamental Law of the Russian Empire.

Ironically, the stated intention of this Law, which was developed by the Emperor Paul, was to ensure that the legitimate heir to the throne of Russia would always be known. In its most basic form, the Fundamental Law provided for a semi-Salic method of succession, that is, by male primogeniture, with women retaining succession rights, but only able to exercise them once the male line became extinct. Important qualifications to the law were that no dynast, including one's parent, could remove an heir from the succession, and, also, that no dynast could be pressured or coerced into relinquishing their succession rights. It is easy to see when considering these qualifications that many scholars regard, with certainty, that Nicholas' abdication on behalf of Alexis Nikolaevich was illegal according to the Fundamental Law. While Nicholas' own abdication was also of questionable legality under this same law, this is by no means as clear cut, as descriptions of his abdication do not definitely indicate that he was pressured into abdicating.

Returning to Alexis, and Nicholas' illegal act, if law prohibited Nicholas from removing Alexis from the succession, then Michael Alexandrovich could not have possibly been the last tsar in the Romanov dynasty. It is apparent from his actions in the days in March 1917 when the dynasty's fate hung in the balance that Michael probably regarded this to be the case. He consulted a number of experts on the Fundamental Law, including Vladimir Nabokov, father of the eventual author of Lolita, in crafting his Manifesto. Unique among political documents of the twentieth century, it is a renunciation of what Nicholas offered Michael without being an abdication of the throne. It left the possibility open for Alexis to claim the throne at a future date, but it also left the possibility of his own political future open. It was also designed to quiet the fears of democratic revolutionaries in one important regard. Michael emphatically took up the mantle of his grandfather, the Tsar-Liberator, and mandated a representative government. This was the very government Alexander II was on the verge of implementing when terrorists murdered him exactly thirty-six years before. In a very real sense, Alexander II's grandson, Michael, while not the last tsar, nonetheless upheld his political legacy at the very moment when Imperial Russia was ending. Michael turned his back on the reactionary politics of his father and the conservatism of his brother. It was, in the writer's view, the crowning achievement of his life and one that required enormous courage.

Michael's manifesto of March 16, 1917 is especially noteworthy, in that it represents a fundamental change in the Romanov family's willingness to use violence to retain its power. His repudiation of force to claim, or regain, the crown, has remained to the present day, the Romanov policy regarding a restoration of the monarchy. Here is what he said:

> *A heavy burden had been laid upon me by the will of my brother, who in a time of unexampled strife and popular tumult has transferred to me the imperial throne of Russia. Sharing with the people the thought that the good of the country should stand before everything else, I have firmly decided that I will accept power only if that is the will of our great people, who must by universal suffrage elect their representatives to the Constituent Assembly, in order to determine the form of government and draw up new fundamental laws for Russia. Therefore, calling for the blessing of God, I ask all citizens of Russia to obey the Provisional Government, which has arisen and has been endowed with full authority on the initiative of the Imperial Duma, until such time as the Constituent Assembly, called at the earliest possible date and elected on the basis of universal, direct, equal, and secret suffrage, shall by its decision as to the form of government give expression to the will of the people.*

In this document, Michael neither accepts nor rejects the crown. It is clearly not an abdication, as some have argued. Michael instead strikes a completely new course, consistent with his call, before Nicholas' fall, for representative government. He or Alexis would rule as constitutional monarchs, or not at all. Misha remained in contact with Alexander Kerensky until the later fled Russia, until the Bolshevik uprising in November 1917. Frequently forgotten is that the elections Michael calls for were actually held, only to have the Constituent Assembly disbanded by the armed force of the Bolsheviks. Thus, all Russian governments to this day lack the basic legitimacy urged by the Imperial successor, Michael Alexandrovich Romanov.

Michael never got his chance because of the interference in Russian affairs by the German General Staff. These men confused the short-term objectives of winning a war with the long-term consequences of sending the Bolsheviks into this fragile democracy. Thus, Michael may have had a chance to gather support and bring about, if not a restored monarchy, at least a representative government. While Bolsheviks were being injected into Russia like mutant bacteria, Michael enjoyed being a private citizen for scant months. As the Bolshevik clouds began to gather, Michael obtained Kerensky's permission to leave Russia but he did not do so. As turmoil festered, he remained on the fringes of politics, never again to be able to initiate history. In July 1917, he discovered that Nicholas, Alexandra and their children were going to be exiled to Tobolsk in Siberia. He received last minute approval for a final visit with his brother. On August 13, 1917, in the presence of Provisional Government leader Alexander Kerensky, he finally saw Nicky for the first time since the Revolution. It was also their final meeting, and the last the former Tsar would see any of his Family, apart from his wife and children. Reportedly little was said, though young Alexis did catch a glimpse of his beloved Uncle Misha. After midnight, in the early morning of August 14, the Imperial Family forever departed their beloved home, the Alexander Palace.

Michael assisted Kerensky with his escape from Russia after the Bolshevik coup, obtaining for the ousted leader a Danish passport through his family connections. The Danish government still rented Michael's home in Gatchina, and it offered Misha's family and connections the tiny bit of safety they had left. Kerensky made his way to the West, finally settling in the United States, and died in 1964. He wrote extensively about Russia while in exile, and became a respected academic. He took such pains to show that he brought no harm to the Romanovs that one would have scarcely thought he had been a revolutionary.

George, Count Brassov, was also spirited out of Russia with a Danish passport. He was educated in England and France. He lived in Paris until his death, at age 21, in an automobile accident that occurred immediately after his college graduation. Because of his premature death, he had no children, ensuring that Grand Duke Michael has no direct descendants.

Both Michael and Natalia were subject to arrest after the Manifesto. Their first arrest took place in July 1917, when Kerensky ordered Michael and Natasha's removal to St Petersburg during the time of the Kornilov rebellion. According to the Crawfords, *"this was just in time (from the viewpoint of their guards). Later in the morning, Michael's old Wild Division rode into the woods around Gatchina."*[11] The elections that Michael had so wanted took place in 1917, but Lenin immediately closed down the Constituent Assembly that it elected. The Reds decided they could not continue the war that had meant so much only months before. To bring the war to a swift end, the Bolsheviks signed a humiliating peace treaty at Brest Litovsk on March 3, 1918. Only days later, the new secret police arrested Grand Duke Michael, and they would never let him go. They ordered him exiled to Perm, which was a provincial capital of the area that included Ekaterinburg. Natasha would follow her husband there for several weeks in Easter. Once again, they hoped for a chance to simply live their lives together. And yet again, the violence and uncertainty of the times in which they lived dashed their hopes. Their final parting at the Perm train station must have been heartbreaking.

Michael Alexandrovich, ever the devoted husband, ordered his beloved wife to leave Russia by whatever means after she returned to Petrograd. Uritsky, the evil Chekist leader in the capital, ensured the Cheka once again arrested her as soon as her train arrived. But, Natasha proved adept at escape, feigning illness and then slipping out of the prison hospital. Once free, she obeyed her husband and escaped from Russia with a Danish passport, disguised as a Red Cross nurse. She lived the good life for some years in London. In 1932, she finally found out what happened in June 1918, to her husband. Impoverished in her later years, she received no help from the Romanovs or their Royal relations. Curiously, the only financial help that materialized came from a cousin by marriage, Prince Felix Yussoupov. Natalia's daughter, Tata, by her first marriage also escaped, married, and had a daughter, Pauline Grey, who wrote Natalia's biography, *The Grand Duke's Woman*. By the time she died, alone and forgotten, in 1952, it was Natalia's favorite title.

Many of the Romanovs remaining in Russia, apart from the contingent headed by the Dowager Empress in the Crimea, were ordered to the Urals where Michael was also imprisoned during the spring of 1918. All were assured by the Bolsheviks of their continued freedom and safety. As we have learned from their history, the Bolsheviks had very curious ideas about 'safety." For instance, they reported that Grand Duchess Elisabeth Feodorovna had disappeared while being evacuated to a "safe place." The"'safe place" turned out to be the bottom of a mineshaft. Alexei and Alexandra were said to be in a safe place after Nicholas' murder. The "safe place" for Alexandra turned out to be a shallow grave in the taiga outside Ekaterinburg.

Michael enjoyed relative freedom for many weeks, and was undoubtedly relieved to know that Natalia and the children either had or would soon escape. It was reported that Michael had many supporters in Perm and its environs, waiting to help him. He resided in a hotel along with his long-time secretary, Nicholas Johnson, who many thought was an Englishman. Not that it would help him, but Johnson was a Russian. Also with Michael in Perm were his chauffeur, Borunov, and his valet, Chelyshev.

According to the latter, on the night of June 12, 1918, a band of gangster-like Bolsheviks entered the grand duke's hotel room and asked him to ready himself for transfer to "a safe place".The Bolsheviks included one Gavril Myasnikov, Andrei Markov, and three others.[12] When Michael protested, and tried to call the local Bolshevik leader who had kept promising his continued freedom, his phone lines were cut. He dressed, and was grabbed by the collar and put into a conveyance, along with his secretary Nicholas Johnson.

The manner in which the grand duke was taken away from the hotel left little doubt in the mind of Chelyshev about what awaited Michael. The grand duke had for many years suffered from ulcers, and he was prevented from taking his medications or any other personal items, such as clothing, with him. One can only imagine what went through the minds of the two friends as they left Perm. They were driven outside of the city and into a forested area near the Motovilikhia factory. Reportedly per the killers, Nicholas Johnson was shot immediately after getting out of the carriage.[13] One report indicates that Michael, after first being wounded and then trying to run away, ran toward his friend with his arms outstretched, only to be shot dead. One of the murderers would proudly wear Johnson's watch for many years, as a souvenir. A few of the murderers reportedly came back the following day to bury Michael and Johnson, but the exact site of their grave is unknown. Historian Penny Wilson noted on the *Alexander Palace Time Machine's Discussion Forum* that the Michael's purported gravesite is now a parking lot. With no survivors, it is not known if this situation will ever be rectified. Certainly Michael and Nicholas Johnson deserve something better.

Their murders were the first in an orgy of Romanov murders that took place between June 1918 and January 1919. In all seventeen members of the Imperial Family were murdered during this time. It is impossible not to recognize the dynastic significance of these brutal acts. They began their rampage with the kind, gentle man, known to Nicholas' children as Uncle Misha. The question remains, why was Michael Alexandrovich killed?

In their chapter on the subject, entitled "The First to Die", published in *The Fate of the Romanovs*, Greg King and Penny Wilson review the evidence and present several possibilities. The prevailing view since the Revolution had been that Lenin and the Bolshevik leadership ordered all of the Romanov killed as retribution for the previous regime's wrongs, real and imagined. However, more recent scholarship, most importantly, Fate, has questioned this view. If Moscow ordered these murders, they say, then some of the actions after the murders simply make no sense. For example, Lenin and his deputy Sverdlov, learned of Michael's murder after it happened, and not before.[14] Another theory, that the assassins acted alone, also will not bear close scrutiny. The only argument that does hold up to examination is that Michael's murder was orchestrated by the Ural Regional Soviet, in conjunction with the Perm Bolsheviks. The reasons for his murder proved to be truly chilling.

In June 1918, the Bolsheviks both in Moscow and in the Perm Government faced myriad pressures. Moscow was fighting to stay in power, having to deal with triumphant Germans because of their war gains, and having to reassure European royals about the safety of their Romanov relations. When rumors, which we now know started with the Ural Regional Soviet (URS), surfaced that Michael had escaped captivity and Nicholas had been shot, there was limited reaction. While questions were asked about Michael's whereabouts, there was virtually no reaction to the murder of the former tsar. Thus, it is now thought that Grand Duke Michael was actually murdered in order to "test the waters" prior to murdering the remainder of the family that was still being held captive in the Urals. In this chilling scenario, had there been a strong public outcry, presumably the massacres that followed in July would not have taken place, or would have been limited in scope. Since the Church and the majority of the people remained silent, the murders took place, but only after the URS had reassured Moscow that the Imperial Family remained alive. Thus was Michael, whose grandfather was murdered after nearly giving his country a constitution, murdered after nearly giving his country a constitutional monarchy.

Michael Alexandrovich, Grand Duke and Imperial Successor, was a vital, intelligent, and interesting man whose character was greatly misunderstood during his lifetime. Without a doubt, his greatest personal happiness, his marriage to his brother officer's wife, Natalia Sergievna Wulfert, came at a very great cost, at the very least, the cost of his good name. He was as guilty as were many others of the latter Romanovs in putting his personal satisfaction ahead of what was best for his country. Ironically, a man who involuntarily became a human sacrifice at the hands of the Ural Bolsheviks was unable to voluntarily sacrifice his relationship with her and possibly save many Russian lives. Yet, this same man was incorrectly viewed as being of weak character and totally living under his wife's thumb. While he was undoubtedly in love with Natasha, she appears to have been as smitten as he in their relationship, regardless of her initial motives. Michael showed true strength of character as he fought in those days in March 1917 to save the monarchy, and possibly his nephew's inheritance. His dreams of democracy may have been premature for Russia, but in fairness, diabolical wartime tactics employed by the Germans disrupted the natural order of things. It was they who sent Lenin back to Russia in a sealed train compartment. Once arriving in Russia, Lenin was able to turn their homeland, at the time, the *"freest country on earth"*, into a newer and deadlier police state. To keep their power and to remain in power, they had to resort to the violence that Michael disclaimed in his Manifesto. In a world still riddled with violence and despair, perhaps it is Michael's refusal to take up arms, the refusal to kill his countrymen to regain power, that is his most profound and enduring legacy.

5

THE SON OF TSAR NICHOLAS II

TSAREVICH ALEXIS NIKOLAEVICH

(1904-1918)

By Janet Ashton

*I*t is one of history's ironies that the last Heir born to a faltering dynasty suffered a genetic defect that left him with an incurable disease. To friends of the monarchy, he was and is a pathetic symbol of its sanctity and vulnerability; to enemies, a tangible symptom of its degeneracy. His is a story so steeped in mythology and symbolism as old as the throne that it is almost impossible to see the real boy. If Grand Duke and Heir Tsarevich Alexis Nikolaevich Romanov had not been born with a flaw in his body, one would undoubtedly have been invented for him.

His birth, on July 30, 1904 (O.S.), was perhaps the occasion for more rejoicing than that of any previous Tsarevich. His father, Nicholas II, who succeeded, unmarried (just) at twenty-six, was almost the first Russian monarch since the Empress Elisabeth in the eighteenth century to come to the throne without a direct male heir. For the first decade of Nicholas's reign, the situation persisted as he and his Empress, Alexandra, whom he married within days of succeeding, produced four daughters and their relatives congratulated them with openly disappointed faces. Even Alexander I, the only monarch since Elisabeth to have no surviving legitimate children of either sex, had had several apparently well-trained brothers to fall back on. But neither of Nicholas II's brothers made a promising heir. The elder, George, although considered an intelligent and spirited young man, was suffering from tuberculosis and died in the Caucasus in 1899. Michael, the younger brother, was generally regarded as feckless and immature, raised in isolation by a possessive mother who herself complained of his attachments to a string of unsuitable girls. After them came the uncles and cousins, and family rivalries as much as any other consideration dictated that Nicholas would never feel comfortable passing his throne onto another a branch of the dynasty, a branch which did not necessarily share his own ideals and priorities for a throne he considered a personal trust. He wanted a son of his own, to raise according to his own, semi-mystical notions of monarchy.

"Your ancestral crown belongs to you alone, as absolute Tsar," declared the Metropolitan of Moscow as he welcomed Nicholas to his own coronation in 1896,

> *but all Orthodox Christians are worthy of the Unction which is given but once. And you should be blessed through this sacrament to perceive a new life, the reason is this – that as there is no power higher, so there is no power on earth more arduous than the power of the Tsar, no burden so wearisome as the duty of the Tsar. Through this visible anointment, may the invisible might of heaven descend upon you to augment your prowess as Tsar and light the way for your autocratic pursuit of the welfare and happiness of your devoted subjects.*[1]

The Tsar did not doubt the literal truth of this pronouncement. He saw his role as a commitment to preserve and protect the inextricably linked Church and Autocracy, thereby ensuring the happiness of his subjects. And, for the first ten years of his reign, he pursued a foreign policy that was equally inextricably linked to these ideas. *"The orient believes in us as far as we cherish the best of what was bequeathed to us by the past: autocracy. Without this, Asia is not able sincerely to love Russia and identify with it painlessly,"*[2] explained a friend and advisor of the young Tsar, underlining the nature of Nicholas's own interest in Asia. The Emperor saw it as a natural extension of Russian territory; he believed in a seamless connection between Russian national interests and those of the Buddhist nations of the east, with their own autocratic traditions and apparently gentle and long-suffering peoples whose character seemed to come close to that stereotypically attributed to the Russian peasant. On an early visit to Germany, Nicholas stated his priorities: to finish the Trans-Siberian Railway, colonize Siberia – and then to confront the emerging imperialist power Japan.[3] The Heir to Nicholas's throne would also be the heir to his autocratic, "Asianist" dream.

But the years advanced and no heir was born. After the arrival in 1901 of Nicholas's fourth daughter, Anastasia, a manifesto was prepared which would allow for the succession of the eldest, Olga. This sent a frisson of horror through government and society: how dared the Emperor meddle with the dynastic laws?[4]

Early in 1902, the Empress again began to put on weight, and confessed to the curious family that she was pregnant once more. No child was ever born. In August there was an announcement that she had suffered a miscarriage, but no one believed it. Even in circles closest to the throne, it was unequivocally accepted that Alexandra had had a false pregnancy brought about by wishful thinking as she dreamed of a son.

The following year, the Emperor and Empress were both personally present at the canonization ceremony for Serafim of Sarov, a popular holy man whose cult Nicholas saw as tangible evidence of the Church's vitality in modern Russia. In the face of some ministerial and synodal opposition, he was more than determined to ensure that the sainthood went through, symbolically uniting him with his people in this gesture of veneration. Also at the ceremony were his favoured advisers, most intimately associated with his Asian policy. Afterward, he and the Empress both bathed in the pool that lay near Serafim's hermitage, relying on his reputation as a healer to strengthen and assist them in their mission.

Not many months later, the escalating tensions between Russia and Japan over territorial claims in the Far East finally brought the two countries to war. It was Japan's actions which actually precipitated the conflict, and things went badly for Russia. Only the most deluded of imperialists had welcomed war with Japan at this point; even the architects of the Far Eastern policy understood that Russia was not quite ready to confront the aggressive, westernized empire of the Rising Sun, its Navy and monarchy rebuilt by the British.

In the middle of it all, Nicholas's sister wrote in surprise and possible disbelief, *"It's been revealed (Mama revealed it!) that Alix is expecting! It is becoming more noticeable now, but she, poor thing, has been hiding it for the moment, as she is probably afraid…"*[5] It was a pregnancy that prompted no real rejoicing. The Empress, whose previous pregnancies had caused her great difficulties with morning sickness and sciatica, this time experienced few problems directly related to her condition. However, she had an ear infection and then flu, and was generally depressed by the war and by her husband's unaccustomed absences, as he traveled the country seeing his troops. Even the relatively easy pregnancy was no automatic cause for rejoicing: the one she had had two years before had seemed easy, and that had ended in terrible humiliation and disappointment. This pregnancy had been welcomed with surprise, since people apparently assumed that her misadventure in 1902 indicated that there would never be another child, but as she had already had four daughters it also seemed unlikely she would ever have a son. The Romanov dynasty had an overwhelming preponderance of male children in its recent generations: Alexander II had six sons to two daughters; his brother Michael six sons and one daughter; michael's son Alexander – married to Nicholas's sister – also produced six sons and a solitary girl. The feminine dominance in Nicholas's family was unique – and ironic in light of the succession law - but given other Romanovs' experience it seemed likely to prove constant.

It therefore came as an enormous surprise to everyone when, on July 30, the Empress calmly ate lunch with her husband in their bedroom at Peterhof, and very shortly afterward was delivered of a boy weighing eleven pounds. Nicholas was moved to rare displays of emotion in his diary: *"A wonderful, unforgettable day when the mercy of the Lord has visited us so clearly: Alix gave birth to a little lad at 1.15. In prayer we named him Alexei. I cannot thank God enough for this comfort."*[6] Three hundred guns fired from the Peter Paul Fortress, and the extended family came to visit the new arrival. *"He is a huge, barrel-chested baby, and generally has the air of a warrior knight,"* recorded Alexis's Aunt Xenia.[7] His name was chosen in homage to Alexei (English: Alexis) Mikhailovich, the second Romanov Tsar, whom Nicholas viewed as the last "Russian" tsar before the modernizing and westernizing efforts of Peter the Great and his successors. It was also the name of the Tsar's favourite uncle, Alexis Alexandrovich, Admiral General of the Russian Navy and a man strongly associated with the far eastern policy: he would be godfather to the new Alexis. St Serafim of Sarov was also to be considered a special patron and protector of the young Heir, whose birth tacitly attributed to Alexandra's bathing near his hermitage almost exactly a year before.

Alexandra nursed the baby herself, as she had all four of her daughters, always supplemented by a wet nurse lest the appetites of the lusty imperial infants prove too much for her. Margaretta Eagar, who had been nurse to all four of Alexei's sisters, arriving with the family when Olga was three and the second girl, Tatiana, eighteen months, at first assumed overall responsibility for the new baby's nursery as well. Within a short while, she was found wanting. Her interest in politics had always been evident – on one occasion she famously became so embroiled in discussion of the Dreyfus case that she forgot to take the Grand Duchess Maria out of her bath, and the child, bored, climbed out by herself and ran naked around the palace corridors until captured and returned by a visiting aunt. Now, it was her views on the Japanese War which were to prove unpalatable. As a British subject (she came from Ireland), Miss Eagar felt some sympathies for Britain's ally, Japan, and on several occasions she rebuked her young charges for racist or otherwise violent comments about the Japanese people.[8] Her views apparently caused great discord in the household, and Nicholas decided that she must be dismissed, despite his wife's "wavering" and reluctance on the matter. The precious Heir to the Throne could not be entrusted to one with sympathies for an enemy power.[9] Henceforth, the chief nurse would be Maria Vishniakova, a Russian, who was called "Mary" by the children, but who apparently talked to them in Russian. It must have been a source of satisfaction to the nationalist lobby that the Heir thus grew up speaking only Russian, despite the fact that English was the domestic language of his parents when alone, and all his sisters – so far as they spoke any language correctly - were bilingual in infancy as well.

It is puzzling that Alexandra, whose Russian is generally supposed to have been clumsy, was the apparently close and doting mother of an exclusively Russophone child. Even when he had passed ten years old and begun English lessons she wrote to him in Russian, with the occasional English word or phrase (*"Be a good boy!"*) rendered into cyrillic lettering[10] – this correspondence indicating either that her Russian was rather better than people gave her credit for, or her relationship with her son was not as close as the popular tale suggests. In truth, her own health began to fail when he was only three or four, so for this reason and because he was a boy she was to prove a less constant a presence in his life than she had been with her elder daughters when they were small and had played in her study while she wrote letters, and greeted guests at her side. Nevertheless, in his infancy, she was for Alexis the same constant presence that she had been to her daughters, keeping him in a crib by her bed and holding him sleeping in her arms while she rested herself. When Nicholas went off to visit his troops, she could now send a pair of their son's socks with him, as a tangible reminder of home but also of the cause for which the troops were fighting: Russia's future; the future of the holy autocracy, which now seemed so much more secure. *"Babysweet is lying across my knees, awake and listening to his musical box,"* the Empress wrote happily to her absent husband. *"Whilst drinking before he was smiling and cooing away. You would have loved him so."*[11]

Ironically, at the very point that Nicholas's autocracy finally seemed assured from within the family, it came under attack from external factors. The mounting disasters of the Japanese War brought to a head several currents of discontent that had been at large during the first decade of Nicholas's reign, ranging from severe labour and student problems to misery in rural communities to issues with subject nationalities. Increasingly, people saw the answer to their problems as being some form of elected representation. After the tragic events of Bloody Sunday in January 1905 in particular, when troops shot unarmed petitioners in front of the Winter Palace, Russian subjects felt they could no longer look to Nicholas to help them. As the year wore on, Russia erupted onto a wave of strikes, riots and increasingly violent demonstrations.

But Nicholas's response underlined his conviction that the autocracy was a divine institution indissoluble from the Russian Empire. With the country collapsing around him, he was forced to take decisive action to save his Throne. He himself favored the idea of declaring martial law, suspending all court trials, and appointing a temporary dictator. Under pressure from several ministers and family members including the Dowager Empress, he finally changed his mind and gave in to calls for some form of governmental reform. Thus, on October 17, 1905, Nicholas signed a manifesto creating the Duma, Russia's first elected legislature.

Practically speaking, he now recognized civil liberties, freedom of religion, speech, and assembly, and had enfranchised the majority of his male subjects; but Nicholas did not view this as the end of the autocracy at all. According to his personal propaganda, presented in Michael Elchaninov's book, *"The Sovereign Emperor,"* (the English title is *"The Tsar and his people"*) which the Tsar personally commissioned and approved, Nicholas granted the October Manifesto not in response to the revolutionary movement, which was not mentioned at all, but out of his own far-sighted wisdom; the Duma itself was compared to the models of medieval Russian sobors, or councils, summoned by the sovereign to advise on important questions of the day. *"It is a fact,"* Elchaninov asserted, *"that the Autocracy of Old Russia was indissolubly bound to 'the voice of the land,' expressed by the Zemsky Sobors. Now by the will of the Emperor this 'voice of the land' has taken a new, more modern aspect, but in spirit it remains the same purely Russian 'union of the Sovereign with the people' that was first born in our land."*[12]

Thus, to Nicholas, the Duma gained its power directly through the benevolence of the Emperor: it was his gift to Russia, subject to his own whims and orders as an extension of the autocracy itself. This allowed Nicholas to claim that he retained intact the autocratic power he had inherited from his father. In 1906, he entered into negotiations with the new powers over the use of the specific terms "autocratic" and "unlimited" in defining the Russian sovereign. After much dispute, Nicholas was forced to abandon the use of "unlimited" when describing his power, though "autocratic" remained to the end of the Dynasty. The Government accepted this definition by reasoning that "autocratic" referred only to the belief that the Emperor had received his authority directly from God, though to Nicholas it continued to imply that he alone maintained full and comprehensive power.[13] To Nicholas, the Duma and other institutions were there on sufferance and subject to their own good behaviour. In this belief, he was ardently supported by the Empress, the mother of his Heir. Nicholas felt fear and contempt for the turbulent behaviour of the Duma he had created, and on several occasions he illegally altered the voting laws, to narrow the chances of troublesome socialists winning the seats.[14] In 1913 he tried, unsuccessfully, to revoke it altogether.[15] This was the political and intellectual background to Alexis

Nikolaevich's upbringing and education.

It quickly became apparent to those caring for him that the little boy had a mind of his own and was by nature disinclined to obey without question. His parents were rather proud of his obstreperous nature; his mother noted with approval that he would "be his own master" when he grew up, and the Tsar cheerfully called him "Alexei the Terrible" and joked that he feared for Russia under the Heir's rule.

Alexis was boisterous and active anyway, but his upbringing did nothing to encourage modesty. From infancy, he was shown off in public in a way that can have left him in no doubt that he was an important person. He accompanied his father to military reviews and heard the troops cheer for him; he had his array of uniforms and military appointments and his own little suitcases that specified his title clearly in gold letters on the lid: "Heir Tsarevich." Sometimes people came to his home to see him personally on business of various kinds, bringing him gifts and kissing his hand. But if he was to grow up an autocrat according to his father's conception of the role, he must be trained to trust the infallibility of his own instincts: perhaps this was why his parents seemed so disinclined to correct his displays of temperament.

There was another, much sadder reason, too. When the Tsarevich was six weeks old he bled for three days from the navel for no discernible reason. On that occasion, the fears of his parents were quieted somewhat by his healthy appearance and cheerful, normal behaviour. It is not known exactly when they realized that their son was suffering from the hereditary bleeding disease hemophilia, which had already appeared in several of Queen Victoria's male descendants. Alexandra knew that her Uncle Leopold – Queen Victoria's youngest son – whose particular favourite she had been and whose gift of a bracelet she wore for the rest of her life had suffered through his life from problems with his joints brought about unchecked bleeding. He was the first known hemophiliac in the British royal family, and it has been theorized that a mutation occurred in the genetic material of his mother the Queen, causing her to give birth to a hemophilic son as well as two daughters who passed hemophilia to their own sons. One of these daughters was Alice, Empress Alexandra's mother. Alice's second son, Friedrich of Hesse, died aged three after a fall from a window, though it is possible that Alexandra, who was less than a year old at the time, may not have known that he too had the dreaded family disease. She did, however, know that the disease had reappeared in the children of her own sister. Only six months before Alexis was born, one of his cousins, four-year-old Prince Heinrich of Prussia, died of a cerebral haemorrhage after a fall while playing, and Heinrich's elder brother also bled excessively from his earliest days. But it is unlikely that either Alexandra or Nicholas understood that this family history meant a fifty per cent chance that Alexandra might herself prove a carrier of hemophilia. Royalty seemed to equate hemophilia with general fragility and did not understand that it was passed on through the generations by hemophilic men themselves and by their carrier daughters, as well as by some of the daughters of other women who carried it. Thus, the Queen feared that another of her grand-daughters, Alexandra's cousin Maud, might be a hemophilia risk because of her poor health, although Maud's father, the future Edward VII, had escaped the disease and her mother did not come from a family that had it at all. Unless by some huge stroke of misfortune a further mutation had occurred in Maud's DNA causing the disease to re-appear in this unaffected branch of the family, she had no possibility of passing the disease to a son. Alexandra, the daughter and sister of known carriers, was another matter. But if Alexandra thought of the subject before her marriage, she probably deemed herself no more of a risk than any of her female cousins.

Those who encountered Alexandra with her son Alexis when he was an infant or toddler were struck by her happiness, her appearance of a woman who had had *"her dearest wish fulfilled."*[16] It is inconceivable, though, that Alexandra did not yet know that he was unwell. As he began to walk, the blue-black swellings which developed at the site of the smallest bruise would have left no doubt that something unusual was happening. Alexandra might have even seen such swellings on the limbs of her nephews. But like any hopeful parent, she probably took refuge in a form of denial, reassured by his boisterous character and sturdy body. How could this big, tough boy be an invalid? He would get better; a cure would be found soon; it wasn't really that bad an illness in his case. *"Relatively speaking,"* agrees Alexandra's well-known biographer Robert Massie, himself the father of a hemophilic child, *"Alexis was a mild hemophiliac. His hemophilia was much less severe than* [Massie's son's] *for example, and he had strikingly fewer bleeding episodes."*[17] But when Alexis reached the age at which a child's more strenuous activity starts to cause painful bleeding into the joints, there could no longer be any pretending that he was totally well. It was at this stage that the Empress herself began to exhibit the symptoms of a cardiac disorder that may have been genuinely organic, brought on by constant stress, or may have been the effects of panic. She was short of breath and spent much of her time lying immobile on a sofa. In the nursery overhead, her children went about their separate lives. When Alexis was ill, though, he saw a lot of her, lying on her bed or in his own while she lay on a sofa near him. The implications are obvious: his mother was a comforter, but she was also associated with weakness, darkened rooms, frustration. Not for Alexis the hikes and pillow fights his sisters had enjoyed in the days before Mama was overwhelmed with worry.

To be fair to the Empress, she fully appreciated that she was often doleful company for her children, and this is reflected in her letters to them. As Alexis grew past nursery age, she introduced a robust, masculine presence into his life in he form of two sailor nannies, Andrei Derevenko and Klementy Nagorny, who played with him, watched over him and kept him company when he was sick. There was nothing in this arrangement to make him feel like an invalid: his sisters were also been followed by protective sailors when they were on board the imperial yacht as young children. The only apparent difference in Alexis's case was that these husky men took the place of the girly governesses, nannies, ladies-in-waiting and Mama when the children were on dry land.

Nevertheless, Alexis's tutors began to worry about the effects of so much supervision. When he was a toddler he charmed people with his looks and spirits; in the words of one of his own future teachers he was then *"a tiny little chap in wee wee white knickerbockers and a Russian shirt trimmed with Ukrainian embroidery of blue and silver."*[18] He had blond curly hair he liked to invade his sisters' classroom and dash around the desks, laughing and waving his arms. When he was excited and happy, Alexis would fling up his hands and shout, *"Hurrah!"* as he had heard the troops do when he appeared.[19] But as he grew, accounts of his activities took on a less rapturous note. Adult relatives complained of his peevish misbehaviour at table, licking his plate and annoying other children. When he interrupted a lesson to send for and greedily cram sweets, his once-enraptured English tutor rightly called him *"piggish"*; and his playmates feared his violent horseplay and tendency to pull rank. It is tempting to blame all of this – as his concerned tutors did – on Alexis's frustrations and boundary-testing as a predominantly healthy child who was not allowed to trip without someone running to catch him, but several of his sisters were also noted for their displays of imperial temperament; his youngest and favourite companion, Anastasia, in particular. The frustrations of hemophilia certainly played a role when he acted up, as did his parents' natural fear of the consequences correcting or thwarting him, but the constant attention that any imperial infant received also had to be a reason for his wildness, as did simply being a normal active child. When Alexis was in a bad or unusually disobedient mood, more people noticed by virtue of his position, just as conversely they also noticed displays of graciousness or good manners and attributed these to a sensitive soul. Even when he was five years old, an older cousin who disliked the bumptious young Alexis would write that he thought the Empress's treatment of her son – far from smothering him – was "incautious", given his condition.[20] As he grew older, Alexis's tutors insisted more and more that he be allowed to take his own risks, have accidents, and cope with the consequences.

Alexis's best-known and probably most serious bout of bleeding was the nightmare occasion in Poland in 1912, when he bled for weeks after an accident in a boat or bathtub that left him with a large bruise in his groin. At first, the bleeding was intermittent, and lessons continued, though he looked pale and was carried from room to room. But at the gloomy hunting lodge of Spala, he had to take to his bed permanently, and for eleven days the corridors echoed with his screams and groans as his leg flexed and the blood that filled the cavity at his thigh began to destroy the surrounding cartilage and tissue. Aware that the boy was growing weaker and weaker and might die, and that all manner of rumours about the cause of his indisposition were appearing in the international press, his doctors for the first time made a public announcement that he had hemophilia.[21] Until then, Nicholas and Alexandra had been intensely secretive about it, and it was only in that spring of 1912 that Nicholas's sisters and mother were officially told of Alexis's hemophilia, though they had seen or heard about his symptoms in the past. *"For the first time she admitted that the poor Little One has that terrible illness,"* wrote Grand Duchess Xenia on March 10, 1912, recounting a conversation with the Empress,[22] *"and that she herself has become ill because of it and will never fully recover."* The reasons for this dissimulation are complex: they feared that the throne might be further weakened at a difficult time if the people of Russia were generally aware of his problems; and perhaps too there was an element of insecurity and pride involved: the Tsar and Empress preferred that their often critical relatives not know that the perfect, long-awaited boy was flawed after all.

Before then, curious stories and inaccurate rumours about his health had inevitably begun to leak out. Ruth Kedzie Wood, an American travel writer who apparently met Alexis and his sisters at Peterhof when he was still *"a stocky little figure in white belted smock and white trouserlets....a dear, plump, pouty baby"* who galloped about the room on a hobby horse, sadly called him *"Heir to the Woe of Russia!"* and observed that his mother, *"knowing his heritage, must yearn to keep him a baby!"* Days later, Wood was told by another friend that the Tsar was *"progeny of a race of alcoholics and epileptics...not one male ancestor for generations back had been normal in mind or body"* and that *"his poor little son also bears the blight of his grand-fathers. It is known that he is a victim of epilepsy, as is his imperial father."*[23] Thus the Romanov dynasty's satanic reputation became mixed up with whispers that there was something wrong with the Tsarevich Alexei, uniting in the person of an heir who would have had a disease invented for him in popular legend even if he had been perfectly healthy. Knowing this, though, many people were skeptical about these stories.

Even the official announcement about his illness changed little. Alexis recovered, apparently through the intervention of the controversial would-be Holy Man, Grigori Rasputin, who telegraphed with the sound advice that the doctors to leave the child alone and stop prodding him in the area of nascent clots. The bleeding had done a lot of damage: the boy was unable to walk for a year, and he wore a metal brace on his bent leg to support it. Mud baths and electrical currents were also prescribed in the effort to relax the muscles, relieve the aches and straighten the poor afflicted limb. For the first time, Nicholas and Alexandra appointed a dedicated hematologist, Vladimir Derevenko, whose son Nikolai ("Kolia') became one of Alexei's most favoured companions. It had all happened at the worst possible time: 1913 was the three hundredth anniversary of the succession of the first Romanov Tsar, and Nicholas hoped for celebrations that promised a bright future for the dynasty. Instead, there were parties and theatre trips which the Empress left early, apparently on the verge of a panic attack. When Alexis appeared in public at church services or parades he was in the arms of a Cossack guard, and a ripple of pity went up from the crowd *"at the sight of the poor, helpless child, the heir to the throne of the Romanovs,"*[24] The symbolism could hardly be more obvious: this frail, crippled child was the best that the degenerate dynasty, shorn of the famous vitality of its ancestors, could manage to produce as an heir.

And, yet, in the same year, in Michael Elchaninov's *"The Sovereign Emperor,"* the hagiographical account which Nicholas commissioned of his own reign, Alexis's illness was again completely ignored. He was, Elchaninov claimed, *"thoroughly proficient in rifle exercises, skirmish orders, the elements of scouting, the rules and requirements of military discipline, and performs the exercises correctly and smartly."*[25] Nicholas hoped to present his son as a strong, capable, and forceful future military leader. Despite the recent public admissions of the Heir's hemo-philia, the Alexis in Elchaninov's book was robust and enthusiastic, a boy who *"delights in gymnastic exercises and has thoroughly mastered the elementary military exercises."*[26] The book's preparation began before Spala made Alexis's illness more obvious, and the boy depicted in it is clearly the Heir Nicholas really wanted and perhaps still hoped his son could develop into.

A year after the Tercentenary of the dynasty, Russia was at war again, this time in Europe, pulled into conflict with Austria and Germany thanks to the complex web of alliances they were all embroiled in. Nicholas spent much of the war at the Stavka, Headquarters, with his troops, infamously leaving many key political decisions to Alexandra. In the autumn of 1915, Alexei joined him there. Spala was now a mercifully distant memory: the boy was walking and running normally, romping with his dog Joy and generally enjoying fine health. When his parents considered releasing a film of him playing in the snow to the public – and perhaps they were thinking specifically that it would be an excellent antidote to the pathetic impression he had created in 1913 – he objected, observing with a rather sharp-tongued humour that since he himself appeared to be pirouetting on screen *"the dog looks more intelligent than I do!"*[27] On high days and holidays his sisters were allowed a break from lessons, but he was not, owing to his reputation for being *"naughty when he has nothing to do."*[28] Nevertheless, he was rather behind in his lessons. *"In the autumn of 1916, Alexis Nikolaevich was already twelve, the age of a cadet pupil of the third class, and yet he still did not know, for example, simple fractions,"* wrote one observer in the household.[29]. Around the same time, he received a book of fairy tales from his mother as a Christmas present and this furnished his reading matter for the time being.[30] His hand-writing was not wonderful, and his diary entries, made under duress, even more simplistic than his father's, often reducing the day's activities to *"Exactly the same as yesterday."* Those well-disposed to Alexis blamed the interruptions in lesssons due to his health for this state of affairs, but it is clear that none of the imperial children was unduly taxed by their timetable. According to their mother's valet, they rose at eight, took lesson until eleven, and then spent much of the rest of the day in walking, driving, sewing or knitting.[31] Like some other princes of his generation, Alexis was taught to knit as if he were to be a soldier who would make his own socks. Family tea also played a big part in the day; even when her health was poor Alexandra liked the children to come and go as they pleased, but the girls who had no governess to supervise them were probably around her more often than her son was.

The timetables kept by the tutors also bear out that scanty attention given to academic matters in the imperial family. On November 29, 1916, for example, the Tsarevich had just four hours of lessons. Four days later, he had only two, the excuse being that he went to the hospital to watch his mother operating on a soldier in her new-found capacity as a war nurse.[32] Alexis's tutors were his most constant companions; both the English tutor Sydney Gibbes and the French teacher (from Switzerland), Pierre Gilliard, eventually had flats in the palaces near their charge, but if his mother's letters and their own testimony are a reliable source for his activities they both spent a great deal of time reading to him or playing games with him while he rested or recuperated from a bout of bleeding.

With the war, he was allowed to abandon the childish sailor suits he had worn since he was three or four, and adopted the uniform of a private soldier with knee-high boots and overcoats. Long-legged, slim and rather tall for his age, he walked beside his father at their encounters with the troops and visits to factories, listening eagerly to the things the soldiers or workmen said. He was an impressive figure to those who saw him thus, a handsome, auburn-headed boy who looked older than he was, particularly when set beside his small, slight father: he was well past the Tsar's shoulder and could have been a fifteen-year-old. *"No babies any more!"* the Empress mourned, but she was proud of him and keen for the army to see him. It is often suggested both by critics of Nicholas and Alexandra and conversely by those well-disposed to them that they cut themselves off from the country and allowed rumour to flourish where simple, solid information about their close family life would have done far more good in terms of the way they were perceived. This is not quite the case, since both Emperor and Empress, while having little to do with high 'society," always made full use of the image of their attractive children in the world at large, publishing photographs and films and taking the youngsters out in public far more often than Nicholas and his siblings, for example, had been shown off by the reclusive Alexander III.

In private, Alexis was still a lot less mature than his appearance suggested. He shared a bedroom with his father at Headquarters, waking early and larking around until the Tsar woke up and sleepily begged him to stop.

"Papa," Alexis once wrote wickedly to his mother, *"made smells much and long this morning."*[33]

When the two were up, the Tsar went to work while Alexis did lessons with the ubiquitous Gibbes and Gilliard – called 'sig" and "Zhilik" by the imperial children. In the afternoon, they went for a drive together, stopping in summer at a convenient location by the river Dniepr for bathing. Alternatively, they might take the electric launch up-river. Alexis spent time with much older cousins such as Prince Igor Konstantinovich, who all took turns serving as the Tsar's ADC, and with foreign generals who came there representing Russia's allies. He would have dinner with his father and the generals, each meal degenerating into a game of football with napkins or other things that came to hand. Intoxicated by the all-male lifestyle, Alexis told his tutors that he found life there with the Army *"infinitely preferable"* to home.[34] Gilliard complained that he was out of control, but the Empress, despite her own constant fears for his health, insisted that he derived far more benefit from being at Headquarters than at home – he was being seen, learning to interact with a broad circle of people, to understand what Russia was fighting for. *"It is so good for him to be your little companion, it develops him quicker,"* she wrote to the Tsar. *"He is not too wild before guests I hope?...you keep him in hand, see that he does not play at table or put his elbows or arms on the table, please – and don't let him throw bread balls."*[35]

Alexis's future rights and duties were a constant theme in his mother's letters to his father. They still clung to the view that they were fighting to pass an inviolate autocracy and undivided Russia onto him almost as a personal estate, and this influenced decisions they took for the worse, forever regarding the Duma as an enemy encroaching upon their rights – much as it did them – at a time when both arms of government should have been working together. Rasputin, the ostensible protector of Alexis as well as his parents' spiritual adviser in a broader sense, also played a role in the breakdown of trust in the Russian government due to his perceived influence over decisions. It is often alleged on scanty real evidence that Alexis disliked Rasputin. This is perfectly possible, but if it is true the boy's feelings are likely to have been those of an always rather recalcitrant youngster for the man his mother held up as an example in some ways – and certainly not a balanced assessment on Alexis's part of Rasputin's character and worth. His exposure to Grigori Rasputin was actually rather limited, in any case: as a small child, he heard the Holy Man tell stories in the nursery and occasionally said his prayers with him; later, they sometimes spoke on the telephone, but Rasputin was certainly not a regular visitor to the Palace.

Late in 1916 Rasputin was murdered by a group of disaffected aristocrats, but it is difficult to know what Alexis was told about this. His diary entry for the day it happened and those that followed are the customary bland records of events (he was still at the Stavka with his father): *"Today was just the same as usual. I wrote to Mama and Aunt Ella...General Janin* [one of the Allied representatives] *gave me some books...It was cold (-6 or -8 degrees Reamur)."*[36] Two days later, he and his father departed for home, where a frantic search was on for the missing man's body. Alexis recorded: *"At quarter past ten I went to church with Papa. Then I played in the garden. Had lunch with everyone. At 3.40 Papa and I went to the station and caught the train...Played 'Nain Jaune'* [his favourite card game]." The diary entries for the days just after they arrived home are missing, and he did not attend the funeral. By December 23rd, he was happily recording skating trips with his friend Kolia again.

Then the food supply system to Russia's cities began to fail. A combination of bread riots, spy stories and ever-escalating hatred for the German-born Empress led senior members of the Duma to converge on the Tsar at Headquarters and seek his abdication, which they won with surprisingly little resistance from him. Alexis was at home suffering from measles, as were all four of sisters, the three eldest quite seriously ill. *"He knows nothing of passing events but feels them all the same,"* noted Sydney Gibbes, without saying how he knew what Alexis was feeling.

Only later, when he was recovering and his father was on the way home, did the boy hear from Gilliard that *"perhaps nobody"* would be Tsar now. For all of Alexis's life he had been prepared for his future role as Emperor; no one had ever acted as if his health might make things difficult for sshim. But now, suddenly, his father signed his rights away on his behalf, unable to contemplate the obvious fact that if he became Tsar while still a minor Alexis would be taken away from the family and raised by those who understood neither his disease nor his parents' plans for him. According to Gilliard, the former Heir did not protest his own rights; most probably, he did not really understand what had happened and expected all to come right before long.

For the first half year after the abdication, the family continued to live in the Alexander palace at Tsarskoe Selo. Alexis's sisters had their hair shaved, as it had begun to fall out in clumps after measles, and he cheerily followed suit. *"Mama was very annoyed about it, but I smoothed things over,"* he wrote insouciantly.[37] With his crew cut, he looked more than ever like a teenage soldier, swimming in the lake and digging vegetable gardens. There were occasional petty humiliations directed at the Tsar in particular during these months, but the children who had never really experienced anything but almost suffocating love and attention from those around them had no real cause to fear the world or take this very seriously. *"He bore unpleasant events without grumbling,"* Gibbes observed of his young pupil,[38] who had in addition been through corporeal suffering by now to take lesser things in his stride.

In August, the day after Alexis's thirteenth birthday, the Provisional Government moved the family for safe-keeping to distant Siberia. It was in

Siberia that news of the fall of that Provisional Government formed from the aspiring democrats of the Duma would reach them. The far more ruthless Bolshevik forces now assumed control, and Russia at large erupted in Civil War.

Dimitri, the son of Ivan the Terrible, was the young heir whose death in 1591 started Siberia's long and dark career as a place of political exile. The child of Ivan's late fifth marriage, he was sent as a fatherless toddler to live in the beautiful city of Uglich with his mother, while nobles and Polish invaders squabbled over the future of the Russian throne inhabited by his half-brother. Parts of Siberia had recently come under the Tsar's jurisdiction: the Russians had taken the towns of Tiumen, Tara, Surgut and the capital, Tobolsk from the ruling Tartars, expanding Orthodox territory into the lands of the faltering Golden Horde which had tormented them for centuries. Slavs had been serfs of this Golden Horde: now suddenly the tables turned and Slavs were ruling Asiatic lands. Russia, a tiny, land-locked state, had now begun its progress toward becoming a huge empire, to which would belong the dubious distinction of being the first European nation to wipe out entire native populations and species of animals. In a sense, here was the origin of Nicholas's Asian dream, to which Alexis was born.

Dimitri the Tsarevich died at nine years old. Officially he fell on a knife in an epileptic fit and accidentally cut his own throat. His hagiography held that he was murdered by the agents of Boris Godunov, the nobleman and future Tsar: in his death throes Dimitri was said to have held onto the baptismal cross at his throat, resisting the attempt of his murderers to remove this most potent symbol of the Orthodox monarchy and state. According to this same legend, the bells of Uglich's cathedral began to toll solemnly, proclaiming the death of the last of the Rurik dynasty. *"What more fitting end to the dynasty of saintly princes could be found than the sacrificial death of its last and most innocent member?"* one modern writer observes, explaining this legend.[39] Boris, incensed by the public mourning, took it upon himself to punish the bell. With one "ear" – the metal lip that took its rope – torn asunder like any prisoner, the Uglich bell was exiled to Tobolsk in Siberia, where it remained for centuries to come.[40]

Siberia would until the last days of the monarchy remain slightly alien, savage, a frontier land with the air of a colony. In the beginning it attracted trappers and explorers, the wild rejects of the Russian state and other European countries as well, drawn east by the promise of wealth and a vast land where the government could barely observe them. Later, the government itself used it for more exiles, the place to which is dispatched every undesirable from religious dissidents to political prisoners.

Rich skeins of myth and implausible tales thus grew up around this bitterly symbolic imprisonment of the last Tsar and his family. They went in the first instance to Tobolsk, the ancient capital, where they were kept in the Governor's house in relatively good conditions and allowed trips across the road to church and other such privileges. Alexis wrote in his diary of his wood-chopping, play-acting, and games with his friend Kolia, the doctor's son. Nevertheless, the Romanovs were following in the footsteps of that first Russian exile, the Uglich bell, sent east in disgrace for proclaiming the death of the Tsarevich Dimitri. In years to come, ardent monarchists made heavy weather of the parallels between Dimitri the last Rurik, and Alexis, the last Romanov heir. Like Dimitri, Alexis by virtue of his youth alone would become a symbol of the martyred innocence of his dynasty, the slaughtered infant behind whose blood the sins of his forebears would disappear: not so much washed away or redeemed in a religious sense as forgotten completely in the horror of the dynasty's last days.

In Ekaterinburg, the scene of his family's stifling final weeks, shut into one floor of a medium-sized house behind painted windows and palisades, Alexis became the subject of a Dimitri-like tale. According to accounts third-hand at best, his sailor nanny or guardian, Klementy Nagorny, was torn from the boy's side and sent away to jail where he was later shot, for helping Alexis to prevent the theft by guards of the Heir's baptismal gold cross. Within six weeks Alexis himself was dead.[41] This dubiously factual story is strikingly reminiscent of the Dimitri legend of the child killed for cleaving to the same baptismal symbol of his Orthodox monarchy, and foreshadowed the nationalist attempts to paint the last Tsar as a saintly victim of foreign – or Jewish – conspiracy, the monarch murdered by aliens solely for his Russianness and his religion.

There was no need for these lurid tales: the reality was bleak enough. After weeks of uncertainty when the only news from outside was the sound of the distant fighting between Bolshevik and anti-Bolshevik forces, Alexis was murdered with the whole of his family on July 16/17 1918, a pathetic figure whose most recent bout of bleeding had left him again unable to walk, as after Spala. Tall and thin, he weighed so little now that his murderers were able to burn his body almost out of existence, burying it and that of one of his sisters in a t-shaped pit apart from the rest of the family and the doctor and servants who died with them, in order to confuse anyone who chanced on the secret graves. In 1991, the discovery of the grave containing the bones of the seven adults was publicly announced, but it was not until the summer of 2007, after repeated fruitless searches, that a party of amateur local historians finally uncovered the resting place of the Heir and his sister, and scientific conferences formally identified them through DNA analysis.[42]

It is difficult to know what manner of man Alexis Nikolaevich might have become. Some recalled his generosity; others said he was careful to the point of being stingy. Some remember a boy whose own experiences made him sensitive to suffering in others; others recall a spiteful little autocrat who enjoyed hurting other children, at least when he was small. He was stoic and optimistic, that is certain, and his sense of humour is an appealing quality, but to those forced to deal with him daily it must have seemed impertinence. It was Alexis's good fortune in a sense that the war came along, as it made an educational virtue of his natural sociability and lack of conventional book learning. It is quite possible that his spirit and curiosity would have served him well had he lived, as those best-disposed to his family like to argue. He might have capitalised on this youthful experience of war and revolution to ask why this had happened and to try to understand the world in depth. But equally, he, like other young aristocrats of his generation, might have conceived a hatred so deep of those who had deprived him of his birthright that he turned to the opposite extreme and threw in his lot with those who sought to wipe the Bolsheviks and their perceived fellow-travelers from the face of the earth. Ironically, the latter-day icon image of Alexis as a big-eyed, murdered boy – who always looks many years younger than his actual age at the time of death – accords in tragic style with the latter possibility. Even the frescos and icons in the Cathedral on the Blood, Ekaterinburg, erected on the site of the house where the imperial family died, underline this point: some were painted by a convicted young murderer, a 17-year-old skinhead named Pavel Ryno who made a career of killing members of racial minorities. When asked why he had committed these terrible acts, the boy replied that he did it for *"Tsar, country and monarchy."*[43] Those who most ardently insist on the saintly character of the last Heir are sometimes also those who seek to avenge him in the most un-saintly of ways.

The Romanov dynasty began with a teenage boy, Michael I, called to his post while in hiding in the so-called Ipatiev monastery on Russia's eastern fringes. It ended with a teenage boy who would have been Alexis II, shot and bayoneted in a house belonging to an engineer named Ipatiev on a bigger Russia's eastern fringe. It is the curious pattern of coincidences like these, the legends and symbols that bound his short life, which hide and eclipse the person poor Alexis really was. But it is the symbols and coincidences, and the poignancy of the position he occupied as the vulnerable heir to a crumbling throne, which also ensure that he remains unforgotten, though he was far too young to be remarkable for what he was as a person and his life itself ended just short of his fourteenth birthday.

E

ENDNOTES

CHAPTER 1: The Sons of Tsar Paul I

Tsar Paul I

1. Catherine II to Melchior Grimm, cited in Martin, 55 [author's translation].
2. Dimsdale, 63-4.
3. ibid., 52.
4. cited in Wortman, 1:196.
5. cited in Hartley, 14.
6. Catherine to Grimm, cited in Palmer, 14.
7. Edling, 57 [author's translation].
8. cited in Hartley, 24.
9. Jerrmann, 72.
10. Elizabeth Alekseevna to Amélie of Baden, 1 August (O.S.) 1800, in Nikolai Mikhailovich, 373.
11. Elizabeth to Amélie, 15 October 1800, ibid., 376.
12. cited in Hartley, 26.
13. Choiseul-Gouffier, 82-3.
14. cited in Wortman, 1:194.
15. cited in Hartley, 45.
16. cited in Wortman, 1:201.
17. cited in Palmer, 77.
18. cited in Markham, 190-1.
19. ibid., 194.
20. ibid., 195.
21. cited in Cronin, 396.
22. cited in Hartley, 117.
23. ibid, 118.
24. ibid., 124.
25. Choiseul-Gouffier, 195.
26. Wassenaer, 129..
27. ibid., 132..
28. Choiseul-Gouffier, 276-8.
29. cited in Wortman, 1:261.
30. Wassenaer, 40.
31. Edling, 266-7.
32. ibid., 268.

33. There is of course no real reason at all to suppose that Rasputin's father was anyone other than the man who registered him and brought him up: Efim Rasputin of Pokrovskoe.

Grand Duke Konstantin Pavlovich

1. Maya Kucherskaya's PhD thesis.
2. Catherine II to Melchior Grimm, cited in Martin, 55 [translation, Janet Ashton].
3. Masson, 178.
4. Karnovich, 8.
5. Pienkos, 3.
6. Karnovich, 28 [translation, William Lee].
7. Czartoryski, 353.
8. Czartoryski, 1: 121-2 [translation, William Lee]
9. Alville, Anna Féodorvna, 21 [translation, Janet Ashton].
10. Masson, 178-9.
11. ibid., 25.
12. Nikolai Mikhailovich, 239 [translation, Janet Ashton].
13. Komarovsky, 75 [translation, William Lee].
14. cited in Martin, 116 [translation, Janet Ashton].
15. cited in Alville, Anna Féodorvna, 49-50 [translation, Janet Ashton].
16. Karnovich, 85 [translation, William Lee].
17. cited in Wortman, 251.
18. cited in Alville, Des course princières, 146 [translation, Janet Ashton]..
19. Pienkos, 11.
20. Pienkos, 15-6.
21. Choiseul-Gouffier, 395.
22. Konstantin to Anna Pavlovna, 15/27 May 1820, in Jackman, 80-1.
23. Konstantin to Alexander I, in British Library "Miscellaneous publications of the Russian Empire" [translation, William Lee].
24. Kwiatowski, 28.

25. ibid.
26. Moriolles, 32.
27. ibid., 132.
28. Konstantin to Anna Pavlovna, 12/24 August 1824, in Jackman, 100.
29. Konstantin to Anna Pavlovna, 28 Feb/11 March 1824, in Jackman, 95.
30. in S.I.R.I.O., 131: 8 [translation, William Lee].
31. Pienkos, 342.
32. Wortman, 346.
33. Anna Pavlovna to Konstantin, 27 Dec 1825, in Jackman, 116.
34. Pienkos, 92.
35. ibid., 104.
36. Moriolles, 353.
37. ibid., 356.
38. Pienkos, 110.

Tsar Nicholas I

1. Catherine II to Melchior Grimm, 25 June, 1796, cited in Grunwald, 19.
2. cited ibid., 24.
3. Maria Feodorovna to Nicholas, 12 May 1815, cited ibid., 33.
4. Schnitzler, 1:277.
5. Nicholas to Anna Pavlovna, 16/28 July 1820, in Jackman. It is not clear if the gun was a toy!
6. cited in Wortman, 261.
7. Hennessy, 28.
8. Cornélie de Wassenaer, diary, 31st May 1825, in Wassenaer, 125.
9. Countess Nesslrode, cited in Grunwald, 1.
10. cited in Wortman, 267.
11. Schnitzler, 1:275.
12. Wortman, 269.
13. Schnitzler, 2:417.
14. Prince Koflofski, cited Schnitzler, 2:434-4.
15. ibid., 2:435.
16. Bourke, 237.
17. M. Kamenskaya, cited in Bott and Faybisovich, 6.
18. Hodgetts, 1: 219.
19. Bott and Faybisovich, 6.
20. Most information about the Cottage Palace is drawn from personal visits.
21. Jerrmann, 36-7.
22. Hodgetts, 2:5.
23. Nicholas to Anna Pavlovna, 11/23 April 1824, in Jackman, 98.
24. Vasilii Zhukovskii to F.P. Litke, cited Kipp and Kipp, 11.
25. ibid., 11.
26. This is the thesis of Jacob and Maia Kipps's article

27. cited in Grunwald, 211.
28. Custine, 120.
29. cited in Lincoln, 241-2.
30. ibid., 246.
31. Wortman, 385.
32. cited in Lincoln, 310.
33. M.P. Pogodin, who had been one of the chief supporters of Nicholas's nationality policy, cited in Kipp, 14.
34. cited in Bassin, 125.
35. ibid., 139.
36. cited in Grunwald, 283.
37. cited in Bassin, 140.

Grand Duke Michael Pavlovich

1. K. Waliszewski, Paul The First of Russia, The Son of Catherina The Great, William Heinemann, London 1913, p. 20.
2. ibid. 390.
3. Nicolas Enache, La Descendance de Pierre le Grand Tsar de Russie, Sedopols, Paris 1983, 45
4. Charlotte Zeepvat, Romanov Autumn – Stories from the Last Century of Imperial Russia, Sutton, Publishing, Stroud 2000, 19.
5. ibid.
6. cited in Enache, 45.
7. cited in Zeepvat, 19..
8. ibid.
9. SW Jackman, Romanov Relations, MacMillan, London 1969, 95.
10. ibid.
11. cited in Enache, 45.
12. cited in Jackman, 153.
13. ibid., 98.
14. ibid., 154.
15. ibid., 163-164.
16. cited in Enache, 55.
17. cited in Zeepvat, 22.
18. ibid.
19. cited in Jackman, 330.
20. http://www.angelfire.com/realm/gotha/gotha/wied.html
21. cited in Enache, 45.
22. Elizabeth Narishkin-Kurakin, Under Three Tsars, E.P. Dutton & Co., Inc., 1931, 34.

CHAPTER 2: The Sons of Tsar Nicholas I

Tsar Alexander II

1 Almedingen, E.M., *Emperor Alexander II* (Bodley Head, 1962) 14
2 ibid 18
3 ibid 34
4 ibid., 288-9
5 ibid., 298
6 Harcave, Sidney, *Years of the Golden Cockerel* (Robert Hale, 1970) 232
7 Almedingen 329
8 Alexander, Grand Duke, *Once a Grand Duke* (Farrar & Rinehart, 1932) 56
9 Ponsonby, Sir Frederick, *Letters of the Empress Frederick* (Macmillan, 1928) 182
10 Alexander, Grand Duke 63

Grand Duke Konstantin Nikolaevich

1. Gavril Konstantinovich, kniaz. *V Mramornom dvortse.*SP, Logos, 1993. p. 259
2. Prince David Chavchavadze. *The Grand Dukes.* Atlantic International Publications. 1990. p. 57
3. Olga Nikolayevna. *Son Junosti.*Zapiski docheri imperatora Nikolaya I. Paris, 1964. p. 74
4. Gavril. *V Mramornom…*p. 261
5. Olga, Zapiski.p. 75-76
6. ibid., p. 77
7. Tiutcheva, Anna. *Pri dvore dvuh imperatorov.* M. 1990, p. 64.
8. Charlotte Zeepvart. *The Camera and the Tsars.* Sutton Publishers. 2004. p. 30
9. Tiutcheva. *Pri dvore….* p.45
10. Kleinmichel, Countess. *Memories of a Shipwrecked World.* Reprint from 1923. p. 52
11. Sheremetev, S.D. *Memuari grafa S.D.Sheremeteva.* M. Indrik.2001, p. 136
12. Chavchavadze. *Grand Dukes,* p. 29
13. Hertsen, Alexander. *Biloye i dumi.* L. 1978, p. 77
14. *Perepiska imperatora Alexandra II i velikogo kniazia Konstantina Nikolayevicha.* 1857-1861.Rossiiski Arkhiv. M. 1992. p. 210-215
15. ibid., p. 147
16. Gavril, *V Mramornom…*p.196
17. The last Muslim leader (Chechen) to surrender to

the Russian army in the Caucasus.
18. The Museum of HIH on the second floor contained collections of arms, coins, medals and other antiques.
19. ibid., p. 269
20. Elizabeth Naryshkin-Kuraki,p. 34
21. Gavril, …p. 263
22. Tiutcheva, *Pri Dvore…* p. 44
23. Kleinmichel. *Memories...*p. 22
24. GARF (General Archive of the Russian Federation). F.681, 0pis 1, ed.hr. 31
25. Kleinmichel…p. 26
26. Sheremetev, *Memuari…*p. 136-137
27. Hoover Institution, Stanford, CA. *Diaries of G.D.Xenia.*
28. Chavchavadze, *Grand Dukes,* p. 61
29. not published
30. Sheremetev, *Memuari…*p. 135
31. Vostryshev, Mikhail. *Avgusteishee semeystvo.* M.2001. p. 173
32. Shestakov, Ivan. *Diaries. RGA VMF.* Fond 26, opis 1. delo 1-7
33. Belyakova, Zoia. *Velikii Kniaz Alexei. Za I Protiv.* St Petersburg. Logos. 1004 p. 164
34. Chief of Gendarmeria
35. ibid., p. 137
36. Vostryshev, *Avgusteyshee...*p.173
37. ibid., p. 173-174

Grand Duke Nicholas Nikolaevich

1. Valerii Sokolovoi and I. V. Kondratiev, *Dom Romanovykh.* St. Petersburg: Lio Redaktor, 1992, p. 139; Zoia Belyakova, *The Romanov Legacy: The Palaces of St. Petersburg.* London: Hazar, 1994, p. 140
2. Chavchavadze, *The Grand Dukes,* p. 117
4. ibid., p. 54
5. Sokolovoi and Kondratiev, p. 139
6. Ibid, p. 139; Chavchavadze, p. 66
7. E. A. Brayley-Hodgetts, *The Court of Russia in the Nineteenth Century,* Two volumes, London: Metheun, 1908, p. 2:72
8. Belyakova, p. 149
9. Count Serge Witte, *The Memoirs of Count Serge Witte,* edited by Sidney Harcave, Armonk, New York: M. E. Sharpe, 1990, p. 91
10. Brayley-Hodgetts, p. 2:72
11. Count Paul Vassili (pseudonym of Princess Catherine Radziwill), *Behind the Veil at the Russian Court,* London: Cassell and Company, 1913, p. 33

12. *Sokolovoi and Kondratiev, p. 139; Belyakova, p. 140*

13. *Belyakova, p. 14.*

14. *Chavchavadze, p. 60; Sokolovoi and Kondratiev, p. 139*

15. *Witte, p. 77*

16. *Alexander Mossolov, At The Court of the Last Tsar, London: Methuen, 1935, p. 39*

17. *Charlotte Zeepvat, Djulber, in Royalty Digest, September 19999, No. 99, Volume IX, No. 3, p. 66; Belyakova, p. 143*

18. *Belyakova, pp. 140-49*

19. *ibid., p. 146*

20. *Chavchavadze, p. 65; Belyakova, p. 140; Sokolovoi and Kondratiev, p. 139*

21. *Belyakova, p. 140*

22. *Private Information from the Romanov Family to the author.*

23. *Witte, p. 78*

24. *Belyakova, p. 145*

25. *In Obshshnee Delo, No. 16, October 1878*

26. *Sokolovoi and Kondratiev, pp. 142-43*

27. *In Obshshnee Delo, No. 16, October 1878*

28. *Brayley-Hodgetts, p. 2:144*

29. *In Obshshnee Delo, No. 16, October 1878*

30. *See Jacques Ferrand, Descendances Natureles des Souverains et Grands-Ducs de Russie de 1762 a 1910, Paris, Repertoire Genealogique, 1995*

31. *Witte, pp. 77-78*

32. *Olga died August 31, 1950. See Ferrand for further details.*

33. *See Ferrand for further details. Vladimir died in 1942; Catherine in 1940; and Nicholas in 1902.*

34. *In Obshshnee Delo, No. 16, October 1878*

35. *ibid.*

36. *ibid.*

37. *Chavchavadze, p. 69*

38. *In Obshshnee Delo, No. 16, October 1878*

39. *See Ferrand*

40. *In Obshshnee Delo, No. 16, October 1878*

41. *E. M. Almedingen, The Emperor Alexander II, London: The Bodley Head, 1962, p. 299*

42. *ibid, p. 288*

43. *Chavchavadze, p. 67*

44. *Edvard Radzinsky, Alexander II: The Last Great Tsar, New York: Simon and Schuster, 2005, p. 264*

45. *Stephen Graham, Alexander II, London: Ivor Nicholson and Watson, 1935, p. 247*

46. *Almedingen, p. 299*

47. *Vassili, p. 82*

48. *Chavchavadze, p. 68*

49. *ibid, p. 69*

50. *Vassili, p. 33*

51. *Witte, p. 176*

52. *Belyakova, p. 153*

53. *Witte, p. 79*

54. *Belyakova, p. 153*

55. *ibid, p. 153; private information from the Romanov Family to the author.*

56. *The Times of London, October 23, 1890*

57. *Belyakova, p. 153*

58. *ibid, p. 140*

59. *ibid, p. 154*

Grand Duke Michael Nikolaevich

1. *William Lee, "Grand Ducal Role and Identity as a Reflection on the Interaction of State and Dynasty in Imperial Russia." Unpublished PhD thesis, University College, London, 2000, p. 178*

2. *Michael's niece, the Grand Duchess Alexandra Alexandrovna, who died in 1849 aged seven, was also nursed by a Miss Hughes, who was probably the same person. While researching "From cradle to crown," her book on royal nannies, Charlotte Zeepvat discovered references to the christening in St Petersburg in January 1852 of twin English girls, Jane and Thomasina Isherwood, whose mother had been a Miss Margaret Hughes before marriage. The babies had as godparents the Empress Dowager Alexandra, her son Michael and her grandson Alexander, perhaps in lieu of his late sister. Michael's presence as godfather suggests that the babies' mother was Miss Hughes the former nanny – it was not uncommon for a former charge to be asked to stand as godparent when an imperial tutor or governess had a child. If young when appointed nurse to Michael, Miss Hughes would still have been able to have a child in 1851: the birth of twins suggests an older mother anyway.*

3. *Dimitri Strukov, Avgustischii General-Feldtseikhmeister Velikii Kniaz Mikhail Nikolaevich. St Petersburg: P.P. Soikina, 1906, p. 46*

4. *Nicholas I to Anna Pavlovna, January 7/19 and November 1/13, 1835, in Jackman, p. 252*

5. *Strukov, p. 49*

6. *F.A. Brokgaus and I. A. Efron, eds, "Mikhail Nikolaevich", Entsiklopedicheskii Slovar', Izdatel'stvo Delo, St. Petersburg, 1896, vol. 38, p. 485*

7. *France Ane Vanne, Marchioness of Londonderry. Extracts from the Russian journal of Lady Londonderry, 1835-1837. London: Royal College of Art, 1980, p. 117*

8. *Zherve, 10 [translation, William Lee]*

9. *Lincoln, p. 58.*

10. *V.V. Zherve, General-Feldmarshal Velikii Kniaz Nikolai Nikolaevich Starshii. St Petersburg: [s.n.], 1911, pp. 12, 16.*

11. *Alexander Mikhailovich, Once a Grand Duke, p. 48.*

12. *Joachim Murat, in Janet Ashton, European Royal History Journal (ERHJ), 9:4.*

13. *Maria Georgievena of Russia, A Romanov diary: the autobiography of H.I. and R. H. Grand Duchess George. New York: Atlantic International, 1988, p. 136.*

14. *Mikhail's diary, 15 August 1857, in Barkovets, 56 [Translation, Janet Ashton].*

15. *Jamie H. Cockfield, White crow: the life and times of the Grand Duke Nicholas Mikhailovich Romanov. London: Praeger, 2002, p. 10.*

16. *Maria Georgievna, 80.*

17. *Cecilie, Crown Princess of Germany. The memoirs of the Crown Princess Cecilie. London: Gollancz, 1931, p. 145.*

18. *Maria Georgievena, p. 77.*

19. *Cockfield, p. 38.*

20. *Witte, Memoirs, p. 20.*

21. *Witte, Vospominaniia, 1:26. It is worth noting of course that in referring to "Caucasians" Witte means the Georgians. He is not implying that Russia's liberal and inclusive policy extended as far as allocating government posts to the mountain peoples of Chechnia and Dagestan.*

22. *Witte, Memoirs, p. 15.*

23. *ibid., p. 20.*

24. *Alexander Mikhailovich, p. 23.*

25. *Letter of Mikhail in Rossiiskii Gosudarstvennyi Istoricheskii Arkhiv, f. 1268, cited in Breyfogle, p. 153.*

26. *Austin Jersild, Orientalism and empire: north Caucasus mountain peoples and the Georgian frontier, 1845-1917. Montreal: McGill-Queen's University Press, 2002, 25.*

27. *ibid, p. 28.*

28. *Miller, p. 68; Zaionchkovsky, 1: 96; Miliutin, 1: 109.*

29. *Heide W. Whelan, Alexander III and the State Council. New Brunswick: Rutgers University Press, 1982, p. 22.*

30. *Countess Kleinmichel, p. 26.*

31. *quoted in Grand Duke Konstantin Nikolaevich [exhibition catalogue]. St Petersburg: Abris, 2002, p. 50.*

32. *Mikhail in GARF, f. 649, op.1, d. 56, 1883, cited in Whelan, p. 111.*

33. *Cockfield, p. 10.*

34. *Polovtsev, Dnevnik, 2:29, cited in Cockfield, p. 31.*

35. *Cockfield, p. 65.*

36. *Mikhail Nikolaevich to Anastasia Mikhailovna, 17th December 1899 (O.S.) and 23rd February 1900, at www.iconastas.co.uk*

37. *Alexander Mikhailovich, p. 147.*

38. *Mikhail Nikolaevich to Anastasia Mikhailovna, 17th December 1899 (O.S.), at www.iconastas.co.uk*

39. *Alexander Mikhailovich, p. 156.*

40. *Cecilie, p. 147.*

41. *ibid., p. 153.*

42. *Cecilie, p. 178; Maria Georgievna, p. 103. The former says his right side was paralysed; Maria says his left.*

43. *Maria Georgievna, p. 113.*

44. *His grandnephew, Andrei Vladimirovich, who died in 1954 aged 78, was proud to be the man who finally beat Mikhail's record.*

45. *A. A. Mosolov, At the court of the last Tsar. London: Methuen, 1935, p. 75.*

CHAPTER 3: The Sons of Tsar Alexander II

Tsarevich Nicholas Alexandrovich

1. *Enache, p. 69.*

2. *Jackman, p. 312.*

3. *Graham, p. 61.*

4. *Zeepvat, Romanov Autumn p. 36.*

5. *Graham, p. 61.*

6. *Zeepvat, p. 36.*

7. *ibid., pp. 36-37.*

8. *Almanach de Gotha 1858, Justus Perthes, Gotha, p. 17.*

9. *Hall, Little Mother, p. 5.*

10. *ibid.*

11. *Maria Feodorovna, Empress of Russia, Exhibition catalogue, 1997, p. 74.*

12. *ibid.*

13. *E. Fricero, The Grand Duke Nicholas Alexandrovich, Crown prince of Russia, (English Edition), Nice, France, p. 4.*

14. *Maria Feodorovna p. 74.*

15. *ibid., p 78.*

16. *ibid.*

17. *ibid.*

18. *ibid., p. 80.*

19. *ibid.*

20. *Zoia Belyakova. Honour and Fidelity – The*

Russian Dukes of Leuchtenberg, Logos Publishers, St Petersburg, 2010, p. 44.
21. Zeepvat, Romanov Autumn, p. 41.
22. Fricero, p. 14.
22. ibid.
24. ibid.
25. Coryne Hall, Little Mother, p. 22.
26. Roger Fulford, Your Dear Letter - Private Correspondence of Queen Victoria and the Crown Princess of Prussia 1865-1871, Charles Scribner's Sons, New York, 1971, p. 23.
27. Coryne Hall, Little Mother, p. 22.
28. Letters of Feodora Princess of Hohenlohe-Langenburg from 1828-1872, Spottiswoode & Co., London, 1874, p. 358.
29. Fricero, p. 15.
30. ibid., p. 22.

Tsar Alexander III

1. Ian Vorres. The Last Grand Duchess. Hutchinson, London, 1964, p. 28.
2. Hall, p. 26; Almedingen, p. 272.
3. Kleinmichel, p. 48.
4. Hall, Coryne, Little Mother of Russia. A Biography of the Empress Marie Feodorovna 1847-1928, Shepheard-Walwyn, London. 1999, p. 22.
5. Barkovets, Olga. 'Proshaite Dushenka!' in Sred shunova bala. Exhibition catalogue, GARF, Moscow. 2001, p. 21.
6. Barkovets, Olga. Nixa, Minny & Sacha, in Marie Feodorovna, Empress of Russia, Exhibition catalogue, Copenhagen. 1997, p. 82.
7. Klausen, Inger-Lise. Dagmar, Zarina fra Danmark. Lindhardt & Ringhof, Copenhagen, 1997, p. 50.
8. Barkovets, Nixa, p. 84.
9. Marie was packed off to Paris, hastily married to Prince Paul Demidov and died in childbirth in 1868
10. A. N. Bohanov, Nicholas II, ACT Press, Moscow, 2000, p. 32.
11. John Van der Kiste & Coryne Hall, Once a Grand Duchess: Xenia, Sister of Nicholas II, Sutton Publishing, Stroud. 2002, p. 12..
12. Alexander Mikhailovich, Once a Grand Duke, p. 174.
13. Prince Nicholas of Greece, My Fifty Years, Hutchinson, 1926, p. 64.
14. Alexander Mikhailovich, p. 174.
15. Hall, Little Mother of Russia, p. 155.
16. Prince Nicholas, p. 116.
17. Hall, Little Mother of Russia, p. 162..

Grand Duke Vladimir Alexandrovich

1. Charlotte Zeepvat, Romanov Autumn, p. 87.
2. Lord Frederick Hamilton, The Vanished World of Yesterday, Hodder & Stoughton, 1950, p. 476.
3. Alexander Mikhailovich, Once a Grand Duke, pp. 137-8.
4. William II, Emperor, My Early Life, Methuen, 1926, p. 320.
5. Ian Vorres, p. 54.
6. ibid., p. 54.
7. Dominic Lieven, Nicholas II, John Murray, 1993, p. 109.
8. Andrei Maylunas & Sergei Mironenko, A Lifelong Passion, Weidenfeld & Nicolson, 1996, p. 108.
9. Lieven, p. 72.
10. Maylunas & Mironenko, p. 147.
11. ibid., p. 222.
12. ibid., p. 261.

Grand Duke Alexis Alexandrovich

1. Rossiiski archiv.1992. Perepiska Imperatora Aleksandra II i Velikogo kniazia Konstantina Nikolaevicha 1857-1861. c.125.
2. unpublished, archive of Z.Belyakova.
3. RGA VMF. F.1247. opis 1, ed. hr.22-59.
4. Alexander II, c.126.
5. Alexander Alexandrovich. c.294..
6. (Meshcherski, Nekrolog. Vestnik, 1908. t.6, kn.12, c. 814-815.
7. Belyakova, Zoia.Velikii Kniaz Aleksei Aleksandrovich. Pro I Contra, p. 50.
8. Peregudova, Z. Imperial Russian Journal, vol.5, number 2, 2001, p. 21.
9. Tolstaya, A.A. Zapiski freilini. M. 1996, p. 93-94
10. Yepanchin,N.A. Na sluzhbe triokh imperatorov, p. 210.
11. Kleinmichel, Memories of Shipwrecked World, p. 21.
12. Ekstut,S. Nadin, ili Roman velikosvetskoi dami .M.2001.
13. GARF. Fond 681. Opis 1, ed.hr.1.
14. ibid.
15. Rossiiski Gosudarstvennii Arkhiv Voenno Morskogo Flota Fond 1247. Op.1 ed.hr.40.
16. Peregudova, Z. p. 23.
17. Belyakova, Z. c.99.
18. RosGosud Istoricheski Arkhiv. Fond 482. Op.6.

ed.xr.71.

19. Maylunas & Mironenko, p. 167.

20. G.D.Cyrill. Moia zhizn na cluzhbe Rossii. p.74.

21. RGA VMF. F.26 Op.1 Ed 40-52.

22. Witte, S. Vospominania.T.3, p.469.

23. Teliakovsky,V.A. Dnevniki Directora Imperatorskih Teatrov. M.2002. p.104, 126.

24. RGA VMF. F.26. Op.1 ed.81.

25. Chavchavadze, p. 117.

26. Maylunas&Mironenko. p. 314.

27.Bogdanovich,A.V.Dnevnik A.V.Bogdanovitch. Tri polednikh samiderzhtsa. 1924, p. 466.

Grand Duke Serge Alexandrovich

1. Queen Marie of Roumania, The Story of My Life (vol. 1).

2. ibid.

3. ibid.

4. Chavchavadze, p. 119.

5. Grand Duke Kirill Vladimirovich of Russia, My Life in Russia's Service: Then and Now, p. 13.

6. Charlotte Zeepvat, Romanov Autumn, p. 123.

7. John Van der Kiste, The Romanovs: 1818 - 1959, p. 39

8. Meriel Buchanan, Queen Victoria's Relations, 92

9. Grand Duke Ernest Ludwig of Hesse and By Rhine, Erinnertes, Aufzeichnungen des letzten Grossherzogs Ernst Ludwig von Hessen und bei Rhein, pp. 76-77.

10 . Zeepvat, p. 124.

11. ibid.

12. Grand Duke Ernest Ludwig, pp. 76-77.

13. Lubov Millar, Grand Duchess Elizabeth of Russia: New Martyr of the Communist Yoke, 51.

14. Queen Marie, p. 93.

15 . Grand Duchess George Mikhailovich of Russia, A Romanov Diary, pp. 85-86.

16. Lubov Millar, p. 23.

17. Maurice Paléologue, An Ambassador's Memoirs: Last French Ambassador to the Russian Court.

18. Richard Hough, Advice to My Grand-daughter Letters from Queen Victoria to Princess Victoria of Hesse, p. 55.

19. ibid., p. 44.

20. Lubov Millar, p. 23.

21. Charlotte Zeepvat, The Camera and the Tsars: A Romanov Family Album, p. 47.

22. Nina Epton, Victoria and her Daughters, pp. 166-7.

23. Van der Kiste, 123.

24. Grand Duke Alexander Mikhailovich, pp. 139-40.

25. Grand Duke Ernest Ludwig, pp. 76-77.

26. Lubov Millar, p. 22.

27. A. E. Almedingen, An Unbroken Unity, p. 28.

28. Count Witte, The Memoirs of Count Witte ed. and trans. by Sidney Harcave, p. 44.

29. Andrew M. Verner, The Crisis of Russian Autocracy: Nicholas II and the 1905 Revolution, p. 68.

30. Peter Kurth, Tsar: The Lost World of Nicholas and Alexandra, p. 66.

31. Prince Felix Youssoupoff, Lost Splendor, trans. by Ann Green and N. Katkoff, p. 90.

32. Count Witte, p. 240.

33. A.A. Mossolov, At the Court of the Last Tsar: Memoirs of A.A. Mossolov, Head of the Court Chancellery 1900-1916, AlexanderPalace.org.

34. Richard Hough, p. 89.

35. ....from Our Own Correspondent, Saturday, March 21, 1891.

36. Almedingen, p. 26.

37. ibid., 41.

38. Robert Massie contends that "...this antagonism [against the Jews] was religious rather than racial ... illustrated by cases of Jews who gave up their faith, accepted Orthodoxy and moved freely into the general structure of Russian society."(Nicholas and Alexandra, p.100n).

39. ibid.

40. E.A. Brayley Hodgetts, The Court of Russia in the Nineteenth Century, pp. 231-3.

41. Lubov Millar, p. 23.

42. E.A. Brayley Hodgetts, pp. 231-3.

43. Grand Duchess Marie Pavlovna of Russia, Education of a Princess, p. 19.

44. ibid., p. 50.

45. Christopher Hibbert, Queen Victoria in Her Letters and Journals, p. 318.

46. Greg King, The Last Empress: The Life & Times of Alexandra Feodorovna, Tsarina of Russia, pp. 143-144.

47. Count Witte, p. 212.

48. Alexander Mikhailovich, pp. 139-40.

49. Ibid., p. 172.

50. Ian Vorres, p. 78.

51. Peter Kurth, Tsar: The Lost World of Nicholas and Alexandra, p. 63.

52. W. Bruce Lincoln, The Romanovs, p. 627.

53. Andrei Maylunas and Sergei Mironenko, p. 150

54. Alexander Mikhailovich, pp. 139-40.

55. Richard Hough, p. 136.

56. Lubov Millar, pp. 91-92.

57. For My Grandchildren: Some Reminiscences of Her Royal Highness Princess Alice, Countess of

Athlone, p. 18.

58. Andrew M. Verner, December 9-10, 1905, p. 137.

59. Grand Duke Ernest Ludwig, pp. 76-77.

60. Baroness Sophie Buxhoevenden, Before the Storm, p. 272.

61. Count Witte, p. 400.

62. The Times of London, January 16, 1905.

63. E.A. Brayley Hodgetts, pp. 231-3.

64. Victoria Milford Haven, Recollections 1863-1914, p. 235.

65. ibid., p. 236.

66. Alexander Ular, Russia From Within, pp. 75-76.

67. The Court of Russia in the Nineteenth Century, pp. 231-3.

68. Princess Marie zu Erbach-Schönberg, Reminiscences, p. 302.

69. Grand Duchess George Mikhailovich, pp. 85-86.

Grand Duke Paul Alexandrovich

1. These were: Nicholas, Alexander, Vladimir and Alexis Alexandrovich. The other being Nicholas Konstantinovich.

2. The rest were: Serge Alexandrovich, Konstantin, Dimitri, and Viatcheslav Konstantinovich, Peter Nikolaevich, and Nicholas, Michael, and George Mikhailovich.

3. These were: "Nicholas Alexandrovich, ViatcheslavKonstantinovich and Alexis Mikhailovich, thus one from every branch of the family except the Nikolaevichi.

4. For an in depth discussion of military modernization and public opinion as they impacted the Imperial Family, see William Lee, Grand Ducal Role and Identity as a Reflection on the Interaction of State and Dynasty in Imperial Russia, unpublished Ph.D. dissertation, University College, London, 2000.

5. Tiutcheva, A.F., Pri dvore dvukh imperatorov, Vospominaniia, Dnevnik, 1852-1882, Oriental Research Partners, Cambridge, 1975, v. 2, pp. 181-182.

6. Grebelsky, Petr, and Aleksandr Mirvis, Dom Romanovykh: Biograficheskie svedeniia o chlenakh tsarstvovavshego doma, ikh predkakh i rodstvennikakh, St. Petersburg, 1992, p. 147.

7. Tiutcheva, Pri dvore, v. 2, pp. 139-141.

8. Lincoln, W. Bruce, The Romanovs, pp. 604-605.

9. Tiutcheva, Pri dvore, v. 1, pp. 18-19.

10. Ignatiev, Aleksei A., Pyatdesyat let v stroyu,

Gosudarstvennoe izdatel'stvo khudozhestvennoi literatury, Moscow, 1950, vol. 1, p. 490.

11. Byrnes, Robert, Pobedonostsev, His Life and Thought, Indiana University Press, Bloomington, 1968, pp 211-212; Tiutcheva, Pri dvore, v. 2, pp. 221-222.

12. Tiutcheva, Pri dvore.

13. Chavchavadze, p. 127.

14. No one should contest this who has not read Grand Duke Dimitri's unpublished diaries.

15. Kozlianinoff, W., Manuel Commemoratif de la Garde a Cheval, Edition de Son Altesse Imperiale Mgr. le Grand Duc Dmitri de Russie, Paris, 1931, p. 58.

16. Witte, S. Yu., Vospominaniia, A.L. Sidorova, ed., Izdatel'stvo Sotsial'no-Ekonomicheskoi Literatury, Moscow, 1960, p. 165; Bogdanovich, Aleksandra Viktorovna, Tri poslednykh samoderzhtsa. Dnevnik, 1880-1912, E. Vavilov, ed. Moscow, 1924, passim.

17. Bogdanovich, Tri poslednykh samoderzhtsa, p. 204.

18. ibid., p. 203.

19. V.P. Semennikov, ed., Nikolai II I velikie kniaz'ia: rodstvenn'ie pis'ma k poslednemu tsariu, Gosudarstvennoe Izdatel'stvo, Leningrad, 1925, p. 142.

20. Semennikov, Nikolai II, pp 54-55.

21. Dimitri to Nicholas (Semennikov); Dimitri to Marie (Mainau letters).

22. Semennikov, pp 55-56.

23. Semennikov, p. 57.

24. Grand Duke Konstantin Konstantinovich, Dnevnik, Entry of 9 February, 1905, GARF f. 660.

25. Konstantine, Entries of 9 and 10 February, 1905

26. Semennikov, Nicholas, p. 53.

27. Semennikov, p. 56.

28. Semennikov, p. 57.

29. Semennikov, p. 58.

30. Semennikov p. 58.

31. Ferrand, Jacques, Le Grand-Duc Paul Alexandrovitch de Russie, sa famille, sa descendance, Paris, 1993, p. 236..

32. Semennikov, p. 60.

33. Nicholas II, Letter to Alexandra, 9 October, 1915, in The Nicky-Sunny Letters, 1914-1917, Academic International, Hattiesburg, 1970, p. 99.

34. ibid., p. 211.

35. ibid., p. 215.

36. ibid., Letter from Alexandra to Nicholas, 13 November, 1915, pp. 218-219.

37. Semennikov, p. 61..

38. Chavchavadze, p. 129.

39. See, for instance, Alexandra's letter to Nicholas of 27 August, 1915, Nicky-Sunny Letters, pp 124-125.

40. *Semennikov, p. 59, letters from Paul to Nicholas, 28 September and 21 October -13 November, 1913.*
41. *Nicky-Sunny Letters, p. 113.*
42. *Paleologue, Maurice, La Russie des Tsars, Librairie Plon, Paris, 1922, pp. 60-65.*
43. *Paleologue, La Russie, v. 2, p. 62.*
44. *Chavchavadze, p. 130.*
45. *Grand Duke Dimitri Pavlovich of Russia, Diaries, entry of 24 December, 1917.*
46. *Semennikov, pp 143-145.*
47. *De Robien, Louis, Diary of a Diplomat, Michael Joseph, London, 1969.*
48. *ibid.*
49. *Chavchavadze, pp. 133-134.*
50. *Grand Duke Dimitri Pavlovich of Russia, Diaries, 1920.*
51. *ibid.*

CHAPTER 4: The Sons of Tsar Alexander III

Tsar Nicholas II

1 1. *Hall, p. 22.*
2. *Ibid. p. 21.*
3. *Macendonsky, Alexander III article.*
4. *Ibid, Mikhail Alexandrovich article. His brother lived to be nearly 80 years old, expiring well into the reign of his grand nephew Nicholas II.*
5. *Massie, ix.*
6. *Alexander Mikhailovich, p. 168.*
7. *Steinberg and Khustalev, p. 368.*
8. *Massie, p. 53.*
9. *Steinberg and Khustalev, p. 168.*
10. *Massie, p. 68.*
11. *Macendonsky, George Alexandrovich article.*
12. *Orthodox website.*
13. *Radzinsky, p.s 65 -68.*
14. *Massie, p. 104.*
15. *Ibid., Chapter 17.*
16. *Steinberg and Khustalev, p. 370.*

Tsarevich George Alexandrovich

1. 1. *Macedonsky, George Alexandrovich biography.*
2. *Hall, Little Mother of Russia, p. 56.*
3. *Hall, ibid.*
4. *Macedonsky, ibid.*
5. *Vorres, p. 18.*
6. *Vorres, p. 18-17.*
7. *Hall, p. 70.*
8. *Alexander, Grand Duke of Russia, Once A Grand Duke, p. 117.*
9. *Maylunas & Mirenenko, A Lifelong Passion, p.20.*
10. *Letters of Tsar Nicholas and Empress Marie, p. 43-45.*
11. *Zeepvat, Romanov Autumn, p. 114.*
12. *Zeepvat, ibid.*
13. *Fabergé website http://andrejkoymasky.com/liv/fab/fab21.html*
14. *Alexander, Ibid., p. 120.*
15. *Maylunas, p. 73.*
16. *Maylunas, p. 106-107.*
17. *Coryne Hall and John VanDerKiste, Once A Grand Duchess, p. 45.*
18. *Letters, p. 111-112.*
19. *Maylunas, p. 163-164.*
20. *Hall, p. 185.*
21. *Ibid.*
22. *Hall, p. 186.*
23. *Macedonsky.*
24. *Maylunas, p. 185.*
25. *Robert Massie, The Romanovs: The Final Chapter, p. 122-23.*

Grand Duke Michael Alexandrovich

1. *King, Greg and Penny Wilson, Fate of the Romanovs.*
2. *Macedonsky, Agnates.*
3. *Trotsky, History of the Russian Revolution.*
4. *Vorres, The Last Grand Duchess.*
5. *Ibid.*
6. *Crawford, Rosemary & Donald. Michael and Natasha.*
7. *Ibid.*
8. *Ibid.*
9. *Letters of Tsar Nicholas and Empress Marie.*
10. *Crawford, Ibid.*
11. *Ibid.*
12. *King, Ibid.*
13. *Ibid.*
14. *Ibid.*

CHAPTER 5: The Son of Tsar Nicholas II

Tsarevich Alexis Nikolaevich

1. Nichols, p. 216.
2. Ukhtomskii, 3:33.
3. Hohenlohe report, 10 Sept. 1896, GP (German diplomatic Archive), vol. ix, no. 2862, 361-2, in McLean, p. 31-2.
4. See extract from the memoirs of Count Witte at http://www.alexanderpalace.org/palace/witte.html
5. Xenia Alexandrovna, diary, 13 March 1904, in Maylunas and Mironenko, Lifelong passion.
6. Nicholas's diary, July 30, 1904, in GARF, F. 601, Op 1, D 247 (author's translation).
7. Xenia Alexandrovna, diary, 16 August 1904, in Maylunas and Mironenko.
8. Eagar, p. 201.
9. Zeepvat, 263-8, is a full examination of this story
10. British Library add. 50850 ff. 31, 32.
11. 18 Sept. 1904, in Maylunas and Mironenko.
12. Elchaninov, p. 128.
13. Verner, 299; Wortman, 2:401..
14. Florinsky, pp. 17-18.
15. Wortman, 2: Chapter 15.
16. Massie, Nicholas and Alexandra, p. 145.
17. Massies, Journey, p. 114.
18. Welch, p. 33.
19. Xenia, diary, March 29 1906, in Maylunas and Mironenko; Massie, p. 130.
20. Dmitri Pavlovich to Maria Pavlovna, in William Lee: "Dmitry Pavlovich, 1908-1914: Portrait of a Young Grand Duke."
21. New York Times, November 6th 1912.
22. in Maylunas and Mironenko, p. 351.
23. Wood, pp. 106-118.
24. The minister Vladimir Kokovtsov, quoted in Massie, p. 227.
25. Elchaninov, pp. 56-7.
26. Elchaninov, p. 56.
27. Alexandra to Nicholas, 5 November 1915, in Complete wartime correspondence.
28. Anastasia Nikolaevna to Nicholas II, April 4th 1916 at http://www.alexanderpalace.org/palace/adiaries.html
29. Memoirs of the priest GI Shavelsky, in GARF, f. 640, op. 1, d. 79, l. 7; in Timms, Nicholas and Alexandra, 322-23.
30. Trewin, 43.
31. Memoirs of the valet Alexei Volkov at http://www.alexanderpalace.org/volkov/8.html, (translation, Rob Moshein).
32. Trewin, p. 43.
33. Alexandra to Nicholas, October 7th, 1915, in Complete wartime correspondence.
34. Welch, p. 48.
35. Alexandra to Nicholas, Nov. 1st 1915 and 25th Sept. 1916, in Complete wartime correspondence.
36. Alexei Nikolaevich's diary, December 16th 1916, in Tsesarevich: Dokumenty, etc; (author's translation).
37. quoted, Eugénie of Greece, 169 (author's translation).
38. quoted in Trewin, p. 74.
39. Cherniavsky, p. 17.
40. Rasputin, p. 86.
41. King and Wilson, p. 178, demonstrate that the chronology of their respective imprisonments makes it impossible for Nagorny to have recounted this tale to Prince George Lvov, a generally unreliable witness who later published it as a story given to him directly. They also make the point that neither of the boy's parents mention this attempted theft in their diaries.
42. See "Mystery solved: the identification of the two missing Romanov children".
43. See Harding, "Putin's worst nightmare."

B | *BIBLIOGRAPHY*

Books and Exhibition Catalogues

Alekseev, A. I. *Fedor Petrovich Litke*. Fairbanks: University of Alaska Press, 1996.

Alexander (Mikhailovich), Grand Duke. *Once a Grand Duke*. Farrar & Rinehart, 1932.

Alice, Princess, Countess of Athlone. *For My Grandchildren: Some Reminiscences of Her Royal Highness Princess Alice, Countess of Athlone*. London: Evan Brothers Limited, 1966.

Almanach de Gotha 1858, Justus Perthes, Gotha.

Almedingen, E.M. *Emperor Alexander II*. Bodley Head, 1962.

Almedingen, E.M. *The Romanovs. Three Centuries of an Ill-Fated Dynasty*. Bodley, Head, 1966.

Almedingen, E.M. *The Empress Alexandra 1872-1918: A Study*. London: Hutchinson of London, 1961.

Almedingen, E.M. *An Unbroken Unity*. London: The Bodley Head, Ltd, 1964.

Alville [pseud.] *La vie en Suisse de S.A.I. Anna Feodorovna, née Princesse de Saxe-Cobourg-Saalfield*. Lausanne: Librairie Rouge, 1942.

Alville [pseud.] *Des cours princières aux demeures helvétiques*. Lausanne [s.n.], 1962.

Anolic, Tamar. *The Russian Riddle – Grand Duke Serge Alexandrovich of Russia (1857-1905)*. Eurohistory, East Richmond Heights, CA 2009.

Barkovets, Olga. *Peterhof ist ein Traum: deutsche Prinzessinen in Russland*. Berlin: Edition Q, 2001.

Barkovets, Olga. Nixa, Minny & Sacha, in *Marie Feodorovna, Empress of Russia. Exhibition catalogue*, Copenhagen, 1997.

Barkovets, Olga. *'Proshaite Dushenka!' in Sred shunova bala. Exhibition catalogue*, GARF, Moscow. 2001.

Bassin, Mark. *Imperial visions: nationalist imagi-nation and geographical expansion in the Russian far east, 1840-1865*. Cambridge: Cambridge University Press, 1999.

Beeche, Arturo E. (Editor) *The Grand Duchesses – Daughters and Granddaughters of Russia's Tsars*. Eurohistory, Oakland, CA, 2004.

Belyakova, Zoia. *Grand Duchess Maria Nikolaevna and her palace in St Petersburg*. St Petersburg: EGO, 1994.

Belyakova, Zoia. *Honour and Fidelity. The Russian Dukes of Leuchtenberg*. Logos Publishers, St Petersburg 2010.

Belyakova, Zoia. *The Romanov legacy: the palaces of St Petersburg*. London: Hazar, 1994.

Belyakova, Zoia. *Velikii Kniaz Alexei. Za I Protiv*. St Petersburg. Logos 2004.

Bloomfield, Georgiana. *Reminiscences of court and diplomatic life*. London: Kegan Paul, 1883.

Bogdanovich, A.V. *Tri poslednikh samiderzhtsa*. 1924.

Bohanov, A. N. *Nicholas II*. ACT Press, Moscow. 2000.

Bokhanov, Alexander, et al., *The Romanovs Love Power & Tragedy*. London: Leppi Publications. 1993.

Bott, I. and V. Faybisovich. *The Alexander Palace*. Tsarskoe Selo: State Museum Preserve Tsarskoe Selo, 1997.

Bourke, Richard Southwell. *St Petersburg and Moscow: a visit to the court of the Czar*. London: Henry Colburn, 1846.

Breyfogle, Nicholas B. *Heretics and colonizers: forging Russia's empire in the south Caucasus*. Ithaca, Cornell University Press, 2005.

Buchanan, Meriel. *Queen Victoria's Relations*. London: Cassell & Co Ltd, 1954.

Buxhoeveden, Baroness Sophie. *Before the Storm*. London: Macmillan and Co., 1938.

Buxhoeveden, Baroness Sophie. *The Life and Tragedy of Alexandra Feodorovna Empress of Russia*. Ticehurst: Royalty Digest, 1996.

Byrnes, Robert. *Pobedonostsev, His Life and*

Thought. Indiana University Press, Bloomington, 1968.

Crawford, Rosemary & Donald. *Michael and Natasha.* London: George Weidenfeld and Nicholson, 1997.

Cecilie, Crown Princess of Germany. *The memoirs of the Crown Princess Cecilie.* London: Gollancz, 1931.

Cherniavsky, Michael. *Tsar and people: studies in Russian myths.* Yale: Yale University Press, 1961.

Choiseul-Gouffier, Sophie de. *Historical memoirs of the Emperor Alexander I and the court of Russia.* London: Kegan Paul, 1904.

Cockfield, Jamie H. *White crow: the life and times of the Grand Duke Nicholas Mikhailovich Romanov.* London: Praeger, 2002.

Corti, Count Egon. *The Downfall of Three Dynasties.* Freeport, New York: Books for Libraries Press, 1970.

Cronin, Vincent. Napoleon. Harmondsworth: Penguin, 1973.

Custine, Astolphe de. *Journey for our time.* New York: Pellegrini and Cudahy, 1951.

Czartoryski, Adam Jerzy. *Mémoires du prince Adam Czartoryski.* Paris: [s.n.], 1887.

De Robien, Louis. *Diary of a Diplomat.* Michael Joseph, London, 1969.

Dimitri Pavlovich, Grand Duke of Russia. *Diaries,* 1920.

Dimsdale, Elizabeth. *An English lady at the court of Catherine the Great.* Cambridge: Quest, 1989.

Eagar, Margaretta. *Six years at the Russian court.* London: Hurst and Blackett, 1906.

Edling, Roxandra. *Mémoires de la comtesse Edling, née Stourza, demoiselle d'honneur de l'impératrice Elisabeth Alexeevna.* Moscow: [s.n.], 1888.

Elchaninov, Andrei Grigorievich. *The Tsar and his people.* London: Hodder and Stoughton, 1914.

Enache, Nicolas. *La Descendance de Pierre le Grand Tsar de Russie.* Sedopols, Paris, 1983

Epton, Nina. *Victoria and her Daughters.* New York: W.W. Norton & Company, Inc., 1971.

Ernst Ludwig, Grand Duke of Hesse and by Rhine. *Erinnertes. Aufzeichnungen des letzten Grossherzogs Ernst Ludwig von Hessen und bei Rhein.* Darmstdt: Roether, 1983.

Eugénie, Princess of Greece. *Le Tsarevich, enfant martyr.* Paris: Perrin, 1990.

Ferrand, Jacques. *Aperçus genealogique sur quelque descendances naturelles des grands ducs de Russie au XIX siecle.* Paris: Jacques Ferrand, 1982.

Ferrand, Jacques. *Descendances Natureles des*

Souverains et Grands-Ducs de Russie de 1762 a 1910. Paris, Repertoire Genealogique, 1995.

Ferrand, Jacques. *Le Grand-Duc Paul Alexandrovitch de Russie, sa famille, sa descendance.* Paris, 1993.

Ferro. Mark. *Nicholas II: The Last of the Tsars.* Oxford University Press. 1993.

Figes, Orlando. *A People's Tragedy.* Johnathan Cape, London. 1996.

Florinsky, Miachel T. *The end of the Russian Empire.* New York: Collier Books, 1961.

Fricero, E. *The Grand Duke Nicholas Alexandrovich, Crown prince of Russia,* (English Edition). Nice, France.

Fulford, Roger. *Your Dear Letter - Private Correspondence of Queen Victoria and the Crown Princess of Prussia 1865-1871.* Charles Scribner's Sons, New York, 1971

George, Grand Duchess (Maria Georgievna). *A Romanov diary: the autobiography of H.I. and R. H. Grand Duchess George.* New York: Atlantic International, 1988.

Gerasimov, V. V. *Bolshoi dvorets v Strelne.* St Petersburg: Almaz, 1997

Grand Duke Konstantin Nikolaevich [book produced to accompany an exhibition]. St Petersburg: Abris, 2002.

Grebelsky, Petr, and Aleksandr Mirvis, *Dom Romanovykh: Biograficheskie svedeniia o chlenakh tsarstvovavshego doma, ikh predkakh i rodstvennikakh.* St. Petersburg, 1992.

Grey, Pauline. *The Grand Duke's Woman.* London: Mac Donald and Jane's, 1976.

Grimm, August Theodor von. *Alexandra Feodorowna, Empress of Russia.* Edinburgh: [s.n.], 1870.

Grunwald, Constantin de. *Tsar Nicholas I.* London: Douglas Saunders, 1954.

Hall, Coryne. *Little Mother of Russia.* Shepheard Walwyn. London, 1999.

Hall Coryne. *Imperial Dancer – Mathilde Kschessinska and the Romanovs.* Sutton Publishing, Stroud, 2005.

Harcave, Sidney. *Years of the Golden Cockerel.* Robert Hale, 1970.

Hartley, Janet M. *Alexander I.* London: Longman, 1974

Hennessy, Una Pope [ed.]. *A czarina's story: being an account of the early married life of Nicholas I of Russia.* London: Nicholson & Watson, 1948

Hertsen, Alexander. *Biloye i dumi.* Leningrad, 1978

Hibbert, Christopher, ed. *Queen Victoria in Her Letters and Journals.* New York: Viking, 1985.

Hodgetts, Edward Brayley. *The court of Russia in*

the nineteenth century. [s.l.]: Methuen, 1908.

Hough, Richard, ed. *Advice to My Grand-daughter Letters from Queen Victoria to Princess Victoria of Hesse*. New York: Simon and Schuster, 1975.

Ignatiev, Aleksei A. *Pyatdesyat let v stroyu, Gosudarstvennoe izdatel'stvo khudozhestvennoi literatury*, Moscow, 1950, vol. 1.

Jackman, Sydney Wayne [ed.] *Romanov Relations*. London: Macmillan, 1969

Jerrmann, Eduard. *Pictures from St Petersburg*. [s.l.]: Longman, Brown, Green and Longmans, 1852.

Jersild, Austin. *Orientalism and empire: north Caucasus mountain peoples and the Georgian frontier, 1845-1917*. Montreal: McGill-Queen's University Press, 2002.

Karnovich, Evgenii Petrovich. *Tsesarevich Konstantin Pavlovich*. St Petersburg: [s.n.], 1899

King, Greg. *The Last Empress: The Life & Times of Alexandra Feodorovna, Tsarina of Russia*. New York: A Birch Lane Book: Published by Carol Publishing Group, 1994.

King, Greg, and Penny Wilson. *Gilded Prism – The Konstantinovich Grand Dukes & the Last years of the Romamov Dynasty*. Eurohistory, East Richmond Heights, CA, 2006.

King, Greg, and Penny Wilson. *The Fate of The Romanovs*. Hoboken: John Wiley and Sons, 2003.

Klausen, Inger-Lise. *Dagmar, Zarina fra Danmark*. Lindhardt & Ringhof, Copenhagen, 1997.

Kleinmichel, Countess Marie. *Memories of a Shipwrecked World*. Roryalty Digest Reprint, Ticehurst, from1923.

Komarovsky, Nikolai Egorovich. *Zapiski*. Moscow: Obschestvo revnitelei russkago istoricheskago provsyschenya, 1912

Kozlianinoff, W. *Manuel Commemoratif de la Garde a Cheval, Edition de Son Altesse Imperiale Mgr. le Grand Duc Dmitri de Russie*. Paris, 1931.

Kurth, Peter. *Tsar: The Lost World of Nicholas and Alexandra*. Boston: A Madison Press Book produced for Little Brown and Company, 1995.

Kwiatowski, Marek. *Lazienki and Belweder*. Warsaw: Arkady, 1986.

Kyrill, Grand Duke of Russia. *My Life in Russia's Service: Then and Now*. Ticehurst: Royalty Digest, 1995.

Letters of Feodora Princess of Hohenlohe-Langenburg from 1828-1872. Spottiswoode & Co., London, 1874.

Letters of Tsar Nicholas and Empress Marie. Edited by Edward J. Bing. London: Ivor Nicholson and Watson Ltd, 1937.

Lincoln, W. Bruce. *Nicholas I: Emperor and autocrat of all the Russias*. London: Allen Lane, 1978.

Londonderry, Frances Anne Vane, Marchioness of. *Extracts from the Russian journal of Lady Londonderry, 1835-1837*. London: Royal College of Art, 1980.

Maples, William. *Dead Men Do Tell Tales*. New York: Doubleday. 1994.

Maria Feodorovna, Empress of Russia, Exhibition catalogue, 1997.

Marie, Grand Duchess of Russia. *Education of a Princess*. New York: Viking Press, 1931.

Marie, Princess of Erbach- Schönberg (Princess of Battenberg). *Reminiscences*. Ticehurst: Royalty Digest Reprint, 1996.

Marie, Queen of Romania. *The Story of My Life* (vol.1). London: Cassell & Co Ltd, 1934.

Markham, Felix. *Napoleon*. London: Weidenfeld and Nicolson, 1963.

Martin, Marie. *Maria Féodorovna en son temps, 1759-1828*. Paris: Harmattan, 2003.

Massie, Robert K. *Nicholas and Alexandra*. New York: Atheneum, 1967.

Massie, Robert K. and Suzanne Massie. *Journey*. London: Gollancz, 1975.

Masson, C.F.P. *Memoirs of Catherine II and the Court of St. Petersburg : During Her Reign and that of Paul I, By One of Her Courtiers*. London: The Grolier Society, 1904.

McLean, Roderick R. *Royalty and diplomacy in Europe, 1890-1914*. Cambridge: Cambridge University Press, 2000.

Michael, Prince of Greece. *Imperial palaces of Russia*. London: Tauris, 1992.

Milford Haven, Victoria. *Recollections 1863-1914*. ms. not published Eingang 4. XII 1969. Hess. Staatsarchiv Darmstadt D 24 64/1.

Millar, Lubov. *Grand Duchess Elizabeth of Russia: New Martyr of the Communist Yoke*. Richfield Springs, New York: Nikodemos Orthodox Publication Society: 1991.

Miliutin, D A. *Dnevnik DA Miliutina*, Moscow: Gosudarstvenaya Ordena Lenina Biblioteka, 1947.

Miller, Forrestt A. *Dmitrii Miliutin and the reform era in Russia*. Nashville: Vanderbilt University Press, 1968.

Moriolles, Alexandre. *Mémoires du comte de Moriolles sur l'émigration, la Pologne, et le cour du grand duc Constantin*. Paris: [s.l.], 1902.

Mossolov, Alexander. *At The Court of the Last Tsar*. London: Methuen, 1935.

Narishkin-Kurakin, Elizabeth. *Under Three Tsars*. E.P. Dutton & Co., Inc., 1931

Nichols, Robert L. "The Friends of God: Nicholas and Alexandra at the canonisation of Serafim of

Sarov", in Religious and secular forces in late Tsarist Russia: essays in honour of Donald W. Treadgold, edited by Charles E. Timberlake, 206-223.

Nicholas and Alexandra: the last imperial family of Tsarist Russia [exhibition catalogue], edited by Robert Timms. London: Booth-Clibborn, 1998.

Nicholas, Prince of Greece. *My Fifty Years.* Hutchinson,1926.

Nikolai Mikhailovich, Grand Duke. *L'impératrice Elisabeth, épouse d'Alexandre I.* St Petersburg: [s.n.], 1908-9.

Olga Nikolayevna. *Son Junosti. Zapiski docheri imperatora Nikolaya I.* Paris, 1964.

Olga, Queen of Wurttemberg (Grand Duchess Olga Nikolaevna). *Traum der Jugend goldner Stern.* Pfullingen: [s.n.], 1955.

Paléologue, Maurice. *An Ambassador's Memoirs: Last French Ambassador to the Russian Court.* Translated by F.A. Holt, 1923. (AlexanderPalace.org).

Paleologue, Maurice. *La Russie des Tsars.* Librairie Plon, Paris, 1922.

Palmer, Alan. *Alexander I, Tsar of war and peace.* London: Weidenfeld and Nicolson, 1974.

Pienkos, Angela T. *The imperfect autocrat: Grand Duke Constantine Pavlovich and the Polish Congress Kingdom.* New York: Colombia University Press, 1987.

Ponsonby, Sir Frederick. *Letters of the Empress Frederick.* Macmillan, 1928.

Radzinsky, Edvard. *Alexander II: The Last Great Tsar.* New York: Simon and Schuster, 2005.

Raeff, Marc. *Understanding imperial Russia.* New York: Columbia University Press, 1984.

Ragsdale, Hugh. *Tsar Paul and the question of madness.* New York: Greenwood Press, 1988.

Rasputin, Valentin. *Siberia, Siberia.* Evanston, Ill.: Northwestern University Press, 1996.

Trewin, JC. *Tutor to the Tsarevich: an intimate portrait of the last days of the Russian imperial family.* London: Macmillan, 1975

Roberts, Ian W. *Nicholas I and the Russian intervention in Hungary.* London: Macmillan, 1990.

Seaman, W. A. L. and J. R. Sewell, Editors. *The Russian Journal of Lady Londonderry, 1836-37.* London: John Murray, 1973.

Schnitzler, Johann Heinrich. *Secret history of the government and court of Russia under the Emperor Alexander and Nicholas.* London: [s.n.], 1847.

Sáemz, Jorge F. *A Poet Among the Romanovs – Prince Vladimir Paley 1897-1918.* Eurohistory, Oakland, CA, 2004.

Semennikov, V.P. ed. *Nikolai II I velikie kniaz'ia: rodstvenn'ie pis'ma k poslednemu tsariu, Gosudarstvennoe Izdatel'stvo.* Leningrad, 1925.

Sheremetev, S.D. *Memuari grafa S.D.Sheremeteva.* Moscow, Indrik, 2001.

Sokolovoi, Valerii and I. V. Kondratiev. *Dom Romanovykh.* St. Petersburg: Lio Redaktor, 1992.

Soloveva, T.A. *Paradnye rezidentsii Dvortsovoi naberezhnoi.* St Petersburg: Evropeiskii Dom, 1995.

Steinberg, Mark D. and Vladimir Khrustalev, Editors. *Flight of the Romanovs.* New Haven: Yale University Press. 1995.

Strukov, Dmitri Petrovich. *Avgustischii General-Feldtseikhmeister Velikii Kniaz Mikhail Nikolaevich.* St Petersburg: P.P. Soikina, 1906.

Teliakovsky,V.A. *Dnevniki Directora Imperatorskih Teatrov.* Moscow, 2002.

The complete wartime correspondence of Tsar Nicholas II and the Empress Alexandra, edited by Joseph T. Fuhrmann. Westport, CT.: Greenwood Press, 1999.

Tiutcheva, Anna. *Pri dvore dvuh imperatorov.* Moscow, 1990.

Trotsky, Leon. *A History of the Russian Revolution.* New York: Simon and Shuster. 1932.

Tsesarevich: dokumenty, vospimananiia, fotografii, edited by A. Iu. Maliutin. Moscow: Vagrius, 1998.

Tuomi-Nikula, Jorma & Päivi. *Kejsaren i Skärgården.* Schildts Förlags Ab, Esbo. 2002.

Ukhtomskii, Esper Esperovich. *Puteshestvie na Vostok' Ego Imperatorskago Vysochestva Gosudaria Nasliednika Tsesarevicha, 1890-1* [Puteshestvie Gosudaria Imperatora Nikolaia II na Vostok']. S-Peterburg: Brokgauz [i.e. Brockhaus of Leipzig], 1893-7.

Ular, Alexander. *Russia From Within.* New York: Henry Holt and Company, 1905.

Van der Kiste, John & Hall, Coryne. *Once a Grand Duchess: Xenia, Sister of Nicholas II.* Sutton Publishing, Stroud. 2002.

Van der Kiste, John. *The Romanovs:1818-1959.* Stroud: Sutton, 1998.

Vassili, Count Paul (pseudonym of Princess Catherine Radziwill). *Behind the Veil at the Russian Court.* London: Cassell and Company, 1913.

Verner, Andrew M. *The Crisis of Russian Autocracy: Nicholas II and the 1905 Revolution.* Princeton New Jersey: Princeton University Press, 1990.

Vostryshev, Mikhail. *Avgusteishee semeystvo.* Moscow, 2001.

Waliszewski, K. P*aul The First of Russia, The Son of Catherina The Great.* William Heinemann, London 1913.

Welch, Frances. *The Romanovs and Mr Gibbes: the*

story of the Englishman who taught the children of the last Tsar. London: Short Books, 2002.

William II, Emperor. *My Early Life*. Methuen, 1926.

Wood, Ruth Kedzie. *Honeymooning in Russia*. Fisher Unwin, London, 1911.

Wortman, Richard. *Scenarios of power: myth and ceremony in Russian monarchy*. Princeton: Princeton University Press, 1995.

Wassenaer, Cornelie de. *A visit to St Petersburg, 1824-1825*. Norwich: Michael Russell, 1994

Whelan, Heide W. *Alexander III and the State Council*. New Brunswick: Rutgers University Press, 1982.

Witte, Count Serge. *The Memoirs of Count Serge Witte*, edited by Sidney Harcave, Armonk, New York: M. E. Sharpe, 1990.

Witte, Sergei Iulevich. *Vospominaniia*. Moscow: Izdvo sotsnalnoekon. litry, 1960.

Youssoupoff, Prince Felix. *Lost Splendor*. Translated from the French by Ann Green and Nicholas Katkoff. New York: G.P. Putnam's Sons, 1953.

Zaionchkovsky, P A. *Krizis samoderzhavia na ribezhe 1870-1880 godov, Moscow*. Moscow University Press, 1964.

Zamoyski, Adam. *The last king of Poland*. London: Cape, 1992.

Zeepvat, Charlotte. *Romanov Autumn – Stories from the Last Century of Imperial Russia*. Sutton, Publishing, Stroud 2000.

Zeepvat, Charlotte. *From cradle to crown*. Stroud: Sutton, 2007.

Zeepvart, Charlotte. *The Camera and the Tsars*. Sutton Publishing, Stroud, 2004.

Zherve, V. V. *General-Feldmarshal Velikii Kniaz Nikolai Nikolaevich Starshii*. St Petersburg: [s.n.], 1911.

Articles, Periodicals, Grey literature and other media

Ashton, Janet. "The coronation of Tsar Alexander II: a translation from a book by Joachim Murat." In the European Royal History Journal, issues 9:4 and 9:5, 2006.

Ashton, Janet and Greg King. "Political dramas and private traumas": the Romanovs in the palaces of the Warsaw region. Royalty Digest Quarterly, 4: 2006.

Hall, Coryne. The Madness of Youth in The European Royal History Journal. Nov/Dec 2002.

King, Greg. "A tyrant's menacing memorial": the Mikhailovskii Castle. Atlantis Magazine, volume 5 issue 2, 72-79.

Kipp, Jacob W. and Maia Kipp. Grand Duke Konstantin Nikolaevic [sic]: the making of a Tsarist reformer, in Jahrbucher fur Geschichte Osteuropas, Band 34, Heft 1, 1986, p. 4- 18.

Konstantin Pavlovich to Alexander I, 14th January 1822. [Copy of the letter held in the British Library: Misc. Official Publications of the Russian Empire.]

Kucherskaya, Maya. "Grand Duke Constantine Pavlovich in Russian cultural mythology." Unpublished PhD thesis, University of California, Los Angeles, 1999.

Lee, William. "Grand Ducal Role and Identity as a Reflection on the Interaction of State and Dynasty in Imperial Russia." Unpublished PhD thesis, University College, London, 2000

Sbornik Imperatorskago Russkago Istoricheskago Obshchestva [S.I.R.I.O.]. Moscow: Russkaia Panorama, 1999-

Charlotte Zeepvat, Djulber, in Royalty Digest, September 19999, No. 99, Volume IX, No. 3, page 66

Websites

www.iconastas.co.uk
www.hermitagemuseum.org
http://www.angelfire.com/realm/gotha/gotha/wied.html
http://andrejkoymasky.com/liv/fab/fab21.html
http://macedonsky.narod.ru/agnates/a10.html
http://www.orthodox.net/russiannm/nicholas-ii-tsar-martyr-and-his-family.html
http://www.alexanderplace.com
http://www.angelfire.com/realm/gotha/gotha/gotha.htm

I

INDEX

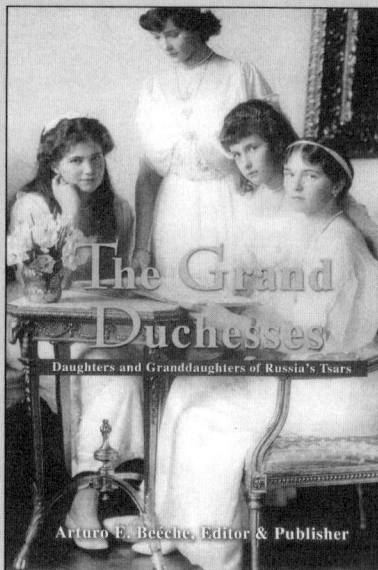

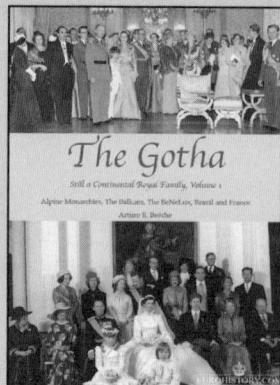

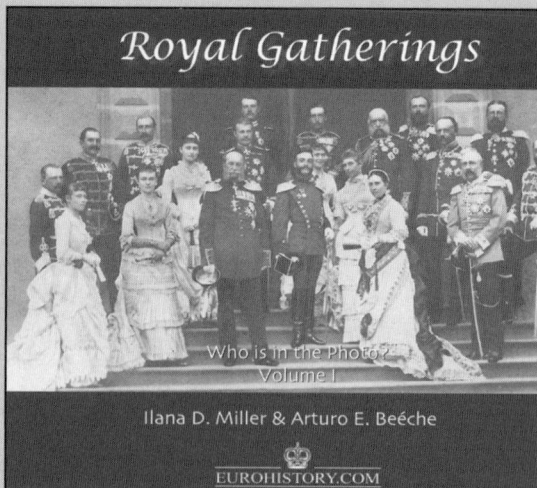

DEAR ELLEN

Royal Europe Through the Photo Albums of Grand Duchess Helen Vladimirovna of Russia

Eurohistory is delighted to bring to you **Dear Ellen – *Royal Europe Through the Photo Albums of Grand Duchess Helen Vladimirovna of Russia*.** This is the latest book by Arturo E. Beéche, ERHJ Publisher. With special access to the Grand Duchess' private photo albums, as well as images from the Eurohistory Archive and the private collections of the grand duchess' descendants, the author built a photographic journey covering the lives of Helen and her husband, Prince Nicholas of Greece. Also included are their three daughters: Olga of Yugoslavia, Elisabeth of Toerring-Jettenbach and Marina, Duchess of Kent. The selection of Romanov photos alone is phenomenal. The book also includes the galaxy of royalty in which the prince and his wife lived. Four of the grandchildren of Helen and Nicholas actively cooperated with the author.

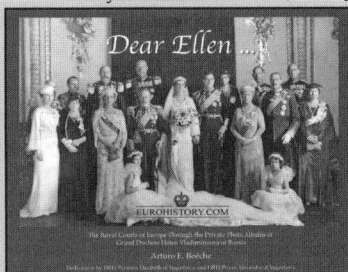

Hardbound, glossy paper and contains more than 350 unique photographs. **Price: $43.95, plus shipping ($8 shipping and handling in the USA. International shipping and handling available for $24). Published by Eurohistory.com. To pay by credit card, contact us at: Phone (510) 510-236-1730**

GILDED PRISM

Eurohistory Exclusive!

Eurohistory is proud to present to you **GILDED PRISM:** *The Konstantinovichi Grand Dukes and the Last Years of the Romanov Dynasty,* by renowned royalty authors Greg King and Penny Wilson.

This fascinating book, brings to life the story of the Konstantinovich line of the Russian Imperial Family, beginning with Grand Duke Konstantin Nicholaevich (1827-1892) and following the lives of his six children (Nicholas Konstantinovich, Queen Olga of Greece, Vera of Württemberg, Konstantin Konstantinovich (the famed KR), Dimitri Konstantinovich and Vyacheslav Konstantinovich) and many of this grandchildren and great-grandchildren. 238 pages, 3 photo sections!

The book sells for $43.95 plus shipping ($8.00 in the USA – $24.00 overseas). **Price: $43.95, plus shipping ($8 shipping and handling in the USA. International shipping and handling available for $24). Published by Eurohistory.com. If you wish to pay by credit card, please contact us at: Phone (510) 510-236-1730 or Email us at: books@eurohistory.com.**

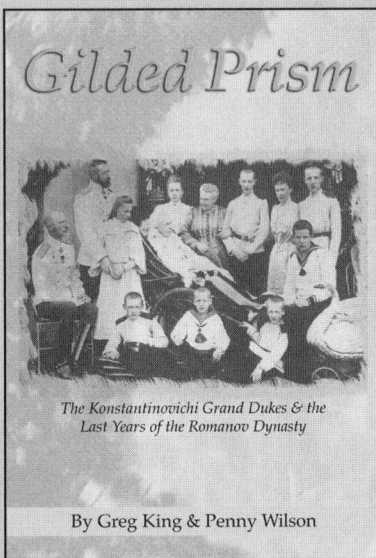

The Konstantinovichi Grand Dukes & the Last Years of the Romanov Dynasty

By Greg King & Penny Wilson

European Royal History Journal

The Engagement of Prin... and Mr. Chr...

The late Margr...

The Wedding of Hereditary Grand Duke Guillaume of Luxembourg and Countess Stéphanie de Lannoy, Luxembourg, 19 October 2012

T his year's *European Royal History Journal* features a fresh new design, and even more wonderful articles written by the best royal biographers and genealogists of today. It's a great time to be a part of the ERHJ community.

To subscribe, please send check or money order to:

Eurohistory.com
6300 Kensington Avenue
East Richmond Heights, CA 94805

Subscription Rates for 2010:
USA: $48.00
Canada: $55.00
Europe and Latin America: $75.00
UK: £45.00
Rest of the World: $75.00

If you wish to pay by credit card, please contact us at ...
phone: 510-236-1730 or email: books@eurohistory.com